Making a Non-White America

Making a Non-White America

Californians Coloring outside Ethnic Lines, 1925–1955

Allison Varzally

UNIVERSITY OF CALIFORNIA PRESS
Berkeley · Los Angeles · London

University of California Press, one of the most distinguished university presses in the United States,
enriches lives around the world by advancing scholarship in the humanities, social sciences, and natural
sciences. Its activities are supported by the UC Press
Foundation and by philanthropic contributions from
individuals and institutions. For more information,
visit www.ucpress.edu.

University of California Press
Berkeley and Los Angeles, California

University of California Press, Ltd.
London, England

Library of Congress Cataloging-in-Publication Data

Varzally, Allison, 1972–.
    Making a non-White America : Californians color-
ing outside ethnic lines, 1925–1955 / Allison Varzally.
        p.   cm.
    Includes bibliographical references and index.
    ISBN: 978-0-520-25344-5 (cloth : alk. paper)
    ISBN: 978-0-520-24345-2 (pbk. : alk. paper)
    1. Minorities—California—History.
2. California—Race relations.   3. California—Ethnic
relations.   4. California—Social conditions—20th
century.   5. Community life—California—History—
20th century.   6. Race discrimination—California.
7. Human geography—California.   I. Title.

F870.A1V37   2008

305.8009794—dc22   2007033313

17   16   15   14   13   12   11   10   09   08
10   9   8   7   6   5   4   3   2   1

For my parents, Joyce and Michael Varzally

Contents

Illustrations

TABLES

Acknowledgments

One of the best parts of completing a book is getting the chance to formally and unreservedly thank the many people who brought it into being. I continue to think fondly of my cohort at UCLA. Amy Sueyoshi, a great friend and guide, John Bowes, Cindy Culver, Lawrence Culver, Cindy Cumfer, Samantha Gervase, Daniel Hurewitz, and Lissa Wadewitz. Josh Sides has always been ten steps ahead and kind enough to explain the way forward. My dissertation advisers were especially influential. While Ruth Bloch taught me to analyze gender in more subtle and sophisticated ways, Min Zhou provided insights about immigration and youth culture from the refreshingly different perspective of a sociologist. When I relocated to the Bay Area during the last stages of my dissertation, Shana Bernstein graciously invited me into her circle of Stanford history students and has offered some of the most careful criticisms of my work.

Archivists who guided me through their collections with remarkable efficiency and humor include Jeff Rankin and Octavio Olvera at UCLA's Department of Special Collections, David Kessler and Susan Snyder at the Bancroft Library, Robert Marshall at the Urban Archives Center of California State University Northridge, and Rosalyn Tonai of the National Japanese American Historical Society. I am also grateful for the resources of the Southern California Library for Social Studies and Research, the East Los Angeles Public Library, the Labor Archives at San Francisco State University, the Los Angeles Human Relations Committee, the National Archives, and Library of Congress.

For financial support I am indebted to the History Department at UCLA, the Bancroft Library Fellowship Program, and the University of California's Kevin Starr Fellowship Program. California State University, East Bay, and my current institution, California State University, Fullerton, also funded my project. Portions of chapters 3 and 5 appeared in different forms in the respective articles "Romantic Crossings: Making Love, Family, and Non-Whiteness in California, 1925–1950," *Journal of American Ethnic History* 23 (Fall 2003): 3–54, and "'What the Heck, at Least He's an Oriental': What Asian American Intermarriage Might Teach Us about Gay Marriage," *Amerasia Journal* 32, no. 1 (2006): 45–60. This material is adapted with permission.

I owe another kind of debt to the many readers who have asked tough questions gently; they pressed me to interrogate my evidence more fully and articulate the significance of my work more clearly. Members of WHEAT (a clever acronym for Western Historians Eating and Talking, a clever group of graduate students at UCLA) and the Los Angeles History Research Group made invaluable suggestions for revising my work. I'm also grateful for the careful readings of Henry Yu, Dorothy Fugita-Rony, and H. Mark Wild, who helped nudge my dissertation into an aspiring manuscript. While Henry's comments prompted me to think more precisely about processes of immigration and racial construction and precipitated a major overhaul of my first chapter, Dorothy offered ideas about space and labor in the American West. Mark rightfully directed me to pay attention to the tensions as well as the connections that surfaced in the state's multiethnic neighborhoods. The book's reviewers, Paul Spickard and an anonymous reader, offered the kind of thoughtful, encouraging, and comprehensive criticism for which every author hopes. At the University of California Press, Niels Hooper, Rachel Lockman, and Randy Heyman patiently guided this project to publication. I have also had the good fortune to work with copyeditor Polly Kummel.

Without those who lent their personal stories and photographs, this book would never have come to pass. Their willingness to speak so openly about issues that so few other sources have addressed helped me to recover a largely hidden history of intercultural relations. And my conversations with Dolores Arlington, Gloria and Eddie Erosa, Clara Chin, Jerry Paular, Sugar Pie De Santo, Vangie Buell, Danny Kim, Jim Fung, Dolores Cruz, Gloria Quan, Peter Jamero, Frances Marr, Bill Sorro, and Rose Mary Escobar were by far the most enjoyable and affirming part of my research. I hope they have a fraction of the fun reading about their lives that I had writing about them.

My greatest professional thanks go to my lead adviser and mentor, Steve Aron, whose boundless energy, mental agility, and downright like-ability continue to impress me. I was lucky to land in Steve's seminar about the American West early in my UCLA career and quickly became a convert to the subject and a groupie of the academic. Somehow I always emerged from discussions with Steve with much more work to do and much more enthusiasm for doing it.

But I am most grateful for my family's unfailing support and love. They helped me realize that history was my passion and should be my career. And to John, without whose insights and kindness I would be lost, thank you.

Introduction

Young Oak Kim, the son of Korean immigrants, recalled sharing city streets, playgrounds, and schools with "Chinese, Japanese, Italians, Mexicans, Jews, and affluent Caucasians" in Los Angeles in the 1930s and early 1940s. Estimating that no more than a handful of Korean families occupied the neighborhood, Kim related how, "right from the beginning, I had to learn to get along with everybody. I learned to get along with Caucasians as well as . . . I had a lot of Japanese friends, as well as Chinese friends." When an interviewer asked him about racial tensions in the period, Kim insisted upon the absence of local prejudice. "No," he began definitively, "as you can see by the way I've broken the groups down, they're almost equal in size, except the Jewish group was smaller. I never had that feeling. I always had a sense that I didn't belong to any group, but that made it possible, I think, early in life to get along with everybody." This "getting along" with other ethnoracial groups, a practical necessity of his youth in a multiethnic setting, became a lifelong habit that took on more political implications as he aged. In 1942, much to the chagrin of his parents, Young Oak Kim married a woman of Chinese and Korean heritage whom he had known since he was five. Kim's propensity for and comfort with crossing established ethnoracial lines shaped his distinguished military career as well. During World War II he took command of an all–Japanese-American unit. Given the long history of hostility between Japan and Korea—hostilities that many immigrants from those nations and their descendants sustained in the United

States—the arrangement had the potential to become untenable. But Young Oak Kim drew from his own interethnic experiences, defused tensions, and rallied Nisei around a panethnic and American version of citizenship.[1] "You're going to do it for the Japanese Americans," he acknowledged to the soldiers, "but in the end you're going to do it for all Asians. That's number one. And that's why I'm here. I look like you. No one can tell the difference, and so when it gets done, it's going to be for everybody."[2] This sentiment of multiethnic connection and responsibility shaped Young Oak Kim's political activities after the war. On his return he joined a service group dedicated to the concerns of Latinos, Blacks, and Asians, helped found the Center for the Pacific Asian Family, and decades later lent his energies to the Japanese American National Museum and the Korean American Coalition in Los Angeles.

The lives of Californians like Young Oak Kim, who inhabited neighborhoods whose eclectic populations resembled that of the state as a whole and presaged the nation's demographics in the twenty-first century, draw us into the past to answer questions of the present, such as what happens to culture, economy, and politics in societies of true heterogeneity? Kim's memories highlight the often hidden history of mingling and mixing among minorities. In multiethnic environments where no single ethnoracial group predominated and minorities became the effective majority, rewarding relationships and panethnic understandings became not only the sociocultural norm but also the foundation for multiethnic civil rights activism. That activism represented mixing among minorities as the realization of democratic principles and the justification for their integration into American society. But told from the vantage point of the late twentieth century, Kim's story of amiable interethnic relations, made possible though they were by White racism, conveys a longing shared by many Americans for positive, practical examples of how diversity plays out. Driving this search for a peaceable multicultural society is the impression, often based upon real events, that ethnoracial distinctions today are sources of disagreement and division.

By analyzing interviews as well as ethnic newspapers, memoirs, personal papers, court records, and sociological writings, this book participates critically in that search. It historicizes concerns about intercultural dynamics, sources of cohesion, and parameters of citizenship in profoundly diverse societies. To better comprehend the variety and character of ethnoracial allegiances possible in environments defined by White racism and remarkable diversity, it explores the social, cultural, and political lives of the many minority Californians who resided in multiracial neighborhoods at roughly midcentury. By the 1930s these largely working-class districts owed their diversity to the Mexican, Asian, European, African, and Native American migrants who had made the state their home. Subject to similar restrictions in employment, housing, and education, minorities tended to cluster in many of the same residential and economic places. In these shared spaces they did not simply coexist but actively intermingled. Minorities argued, empathized, fought, allied, collaborated, and then revised their notions of community to accommodate these complex interactions.

This study is about the ways in which non-Whites shaped ethnoracial categories along one end of the state's ever-shifting ethnoracial spectrum. They expanded and reconfigured group boundaries by making original, repeated connections across the cultural lines that were immediate and accessible. These panethnic affiliations—attachments that were cumulative and multiple, permitting individuals to simultaneously perceive themselves as members of smaller and larger groups—opened up more opportunities than were available to them as members of single ethnic communities.

Many scholars have written about the coming together of European immigrants and their offspring to make a unique White racial identity during the nineteenth century and the first half of the twentieth century. These ethnics frequently acquired power and incorporated themselves into American society by disassociating themselves from other ethnoracial groups. Such strategies were made possible by, even encouraged by, naturalization, property, and marriage laws, the courts that enforced this legislation, the U.S. census, "race science," newspapers, real estate agents, politicians, political parties, unions, and employers who extended privileges to European ethnics that they denied African, Asian, Native, and oftentimes Mexican and Jewish Americans. Certainly, European Americans suffered discrimination and prejudice. Negative sentiments with explicitly racial overtones faded at different rates for different groups in different locations. For example, Irish Americans, portrayed in many regions of the country as brutish and simian, instigated anti-Chinese campaigns in California that won Irish Americans almost complete social acceptance and political importance as early as the late 1800s. Simultaneously, Italian immigrants in California claimed solidarity and identity with immigrants from all parts of Europe and their descendants in order to protect themselves from the kinds of restrictions imposed upon Asian ethnics. Although the Italian Americans were less successful than the Irish—the National Origins Act of 1924 effectively defeated Italian Americans' defense of an open-door policy for all European immigrants—their effort to distinguish Europeans from Asians and Mexicans highlighted the important ways in which these groups were racially constructed and controlled. As naturalized citizens, Italians and other southeastern Europeans had more opportunity for political participation. Moreover, the 1924 act established Europeans as Whites and set them at a distance from Asians and Mexicans, who were classified as aliens and illegals, respectively. Thus over time a similar trajectory of integration and consolidation set the experiences of Irish, Italians, and other European groups apart from those on the other side of an increasingly visible color line. As White ethnics became more secure in their advantages, the salience of the differences among them faded even as their differences with other ethnics became more conspicuous.[3]

But such treatments of race making and assimilation neglect the perceptions and consolidations of those minorities of color: those long denied entry to the pathway to socioeconomic and political incorporation. *Making a Non-White America* highlights the ways in which non-Whites judiciously constructed their own panethnic links in diverse spaces throughout California. It addresses the emotional, political, and economic significance of ethnicity and race among neighboring individuals of color. During the second quarter of the twentieth century, a realization of shared misfortune and a will to correct ethnoracial discrimination drew California minorities closer together. Unlike Whites, for whom shared privileges became the glue that loosely stuck them together, minorities bonded over their lack of power. However, their periodic affiliations rested upon a foundation firmer than frustration with common restrictions in employment, education, citizenship, marriage, and the military. Discovering opportunities and commonalities within other ethnoracial groups, non-Whites selected and blended new cultural forms, political approaches, and economic arrangements. Whites combined multiple traditions as they gathered together, but the desire to preserve or gain authority made them hesitate. Besides, their more homogeneous living and working situations left them fewer chances to sample cultural differences. In contrast, non-Whites embraced exchanges and combinations with less inhibition because they had less to lose and more to gain in crossing ethnoracial boundaries of all kinds, especially those between one another.

A spirit of quasi-cosmopolitanism guided the connections among minorities. Although their interethnic and panethnic relations concentrated along one end of the ethnoracial spectrum and were informed by White racism, minorities considered such relations neither exclusive nor separatist. Instead, like many White liberals of the period, they believed that cultural diversity was best managed when *all* ethnoracial groups interacted respectfully and regularly. However, a consciousness of how their lives differed from many European ethnics' muted the non-Whites' cosmopolitanism and made them more reluctant to cross the hardening color line that divided them from Whites. Minorities were willing to recognize the value of coordination with Whites, but the minorities more conspicuous social similarities and physical proximity encouraged them to first join with one another. Furthermore, they hoped their ethnic transgressions would not only cure collectively felt racism but would also prove their American identities, proof, the minorities realized, that even the most fair minded of Whites already possessed for themselves.

Minorities more warily crossed over and more effectively reinforced the color line that separated them from Whites, but in all cases of crossing, minorities proceeded with caution. Concerns about color, culture, gender, politics, and class scripted their engagements and commitments with one another. Most ethnoracial groups had informal but well-understood preferences about ethnicity and race that guided their choices of friends and romantic partners. Japanese immigrants discouraged contacts with Chinese Americans but most passionately resisted connections with African Americans. Mexican and Filipino Americans, with their similar skin tones, often-shared religion, and agricultural roots, regularly connected across ethnic lines. So did political progressives who embraced an interracial ideology, as well as Koreans and Chinese disgusted by the expansion of Japan in the Pacific. The sense that familiar gender roles were too unbalanced or expressions of sexuality too restrictive within one's own cultural group motivated mixing among minorities, too.

Relative differences in their disadvantages determined who associated with whom and for how long. Mexican and Jewish Americans, groups closest to a still-developing color line, were the groups that integrated most imperfectly into allegiances with other minorities.[4] Classified by state and federal officials as "White," they enjoyed legal freedoms of which Asian, Native, and African Americans could only dream. The ability of these former groups to naturalize, to marry European ethnics, to serve in regular units of the armed forces, to call themselves "White" built tensions into their relations with other minorities. The everyday prejudices that Jews, and especially Mexican Americans, encountered in housing, education, and employment were sometimes not enough to convince other minorities that they had reason to associate or collaborate.

Threads of identity could be pulled apart as easily as they were spun together. However, precisely because of the socioeconomic and geographic
limits they faced, Mexican Americans and Jews who lived in mixed areas
through the early 1950s more often became involved with nearby minorities than did Whites who lived at a distance.

Thus Asian ethnics, Blacks, Native Americans, Mexican Americans,
and Jews in multiethnic spaces tested, passed over, and repositioned the
many ethnoracial lines that cut through their communities. In doing so,
they not only exposed the mechanisms of race and ethnicity in spaces of
great diversity but also demonstrated the authority they possessed over
ethnoracial boundaries despite and because of White racism. These manipulations by the ethnic communities happened in tension with and
alongside manipulations of White Europeans, who were wrestling with
their own differences and their relationship to less privileged Americans.
These simultaneous and overlapping processes decided the ethnoracial
structure of mid–twentieth century California society.

This story of how social relations and cultural exchanges among minority residents of diverse spaces generated panethnic affiliations and political collaboration unfolds in six chapters. The first chapter establishes
the demographic and economic context as well as the regime of discrimination that encouraged interethnic mixing in California. Between
1925 and 1955 the arrival of new immigrants and migrants accentuated
the already-impressive diversity of the state. Although many intended to
live and work in ways that preserved their ethnoracial integrity—an integrity that was itself a construction of the experience of immigration—
the very diversity of California and its prejudicial laws and practices frequently undercut these efforts. In other words, these non-Whites mixed
because it was difficult not to.

Chapter 2 stresses the powerful role played by interracial peers in the
making of youthful identities and explores the construction of a multiethnic youth culture immediately before World War II. Building in part
upon the easy connections they had made with varied other ethnics as
children within heterogeneous spaces, young adults crossed ethnic lines,
challenging their parents' and often the larger society's preference for
ethnic isolation. Certainly, not all youngsters ventured into other cultures with the same comfort or regularity. Communities more closely policed and more narrowly defined female sexuality, making intercultural
heterosocial contacts much riskier for young women than for young
men. An attachment to ethnic conventions and fear of disapproval directed youths' social and cultural choices as well. But even those who

shied away from ethnic crossings often championed the ideal of cross-
cultural friendships in a multiethnic society. Thus whether as rhetoric
or practice, a certain cosmopolitanism distinguished most minority teens
in the second quarter of the twentieth century and highlighted how non-
White youth managed their acculturation and pursued alternatives to
standard assimilation. A much smaller and deliberately provocative
group of adolescents blended cultural traditions more aggressively
and exclusively. They dismissed the cosmopolitan perspective of their
peers as an inept response to persistent discrimination, foreshadowing
the more separatist and minority-centric views of a later generation of
youths.

The third chapter addresses a more permanent and committed ethnic
crossing than those made by youth: the creation of intercultural families.
Minorities found love and company with one another as well as with
Whites, expanding and relocating ethnoracial boundaries along one side
of a strengthening color line. As working-class minorities within multiethnic spaces who met on relatively equal ground, partners faced contentious compromises of cultural differences. Because neither could offer
the obvious advantages of White culture, each had to and did argue for the
strengths of her or his own, believing it was possible to preserve ethnic distinctions within a cross-cultural setting. With the help of their multiracial
children, they consolidated rather than erased racial or social bonds, coming together rather than pushing toward a monoethnic identity.

In chapters 4 and 5 the contribution of wartime stresses to the development of panethnic relations takes center stage. Previous chapters established how minorities cultivated social and cultural ties in shared
spaces before the war, but the events surrounding World War II reinforced the sense of connectedness among non-White Californians. Chapter 4 features the dramatic acts of discrimination—the Zoot Suit Riots
and Japanese internment—that exposed the depths of American ethnoracial prejudice and thus invited minorities to look with fresh eyes upon
California society, their place within it, and the prospects for collective
action. What they saw was not only the precariousness of their own lives
but also misfortunes shared with other non-Whites and the immediate
ways they could work together. Minority families, singles, and adolescents expressed sorrow as they witnessed or personally experienced violence and displacement that steered them toward cooperative activity
after the war.

Although it too interprets World War II as a critical moment in the
evolving relations among minorities, chapter 5 brings a more national

and global perspective to bear upon that history of intersection. It highlights the ways in which minority soldiers whose tours of duty took them beyond the boundaries of California discovered new peoples and ethnoracial etiquettes that altered the Californians' views of other minorities and made them sharper critics of the American ethnoracial system. For minorities already oriented toward multiethnic notions of community, the service of these Californians reinforced this orientation and deepened their desire to win equality for multiple minority groups. Non-Whites who had been less attuned to White racism and the panethnic possibilities of diverse environments became more interested in the conditions of other ethnoracial groups and how they might join together. These soldiers of World War II saw injustice within a broadened context, one that emphasized their shared disadvantages.

The final chapter moves beyond wartime California to explore how minorities reshaped long-emerging social and cultural connections into political relationships. Until this period the ties among the various minority groups remained largely informal and apolitical. But their experiences of intermingling, the shocks of wartime, and a hospitable climate for reform emboldened them to challenge prevailing discriminations. As they did so, the possibilities and complexities of panethnic affiliations became clearer. Many of the concerns about color, class, gender, or age that informed their social and cultural interactions guided their political choices. Thus minorities' attempts at a panethnic or minority-centric politics often ended in unrealized, incomplete, or short-lived coalitions. However, collaboration among neighbors sometimes worked in multiethnic California. By the late 1940s and early 1950s their activism had helped to collapse much of the legal apparatus supporting White privilege: housing covenants, antimiscegenation statutes, school segregation, and immigration restrictions.

Like all history books, this one is indebted to those written by others. Recent works on race, immigration, Whiteness, and American nationalism have made my study possible. In defining the most elemental and complex concepts of my work—race, ethnicity, color—I depended upon answers offered by Henry Yu, Matthew Frye Jacobson, and David Hollinger. A dramatic drop in European immigration following restrictions in 1924, the rise of Nazism in the 1930s and early 1940s, and the migration of millions of African Americans to the North and West made Americans more concerned about the position of the color line. *Race,* which had often been used to describe the physical and cultural characteristics of various

Europeans, now came to mean color and referred to larger groups like "Whites," "Negroids," and "Orientals." The terms *ethnicity* and *nationality* emerged to explain differences once understood as racial. To accommodate these changing definitions and still acknowledge the distinct positions of groups and the contingent character of those positions, I use the term *ethnoracial*. This captures the perceived biological, historical, and behavioral qualities by which groups bounded themselves and were bound by others at different times and different places. The relative salience of these criteria for membership obviously differed across groups, with African Americans more heavily and enduringly burdened by the presumed importance of the physical.[5]

But I hope *Making a Non-White America* is as much a challenge to as a commendation of recent scholarship about race and ethnicity, particularly writings on Whiteness. Historians, sociologists, and cultural critics responsible for the new "Whiteness studies" have contributed to our understanding of how race is invented, interpreted, and enacted. They have debunked romantic assumptions about cross-race, working-class solidarity and reminded us that race is not the exclusive possession of non-Europeans. Despite these strengths, as critics have noted, the studies rob Whiteness of its explanatory power by deploying it so frequently and carelessly. In many instances the meaning of the concept has become alternatively too elastic or too static. The specific contexts and mechanisms of "Whiteness" remain unclear. So does the relative significance of other lines of distinction. A related and perhaps more damning criticism faults Whiteness studies for shifting attention away from racism, neglecting the views of non-Whites, and suggesting the false equivalence of White racial identities and those of people of color. This book participates in and seeks to answer these complaints. It addresses concrete social relations at a specific moment in California history and privileges the perspectives and activities of groups named "un-White" by laws and social customs. Finally, I emphasize the contingent nature of the panethnic practices and ideas of minorities, a contingency much influenced by their interactions with different White groups or institutions and differences of gender, religion, work, and sexuality.[6]

This book also draws on immigration historiography and its theories of incorporation. The theory of assimilation, once understood and then discredited as a melting pot or drift toward a stable Anglo-American cultural core, has been revised by scholars to mean the narrowing of differences between groups.[7] They have reimagined the United States as a pluralist society composed of many distinct cultures. In this conception immigrants do not conform to a central "Americanism." Instead they influence the larger public culture even as they are influenced by it. Change becomes a matter of mutual or multiple acculturations. The persistent flaw in this version of how newcomers get folded into American society is that it more accurately describes the experiences of European than non-European ethnics. Asian, Mexican, African, and Native Americans have historically not enjoyed the same powers of persuasion. They inhabited the same United States but did not equally shape its economics, politics, or other power relationships. But if their struggle to have social and cultural influence in a multicultural nation did not dislodge the dominance of European ethnics, these non-European minorities did influence one another. I explore this incorporation over time—the selective, fleeting affiliations of non-Whites between 1925 and 1955. Rather than remain fragmented outsiders who simply observed the growing authority and solidarity of European ethnics, these groups found their own sources of connection and commonality.

In addition, *Coloring outside Ethnic Lines* builds upon the group-specific histories of immigrants and their descendants that usually are produced under the auspices of ethnic studies. These works typically depict the complex process of cultural adjustment by which second-generation immigrants blended familiar, inherited traditions with those of the American mainstream. In these accounts conflicts with elders and White peers complicated the cultural negotiations. Nevertheless, these ethnic Americans made original, bicultural identities. Rather than choose between being American or foreign, as previous scholars envisioned, these non-European ethnics located positions between.[8] They also struggled for secure positions within their ethnoracial group. Even though co-ethnics typically shared many ideas, values, and institutions, their common ethnicity did not ensure homogeneous experiences. Differences in gender, class, religion, age, and sexuality fractured communities. Studies of White and Black migrants, as well as Mexican immigrants, to California have emphasized divisions between old-timers, or American-born residents, and the newcomers.[9]

Looking outside ethnic borders, historians have addressed connections between groups. These works have illustrated the interdependence of Whites and non-Whites and helped integrate minority histories more smoothly and completely into the general narrative of the development of the United States. Some have spotlighted the clash and readjustment of distinct gender systems as cultures come into contact, bringing specificity to the now often-repeated assertion that race, class, and gender mutually constitute one another. Yet another school of historians has attempted more synthetic accounts of the history of non-Whites in relation to Whites. Despite differences in the interactions of the majority with the West's main minority groups—African Americans, Asian Americans, Native Americans, and Mexican Americans—these relationships similarly served the economic and political ambitions of European Americans. Unique racializations of groups structured the same White supremacy.[10]

In all these studies of ethnoracial groups, though, Whites and their dominant culture remain leading characters shaping the fortunes of minorities. For the most part the interplay *between* minorities is overlooked. This book contributes to a new and thankfully growing body of scholarship that addresses how the lives of minorities intersected and how those intersections shaped the larger contours of politics, culture, and society. These studies take seriously the unique multiethnic composition of the American West, going beyond black and white or brown and white or even yellow and white to consider the experiences of many ethnoracial groups simultaneously and interdependently. In not focusing on Whites and by discarding biethnic frameworks, this book specifically explores the many ways of mingling that took place on the margins of California society between 1925 and 1955.[11]

Finally, this book depends upon writings in which race and immigration are part of a larger conversation about citizenship in multidescent nations. Historians interested in the meaning of the nation and civic identity have long observed the tendency in the United States by which certain groups "get in" by keeping certain groups out. One's religion, political affiliation, ethnicity, and, most enduringly, race, they note, have mattered to one's incorporation. One of the earliest and most prominent historians of American nationalism, John Higham, discussed a habit of defensive national unity or nativism in U.S. history that variously manifested itself in anti-Catholic, antiradical, or racial forms. As American confidence about the ability of the United States to absorb newcomers ebbed and flowed with changes in the economy and foreign relations, so did fears about internal minorities. More recently, Gary Gerstle has described the tension in American nationalism as that between inclusive "civic" expressions based upon tolerance of difference and exclusive "racial" expressions premised upon conformity or sameness. Even during the 1930s, a period of celebrated liberalism, he noted, eastern and southern Europeans seized upon the opportunity to whiten and assimilate by supporting legislation to restrict Japanese immigration. Reflecting upon today's society, Gerstle pondered whether civic or racial nationalism will prevail. While the former would mean a strong, solidaristic, though exclusive, nation, the latter would create an inclusive but loosely bound one. George Sanchez, Michael Omi, and Harry Winant have similarly highlighted the theme of racial exclusion in U.S. history. David Hollinger has framed these concerns about citizenship and solidarity in a diverse society slightly differently. Critiquing contemporary multiculturalism as a suitable orientation toward cultural diversity and foundation for national unity, he proposed a "postethnic" perspective. In its respect for cultural differences, Hollinger argued, multiculturalism reifies these differences and thus fragments Americans. "Postethnicity" combines cosmopolitanism—an "impulse towards worldly breadth"—and the ethos—an appreciation of smaller, separate affiliations.[12]

The panethnic attachments of midcentury minorities, which are the focus of my study, demonstrate this voluntary, multiple, and shifting version of boundary making. When diverse ethnoracial groups met on an almost level playing field, they freely interacted and became attached even as they retained original ethnoracial ties. Although fragile, momentary, and interrupted by interethnic tensions, these connections among marginalized Californians represented an alternative way of belonging and interacting, one based upon positive assertions of compatibility rather than negative comparisons and exclusion. That such a model of a multicultural society once existed, even briefly, is intriguing and encouraging in a state that is today truly multiethnic as well as in a nation that is becoming increasingly so; it suggests the possibility of an inclusive nationalism despite and even because of greater diversity. Amid fears that a more multiethnic population makes for a more volatile society, the experience of California has relevant lessons to offer.

Indeed, California provided an ideal vantage point from which to observe the making and meaning of ethnoracial categories. Although varied peoples and their complex interactions have long defined U.S. history, this variety was most pronounced in the twentieth century and most visible in California. Mexican, Asian, Native American, European, and Black migrants in search of better lives joined established residents there. Many of these newcomers arrived and took up jobs in booming defense industries during World War II. The suddenness of their presence and Japanese Americans' absence created new spatial and economic arrangements that both altered and invigorated patterns of integrated living. Other regions of the country were unsettled by the prosecution of war and claimed a polyglot population of European ethnics and African

Americans. However, the relative absence of Asian ethnics and Mexican immigrants in these places narrowed their diversity and directed their gaze toward other foreign countries and issues. At the same time the concentration of military bases, Japanese Americans, and war-related manufacturing in California meant the Golden State underwent more disruptive changes in the period. Certainly, the precise collection of ethnoracial groups varied from location to location in California, with Mexicans and Japanese more abundant in Los Angeles, Chinese in San Francisco, and Filipinos in Stockton, but these distinct locales had highly mixed populations in common. But if the timing and uniqueness of the state's demography explain the setting of this study, so does its representativeness. During the last half of the twentieth century, the kind of broad diversity that, by the mid-1940s, so distinguished California from so many of its more eastern neighbors came to characterize those very neighbors. This book makes the case that the ethnoracial dynamics on display in California have national importance.

While histories of race, immigration, and citizenship have shaped the argument of *Making a Non-White America,* works about or heavily dependent upon oral histories, memoirs, and interviews have informed its methodology. These kinds of primary sources may be problematic because they represent the experiences of individuals rather than groups and suffer distortions as time passes, but I believe they are invaluable, and I tried to manage their limitations. Learning from practitioners like Vicki Ruiz and Willa Baum, I drew upon oral histories produced in recent years as well as interviews conducted during the period in question to balance out errors related to distortions of memory. As an interviewer for some of the oral histories integrated into this book, I followed the advice of Judy Yung, listening carefully and unobtrusively and permitting the speaker to tell her own story even when it ran against my own narrative expectations. In these and other firsthand accounts I treated with more caution those statements spoken with uncertainty and vagueness: volunteered details typically indicated a stronger memory. Mixing different types and depending upon a breadth and diversity of personal accounts strengthened the representative quality of the material, too. Ultimately, the memories may have skewed toward the positive and the nostalgic, but they also conveyed the reality of interethnic connection. I answer the other criticism made of these sources—Can we generalize attitudes and practices from the stories of a handful of individuals?—by acknowledging the relative rarity of many of the experiences described. Yet if the interethnic and panethnic connections depicted in this book were not always typical, they were still significant illustrations of the social, cultural, and political creativity of minorities who shared segregated settings.

"A kaleidoscope of colors and languages" was Ernesto Galarza's description of his mixed neighborhood in Sacramento just before World War II.[13] I use this optical device throughout this book to see the varied cultural patterns and combinations of multiethnic California. It rotates discussions of ethnoracial formation and multicultural communities toward the shifting interactions among California minorities in common spaces. These non-Whites selectively leaned on, borrowed from, and dared to organize politically with one another. But they did not do so indefinitely. This book ends just as the legal, spatial, and political shards of that kaleidoscope shifted in ways that unsteadied the colorful combinations that minorities had pieced together. By the early 1950s the cautiousness of Cold War anticommunism had begun to eclipse the enthusiasm for reform that was a legacy of World War II. Heterogeneous downtown spaces became more homogeneous, and the most egregious legal underpinnings of White privilege had fallen away. Yet if the particular panethnic affiliations created among non-Whites in particular multiethnic spaces did not last, the example of their cooperation did and would guide the formation of new multiethnic coalitions later in the twentieth century. It is this past of ethnic crossings and consolidations of which contemporary Americans might take note as they negotiate ways of cohering and belonging in a society of such heterogeneity.

CHAPTER I

California Crossroads

"Like many other small villages in the wild, majestic mountains of the Sierra Madre de Nayarit, my pueblo was a hideaway," Ernesto Galarza wrote of Jalcocotán, Mexico, his birthplace. As a result of economic and political instabilities wrought by the Mexican Revolution and capitalist expansion, however, this hideaway ceased to be a refuge. Seeking work and safety, the Galarzas and other peasant families began a series of migrations that would carry them across the Mexico-U.S. border. Passing through Tepic, Mazatlán, Nogales, and Tucson, the Galarzas finally reached Sacramento. They settled into the "Lower Sacramento . . . the quarter that people who made money moved away from." It was, he wrote, "not exclusively a Mexican *barrio* but a mix of many nationalities," including Japanese, Chinese, Filipinos, Hindus, Blacks, Koreans, and Portuguese, a neighborhood that was a truly multicultural setting.[1]

The Galarzas' long journey and diverse neighborhood typify the migration and settlement experience of so many working-class minorities in roughly the second quarter of the twentieth century. Inside California's big cities and small towns, non-Whites lived and socialized in truly mixed neighborhoods rather than ethnically specific enclaves; they regularly bumped into and brushed up against one another as they went about their daily routines. These integrated spaces demonstrated not only that the Golden State had accumulated a varied population but also that this population was distributed in ways that made diversity visible and important to everyday experience. In part, making ethnoracial communities in California was about discouraging physical and social contacts with other groups. But in the end, the spatial concentration of non-Whites made their intermixing almost inescapable.

Patterns of migration, discrimination, and ethnoracial formation created the state's heterogeneous spaces. During the late nineteenth and early twentieth century, the spread of capitalism generally and American power specifically encouraged the migration of the Galarzas and many others to the United States. California loomed large in the imaginations of Asians, Mexicans, and Europeans as a place of particular promise. It also beckoned to Americans from other states, including Black southerners and Native Americans, who thought their lives could be better out West. These new arrivals set up and settled into systems of difference that expressed the stresses of their migrant experiences. Informed by local diversity, the rise of nationalist movements, and the racial assumptions of long-time Californians, the new arrivals expanded their notions of kinship beyond the familiar borders of village or region. Established Whites participated in this process of making ethnoracial categories by building stronger boundaries around their privileges. In addition to sweeping revisions in immigration and marriage law, Whites' skillful, increasing use of real estate covenants, as well as prejudicial hiring, housing, and educational practices in the decades before World War II, severely restricted the opportunities of minorities.

The consolidation and segregation of ethnoracial groups resulted in multiethnic, working-class communities in the least desirable sections of metropolitan and rural areas. There, a mixture of ethnoracial groups met in schools, community centers, religious institutions, restaurants, and shops. Although European immigrants inhabited these districts, advantages attached to their legal status as White made their residence more voluntary and temporary; thus their attachment to the place and its occupants was more often attenuated or tentative. In the end, the physical closeness of so many distinct groups constituted the fertile ground from which panethnic social and cultural connections sprouted.

ACCENTUATED DIVERSITY

The rush of so many immigrant and migrant groups into California created a place of pronounced diversity by the middle decades of the twentieth century. The state had long boasted of a special demography, but the convergence of new peoples strengthened this claim. States of comparable population size—New York, Florida, Texas, and Michigan—had accumulated large numbers of non-Whites, but none had California's variety. For example, the 1940 census found that Whites represented 95.6 percent of the total population of New York State, whereas Blacks accounted for 4.2 percent, and "other races" a mere 0.2 percent. In Texas Whites constituted 82 percent of the population; 14 percent were Black and a paltry 0.03 percent were of other races. In California 95.5 percent of the population was White, 1.8 percent Black, and 2.7 percent belonged to "other races." The significant presence of American Indians, Chinese, Japanese, Filipinos, and Mexicans widened the range of the Pacific state's peoples. The newcomers who hailed from Asia and Mexico as well as eastern Europe and the American South were pushed and pulled by many of the same forces. Shaping their movement were political unrest and economic distress in home areas—often precipitated by, or at least related to, U.S. engagements overseas—as well as abundant work opportunities in California. Men migrated more regularly than women, a pattern that engendered unique family and sexual dynamics.[2]

As a result, through much of the second quarter of the twentieth century, California had a much larger and more male population of minorities than in previous periods and most other American regions. Although not the most lopsided, its 1940 sex ratio of 103.7 males per 100 females was the thirteenth highest in the nation. Of those primarily western states that boasted more severe imbalances, such as Montana, Washington, Oregon, Nevada, and Arizona, none had populations as large *and* as diverse as California's. Washington, for example, had an aggregate sex ratio of 109.1:100, with twice as many Chinese men as women, and 1.25 times as many Japanese men as women. But the total Chinese and Japanese populations reached only 2,086 and 4,071, respectively, tiny populations when compared with the 39,556 Chinese and 93,717 Japanese who made their homes in California. The larger size of these Asian groups made demographic imbalances more conspicuous and meaningful.[3]

Among the immigrants who chose California as their destination in increasing numbers during the early twentieth century were Mexicans. They joined an established population of residents of Mexican origin with local roots that often preceded the U.S. conquest. Dramatic changes in Mexico introduced during the Porfiriato political period (1876–1911) prompted many citizens to travel northward. Hoping to modernize his country's economy by improving transportation, raising agricultural productivity, and attracting foreign investment, Porfirio Diaz ordered the privatization of communal land, the construction of railroads, and the introduction of new machinery. As in other parts of Latin America, U.S. businesses played an active role in this economic development, becoming major shareholders in Mexican railroads, establishing industries, and selling manufactured products. The historian George Sanchez has reported that almost two-fifths of all foreign investments by Americans were made in Mexico by 1911. As the U.S. and Mexican economies became more entangled and capitalism more far reaching, land became more expensive and more concentrated in the hands of a few. Formerly independent farmers suddenly found themselves working for wages on land they had once owned. Those dispossessed who could not find work as tenants or sharecroppers wandered into the cities of northern Mexico and searched for industrial jobs. Food prices climbed even as a labor surplus forced wages lower. This dim picture darkened when revolution broke out in 1910, forcing Mexicans to contend with political turmoil in addition to economic difficulties. Increasingly, Mexican workers contemplated a longer migration—one that took them, like members of the Galarza family, across the border into the American Southwest.[4]

Shifts in the economies of states such as New Mexico, Texas, Arizona, and California also encouraged the migration of Mexicans. New and widespread irrigation projects, the extension of railway lines, and the introduction of refrigerated boxcars contributed to the impressive expansion and productivity of the region's agriculture. In the first decades of the twentieth century, California became the nation's leading agricultural producer, a feat made possible by economies of scale introduced by new technological innovations as well as inexpensive labor. Recognizing the advantages of Mexican workers who accepted wages comparatively better than those prevailing in their native country but low by American standards, large agribusinesses sent labor recruiters to border towns. These agents staffed railroads, mines, factories, and farms throughout California. As American workers joined the military or entered defense work during World War I, the depletion of the labor force only intensified the recruiters' efforts and boosted immigration rates.[5]

A disproportionate number of adult Mexican men chose work across the border. In 1910 the El Paso immigration station reported women as only 6.8 percent of those arriving from Mexico. Typically, Mexicans practiced a kind of circular migration in which the men would travel back and forth across the border in rhythm with the seasonal demands of their work. However, the tightening of U.S. immigration policy in 1921 and continued political chaos led some Mexican families to make their migration more permanent, moving wives and children into California.

By 1920 the Mexican-born population, concentrated in the state's southern half, had risen to 478,000 from 103,000 in 1900. By 1940 the Mexican population in Los Angeles alone stood at 61,248.[6]

Asian immigrant groups, hailing primarily from the Philippines, China, and Japan, joined Mexicans in the state in the late 1800s and early 1900s as they too fled political unrest and sought better economic opportunities. Chinese were the first Asian group to arrive in California during the gold rush, and the treatment they received would set the standard for later Asian arrivals. A large-scale diaspora beginning in the 1840s sent Chinese to Canada, Australia, New Zealand, Southeast Asia, and Africa, as well as Hawaii and California. Political conflicts, namely, the Opium Wars and peasant rebellions, encouraged the migration. So did economic troubles caused by flooding, imperial taxes, and foreign competition. Yet more than misfortune in China propelled the migrants. The majority originated from the province of Guangdong, a region whose economic development and coastal location meant greater familiarity with the United States. Residents of this delta of the Pearl River enjoyed greater contact with missionaries and traders, who shared news of the gold rush and other California opportunities. Many men acted upon this information, borrowing money, saving, or signing labor contracts to pay for their eastward passage.[7]

Chinese wives remained behind in greater numbers than in Mexican families. The cost of the journey, the men's hope of a quick return, and responsibilities to in-laws discouraged the women's travel. Employers in California also objected to the emigration of wives and families whom they believed would distract workers from their migratory routines. Therefore, although 50 percent of the immigrants were married, most had not brought their wives. In 1885 Chinese women represented less than half the Chinese population in America. Thirty-five years later the sex ratio was a shocking 27 males per female. The gap narrowed during the twentieth century but never closed completely. In San Francisco, where Chinese were most numerous, Chinese men still outnumbered Chinese women by approximately 3 to 1 in 1930. By 1950 a statewide Chinese-American sex ratio of 161.8:100 marked the continued surplus of men.[8]

Japanese began coming to California via Hawaii in the 1890s, a few decades after the first Chinese. As in Mexico and China, the economic problems in Japan in part explained the movement. To pay for its expensive program of modernization and Westernization, the Meiji government placed new taxes on land and adopted a deflationary policy, leading many small farmers to lose their land. The high wages promised by American agents for work in Hawaii and on the mainland convinced many Japanese to leave their homeland. Their government tightly controlled the exodus, viewing Japanese abroad as representatives of their country. To ensure a more stable overseas community, the Meiji regime encouraged the emigration of women. This prescription, along with the picture-bride system, in which immigrant single men would choose wives after viewing a set of photographs sent from home, created a more sexually balanced society. The eventual Japanese sex ratio of 2.5 males per female approximated that of European immigrants'. By 1920 women constituted 34.5 percent of the Japanese population in California. As the century advanced, the Japanese became both a more stable population, reaching a comfortable sex ratio of 116:100 in 1950, and, unlike the Chinese, one that was more concentrated in Los Angeles County. Seattle had enjoyed the largest Japanese population in 1900, but two decades later Los Angeles could rightfully call itself the "metropolis of Japanese America."[9]

Filipinos, the third most prominent group of Asian immigrants, became Californians in large numbers during the 1920s and 1930s. Perhaps more than the migration of any other group, their movement demonstrated the destabilizing consequences of U.S. imperialism. As residents of a U.S. territory who often spoke English, understood American customs, and carried the status of nationals, these arrivals enjoyed a familiarity with and an ease of entry into the United States unknown by Chinese, Japanese, or Mexicans. The majority of Filipinos who chose California as their destination were young laborers from poor families in the Ilocos region who found it increasingly difficult to make ends meet. Changes in the Philippine economy, brought about by the United States, favored large landowners and commercial agriculture. Dispossessed peasants responded eagerly to American labor contractors who were offering jobs in Hawaii plantations or California fields. Between 1920 and 1927 most Filipinos arriving at the ports of San Francisco and Los Angeles had spent time in Hawaii, but by the late 1920s and early 1930s most came directly from the Philippines. Men dominated the immigrant flow, resulting in bachelor societies that resembled those of the Chinese. In fact, between 1924 and 1929 only 16 percent of the twenty-four thousand Filipinos coming to California were women. This imbalance reflected employment demands, the expectation of a short stay, and restrictions that Filipino families placed on the travel of single women.[10]

Adding to the variety of Asian immigrants were Koreans and Asian Indians. The small numbers of these arrivals made them less conspicuous in California communities and explain the more limited attention they receive in this history of intercultural relations. Encouragement by American missionaries, a desire to escape from Japanese imperialism, and economic troubles all contributed to the movement of about eight thousand Koreans between 1903 and 1920 to Hawaii and the mainland (with the vast majority settling in Hawaii). As in the Japanese community, the picture-bride system helped create nuclear families on American soil. The community never reached significant size in the years before World War II, though, largely because Japan severely limited Korean emigration after 1905.[11]

Asian Indian immigrants constituted a similarly small proportion of California's diverse minority population. Sixty-four hundred Indians came in search of economic opportunities better than those at home, where British land-tenure policies had hurt small farmers. Even more male in composition (about 99 percent) than other Asian immigrant groups, the Indians usually labored in California fields in ethnic group–specific gangs, with some rising to the rank of tenant farmer by the 1920s.[12]

Although the timing and scale of their emigration differed, Europeans found their way to California, too. Jews participated in the surge of emigration that peaked in the first part of the 1920s and prompted new restrictions by 1924. A healthful climate and political refuge from the pogroms of 1905 through 1907 attracted Jews to the Golden State. San Francisco boasted the oldest, largest community. After World War I, though, the westward relocation of Jews already settled in the United States outpaced the flow of Jewish immigrants. In Los Angeles—a destination of growing popularity—the Jewish population grew in step with the city. Although only 2,500 Jews called Los Angeles their home in 1900, by 1945 that number had increased to 168,000. Distinguishing these immigrants from their Mexican, and especially Asian, contemporaries was their tendency to move as a complete family and the rarity of return migration. Jewish communities in California enjoyed more balanced sex ratios and stability than did other groups. So did the state's Italians. In the late nineteenth and early twentieth century, what Donna Gabaccia called "worker diasporas" scattered laborers across the globe from particular villages across Italy. Although many of these men and women settled along the East Coast of the United States, significant numbers relocated to Los Angeles, rural California, and, especially, San Francisco. By 1940 California's Italian population had reached 100,911—the largest of any western state. These immigrants, who more likely hailed from northern regions of Italy than southern ones, settled into jobs ranging from construction and agriculture to truck gardening and small trades. A relatively balanced sex ratio prevailed for "foreign-born whites" a census category that included Italians and Jews as well as Mexicans. Although slightly more Italian males than females populated the state, the gap was far smaller than for all other groups except native-born Whites.[13]

Well before the majority of these Italians, Jews, and other southern and eastern Europeans had migrated, Irish migrants had come to California. Like Italians, most Irish first settled in East Coast cities. But the lure of gold drew them west in large numbers during the mid-nineteenth century. When the dream of getting rich quick proved elusive, these Irish at least had the good fortune to find sufficient, well-paid work across the state, work withheld from their Mexican and Chinese contemporaries. By 1870 the Irish represented the largest overseas-born group in California, about 25 percent of the total. They would lose this ranking as the century advanced and emigration from Ireland dwindled.[14]

As much as the arrival of a wide spectrum of immigrants from foreign countries, the entry of African Americans, White southwesterners, and, to some extent, Native Americans in the twentieth century further guaranteed California's special diversity. African Americans were certainly present in the state as early as the gold rush when they had headed west in the company of slave owners or as freemen to make their fortune. Enjoying the break from southern-style discrimination, the African-American community made San Francisco its cultural and political center. The expense of housing pushed some out of San Francisco into more affordable housing in Oakland, a logical choice for Blacks working on the railroad, which terminated there. Not until the wartime demands of the 1910s, and the economic dislocations of the '20s and '30s, though, did migration make the group more visible in the California landscape. The new waves altered the distribution of the African-American community, with Los Angeles displacing San Francisco as the California city with the largest Black population. Propelled by the promise of freedoms denied them in the South—home ownership, integrated schools, minimal racial violence—they came in large numbers. From only twenty-one hundred in 1900 LA's African-American community had expanded to forty thousand by 1929.[15]

White migrants from Oklahoma, Arkansas, Louisiana, Texas, and Missouri may not have added to the racial diversity of California, but as newcomers with distinct cultural traditions they contributed to its heterogeneity. Migration that began as a steady stream during the 1920s became a fast-moving river in the Depression decade. More striking than the increase in numbers were the changed characteristics and intentions of the arrivals. After the stock market crashed in 1929, an already-struggling southwestern economy collapsed. Low crop prices, combined with environmental disaster, drove desperate farmers westward. As the historian James Gregory explained, unlike previous generations, these people seemed poorer and more driven by bad circumstances than pulled by opportunities. The majority chose California as their final destination, motivated by positive representations by boosters, writers, relatives, and friends. Although by 1940 more than half of the 701,300 had selected cities—especially Los Angeles, which drew three times as many migrants as San Diego, San Francisco, Oakland, and San Jose combined—almost 300,000 settled in rural areas where they became critical components of agricultural workforces.[16]

Already a diverse state, California became even more so in the first few decades of the twentieth century. The economic and cultural reach of the United States, the general expansion of capitalism, and political problems particular to European, Latin American, and Asian nations encouraged the migration of thousands. White and Black southwesterners, who increasingly saw opportunity in the fields and factories of California, joined these new immigrant minorities. In the end, this movement enhanced the state's distinctive heterogeneity.

BECOMING AMERICAN ETHNICS

This motley collection of migrants slowly settled into new routines and new ways of perceiving and ordering their distinctions. Established residents concerned about preserving or expanding their privileges and setting standards of difference determined the contours of ethnoracial groups, too. As historians who increasingly speak about the transnational nature of immigration have argued, assimilation and ethnicization were always two-way streets. While immigrants and ethnic migrants created their own affiliations, mediating between cultures of origin and cultures of the United States, they retained or evolved "diasporic sensibilities." Their awareness and active links to events and peoples of their homeland or, in the case of American-born migrants, home regions, became central to the "emergence . . . of nationally specific ethnicities." In early to mid–twentieth century California, this process of making ethnoracial distinctions or claiming membership in a community was informed by nationalist movements abroad, a multiethnic population, and racial definitions inscribed in American law.[17] Overall, the new arrivals stretched their notions of belonging, a habit they would repeat as the century wore on. The examples of Italians, Japanese, Filipinos, and White southwesterners represent some of the ways in which all newcomers to California carved out these early categories of connectedness.

For many immigrants, coming to California meant coming to see themselves as descendants of nations rather than regions, provinces, villages, or towns. Despite their physical separation they actively participated in making distant nation-states important units of their political and social experience. Italians arriving in the late nineteenth and early twentieth century considered themselves Ligurians, Tuscans, or Calabrians. They departed from a country that, until then, had faltered in its efforts to create self-conscious citizens of Italy. But as nationalist efforts gained momentum and the unifying, if fear-inspiring, leaders like Mussolini gained power, these immigrants broadened their self-definitions. The failure of Americans to observe the immigrants' regional distinctions mattered, too. Through everyday slights, slurs, and laws Americans constructed the members of villages or regions as Italians. The 1924 immigration act invented or acknowledged European nations, including Italy, in order to set its quotas. Meanwhile, census takers, labor organizers, and politicians counted, mobilized, and courted the votes of "Italians."[18]

California's multiethnic setting contributed to the broadened identity. Scholars have repeatedly distinguished the experience of the state's European ethnics from those of their East Coast counterparts, who suffered more sustained and harsher discrimination. Historians attribute the difference to the presence of Asian, Mexican, and Native Americans, who deflected White racial animosities away from White ethnics.[19] The targets of California's nativist movement and the ethnoracial expressions of Italians themselves support this interpretation. While preoccupied with harassing Catholics in the eastern United States, the California branch of the infamous nativist organization the Know-Nothing Party confined its attacks to Chinese at the turn of the century. And Italians did not stand on the sidelines. Italian fishermen of San Francisco Bay protested an attempted repeal of a tax levied against their Chinese competitors, insisting the payments were necessary protection for "White fisherman" against the "Mongolians." Italian-American leaders echoed this defensive notion of community when they condemned the goods, shops, and manners of Chinese and Japanese in the early 1910s.[20]

As the century progressed, an Italian identity was often defined by what or who it was not. The recollections of Joe Cruciano and Teresa Angeluzzi reflect the changing sensibilities of so many Italian Americans. Cruciano remembered playing with Black peers who "were very nice, very funny" in the state's Central Valley during the 1930s. Yet he never felt completely at ease in their company. "But they were oppressed, you could see it," he stated. "And I felt deprived as I was." This instinct to distinguish themselves from other minorities, to prove how American they had become, motivated the prejudices of Teresa Angeluzzi's in-laws. With the worst of the Depression years behind them, the Italian immigrant couple hired Mexicans for their expanding farm. Although Teresa Angeluzzi's mother-in law sympathized with the plight of migrant laborers, she treated the men as her inferiors. Angeluzzi's father-in-law conveyed this distaste and sense of hierarchy more starkly, referring to his employees by the pejorative "Messians."[21]

While Ligurians and Sicilians were becoming California Italians, men from many areas of the Philippines were inventing and being invented as "Filipinos." The 1896 revolution that liberated the Pacific islands from Spanish rule sparked a spirit of nationalism. But despite this enlivened sense of connectedness, few residents considered themselves in geographic terms broader than the town, province, or region in which they lived. These narrower loyalties initially survived the transition to California. Language differences and ideas of kinship divided Ilocanos, Visayans, and Tagalogs. But as Dawn Mabalon has argued, though their paths may never have crossed back home, the time they spent together in fields, dance halls, and gambling dens in the United States brought the men together. As exploited workers who hailed from a territory effectively controlled by the United States, they found things in common. For example, union organizers slowly convinced men to set aside their sectionalist feelings and act as a unified group. Their nationalist expressions remained more muted than those of Chinese or Korean immigrants who, from the safe distance of California, angrily denounced Japan's occupation of their respective countries in the early twentieth century. Tasked to resist colonization from inside the land of the colonizer, Filipinos adopted quieter, more indirect tactics.[22]

American citizens and their legislators described the diverse islanders as "Filipinos." Alarmed by the volume of emigration from the Philippines in the 1920s and 1930s, U.S. officials moved to redefine the political relationship of the United States and the Pacific nation and to dramatically reduce the movement of its citizens to the United States. The

1934 Tydings McDuffie Act reclassified Filipinos as aliens and limited their entry to fifty people annually. Revisions to the state's antimiscegenation law blurred the significance of regional distinctions as well. Regardless of their provincial origins, all islanders were categorized as "Malays" and added to those racial groups prohibited from marrying "Whites." Momentum for these statutory changes originated from diverse Californians. While established Whites characterized Filipinos as clever brown men on the make, Japanese and Chinese immigrants were as ready to stereotype and slander, portraying Filipinos as savage and dirty.

But the Japanese were themselves an ethnoracial group generated from experiences of movement and settlement in California. Many of these immigrants had left Japan at a moment of ascendant nationalism. The newly installed Meiji regime challenged regional and feudal loyalties in its attempt to create a more capacious community. Imagining a more unified Japan involved drawing lines of cultural and racial distinction. Although the Japanese acknowledged affinities with other Asians, whom they called common members of the "yellow" race and allies in a global struggle against the West, they simultaneously claimed physical and intellectual superiority over Chinese, Koreans, and Filipinos. These notions of kinship played out and evolved among the Japanese of California. Eiichiro Azuma has described the process by which Issei built collective memories and an "undifferentiated identity" through their writing of informal histories during the 1920s. These narratives celebrated Japanese as brave pioneers integral to the development of the American West and the overseas expansion of Japan. Glossing over the realities of their racial troubles as aliens ineligible for citizenship, landownership, or open immigration, Issei declared their equality with Whites and distance from other minorities.[23]

The Japanese of California enacted this historical understanding when they spoke and thought about Filipinos. Between 1930 and 1941 Japanese of the San Joaquin delta constructed themselves as a race distinct and superior to the Filipinos who worked their farms. The unpopular marriage of a Filipino man and Japanese-American woman initiated a decade of clashes. Filipinos boycotted Japanese businesses or struck against farmers in retaliation for what the Filipinos perceived as unfair wages, prices, and labor conditions. The Japanese answered these complaints by collaborating with local law enforcement, hiring strikebreakers, and convincing sympathetic Japanese workers to favor an imagined ethnic community over one of mistreated laborers. These delta residents increasingly conceived of their fight against Filipinos in racial and national terms; the struggle was the domestic corollary of the battle that Imperial Japan waged for supremacy over other Asian nations. In other words, by subordinating Filipinos, Issei believed they contributed to the strength of their homeland. Filipinos in turn forgave ethnic differences when faced with hostile Japanese. Capitalizing on deteriorating relations between Japan and the United States, Filipinos boasted of their American loyalty in contrast to that of the Issei. Such interethnic rivalries and the racial understandings they helped generate were not consistent throughout California. However, the case of the delta demonstrates how nationalism and international competition shaped ethnoracial groups in California.[24]

Regional loyalties conditioned the attachments of American-born migrants, too. The thousands of Whites who left behind the poverty of 1930s Oklahoma, Arkansas, Louisiana, and Missouri for the promise of California were discomfited by a population more multiethnic, and a racial tolerance seemingly greater, than the South's. White southwesterners resented that culturally unfamiliar Filipinos and Mexicans competed for and often won the agricultural jobs they coveted. That foreign-born Whites or Japanese immigrants were sometimes their employers or their contractors further disoriented the White southwesterners. But the position of Blacks bothered the "Okies" most of all.[25] Although African Americans in California suffered more than the Okies, Blacks gained new opportunities in education and the economy. Such relative advantages brought African Americans uncomfortably close to White migrants; the most startling break in racial segregation happened in schools, where Okie children learned alongside Blacks for the first time in their educational career. This social proximity infuriated Whites already disappointed by the prejudices they had encountered. In the context of a depressed economy, resident Whites came to perceive the Okie newcomers not as fellow citizens in desperate straits but as an alien social group. They derided Okies as social and physical inferiors, as those whose poverty and limited education were innate characteristics. Such perceptions clashed with the migrants' own view of themselves as "true" Americans whose ethnic background guaranteed them certain advantages. In maintaining the distaste for Blacks so characteristic of their southern homes, the Okies found an outlet for their frustration and potential source of affiliation with other Whites. James Gregory has described this California-grown sensibility as neither particularistic nor strictly exclusive. Rather, Okies claimed solidarity with all Whites who shared their values of independence and individualism. This vision of group identity firmly set the White southwesterners apart from California's Blacks, Asians, Mexicans, and even foreign-born Europeans.[26]

Integral to the process of making ethnoracial communities of Italians, Filipinos, Japanese, and "Okies"—as well as African Americans, Mexicans, Jews, Chinese, and Native Americans—were immigration policies, property laws, marital statutes, employment practices, and housing covenants. While the 1924 immigration act established national quotas that hurried the transformation of Ligurians into Italians, it also codified racial understandings that would facilitate the consolidation of European ethnics as Whites and the long exclusion of Asians and Mexicans. In her review of the statute Mae Ngai described how the act disentangled concepts of race and nationality, differentiating European ethnics even as it aggregated them as part of the White race. But for Chinese, Mexicans, and Filipinos, racial and ethnic identities remained the same. Rather than national quotas, the racial creation of "Asiatic" governed the migration of Filipinos, Chinese, and Japanese. In the case of Mexicans the dictates of foreign policy, privileges promised under the Treaty of Guadalupe Hidalgo, and labor market demands made it more difficult to block their entry on a racial basis. Yet administrative devices achieved the desired outcome. The enforcement of a ban on contract labor, the admission of a literacy test, and the screening out of those deemed "likely to become a public charge" effectively reduced legal, and increasingly illegal, Mexican emigration. Follow-up legislation—laws that made unlawful entry a felony and lifted the statute of limitations on deportation—not only criminalized illegal entry but also racialized such behavior as "Mexican." Illegal, in other words, became associated with Mexicans, regardless of their citizenship or immigration status.[27]

Marital and property laws drew similar lines of demarcation that helped create Mexicans, Asians, and Blacks as groups apart from most European ethnics. Alien land laws prohibited Asian immigrants from owning property, a prohibition that made more onerous the already heavy burden of being ineligible for citizenship, as established in the Naturalization Act of 1790. Other restrictions on property affected a broader cross-section of minorities. In addition to the informal acts of real estate agents and landlords who refused sales and rentals to non-Whites, housing covenants dramatically constrained residence. Devised by homeowners concerned about maintaining the "Whiteness" of their community, these agreements prohibited Asians, Mexicans, Blacks, Native Americans, and, customarily, Jews from buying or renting property.

First introduced during the 1890s, covenants were used by about 20 percent of Realtors in 1920. However, the figure had risen to 80 percent by 1940. Not until the 1948 U.S. Supreme Court decision in *Shelley v. Kraemer* did states lose the right to enforce racial restrictions on real estate.[28]

Access to housing influenced notions of ethnoracial community, but so did rules of marriage and employment practices. In response to rising rates of immigration and coincident fears about interracial intimacy, the California legislature passed a statute in 1850 prohibiting marriage between Whites and Blacks. In 1880 it expanded these limits by inventing new ethnoracial categories. Neither a "Negro Mulatto, [nor] Mongolian" could marry a White person. Although legislators originally designed the classification of "Mongolian" to restrict the rights of Chinese, officials soon applied it to Japanese as well. That an immigrant from Japan or China might conceive of himself in narrower, more national terms—conceptions formed out of his diasporic experiences—failed to register among or concern California Whites. Nor, as I mentioned earlier, did they notice the distinctions that divided Filipinos. These islanders were merged together under the label "Malay."

This disinterest in the origins and ambitions of minorities also confined them to the most disappointing jobs. Through the late nineteenth and early twentieth century, California saw the evolution of a system of capitalism premised upon a racialized division of labor. Under this regime ethnic and racial differences came to closely parallel class distinctions. Large-scale farming, food processing, construction, and petroleum industries depended upon the presence of a sizable, mobile, and inexpensive supply of labor. Aggressively recruited and deftly shuffled Asians, Mexicans, and Blacks fulfilled this economic need and assured California's prosperity. These groups were largely responsible for constructing the state's physical infrastructure, extracting its precious minerals, and growing its fruits and vegetables. Yet they endured the lowest wages, longest hours, and slimmest chances for upward mobility. Many native-born Whites had abandoned occupations in these areas for more lucrative opportunities as independent farmers, skilled industrial laborers, and business owners. The national economic crisis of the 1930s only darkened this already-bleak employment picture. For those lucky enough to keep their jobs and, in the case of Mexicans and Filipinos subject to repatriation, keep their homes on American soil, the Depression reinforced a racially stratified labor system. It was within this environment structured around the customary and legally embedded ethnoracial expectations of Whites that Californians made social and eventually political ties.

The expansion and accumulation of affiliations were essential to the integration of California's newcomers. After becoming American ethnics, they would become American panethnics; they multiplied their attachments as they confronted White racism and discovered cultural commonalties or opportunities with other groups. This pushing out of self and group boundaries took place in spaces of remarkable diversity.

NEIGHBORS

The separations and connections among California's diverse peoples in the first decades of the twentieth century were imprinted upon the physical landscape. Although the early ethnoracial thinking of these varied migrants predisposed them to keep apart, their paths intersected within California, thanks to formal and informal restrictions. In other regions of the nation, living on the other side of the tracks often meant living in monoethnic ghettos. But in California those districts most segregated from Whites were often those most integrated with multiple minorities (see table 1). This physical reality made possible, if not inevitable, the interethnic mixings and mingling that ultimately broadened the systems of difference upon which migrants had first settled.

Restrictive housing practices and laws concentrated non-Whites in the same neighborhoods, but the de facto segregation of public areas, schools, places of worship, and businesses made the intermingling of non-Whites even more likely. Mexicans, Asians, and Blacks frequently watched films from special balconies reserved for minority customers or patronized theaters more accepting of their business. "You could go to this one theater, and that was all right because that was where all the people of color would go," explained Connie Tirona, a Filipina from Vallejo, "but if you went beyond to the next block, people would stare at you." Restaurants refused service to those of darker complexion or seated them in distinct sections. Public pools reinforced White privilege as well. Hoping to prevent perceived contamination, administrators typically scheduled swimming days for minority children immediately before pool cleanings. At a pool in San Francisco the ticket taker told a young girl that "all Mexicans have to have a health card to get in" before turning her away. Beginning in the early 1920s city ordinances in Los Angeles kept Issei off public golf courses and tennis courts.[29]

TABLE 1. ETHNORACIAL COMPOSITION OF SELECT CITIES AND NEIGHBORHOODS
(% populations, 1950[1])

	Boyle Heights	Watts	Central Downtown	L.A. City	Fillmore District[2,3]	S.F. City[3]	West Oakland[2,3]	Oakland City[3]	East Sacramento[2]	Sacramento City	West Berkeley	Berkeley City
Asian[3]	15.0	0.5	8.4	2.0	15.0	5.0	7.8	2.1	19.0	4.4	5.0	3.7
Black	6.0	28.0	41.0	8.7	44.0	6.0	38.0	12.0	13.0	3.2	30.0	12.2
Foreign-born White	27.0	8.0	9.9	12.0	10.0	16.0	12.8	10.0	13.0	8.9	8.6	13.0
All White	79.0	71.0	50.0	89.0	40.0	90.0	43.0	85.0	66.0	92.0	60.0	84.0
Mex/Hisp[4]	46.0	13.0		2.0		0.7	1.6	0.5	2.6	1.1	0.5	0.4

SOURCE: U.S. Bureau of Census, *Seventeenth Census of the United States: 1950, Population and Housing Statistics for Census Tracts*, San Francisco—Oakland Census Tracts, Los Angeles Census Tracts, Sacramento Census Tracts (Washington, D.C.: GPO, 1952). Blank spaces in the chart indicate where data were incomplete or the ethnoracial group made up less than 0.5 percent of the neighborhood's or city's total population.

[1] Averaged and rounded, figures do not add up to 100 percent in most cases.

[2] Figures for the Fillmore District, East Sacramento, and West Oakland are averages of relevant census tracts.

[3] In the San Francisco and Oakland census Asian ethnics are categorized as "other race."

[4] The category "Mex/Hisp" counts only those born in Mexico for all census tracts except those of Watts and Boyle Heights. In these latter locations the census counts all residents of Hispanic descent.

Even at school and places of worship Whites deliberately separated themselves from minorities. They drew or redrew district boundaries or counted upon residential segregation to exclude non-White students, especially Mexican- and African-American youngsters. When challenged, educators and administrators argued that minorities' poor language skills and low intelligence justified the arrangement. Because of geography and deliberate policy, non-Whites worshiped separately as well. Many White churches either barred minorities or offered segregated services, hostile officiants, and specially reserved back pews. But as local institutions, houses of worship reflected a neighborhood's ethnoracial makeup. Thus a multicultural environment often explained an institution's diversity as much as its procedures of selection. As examples, Peoples Church in Berkeley, St. Patrick's in Los Angeles, and Trinity in Sacramento had Black, Filipino, Chinese, and Japanese congregants.[30]

Commercial districts tucked inside mixed neighborhoods brought minorities together as well. The reluctance of Whites to service and fairly compensate minority populations meant minorities frequently served and employed one another. Thus whether shopping nearby for groceries or seeking medical attention, a stiff drink, or an after-school job, non-Whites often found that the face on the other side of the counter, the stethoscope, the bar rail, or the paycheck belonged to another non-White. Economic depression only encouraged these patterns of interethnic interdependence as minorities, largely denied the levels of governmental aid offered to Whites, turned toward the local community for relief. Jews and African Americans opened small businesses, but Chinese and Japanese Americans were among the most entrepreneurial. On the edges of or inside the Black and Mexican communities of San Francisco, Oakland, and Los Angeles, Chinese and Japanese Americans established their operations and attended to local needs. Also, enterprising Asian ethnics, especially Chinese and Japanese, most commonly provided sites of rest and relaxation for other Asian men excluded from White restaurants, parks, theaters, dance clubs, and other social venues. Minorities spun a localized web of economic connections as a convenient and available strategy for survival in a time of economic discrimination and depression.[31]

A distinctive, racialized geography resulted from the scarce resources of non-Whites as well as the restrictions on housing, worship, education, public facilities, and employment. Those of the same ethnicity often congregated together, but they did not form isolated or perfectly self-contained enclaves. Instead, non-Whites *as a group* tended to be segregated. "Far from being randomly distributed," observed urban demographers in 1949

Los Angeles, "these five groups, Negroes, Orientals, Russians (mainly Jewish), Mexicans, and Italians are found in greater concentration in some census tracts than in others, and they tend to be closely associated with one another in their distribution." The scholars went on to conclude that "Negroes, Mexicans, and Orientals" were the most isolated groups and most likely to live in adjacent or mixed city blocks. Residents of these neighborhoods scored lowest in income, schooling, and level of occupation. A survey of housing in central Los Angeles—only Japanese and Mexicans had any significant presence outside this area—stated that Whites occupied a mere 18.3 percent of substandard housing compared with 28.6 percent of Blacks, 47.2 percent of Asians, and 59.6 percent of Mexicans. In contrast, the city's White southwesterners demonstrated a pattern of residential dispersion. The closest the White migrants came to concentrated settlement as a migrant group was in newer subdivisions on the outskirts of Los Angeles. Thanks to their citizenship and color, they had the freedom, a freedom they happily exercised, to live wherever they could afford to.[32]

In the San Francisco Bay Area officials noted a similarly skewed ethnoracial and socioeconomic distribution. In 1954 the San Francisco Department of City Planning concluded: "More than half of the dwellings occupied by non-White families are concentrated in about 175 city blocks which contain 50 percent or greater non-White occupancy." This pattern of residence roughly repeated itself in Oakland, where the housing authority in 1945 reported the confluence of poverty and a large minority population. This pattern of concentrated residence continued throughout the 1950s; by the 1960 census, the concentration of non-Whites had only deepened, with 89 percent of them squeezed into 22.2 percent of the city's census tracts (see map 1).[33]

More recent evaluations of race, ethnicity, and space in California have confirmed the convergence of non-Whites. The Center for Geographical Studies at California State University, Northridge, has determined that in Los Angeles between 1935 and 1955, not only were Mexicans "living close to or somewhat intermixed with immigrants from Europe or with Blacks, Japanese, or Chinese" but also that "pockets of multiethnic neighborhoods were quite common in poorer areas and were usually distinct from neighborhoods in which U.S.-born whites lived."[34] Historians of both the Bay Area and Los Angeles have acknowledged how "ethnic intermixing characterized most but not all central and east side communities," creating a "heterogeneous ethnic population," in the first half of the century.[35]

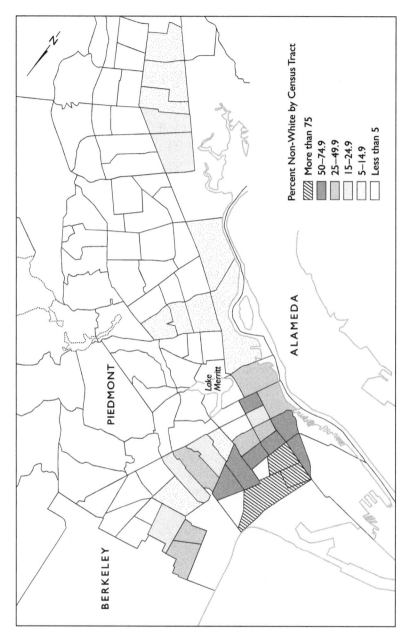

Map 1. Distribution of non-White population, City of Oakland; based upon U.S. Census data, 1960. Source: Bryce Young, *Oakland's Changing Community Patterns* (Oakland City Planning Department, 1961).

The most recognized and largest minority districts appeared in California's major cities during the second quarter of the twentieth century. In Los Angeles Whites, who represented almost 93 percent of the county's population, separated themselves on the West Side, surrendering downtown and East Los Angeles to new immigrants and Blacks.[36] Specific ethnoracial clusters dotted the area, yet they proved porous and imprecisely defined. Almost one-third of Jews resided in Boyle Heights, with significant pockets in South Central and on Temple Street. Meanwhile, African Americans clustered around Central and Slauson streets, with smaller settlements in West Jefferson, Watts, and South Pasadena (see map 2). Large numbers of Mexicans mingled among Blacks in these same sections or joined Jews and Japanese in Boyle Heights (see map 3).[37]

Like their non-White peers, Japanese were shoehorned into neighborhoods near commercial and industrial sections of Los Angeles. Some Japanese established homes as distant from downtown as West Los Angeles and Hollywood, but Little Tokyo (adjacent to Central Avenue), the West Jefferson area, and Boyle Heights absorbed almost all others. Japanese frequently shared blocks with Blacks. Within 1940 census tracts roughly bounded by Alameda, Central, Washington, and Jefferson streets, Blacks comprised 58 percent and Asian ethnics 29 percent of the population totals. Given that Blacks represented less than 3 percent and Asian ethnics not even 2 percent of the citywide population, these figures are striking. Japanese spread steadily westward from West Jefferson Street toward Van Ness Avenue. African Americans, who also were eager to capture space that opened up as Whites suburbanized in the 1940s, accompanied these Asian pioneers (see map 4).[38]

The much smaller populations of Chinese, Filipinos, and Koreans blended in with other minorities in Los Angeles. After the razing of Chinatown in 1933, Chinese relocated among Mexicans, Japanese, Blacks, and Jews in city sections marked by Hill and Broadway as well as San Pedro and Central. Chinese and Filipinos typically shared residence in 1940 (see maps 5 and 6). Although smaller in numbers, Filipinos as well as Koreans gathered near the larger Chinese community between Main and Los Angeles, west of downtown, or between Vermont and Western avenues. Sections of San Francisco and other metropolitan areas reproduced this same overlap of Asian ethnics. But enterprising Chinese also located themselves and their businesses in largely Mexican neighborhoods farther east. There, as Marshall Hoo explained, Chinese Americans found a ready supply of minority customers and rents that were much less expensive.[39]

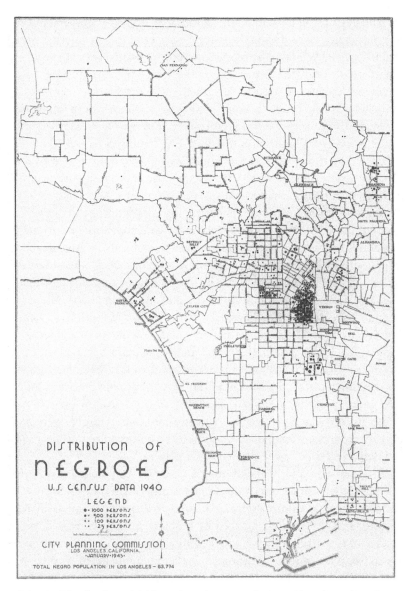

DISTRIBUTION of
NEGROES
U.S. CENSUS DATA 1940
LEGEND
●・1000 PERSONS
●・ 500 PERSONS
+・ 100 PERSONS
・・ 25 PERSONS

CITY PLANNING COMMISSION
LOS ANGELES, CALIFORNIA,
·JANUARY·1945·

TOTAL NEGRO POPULATION IN LOS ANGELES - 63,774

Map 2. Distribution of African-American population, City of Los Angeles; based upon U.S. Census data, 1940. Source: Courtesy of the John Randolph Haynes and Dora Haynes Foundation. Earl Hansen and Paul Beckett, *Los Angeles: Its Peoples and Its Homes* (Los Angeles: Haynes Foundation, 1949), following p. 36.

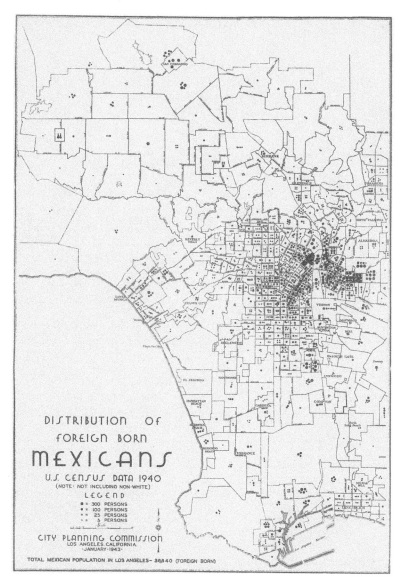

Map 3. Distribution of foreign-born Mexican population, City of Los Angeles; based upon U.S. Census data, 1940. Source: Courtesy of the John Randolph Haynes and Dora Haynes Foundation. Earl Hansen and Paul Beckett, *Los Angeles: Its Peoples and Its Homes* (Los Angeles: Haynes Foundation, 1949), following p. 36.

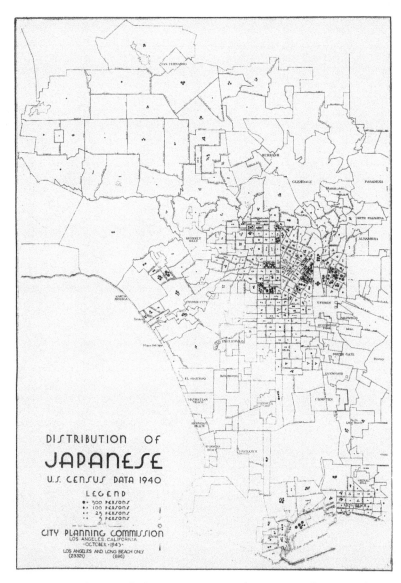

Map 4. Distribution of ethnic Japanese population, City of Los Angeles; based upon U.S. Census data, 1940. Source: Courtesy of the John Randolph Haynes and Dora Haynes Foundation. Earl Hansen and Paul Beckett, *Los Angeles: Its Peoples and Its Homes* (Los Angeles: Haynes Foundation, 1949), following p. 38.

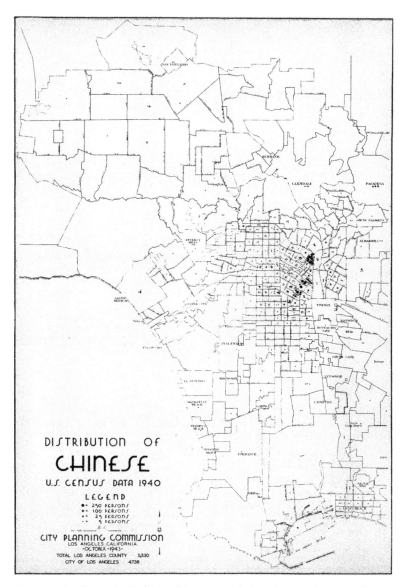

Map 5. Distribution of ethnic Chinese population, City of Los Angeles; based upon U.S. Census data, 1940. Source: Courtesy of the John Randolph Haynes and Dora Haynes Foundation. Earl Hansen and Paul Beckett, *Los Angeles: Its Peoples and Its Homes* (Los Angeles: Haynes Foundation, 1949), following p. 40.

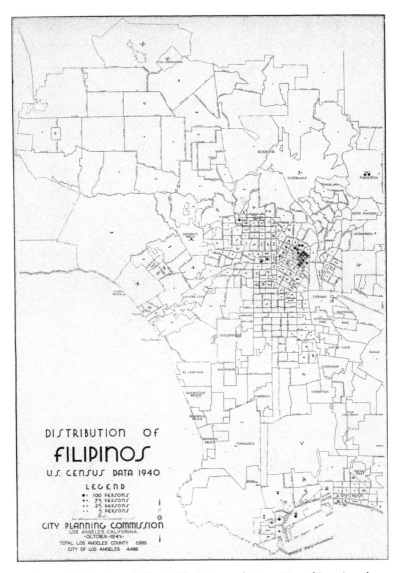

Map 6. Distribution of ethnic Filipino population, City of Los Angeles; based upon U.S. Census data, 1940. Source: Courtesy of the John Randolph Haynes and Dora Haynes Foundation. Earl Hansen and Paul Beckett, *Los Angeles: Its Peoples and Its Homes* (Los Angeles: Haynes Foundation, 1949), following p. 40.

Within this minority medley of east and central Los Angeles, some sections stood out as particularly eclectic. Before World War II Boyle Heights boasted a population of 25,000 Jews, 15,000 Mexicans, and 5,000 Japanese. "The neighborhood was very diverse," recalled Harry Honda, a Nisei. "We had Chinese families, Korean families, Latino families, Jewish families." Art Takei confirmed this portrait, explaining that although Boyle Heights would become "predominantly Latino," he "was brought up in a real diversified community" where "it was just everyone." Based upon the 1940 census, African, Asian, and Mexican Americans accounted for approximately one-third and foreign-born Whites another one-quarter of Boyle Heights's population, much higher fractions than their presence in the city's population overall. Foreign-born Whites accounted for 21 to 28 percent, again, a rate higher than the city's average.[40] Those who settled in Watts during the second quarter of the twentieth century remembered the neighborhood as similarly mixed with non-Whites. "The environment there was almost all races, and we got along very well. There were Whites, Mexicans, Orientals, Jewish people," explained William Woodman. Another resident suggested that the town's blacks, Mexicans, and Japanese "kept out" of White areas and remained among themselves, respecting the unspoken racial divide.[41] Census data supports these recollections. Almost equal numbers of foreign-born Whites, Mexicans, and Blacks—4 to 9 percent, 13 percent, and 14 percent, respectively—called Watts home in 1940.[42]

San Francisco's Fillmore District and Western Addition also supported a blended and changing minority population. A majority of the city's Black residents made their home in the area roughly bounded by Post, Sutter, Bush, and Pine streets. Adjacent and melting into the African-American district was a Japanese section bounded by Geary, Pine, Octavia, and Webster. But as in Los Angeles these ethnic clusters were no more than loose collections of peoples. Jews, Filipinos, and, to a lesser extent, Mexicans added to the diversity of the Fillmore and Western Addition. According to *Crisis,* the official publication of the National Association for the Advancement of Colored People, in 1945 "even the area of Negro concentration, the Fillmore district, did not constitute a 'Black Belt'" because "sizeable groups of Whites, Filipinos, Chinese and Japanese resided in the same area." Former residents remembered its eclecticism. We grew up "with every color you could think of," explained Sugar Pie De Santo, a Filipina-Black woman, of her 1940s neighborhood. Jerry Flamm, a Jewish storekeeper, recalled the important place of Jews within the "ethnic and cultural mix" of the Fillmore. In fact, the district's demography was so unusual that it became a point of curiosity among adventure-seeking tourists and locals. "In two chief Negro neighborhoods, between Fillmore and Divisadero streets, from California to Fulton streets, a great cosmopolitan neighborhood has grown up," stated one guidebook. The presence of "the Negro and the White man, Orientals of many sorts, East Indians, West Indians and American Indians" as well as "many inter-racial families" who supposedly lived "amicably side by side," made the area "San Francisco's melting pot." In 1940 minorities (classified as Black, "other races," and people born in Mexico) constituted no more than 5 percent of the city's population overall, but they represented 39 percent of residents in the district.[43]

Given the diversity of its business owners and clientele, San Francisco's Chinatown section was misleadingly named. Filipinos and Japanese filled the district, operating small businesses or consuming local services. Japanese Americans in particular competed with Chinese-owned enterprises in providing food, hotel rooms, medical advice, or Asian-imported collectibles to local Asian Americans as well as curious White tourists. Taking advantage of the tendency among White Americans to conflate Asian ethnicities, Japanese, Koreans, and Filipinos served up "Oriental" goods and Americanized Chinese food to outsiders who imagined the proprietors as representatives of an exotic China. In a pattern repeated across California cities, single young Filipino men looking for leisure activities and blocked from most White-owned and -patronized establishments, dined, played pool, gambled, danced, and slept in businesses run by Japanese or Chinese Americans. Japanese youth and families gravitated toward San Francisco's Chinatown for fun and festivity, too. In a recent interview Tarao Neishi, a Japanese American, explained that Chinatown was "the only kind of place we could go" before World War II. The report of the sociologist Rose Hum Lee and disgruntled comments made by Chinese-American residents on the eve of World War II documented exactly how sizable was the presence of non-Chinese Asians in the neighborhood. Rose Hum Lee counted as many as fifty Japanese shops ringing Chinatown. Meanwhile a writer for the *Chinese Digest* in 1935 editorialized that "the Japanese have already taken the southern half of Chinatown—our best bazaar section—and we are reminded of what harm is being done our bazaars when cheap imitations and flimsy curios flood Grant Avenue." Thanks to White prejudices, cultural preferences, and economic opportunities, Asian ethnics collected in Chinatown.[44]

Unlike the city's Asian ethnics, Jews, Mexicans, and African Americans, its Italian immigrants were more dispersed and more likely to live alongside other European ethnics. By 1940, 47 percent of Italians owned homes compared with 41 percent of non-Italian foreign-born families. In those census tracts that contained the largest numbers of Italians, the ethnic group still comprised little more than one-third of the total population. Germans, French, and Spanish speakers made up the remainder. Less than 2 percent of residents in the Italian-heavy tracts were non-White. In San Francisco the relative integration of European ethnics and their collective separation from minorities likely contributed to those sensibilities related by Italian Americans to researcher Micaela Di Leonardo. Looking back upon their lives in mid–twentieth century California, her middle-aged informants remembered Irish and Germans as "people like themselves." For European ethnics, as much as for Blacks, Mexicans, or Asians, where they lived and who lived nearby had a profound effect upon their ethnoracial notions.[45]

Across the bay from San Francisco, Oakland's established Whites similarly arranged their residential space. Minorities converged in the city's western end near local manufacturers and the terminus of the railroad. In this densely settled section west of Grove Street and San Pablo Avenue and south of Emeryville, non-Whites lived in housing that officials declared to be the worst in the city. Mexicans, Blacks, Japanese, and Chinese readily mingled. Rose Mary Escobar and her mother rented upstairs rooms from a Japanese family that occupied the flat below. In the same neighborhood Mexican Americans "coexisted with the growing African American community" that settled there in growing numbers through the 1940s. Although West Oakland would become a more singularly Black district during the 1950s and 1960s, in the second quarter of the twentieth century it integrated a remarkable collection of non-Whites. The two census tracts with the highest density of African Americans, 35 to 38 percent (compared with a citywide percentage of just 3 percent), also had twice as many Asian ethnics and four times as many Mexican immigrants as Oakland's overall population. In an adjacent tract the mix of non-Whites was even more balanced. Blacks and Asian ethnics represented 11 percent and 5 percent of the total, respectively. Where Asian ethnics were most concentrated, making up as much as 45 percent of two census tracts within West Oakland, Blacks still appeared in significant numbers. Alternatively, the 1940 census reported how evenly foreign-born Whites were distributed. In no single tract did they exceed 22 percent or dip below 7.4 percent of the total, figures that fell close to their 14.1 percent share of the city's total population.[46]

Minorities lived in the easternmost sections of Berkeley, just along the city's border with Oakland. Asian ethnics and Blacks most conspicuously converged in two census tracts marked by Grove Street on the north, San Pablo along the south, Dwight Way to the east, and Russell to the west. Combined, the ethnoracial groups represented no more than 6 percent of Berkeley's total, but in these eastern neighborhoods Blacks made up 31 percent and Asian ethnics between 7 and 22 percent of the residents. In contrast, and as in other metropolitan and nonmetropolitan areas of California, foreign-born Whites were found in relatively equal numbers across the city.[47]

Although smaller in size, California's rural towns segregated non-Whites as decisively as their big-city counterparts. Chinese, Mexicans, Filipinos, Japanese, and some Blacks resided in the state's fertile valleys, where they shared bunkhouses, makeshift camps, hotels, or old houses. In cities like Fresno and Stockton, where migratory laborers rested from fieldwork and waited out rainy winters, non-Whites occupied clearly defined territory. "Fresno shows a rather interesting situation," a surprised reporter wrote in 1936. "This town is divided into two parts. One 'west' and one 'east' of the railway tracks. 'West' of the tracks is the foreign-born residential section, in which at least thirty different nationalities are represented." In central Stockton Japanese, Chinese, and eventually Filipinos converged in what became known as the "Oriental Quarter." Chinese immigrants first settled the area bordered by Market, Lafayette, El Dorado, and Hunter streets in the nineteenth century. Japanese soon joined them, building a residential and commercial presence that overlapped with and extended west of Chinatown. When Filipinos arrived in larger numbers in the 1920s and '30s, they too blended into the mostly Asian district; their attempts to find housing, leisure, and basic goods outside the quarter met with immediate opposition. Along El Dorado Street they frequented restaurants, gambling dens, and pool halls, many operated by Chinese or Japanese Americans. A comparable split marked the landscapes of Sacramento and Watsonville. The 1950 census corroborated Ernesto Galarza's depiction of California's capital as a city where Blacks, Asians, and Mexicans concentrated in the easternmost and northernmost sectors. Although these ethnoracial groups represented 3.2 percent, 4.5 percent, and 1 percent, respectively, of the city's total population, in the area bounded by R, Capitol, and 7th streets they comprised 23 percent, 45 percent, and 6 percent of the total. The neighborhood's large number of Mexicans is even more apparent when calculated as a percentage of the district's foreign-born White population: 62 percent.[48]

Watsonville's demographics conformed to the same pattern of segregation. There, "an understanding prevailed," remarked local resident Duncan Chin, that "Asians, Africans, and Mexicans . . . would stay south of
the plaza."[49]

Even in more sparsely populated areas such as the Imperial Valley,
non-Whites generally became neighbors. "The Mexican and Negro settlement is found 'across the tracks' as a rule," one citizen observed of
towns in the valley, and were "fairly well marked off from the sections
inhabited by the Whites." According to a study of housing in the valley,
sections east of the Southern Pacific railroad tracks held the majority of
substandard housing. In towns such as Brawley and Calexico, Mexicans
resided in approximately three-quarters of the properties deemed unin-
habitable. This pattern proved typical of the region: Mexicans, Punjabis,
Japanese, Chinese, and Blacks established businesses and residence in
self-contained eastern sections, rarely venturing into the White western
end.[50]

Chinatowns, Little Manilas, Mexican barrios, Black districts, and
Japantowns occupied the residential and commercial landscape of California, but these settlements were more flexible and fluid than self-
contained. Black districts bled into barrios, while Filipinos lived inside
Chinatowns. Small numbers of European immigrants inhabited these
areas, too. Thanks to housing discrimination and financial constraints,
minorities occupied multiethnic rather than ethnically singular territory.

CONCLUSION

Coming together in California, ethnic migrants, immigrants, and established residents collectively and often competitively created systems of
difference. Notions of nationalism, American laws, cultural diversity,
and misperceptions fixed, at least temporarily, the parameters of groups.
These conceptual and emotional borders of distinction took on spatial
forms. Minorities converged in many of the same city and rural districts,
forming multiethnic swaths within the larger, more monoethnic field
of California. Inside and outside these integrated environments, which
were segregated from White neighborhoods, panethnic social, cultural,
and eventually political relationships evolved.

CHAPTER 2

Young Travelers

Born in 1912, Dora Yum Kim grew up in San Francisco's Chinatown, where her parents operated a pool hall frequented by single Chinese, Filipino, and Korean men. Despite the ethnic differences among the men, Dora remembered the district as a space where "you never thought about nationality" because "we were all Orientals to Americans, and we were all just here together." Her own social and cultural choices reinforced her view of inter-Asian harmony during the 1920s and 1930s. She befriended local Chinese and Japanese Americans from whom she learned of new foods, games, celebrations, and vocabulary. Yum Kim learned from her parents too but reinterpreted their lessons about Korean politics and traditions to fit her multiethnic setting. Try as she did, she could not appreciate or apply their animosity toward Japanese. Her local contacts and experiences made it difficult. "Your parents tell you that in Japan the Japanese hate the Koreans, and they still fingerprint them even though they have Japanese names and all that," she explained. "But within the community of people we knew, we had a Japanese doctor, Dr. Clifford Uyeda, who went to Japan to try to fight against that. . . . You can't tell what people believe based upon appearance."[1]

Despite geopolitical and parental pressures, a sense of solidarity with other non-White ethnics, especially other Asians, shaped Yum Kim's acculturation. At a dance sponsored by Girls High School in San Francisco, Yum Kim and a close Chinese-American friend watched from the sidelines as, "sure enough, every white girl was asked to dance, but this girl and I were never asked." The young women reacted with disgust as the rejection they had anticipated played out in practice. The pair found comfort, however, in one another's company. "I'm really glad I went with my girlfriend because imagine how I would have felt if I had gone there alone as the only Asian girl, being ostracized like that," Yum Kim said. Such conspicuous acts of prejudice reminded her of the parallel positions occupied by other minorities in California.[2]

Dora Yum Kim's story highlights the complex, often competing attachments available to non-White youth who inhabited residential and economic spaces of remarkable diversity. These young people, whose contacts and conversations with one another mattered as much to their socialization as the teachings of families and community institutions, experimented with and expanded ethnoracial boundaries. The demography of their neighborhoods and a youthful propensity to risk encouraged their crossing over into other cultures. Such travels did not happen equally or evenly. Political and familial concerns, ethnic stereotypes, and gender standards structured their interactions. Training for the prerogatives of manhood, non-White boys enjoyed a greater freedom than girls did to engage with other ethnics, especially those of the opposite sex. The cultural and political preferences of parents conditioned their meetings, too. Not all teens shook off the nationalist beliefs of immigrant elders as easily as Dora Yum Kim. Finally, a desire to win the privileges of better-off White ethnics, and a conviction that associations with other non-Whites might delay those gains, motivated young Californians to limit their outside connections.

If non-White youth in multiracial environments of the 1930s and early 1940s did not collapse ethnic borders altogether, they did expand them to accommodate more cultural contacts and to better realize the inclusive principles of California society. Most California youth borrowed selectively: they tasted a new dish, copied a hairstyle, or learned a few words in another language. But in these multiracial spaces even those who preferred the company of coethnics and integrated cultural variations more superficially often embraced a multicultural ethos. They celebrated the ethnic diversity that described their surroundings as the essence of American democracy and identity. In doing so, they lent credibility to cosmopolitanism—an ideology increasingly popular among educators, policy makers, and liberal Whites—that valued cultural diversity and promoted intercultural harmony. Rather than merely listening to the hopeful rhetoric of authorities from distant places, these youth demonstrated how ordinary and workable the everyday practice of cultural difference could be. Although they primarily learned this tolerance through relations with other minorities and they primarily promoted cultural exchanges *among minorities* as central to Americanization, they allotted White ethnics an equal place in the multiethnic, democratic society they envisioned. Theirs was not the exclusive understanding of ethnoracial identity as conceived by more radical African-, Asian-, Mexican-, and Native American activists in the late 1960s and 1970s.

However, a small but highly visible number of youth adopted a more separatist and minority-centric sociopolitical perspective. They consistently bent ethnic lines, opening up space for pronounced panethnic affiliations. For them the cosmopolitanism in which their peers trusted as a strategy of integration seemed inadequate and naive. In seeking to level ethnoracial inequalities by celebrating cultural diversity, these disaffected youth reasoned, cosmopolitanism ignored privileges that European ethnics enjoyed and they did not. Their cross-cultural relationships reinforced their critique of social inequities. But as a group, when thrown together in these spaces, minority youths mixed more willingly and regularly than previous generations, producing new cross-cultural tensions and understandings.

MULTIETHNIC SPACES OF YOUTH

Stepping out onto the bustling streets, sidewalks, and parks of their communities, young minorities of distinct backgrounds struck up impromptu conversations and play sessions that frequently evolved into more regular and planned encounters. This was the case in such demographically eclectic places as West Oakland, the Fillmore District, Boyle Heights, and West Stockton. A liberal sprinkling of White ethnics, mostly immigrants and their children from southern and eastern Europe, inhabited these spaces and entered into the social circles of minorities, too. The ethnic makeup of many rural areas also supported the cultural experimentation of children and adolescents. Youth often grew up in the company of minority adults to whom their parents provided food, entertainment, housing, or work. And because school populations and religious congregations typically mirrored the composition of urban neighborhoods or small agricultural towns, non-White youth had ample opportunity to mingle as they participated in classes, services, and extracurricular activities. Pardee Lowe spoke affectionately of the educational melting pot that was his San Francisco elementary school, where "no two in the entire group [were] of the same nationality." Yori Wada, who would dedicate himself to social work in postwar San Francisco, summed up this pattern of diversity amid segregation in Hanford, California. "In some ways we had a segregated elementary system," he related in a 1990 conversation. "It was geographically based and most of the minorities lived on the southside of town so they had elementary school southside where most of the Asians, Blacks, and Hispanics went to school." This diversity mapped itself across local religious and community centers as well. Sports teams, summer camps, and day-care programs sponsored by All People's Christian or All Nation's Churches in Los Angeles, for example, brought together Korean-, Mexican-, European-, Chinese-, and African-American children.[3]

These centers, schools, and churches contained a youthful, increasingly American-born, as well as racially diverse, population. Among Mexicans and Asians, a second generation was emerging and preparing itself for leadership. Asian Americans appeared in California as early as the 1850s but constituted a small subgroup until the 1920s. Between the world wars American-born Chinese and Japanese gained numerical dominance in their respective ethnic communities. By 1940 the second generation represented one-third of the Japanese adult population in Los Angeles, and one-half by 1945. Japanese offspring throughout California organized social clubs, athletic teams, and political organizations— most prominently, the Japanese American Citizens League (JACL)—that expressed their distinctiveness from their parents. The children of Chinese immigrants also advanced a generation-specific ethnic identity that was oriented more toward American education and middle-class aspirations.[4]

Like their Asian-American peers, U.S.-born Mexicans and African Americans assumed new importance in the years before and during World War II. Mexican descendants had long resided in Southern California, but not until the Mexican Revolution and the mass migration it stimulated did Mexicans create large settlements there. As a result a sizable, mature second generation became influential only during the 1930s. By the 1930s and 1940s, 70 percent of the population of Mexican origin in California were the offspring of Mexican immigrants or Americans of Mexican descent.[5] During the same period African-American families escaped to the state in increasing numbers and brought with them adolescents who joined the sons and daughters of immigrants, including American-born European ethnics whose parents had crossed the Atlantic at the turn of the century, in shaping the local scene. This general shift toward a younger, more native minority population in the second quarter of the twentieth century helps explain the emergence of a unique set of youthful attitudes and behaviors.

In the decades leading up to World War II minority youth were numerous enough, and concentrated enough, to mix and mingle. Out of their regular meetings came a multiethnic youth culture torn between a faith in cosmopolitanism and doubts that cosmopolitanism could improve their condition.

CROSSING OVER

If young minorities were encouraged by demographics to engage with other ethnics, they did so strategically. Familial pressures, international politics, ideas about appropriate gender roles, and socioeconomic aspirations set limits on their intercultural contacts. Thus youth were not perfect cosmopolitans indifferent to the advantages of drawing distinctions amid social and cultural complexity. Even as they took notions of equality and inclusiveness further than their peers in more monoethnic settings, they still clung to certain exclusions in order to manage their multiethnic surroundings.

For Asian-American youth in particular, international events and economic inequalities had important local consequences. Their own relations were complicated by the competing political and economic positions taken by their parents. Although these Asian immigrants resided in the United States, many, like those from Europe, felt passionately about and participated in events in the countries of their birth. Thus, when Japan began to covet and conquer new territory in the Pacific during the 1930s, many Chinese, Filipinos, and Koreans in the United States were outraged. Communities acted out their frustrations by organizing fund raisers, boycotts, and propaganda campaigns. Although the hostility of Koreans, Chinese, and Filipinos was primarily directed at Japan and Japanese abroad, it frequently corrupted their associations with Japanese in California. Anti-Japanese acts perpetrated by Filipinos increased through the 1930s, prompting a commensurate increase in anti-Filipino feeling in the Japanese community. Frustration about wages and working conditions reinforced their political disagreements. Because the Japanese often owned and managed farms, they had a much-resented economic leg up on Filipinos. In one instance that was illustrative of the resentment this relative advantage caused, a group of Filipinos attempted to cash checks forged in a Japanese man's name. The thieves were captured at a Mountain View, California, bank and found guilty in 1937.

Another instance in which economic disparities strained Filipino-Japanese relations occurred two years later, again in Santa Clara County, when seven Filipino men plotted to rob a Japanese farm owner. Police apprehended the thieves in the midst of their crime. Even when Japanese and Filipinos shared the same economic footing, as in a case that Charles Kikuchi chronicled in his diary, distrust and violence could prevail. While laboring as a farm picker in the late 1930s, Kikuchi befriended a mixed work crew of Japanese and Filipinos. Although he noted "distinct parallels between the situations of the two colored groups," an interethnic riot broke out during which his nose got sliced. After the fight each ethnic group asked its employer to fire the other. These economic gaps and political differences became significant obstacles around which Filipinos and Japanese youths would construct their relationships.[6]

Although Chinese communities in California enjoyed relative economic parity with the Japanese, their political differences brought the groups into confrontation. In 1930s San Francisco, Chinatown merchants launched a protest by burning their Japanese curios in a huge bonfire. Young men delivered speeches denouncing Japanese aggression and urging local activism. Families brought silks, bracelets, rice, and ornaments purchased from Japanese stores and tossed them into the pyre. As the crowd grew in size, so did the sense of festivity and commitment to the anti-Japanese action. Outside San Francisco, Chinese Americans expressed discontent with less drama but familiar dedication.[7]

As American-born residents of multiracial neighborhoods, Asian-American youths had more attenuated connections to Asian nations, but the views of their elders still influenced the everyday encounters and political behavior of the youths. Monica Sone, a Japanese American, could not help but notice how global events, especially Japan's invasion of North China in 1937, heightened ethnic tensions as she strolled through Chinatown. The "pointed, icicled glare" of the Chinese storekeepers who paused in their gossiping as she passed was unmistakably hostile. Some of her Asian peers learned and acted upon this antagonism. Taking cues from her mother, who had joined a women's auxiliary in San Francisco that opposed Japan's expansion in Asia, Lorena How made special coins to sell as part of a war relief fund-raiser. More confrontationally, she stood outside Japanese gift shops lining Grant Avenue and urged customers, "Don't buy, lady, Japanese store!" Angry Japanese proprietors chased her away with their brooms. Paul Paular confessed that he too fell under the spell of anti-Japanese fervor. Soon after the bombing of Pearl Harbor, he and his Filipino friends spent an evening meting out their version of justice: they stole bikes and candy that belonged to Japanese Americans.[8]

But many Asian Americans reacted to conflict overseas much like Dora Yum Kim, by questioning parental loyalties and differentiating Japanese in California from Japanese in Japan. Jeanne Wakatsuki Houston's account of her first day at school highlights the difficulty of the second generation in perfectly reproducing the ethnic rivalries of their elders. As a child on Terminal Island in Southern California, she grew up under the firm control of her father. To discipline his periodically unruly daughter, he would threaten to sell her to "a Chinaman." Taking her father's promise to heart, she screamed and cried during her first day at kindergarten when a Caucasian girl, "who happened to have very slanted eyes," sat beside her. Though prepared to fear and separate herself from Chinese, Houston's poor powers of identification turned an act of ethnic separatism into a comedic mistake.[9]

Older youth had the maturity to make more deliberate and independent political decisions reflective of their close encounters with one another. In a 1943 interview Yuri Kosamoto claimed that he had long felt disconnected from Japan and "sorry for the way Chinese were being treated by the Japanese." He credited his sensitivity to a scene that he witnessed in the San Francisco Bay Area months before Japan's invasion of China. The vulgar, aggressive behavior that Japanese sailors on leave displayed toward local Nisei disgusted him. Although grateful for the relative respect that Japanese immigrants in the United States enjoyed because of Japan's power, Kosamoto did not express this gratitude as hatred toward Chinese Americans. Such careful distinctions defined the positions of so many second-generation Asians who, in contemporaneous and later interviews, remembered separating American-born Asians from Asian nations. Mary Lew Shepard's account of an enduring friendship with a Nisei girl highlights this propensity for parsing ethnic differences. The pair became close companions at their San Francisco high school and remained close even after Japan invaded China. "I didn't hold it against her because it wasn't her fault but her government, her ancestors," said Shepard, who was of Chinese descent. Even when Shepard picketed at Pier 45 against scrap iron shipments to Japan, the two remained friends "because we didn't connect sometimes with China, so we didn't connect her with Japan." Overall, the conflict in Asia made American-born Asians more cautious in their intercultural contacts, but they did not end those contacts because of their proximity to one another and distance from Pacific Rim nations.[10]

As much as competing political loyalties, competing definitions of gender mediated the meetings and affections of non-White youth. Although both sexes sampled the multiple cultures of their mixed neighborhoods as a rite of passage and opportunity to elaborate identities, standards for exemplary women's behavior limited the experimentation of many girls. Such cross-cultural contacts, especially those involving young men, were more difficult, more discouraged, and more damning to their reputations. Certainly, ethnoracial communities and individual families varied in their expectations, but it was generally true that boys enjoyed greater autonomy and acted within a larger physical expanse than their female counterparts. This pattern reflected the conviction common in so many cultures that women were vulnerable and men powerful. As the historian Mary Odem has noted in her study of teenage girls in early twentieth century Los Angeles, a concern for female chastity was not a value exclusive to the Protestant middle class. The patriarchal family structure, code of honor, and religious traditions of many working-class and immigrant families circumscribed the social activities of young women. Chaperones, tighter curfews, and more home-oriented chores were parental attempts to protect their daughters. Daughters who accepted these prescriptions about the ideal behaviors of and interactions between women and men were not only pacifying their parents but also practicing their own beliefs. Proximity to the young, frequently lonely, young men, with whom their parents did business as labor contractors or operators of pool halls, restaurants, and boardinghouses, often made the young women feel as if they had to obey.[11]

Taking advantage of their freedom, many minority boys of the period tested the cultures of those all around them. Their drive for adventure made them active explorers of California's multicultural places. In his memoir about growing up in the southern section of Watsonville during the 1930s, Duncan Chin describes watching Mexicans leave the pool halls and beer joints that surrounded his Chinese-language school, listening to customers at the barbershop pass the time by strumming "Celito Lindo'" on their guitars, seeking fishing advice from the Japanese American who ran the town's tackle shop, and smoking cigarettes that "Blackie," a Cherokee, gave to him. This spectacle of diverse activities and peoples offered Chin both engaging entertainment and a thorough education about different traditions, occupations, and languages. Similarly, the camps where the Mexican workers of Japanese and Filipino employers rested became informal schools for the curious sons of the contractors. The laborers invited these children to sample freshly made tortillas and listen to the stories they shared of home and family far away.[12]

Perhaps even more than their leisure-time encounters with non-White adults, the small jobs that boys often assumed gave them insight into other cultures and an understanding of diversity as both an ordinary and essential dimension of community. In the "lower quarter" of Sacramento, Ernesto Galarza worked easily among a diverse network of acquaintances. Big Singh, the Asian Indian who operated a boardinghouse for Hindu laborers adjacent to Galarza's home, hired him to prepare the "thick flour cakes" called roti. Simultaneously, Galarza learned about the Chinese laundry business as an errand boy, sold catfish to the Japanese fish peddler, and convinced a Black woman to save her empty bottles for his collection. After distributing handbills for a sumo wrestling troupe that was passing through the city, Galarza sat down in the crowd and watched in amazement. Becoming an integral link within his neighborhood's diverse local economy required him to understand individual cultures and negotiate between them. Bill Sorro, a Filipino American, had less entrepreneurial energy, but his paper route among the Black bars of the Fillmore District in San Francisco widened his own awareness. "The beautiful sounds of Black music" that he heard wafting from the district's clubs introduced him to the jazz, gospel, and blues that would captivate him through his middle age.[13]

Work also introduced young boys to the racial inequalities and distinctions that so frequently separated Whites from other ethnoracial groups. Duncan Chin, who was Chinese American, picked apricots at a Watsonville ranch during his summer breaks from school. He regularly caught rides to the fields in the trucks of Mexican laborers who also harvested the summer crop. Chin related that "I blended in okay," but his White friend from Arkansas did not. The southerner's "Whiteness made him stand out like a turnip in a bucket of tomatoes." Chin's experiences highlighted his developing awareness of color in California society and how comfortably certain minority groups blended together, a comfort only the incongruous presence of a White boy made him realize. Having seen ethnoracial differences in his neighborhood as occasions for profit and discovery, the sudden realization that differences were divisions startled him.[14]

Using the space permitted by their parents to explore, minority boys tried out the attitudes and behaviors of those more persuasive than adults, their peers. With a boldness that few girls could or would exhibit, Kazuo Inouye cut school with his Jewish friends in Boyle Heights. Inouye

already knew a few Yiddish expressions, but he advanced his Jewish education by playing hooky. He attended bar mitzvah classes where the
local rabbi showed him how to write his name in Hebrew. For Inouye
his neighborhood and the mixed people he met there provided more intriguing information than the books he read at school and the lessons
taught by his Japanese parents.[15] Peter Jamero, who was Filipino, thanked
a Mexican-American neighbor for instructing him in the ways of Americans. Ralph Perez, "the most convenient older role model in my own
acculturation process," Jamero explained, "drove a car, and spoke English
better than anyone I had ever heard."[16] Unlike many second-generation
youth who accessed American habits and values through White peers,
Jamero became more American through his relationship with an ethnic
Mexican. Jamero's story suggests how cultural mentoring of minorities close in age and location could ease the adjustment to mainstream
society.

But the greater ease with which minority boys could admire or date
individuals of other ethnoracial groups was what most distinguished
their developing gender identity from that of girls. Certainly, communities and parents pressured boys to stay within the ethnic circle, a pressure
that I will discuss in greater detail in chapter 3, but interracial, heterosocial
contacts were still easier than they were for girls. At a Chinatown dance,
for example, Roberto Vallangca, a Filipino, attended under the ethnic
alias "Ben Lee"; he waltzed for the first time with a Chinese-American
girl. Though initially petrified, Vallangca/Lee soon relaxed and enjoyed
the "heavenly" company of the young woman. Given the reluctance of
some Japanese- and probably Chinese-American women to receive the
advances of single Filipino men, his posing allowed him to experience a
warmer, friendlier set of interactions between the sexes. If discovered by
his dance partner, Vallangca could expect her contempt, but as a young
man the exposure posed little risk to his reputation among Filipinos.
Wooing girls of other races was an expected, assumed privilege of the
mostly male community. In the more demographically balanced Japanese-
American community, young men talked breezily about dating non-
Japanese. Allen Ihara recalled in a 1944 interview how he and his Nisei
pals from Pasadena had had "their fling in sowing the wild oats too like
most of the fellows do." These boys dated Chinese, Korean, and White
girls whose lively spirits, they believed, favorably contrasted with those
of Nisei who "didn't know how to be casual and friendly." That these
girls did not belong to the intimate circle of Nisei added to their appeal
for adventure-seeking young men.[17]

If boys could comfortably satisfy their appetites for the culturally different, the spaces and familial codes that constrained the lives of minority girls made it much more difficult and anxiety provoking to do so. Geography and economics brought minority girls into regular contact with
older men of unfamiliar ethnic backgrounds, but familial and personal
notions of appropriate female behavior often led the girls to withdraw.
Chizu Iiyama and her sister initially enjoyed the presence of single Black
men who rented rooms at their father's hotel in 1930s San Francisco. The
men "were so kind to us. They gave us 'Black names' and 'Black dolls'
for Christmas," Iiyama recalled. Yet one day, while bathing in a bath-
room shared with hotel guests, Iiyama's sister spotted "these skinny
Black legs under the stall" and screamed for her father. When he arrived,
he found "the guy just looking," but the girls were surprised that such
an event occurred "in a time when people were so respectful of one another that nothing ever happened to us." The incident betrayed not only
the girls' naïveté but also how the proximity of minority men could be a
source of danger and fear.[18]

As the girls became young women, the proximity of older men and the
prospect of interethnic dating appeared even more unsettling. Motoko
Shimosaki helped her father operate a pool hall in rural Guadalupe that
served a primarily Mexican and Filipino clientele. Despite the proximity
of the men and her father's likely advice that she act hospitably, Shimosaki avoided them because they "caused trouble," "went around
murdering," and "seemed too sexist." Clearly, these men violated her
sense of how men should interact with women. In protecting her space
she held out for a preferred set of gender relations. So did Yone Mizuno,
a Japanese American who also lived in Guadalupe in the 1930s. Although Mizuno had gotten along well with Chinese and Italian children
at her school, she felt nothing but disgust for Filipinos. She disdained the
Filipino customers of her father even as he implored her "to be patient"
for the sake of the family business. Instead, she fed the frustration of Filipinos, talking to, joking with, and dating only Nisei boys. She confirmed
ethnic barriers even as unmarried Filipino men hoped to lower them.[19]

Empathy for the loneliness of minority men and awareness of the discrimination underlying their single status did little to allay the personal
fears of young women. In Oxnard during the mid-1930s Nikki Bridges's
Japanese father hired gangs of non-White men to harvest his strawberry
crop. She understood the dilemma that restrictive legislation created for
these laborers, who "could never have a wife" and because of "the antimiscegenation law couldn't get married to Caucasians." But despite her

appreciation of these restraints, Bridges distanced herself from the men and what she perceived to be their aggressive sexuality. Among the group were Koreans whom she described as "a desperate group" and "very silent." She surmised that these characteristics encouraged her father to keep "a good eye on me and my mother because those men—who knows what they would do?"[20] This sense of threat and attempt to keep at a distance contrasted sharply with the easy mingling that boys like Peter Jamero enjoyed with Mexican fieldhands.

When the reluctance of girls to associate with neighboring non-White men clashed with the expectations of parents, generational tensions, conveniently avoided by boys, surfaced. Like many young Japanese Americans whose fathers contracted labor, Frances Nishimoto grew up among Filipino fieldhands. She could identify the exact moment when she began hating these single men. "When I was ten years old," Nishimoto explained in a 1943 interview, one of the workers "got fresh with me on the farm" and "I talked back to him." She refused to give the Filipino a ride back to the house, an act that so angered her father that he slapped her and urged her not "to be nasty to the Filipinos because they are good workers." Despite the reprimand, she continued to distrust Filipinos because "they were desperate for a mate" and "always looking at girls funny." Polite and regular interactions between daughters and non-White men were sometimes a business practice that fathers insisted upon.[21] In these cases the fathers must have trusted their workers and clients, dismissing their daughters' feelings as foolish or selfish. Yet when young women like Frances Nishimoto continued to avoid contact with or disrespected minority men, generational conflict ensued. Surprisingly, parents could find themselves in the position of advocating ethnic crossings that their daughters resented. Boys typically escaped this familial stress.

The worries and self-protectiveness of girls were not unfounded. What could happen became painfully clear to a Mexican American in East Los Angeles. A Black shopkeeper invited the young woman into his store to look for a dress. On previous occasions she had safely shopped at the establishment. But on this day the owner offered her discounted prices and a spiked ginger ale. When she returned home, wobbling and sporting bruises on her arms, knees, and lips, her mother had the African-American proprietor arrested for "contributing to the delinquency of a minor by offering her intoxicating liquor." This case emphasized how seemingly innocent and regular interethnic, heterosocial interactions could become dangerous. From an early age these young women were learning to treat non-White men with suspicion and missed out on much of the cultural adventuring of boys.[22]

Despite a general wariness, many young minority women still sought and found relief from uncomfortable gender roles in the company of male peers of other backgrounds. Those willing to make friends and dates with cultural outsiders may have considered White boys fair game but not a better game. These young women sought not so much the general advantages of White culture but the more particular and varied opportunities of other cultures in their midst. As schoolmates, neighbors, or friends of friends, these teenage boys were familiar and safe in ways that older men were not. Yet, they appeared different enough to fulfill girls' longing for cultural escape or adventure. In contrast to her first Nisei boyfriend, "who was so bashful that he sent me a scarf for a Christmas present and he didn't put his name on it," Sammy, "a cute Jewish boy," was fun and interesting, Tamie Ihara said. She enjoyed how differently he behaved from the shy, boring Japanese Americans she typically dated. The notion that coethnic boys lacked the charisma and daring of others motivated the dating choices of Jane Kim, too. She rejected the tentative advances of Japanese Americans at her Boyle Heights school in favor of her Mexican classmates. Mexican-American girls complained that Nisei got "all the good Mexican boys," which suggested that Kim's romantic choice was not a unique one. Characteristics that were too familiar to coethnic girls could seem appealing and exotic to those outside the group. Rose Mary Escobar of Oakland admired in her Nisei boyfriend precisely those qualities that Ihara, Kim, and other young Japanese-American women disliked. "A perfect gentleman," Escobar fondly remembered of her boyfriend's politeness and kindness years after they had broken up. Amid the Armenians, Germans, Italians, Mexicans, and Chinese of her Fresno neighborhood, Clara Chin, a teen of Mexican and Chinese descent, chose a Mexican-English lad as her first boyfriend. Not only did he share her tastes for football, movies, and dancing, but he also felt comfortable in mixed ethnic company because of his own background; neighboring Jews, Irish, and Chinese were part of their social crowd. These cases demonstrate how multiethnic zones created risks for young women but also chances for more complex, fluid self-definitions.[23]

As much as ideas about appropriate gender roles, relationships among minorities were structured by a longing for the full privileges and status of many White Americans. Oftentimes, this striving for acceptance was a competitive process in which non-White youth traded stereotypes and kept at a distance. Prejudices of families, friends, and the larger society colored their own thinking. At a very young age non-White youth showed sensitivity to ethnicity and race. On the playground of Ernesto Galarza's Stockton school, children called each other "wop, chink, dago or greaser." Yet the pejorative names "were simply insults we heard from our elders, uttered without malice or real understanding of their meaning," Galarza insisted. Hours later these same children played easily together. However, even if the boys made nice quickly, their use of ethnic slurs revealed an early awareness of racial difference and a willingness to enforce those distinctions through names and taunts. Kimbo Kurihara acknowledged that he and his childhood friends in the early 1940s used epithets in moments of heated argument, but he too believed that these words had little significance. They may have lacked the malevolence or consistency of racist expressions spoken by adults, but the tendency of even very young children to reach for race as a point of demarcation suggested an evolving ethnoracial consciousness. And part of that evolution was the recognition that certain European ethnics enjoyed greater privileges. Looking back upon his youth in the 1930s, a Chinese American from Los Angeles rosily related the absence of prejudice in his neighborhood. His large social circle included children from the usual proximate minority groups: Japanese, Chinese, Mexicans, and Jews. But he was not as free of discrimination or discernment as he claimed. As a boy he deliberately avoided association with "ritzy whites," an avoidance that captures not only how class influenced relations among youths but also their willingness to consider certain European ethnics, but not others, as their compatriots and equals.[24]

Aspirations for and strategies of acculturation prompted non-White children and adolescents to more consistently separate themselves from one another. For Asian ethnics imitating the racial preferences of their parents and White peers, this often meant disparaging African Americans. Richard Moto, a Japanese American, grew up in a predominantly Black neighborhood of Berkeley, where he and his brother hung around with African-American neighbors. But prejudice tinged these friendships, thanks to his father's repeated warning that Blacks "were dirty and filthy" carriers of disease. The lesson taken by Moto and his brother was the risk to one's health and socioeconomic prospects posed by association with Blacks. A new student at a Pasadena grammar school in the 1930s, Doris Ihara, immediately noted how definitively this assumption shaped the interactions of her peers. Nisei shunned a Japanese-American girl "because she played with the Kurombos [derogatory Japanese term

for Blacks] and she was not so good looking." Despite their limited
years, these young Nisei were actively separating themselves from other
groups with the hope of assuring their own mobility.[25]

Among Asian ethnics, the drive for acceptance expressed itself as
a competition about who most acted, talked, and thought like White
Americans. Tadashi "Blackie" Najima, a San Francisco Nisei, sharply
distinguished himself from Chinese Americans at his school. "I didn't
like the Chinese kids at all," he said in a 1944 interview, "because they
stuck to themselves too much. These kids were always talking Chinese
in school and that griped me to hell. I used to fight with the Chink kids
every time." Why did Najima so heatedly criticize his Chinese-American
peers? He did not specifically explain his feelings, but his depiction
echoed that of so many Whites who labeled Chinese as "clannish" and
unable to assimilate. In categorizing them as foreign, Najima could claim
the status of an insider. He was not alone in his attempt to elevate Japanese Americans by putting down Asian neighbors. Laura Tanna's 1932
column in California's *Kashu Mainichi* affectionately personified LA's
Little Tokyo as a "modern maid" whose wide-flung arms embraced "oc-
cidental sophistication" and rejected "aged traditions and hovering elders." In sharp relief Tanna portrayed the city's Chinatown as a "tired old
woman, inimical, crouching in the sun," who "holds to traditions and
frowns upon her too modern children." In portraying Little Tokyo as
modern and Chinatown as traditional, she implied the greater preparedness and worthiness of the Japanese community for full inclusion
in American society. Filipino-American youths in close contact with
other Asian ethnics made comparisons similarly designed to prove how
American they were. During a recent conversation Jerry Paular contrasted the open, easy interracial relations of Filipino boys in the 1930s
and 1940s with those of highly academic and prejudiced Chinese Americans, who, he argued, cut themselves off from other students.[26]

The longing for full acceptance into American society prompted other
efforts of demarcation among non-White youth in multiethnic settings.
For fairer-skinned Jews and Mexicans, whose technical position as
Whites already set them apart, the temptation to disidentify from other
minorities proved especially difficult to resist. Second-generation Mexicans involved in the Mexican-American Movement (MAM) often surrendered to it. A group of up-and-coming youth, MAM championed a
middle ground between the Mexican traditions of their parents and the
norms of Anglo Americans. MAM members stressed education, citizenship, and subdued displays of ethnic heritage as a means of improving

their lot. Leaders extolled the civil rights efforts of African Americans and urged members to emulate their activist course. "As the Negro grows in education he also grows in political strength and presents an important factor in American politics which cannot be overlooked," observed a columnist in a 1938 issue of MAM's *Mexican Voice.* "They are trying to better themselves. Why can't we engender the same spirit?" Yet the writer stopped far short of endorsing an alliance of Blacks and Mexicans against segregation. A Black friend had advocated such cooperation, which he firmly rejected. "Why should one of Mexican descent join forces with colored people to fight segregation? We're of a totally different race. We're of the same white race that segregates us. No, the only thing to do is to elevate ourselves; to command respect by becoming educated. This segregation is a challenge, not a combined fight. But yet we could profit by following the colored man's example in ambition and pride in our national descent," he concluded. MAM's reluctance to join with Blacks reflected its belief that, as Whites, Mexicans deserved the full privileges of that racial status. Associating too closely with African Americans would challenge this bid for equality.[27]

Jewish Americans also worked to position themselves, and were sometimes seen, as fully accepted Whites. James Alex Tolmasov, Boyle Heights resident, recalled that "Russians and Mexicans used their backs" and "weren't as educated and smart" as Jews, who emphasized education, owned businesses, and "were prominent." Asked in 1996 to reflect upon his early days in Watts, Marshall Royal, a jazz musician, was less persuaded by the success of Jewish American strivers. In his neighborhood of working-class Italians, Jews, Mexicans, Asians, and Blacks, certain families changed their names and those of their children from ethnically specific to ethnically neutral ones. The process by which "Navakoffs" became "Novas" did not fool Marshall, who knew "Jewish people were running to be considered as being all white." However, their working-class and multiethnic settings limited the distance that Jewish American youths actually ran. Leo Frumkin of Boyle Heights explained why certain Jews remained within the orbit of Mexicans, Blacks, and Asians despite their European heritage. East LA Jews like himself "never thought much of the kids—Fairfax, or wherever else they lived," mostly because these West Side Jews "were already the little more wealthier kids. These were kids whose parents weren't chicken peddlers." Jewish efforts to share the privileges of other White ethnics still fell short in the 1930s and early 1940s, and plenty of Jewish youth built their identities around this shortfall. However, even the efforts of some to escape segregation and exclusion expressed a desire that helped them relate to, instead of separating them from, other minority youth.[28]

Decisions about friends, dates, clothes, music, and food revealed the self-consciousness typical of aspiring adults. But unlike the choices made by children or teens in more homogeneous environments, those of minorities in mixed neighborhoods were as varied as the people they lived among. Well aware of the perils and promises of crossing into other cultures, youth did so cautiously but consistently.

COSMOPOLITANS

The ambition to win the privileges of many White Americans motivated minority youth to compete with one another, but it also fostered collaboration. Because of their multiethnic environments certain non-Whites thought about Americanization as a cooperative or mutually beneficial process. They imagined a society in which all cultural groups enjoyed equal standing, not one in which a single group advanced at the expense of another. This version of American identity was a capacious and hybrid one in which youths could selectively borrow from varied cultures in their midst even as they preserved vestiges of their own. Youths embraced these ideas not as deliberately defiant but as consistent with democratic principles and the teachings of progressive educators and officials. Exchanges of foods, words, clothes, and manners demonstrated how thoroughly young minorities enacted these notions in their everyday lives.

Educators of the day introduced youth to the cosmopolitan ideals so many would accept as a description of and model for their own multiethnic communities. As historians of education have noted, reformers and government officials had long viewed schools as ideal institutions for teaching citizenship and mainstream American values. Experts committed more completely to this pedagogical perspective in the 1920s, '30s, and '40s, as a rush of new immigrants raised concerns about sources of stability in a society with so many newcomers. The historian Mark Wild has described the programmatic realization of this perspective as "internationalism," a precursor of postwar ethnic studies. Schools promoted cultural understanding among California's diverse youth by frequently using international relations to model positive local interactions. Ernesto Galarza fondly recalled this curriculum as a student in 1930s Sacramento. His kindergarten teacher organized a kind of cultural "show and tell" in which first-graders shared objects or experiences that reflected their background. A Chinese boy unfurled a scroll, a Filipino demonstrated native fishing methods, an Italian shared his mother's quilting secrets, and Galarza related the tale of his trip on a stagecoach in Mexico. He credited this exercise, and others that stressed the value of difference, for helping to "warm knowledge into us and roast racial hatred out of us." By structuring and institutionalizing displays of cultural difference, Galarza's teacher helped him appreciate his everyday encounters with diversity. Los Angeles pupils of the Amelia School also enjoyed lessons that reflected their daily experiences. Educating mostly minority students, the school organized Cinco de Mayo and Japanese Boys' Day celebrations that showcased the traditions of the diverse neighborhood. Children also had the opportunity to ask questions of Native American visitors during special assemblies. In a neighborhood school less mixed with minorities, multicultural assignments such as these may have inspired curiosity. However, the children of multiethnic spaces were more than curious: practical, immediate considerations encouraged them to implement the lessons.[29]

Efforts to teach students to appreciate their differences motivated performances of and comfort with diversity in Los Angeles and San Francisco Bay Area high schools. At Roosevelt High School in Boyle Heights, where no single ethnoracial group predominated, special demonstrations of Chinese lion dances and Spanish songs educated students about the variety within their midst. So did speeches, exhibits, and parades for which students and teachers sported costumes representative of "the racial background of their families" as part of annual "International Days." Officially sponsored and faculty supervised "Cosmopolitan" or "World Friendship Clubs" at Roosevelt, neighboring Belmont and Lincoln, Oakland's Technical High School, and Berkeley High School, and even Los Angeles's City College, further reflected the efforts of educators to bridge different backgrounds. These clubs gathered students for discussions about the importance of brotherhood among various races and nationalities. All these plans and programs forwarded the notion of an American identity based upon an understanding of varied cultures. In doing so, educators created opportunities for students to cross ethnic lines and to conceive of those crossings as exercises in democracy.[30]

Indeed, in multiethnic high schools and colleges students did not simply tolerate a multicultural curriculum but embraced and advanced its principles. At Roosevelt High students celebrated their diversity in the pages of yearbooks and newspapers. A 1940 edition of the student newspaper, the *Rough Rider,* praised the school as a "typical American institution" where "students of Mexican, Jewish, Negro, Russian, French, Turkish, Finn, and Japanese parentage work and play together without any feeling of antagonism toward each other. We are truly a melting pot." The writer concluded the article by noting that "students with different ideas and customs are melted together to form a better American. All their efforts are eventually put toward bettering themselves and their country." Even when differences of background raised the potential for conflict, Roosevelt students expressed faith in an integrated environment. In a 1942 piece titled "Brotherhood at Roosevelt" a reporter for the *Rough Rider* observed, "Troubled days have descended upon American youth. Even stormier winds lurk ahead." The warning echoed that made three years earlier by student body president Masamori Kojima, who had coached classmates "to expect that we have sympathizers for both warring factions" and to "take care not to raise enmity amongst the students out of this institution." Despite concerns about the local effects of events overseas, students reaffirmed the value of their diversity. "It seems that Roosevelt High is a crucible of all nations," the *Rough Rider*'s 1942 article continued. "Russian, Jew, Japanese, Mexican, Chinese, Negro—all help to make their school the better for their having been there."

However, this conviction, that different cultures deserved respect, expressed itself beyond the printed page and the formal requirements of school. Atoy Rudolph Wilson recalled International Day as "quite interesting." He joked that he had not dressed up because he "didn't know what part of Africa [I] came from" and "didn't know whether I ate people dressed in a loin cloth." Even though Wilson's remarks emphasized the awkwardness that Black students felt because their ethnic histories were less easily traced or reduced to costumes, the sense of importance with which he remembered the event suggested that students took pleasure in and supported it. They did so in large part because the multicultural program was a practical guide for negotiating the cultural differences of their everyday lives. "You slept in each other's homes. You'd eat at each other's homes," Leo Frumkin fondly related about his Boyle Heights youth. "It was this interchange, this fellowship. I don't know what term you would use, except that you became internationalists." Like Frumkin, many minority youths chose cosmopolitanism as the perspective that most comfortably and accurately represented their intercultural relations.[31]

Roosevelt students were not alone in embracing an inclusive, multiethnic model of American citizenship. The 1940 yearbook of Roosevelt's near neighbor, Lincoln High, opened with a message entitled "Americans All" that celebrated the school as a "remarkable demonstration of the way in which many racial groups can be united in peace and harmony." Rather than "suppressing their admirable qualities," the author explained, "each brings the best he has to offer and benefits from the contributions of others. We find that there are leaders from every race in every field." And to relate these positive relations to the world beyond school grounds, the message asked Lincoln students "to remember the lesson we have learned in racial tolerance."[32]

Youth advocated a more cosmopolitan version of American identity through their choice of extracurricular organizations as well. What Paula Fass noted of New York public high schools in the 1920s holds true for multiethnic California high schools and junior colleges a decade later: ethnicity shaped and was shaped by student choices about the clubs to which they should belong. Involvement in "World Friendship" or "Cosmopolitan" groups most starkly expressed a panethnic or multicultural orientation. The smiling faces of World Friendship Club members peered out from the pages of the 1934 yearbook of Los Angeles City College (LACC). Beneath the photographs and surnames, which suggested origins in Latin America, Asia, and Europe, the club explained its mission:

> There is no institution in the U.S. that has the variety of races represented in its student enrollment, for its size, as has Los Angeles Junior College. In one of the industrial centers of the U.S. and near the Pacific Coast, the college serves as an educational melting pot for innumerable nationalities. Many collegians on the campus are of foreign birth and hundreds more of the first generation, born on American soil. Traditions and customs of their countries are woven into their daily life through home environment. These many representatives are drawn together in the classroom, and have established a medium of expression and better understanding.[33]

Freda Ginsberg Maddow, a Jewish American, recalled that she joined the club in the 1940s because "it was an important idea to me to be friends with all the different ethnic groups of people, to know their music, and to know what kind of dance, and to know everything about the culture." She lamented that the group may have met too infrequently to generate friendships that lasted more than the length of the meetings, but she still admired and believed she benefited from its multicultural intent.[34]

Even the ethnicity-specific school-based clubs that attracted so many young minorities articulated a cosmopolitan vision. Groups such as the Cathay Club, Rizal Club, La Società Dante, Le Collegian Français,

Hawaii Club, and Nisei Club offered members a sense of ethnic continuity amid diversity. Yet even as these organizations reaffirmed ethnic identities to some degree, they also promoted intercultural relations and exchanges. In Lincoln High's yearbook the Mikado Club stated its purpose as "creating a better understanding between the Japanese and most of the student body." The Russian Molokan Club had a similar objective: "International friendship among the students and faculty." At the college level non-White youth intended to include and educate ethnic outsiders as well. LACC's Rizal Club brought Filipino students together to foster friendship not only "between students of their own nationality" but also with "those of other races" and to promote "the intellectual and cultural life of the members." In 1933 La Società Dante and Le Collegian Français, whose participants were second-generation Italians and French, respectively, organized a joint Christmas party. Still other clubs expressed this awareness of and desire to connect with the student body as a whole. Founded in 1935, the James Johnson Club had originally excluded non-Black students from its efforts "to further the study and advance of Negro culture" but by 1939 welcomed "anyone who is interested in the accomplishments and problems of this often misunderstood race." Two years later it sponsored LACC-wide lectures about African-American life. In a request that foreshadowed that of a later generation of young activists, members proposed a "Negro Culture Class"; it quickly won the approval of the student council. Such acceptance demonstrated the appetite for teaching and learning about cultural differences on the multiethnic campus. In joining ethnically specific organizations, young people sought not only the comfort of familiar companions but also the promotion of their culture to a larger audience.[35]

The cosmopolitan ethos championed in the clubs and publications of multiethnic schools reinforced and reflected the cultural trades of minority youth. In spaces of pronounced diversity many young people comfortably swapped words, foods, songs, dance steps, and attitudes. Looking back upon their past in these places, minorities consistently recalled how flexible notions of ethnic and racial difference invited such crossings. As a Chinese girl growing up in Stockton, Maxine Hong Kingston had no "sense of very clear boundaries" between herself and her Japanese, Black, and Filipino friends. At their young age and in their diverse settings, these children reported feeling no different from their peers.[36] Ethnoracial distinctions also failed to impede or direct the interactions of Young Oak Kim and the Japanese, Chinese, Jewish, and Mexican kids with whom he grew up. "So right from the beginning I had to learn to get along with everybody," he said. Young never sensed that he "belonged to any one group," in part because no ethnic community held a numerical majority in his neighborhood.[37]

This hazy awareness of boundaries encouraged youths to regularly sample and swap the most immediate and accessible aspects of other cultures: food, language, and music. Vangie Buell, a Filipina born in Oakland, followed African-American friends into their churches, where she first listened to and fell in love with gospel music. Well into adulthood, she maintained a passion for the soulful lyrics and melodies. Buell returned the cultural favor of her companions, bringing them to the Catholic services she attended weekly with her family. Other kinds of ceremonies excited Ruth Takahashi. She recalled feeling a rush of delight when invited to the birthday parties of her Mexican-American girlfriend. Her own family "didn't have much of that," making the event particularly special. She could take part in celebratory traditions missing from her own ethnic repertoire. New words and phrases also imprinted diversity into the lives of minorities. Looking back to his youth in Boyle Heights, George Yoshida, a Nisei, described the Hebrew poem he had learned from a Jewish classmate and the sweet Japanese inscription a Black classmate had written in his yearbook. "I guess he wanted to learn a bit more about who we were and so forth, and he learned a few bits of *katakana*." These forays into other cultures were not necessarily long-term commitments to cultural change, but they suggested the much more fluid and potentially transformative pattern of sociocultural relations that prevailed among youth in multiethnic neighborhoods.[38]

Food and customs of eating were the cultural forms most commonly tested by youth. Maya Angelou related the multicultural education she gained as she ate her way through the restaurants of West Oakland. Biting into Chinese, Italian, Hungarian, and Irish dishes with her mother in the early 1940s taught her "that there were other people in the world." More informal culinary exchanges occurred at the cafeteria of Gloria Quan's Los Angeles high school, where the Filipina traded with Nisei for the sushi she so craved, and in the kitchens of Lisa Tsuchitani's Korean-American friends, where she enjoyed the peppery foods forbidden by her Japanese mother. Eddie Ramirez, a native of Boyle Heights, hungered for the rice with soy sauce and the sweet potatoes that his Nisei and Black pals offered him in exchange for his mother's famous burritos. When asked to recall what they liked or learned from other cultures as they grew up in diverse places, minorities most vividly and consistently mentioned food. As scholars have

Figure 1. Vangie Canonizado Buell (bottom left) and family. Private photograph of Vangie Buell.

argued, strong memories of specific foods signal the importance of what
we eat to notions of personal identity as well as individual bodies. Enjoying unfamiliar cooking made non-White youth more familiar with
one another. Food acted as the gateway through which they could discover other dimensions of difference.[39]

More than just stumbling into an appreciation of the most visible distinctions of their neighbors, youth deliberately emulated attitudes and habits that enhanced their evolving identities. In her semiautobiographical novel *The Woman Warrior* Maxine Hong Kingston explained how she shrugged off the polite demeanor expected of Chinese-American girls in favor of the toughness she observed in her African-American friends. She felt powerful as she bullied a quiet Chinese classmate at the Stockton elementary school. Emulating her Black classmates, Kingston detached herself from unappealing ethnic traits. She could become less foreign and more American by becoming Black. The notion that African-American culture fostered a strength and boldness lacking in Asian ones was neither uncommon nor consistently accurate. Whites and minorities alike often characterized Blacks as assertive. But Kingston's cultural understanding developed out of a close friendship rather than her imagination or popularly accepted stereotypes. While her Black companion coached her in unfamiliar ethnic behaviors, she shared a bit of "Chineseness." The friend "had her mother coil braids over her ears Shanghai style" to resemble Kingston's hair, transforming the pair into an unlikely set of twins.[40]

Such intimacy and careful observation informed the more extensive cultural changes made by other minority youths. Ruben Leon, a Mexican American, admired and copied the manners of his Boyle Heights neighbor James Tanaka with whom he talked and walked to school each day. The pair became "real close friends," close enough that Leon hoped "to keep up" with Tanaka in scholastics and athletics. Leon explained that he "started making A's, working toward A's and all that," as if competing in a contest. The results were grades better than he had ever received. But Leon credited his friend for more than his higher grades and fitter body. From the Nisei he learned a system of self-defense that protected Leon from bullies at school. Such skills gave young Leon "a sense of dignity" that made his adolescent years more pleasant. Charles Mingus similarly benefited from a cross-cultural education. The aspiring musician, whose timidity at twelve left him vulnerable to the taunts and teasing of peers, came to depend upon the confident example of Noba Oke, one of the few Japanese Americans in their mostly Black and Mexican high school in Watts. One day on his way home from orchestra practice, Mingus was intercepted by local bullies who kicked and tormented him until Noba Oke arrived. The Nisei not only rescued Mingus from the scene of abuse but also introduced him to the art of fighting. "That's right, Charles. Forget your cello. Be a fighter," urged Noba's brother Masa.

The variety and kind of lessons that Leon and Mingus learned from Japanese-American companions inverted the stereotype of the "quiet Oriental" that Maxine Hong Kingston so scrupulously tried to avoid. In these multiethnic environments more precise cultural trades could and did take place.[41]

At times these cultural discoveries and attachments went so deep that children lost sight of their own ethnic roots. Kisako Yasuda, a Japanese American, grew up among Native American girls in Long Beach during the 1930s and developed "the idea that I was an Indian." When her Japanese parents did not comprehend her speech, they falsely assumed she was speaking English rather than an Indian language. Yasuda's durable connection to "Indianness" isolated her from classmates as well as her parents. Why her peers "could not speak Japanese or Indian" puzzled her. Her unique acculturation drew her away from the traditions of both her immigrant parents and those of mainstream society. As a result this young girl's notion of what was normal—speaking Japanese or a Native American language—clashed with that of the people around her. Spending most of his days in the company of Jewish friends in San Francisco also complicated Tom Kawaguchi's ethnic awareness. The imprint of Jewish culture upon Kawaguchi appeared in his facility with Yiddish and his complete surprise upon learning that "there was a Japantown and all these Japanese."[42] More Jewish than Japanese because of his associations, Kawaguchi had trouble recognizing the ethnic community that could claim him as one of its own.

For Hazel Nishi a near disappearance into the culture of another was a more deliberate act of ethnic separation. In Santa Cruz at the close of the 1930s she mixed with Chinese Americans as regularly as with Nisei because she believed that, unlike the Japanese, who "were a very uninteresting lot" and "too Japanesey," Chinese Americans were sincere and "not so rural-like."[43] While Maxine Hong Kingston found a way into what she understood as American culture through associations with Blacks, Nishi did so by accessing another Asian group. In her own mind the Nisei had resolved the periodic debate between second-generation Asian ethnics about who was more assimilated: Chinese Americans. More generally, her experience represents one end of a spectrum of cultural experimentation available to youth who inhabited multiethnic spaces and learned cosmopolitan ideals.

Youth practiced the multicultural ideals preached by school administrators because they were compatible with the details of their everyday experiences. An ideology that emphasized respect for cultural differences and getting along became more than a wishful set of words. To minorities seeking both descriptions of and strategies for coping with their integrated, segregated spaces, cosmopolitanism was exactly that.

THE ULTIMATE CROSSERS

Within these heterogeneous neighborhoods a small but highly visible population of minority youth aggressively crossed ethnic lines and scoffed at the schemes of Americanization pursued by their peers. This subset of adolescents designed a street-centered, oppositional version of the youth culture that was defined by particularly permeable ethnoracial and gender lines. Not surprisingly, given the relative freedoms afforded their gender, boys were more prominent members. Although their active mixing expressed the experimentation and adaptation typical of many youth, it atypically challenged the segregated character of society. Too much interracial intimacy alarmed most White and middle-class Americans, who depended upon stable borders to protect their social privileges. At the same time these young women and men disappointed their own cohort by cynically rejecting cosmopolitanism as the solution to inequality among ethnoracial groups.

Mexican Americans were the most visible and talked-about participants (often described as *pachucos,* a word of Mexican origin) of this youth counterculture, but a wide variety of minority adolescents chose defiant styles and attitudes. As marginalized members of urban, immigrant, and working-class communities, African, Mexican, Asian, even some Jewish, Italian, and Russian Americans had reason to resent the conditions of their lives and similarly express that frustration. A sense of particular connectedness developed among these teens who felt themselves displaced and downtrodden. Barry Shimizu's first childhood friends were exclusively Japanese, but as he got older he palled around with Mexican and Italian kids. By the time he reached high school in Stockton, he had joined a casual gang of Nisei who periodically fought with White and Mexican rivals. But they "liked the Mexicans a little more"— so much more that they joined forces in a coordinated assault on White students. Shimizu and his buddies disputed the lessons of cosmopolitanism, learning instead to treat European ethnics as enemies. During a 1998 interview the African-American jazz musician Britt Woodman confirmed the sense of solidarity among similarly poor and persecuted Black and Mexican teens that set them apart from Whites in the neighborhood. "Mexicans were beautiful. Mexicans were like us in a sense—minority,"

Woodman explained of his friends in Watts who, like African Americans, stayed away from White districts and White peers at the local high school. In choosing to cross one ethnoracial line and not another, Woodman and his compatriots forgave what divided Mexicans and Blacks but preserved, even strengthened, what divided those groups from White ethnics. Jerry Paular articulated this collective disaffection with White ethnics more clearly. Thinking back to his 1930s youth, he described the zoot suit as a defense. You "put Whites on notice, I'm no fool, I'm ready," the clothes signaled. "Not all whites hated you," and, in fact, some "Okies" joined the crowd, Paular added, but "you couldn't distinguish among them." The zoot suits may have said more loudly than words that one belonged to a community of the disenchanted, but words communicated this membership, too. In his detailed 1938 study of young Filipinos in downtown Los Angeles, the sociologist Benicio Corpus reported their colloquial phrases. While the single Filipinos described White girls who dated Filipino men as "nigger lovers" and women who rejected the advances of Filipinos as "staying white," the Filipinos used the term *cousin* when referring to African Americans. Such language conveyed the Filipinos' feeling of fellowship, almost family, with nearby Blacks.[44]

Signature attributes of this mixed cohort included a style of speech, dress, and music that pieced together varied cultural sources. The zoot suit was the most visually dramatic and identifiable. Consisting of long, baggy pants, often in bright colors; an oversized jacket with padded shoulders; a wide-brimmed hat; and metal watch chain of exaggerated length, this distinctive outfit set the adolescents apart from more traditionally dressed Americans. Reports suggested the zoot suit's multiple lines of origin. Long before the garments became popular among California teens, they reportedly appeared on the backs of African Americans in Harlem as well as Mexicans in urban Mexico. California's Filipino Americans, such as Jerry Paular, offered still another theory of its beginnings, one that symbolized the phenomenon's interethnic and minority-centered character. Paular insisted that zoot suits were developed by style-conscious single Filipino men who convinced a Jewish tailor in Los Angeles to adjust ready-to-wear pants and jackets to fit the Filipinos' smaller frames. Pleats, zippers, and padded shoulders, which had been added for practical reasons, soon became must-have fashion features.[45]

Perhaps attracted by the zoot suit's mixed pedigree, California's adolescent minorities adapted it for themselves. And sometimes, in a gesture that made explicit the defiance implicit in the suits, youths stole or bought them from underground sources. According to the state's Youth Authority, Mexican and Black teens in 1937 broke through the skylight of a Hollywood-based clothing store, collected armfuls of men's suits, and proceeded to sell them "up and down Central Avenue," the commercial and cultural hub for much of Black and minority Los Angeles. Officials claimed that "two gangs of men or boys, mostly Mexicans and Negroes [are] operating along similar lines of action." Although authorities may have overstated the criminal activity, the robberies still represented the collaborative and rebellious character of the zoot culture.[46]

Hybridity and irreverence defined the speech as well as the dress of these teens. Combining English dialects and foreign languages, they communicated easily with one another, often-mystifying parents and other youth unschooled in their way of speaking. The jargon consisted of such catchphrases as "slick chick," "he's sharp, man," "so keen," and "everybody's jiving in his seat" that Mexican and Japanese youth had lifted from their Black peers. In the internment camps during World War II, Charles Kikuchi noted the extroverted Nisei zoot-suiters who spoke "the same jitterbug language with the same facial expression" that they had "copied from the Negroes." As minorities imitated rhythms of speech and traded words, language changed, becoming more expressive of zoot-suiter experience. In the tradition of Black jive talk Mexican-American youth invented the popular saying "He threw me a shine," said by one Mexican American to mean, "When you pass shoe-shine kids and they always say 'shine-shine?' Well, when you don't pay them attention, it's 'throwing them a shine,' see? Thus 'to throw a shine,' means to snub."[47] Observations made on urban streets informed a language intended to set zoot-suiters apart from their more conventional coethnic and White peers.

These ethnic sojourners actively blended their musical traditions in addition to their speech. Jazz and jitterbug had their roots in the African-American experience and were most regularly performed in Black areas such as LA's Central Avenue and San Francisco's Fillmore District, but the music soon gained broader audiences and venues. Among their most devoted fans were zoot-suiters who stretched and diversified the music's character. Through the 1930s and 1940s Mexican and Asian teens increasingly joined African Americans at nightclubs and cabarets. In a letter to a jailed boyfriend a young Mexican woman urged him "to get a Black finger tip coat, and when you come home we'll go to the Orpheum," where Duke Ellington performed and "everybody's jiving in his seat." As Eduardo Pagán noted, the excited fans were not passive consumers but active participants in the reshaping of these cultural forms. Mexican Americans transformed the lindy hop, a popular dance with beginnings in Black communities of the East, into the "pachuco hop," a much slower, more subdued set of movements.[48] African Americans did not always appreciate such revisions. In a 1997 interview Anthony Ortega, a musician, recalled being fired from Marty's, a Mexican-American–owned club, after Black customers demanded an African-American saxophonist. Disgruntled at the time, Ortega later came to respect the protest by Black Americans concerned about jobs and the integrity of a musical form some claimed as their own.

But most African Americans did not carry these racial preferences very far, accepting the interest and alterations introduced by Mexican and even Asian Americans. After losing his gig at Marty's, Ortega found regular work performing before largely Black crowds at LA's other Central Avenue hotspots. At the same time African-American performers and composers acknowledged their broadened audience of Asians and Latinos by changing their product. Black groups like the Woodman Brothers Biggest Little Band in the World acknowledged that they became more Mexican in their music, adding traditional folk songs to their play list when the crowd demanded it. At Sweet's Hall in West Oakland a Latino band alternated with a Black one, singing songs as ethnically varied as the audience itself. Asian Americans enjoyed jazz, joining the ranks of Mexican and Black artists and elaborating an already-diversified musical form. Chinatown restaurants frequently hired Nisei jazz bands, and Tote Takao, a Japanese American, performed with Lionel Hampton's all-Black band to great acclaim. Before Japanese internment Paul Bannai played the drums alongside Italian, Mexican, and Slavic musicians, and "because we had a mix," he related, the band played at "Slav dances," "Mexican dances," and "Italian things." By the mid-1940s a predominantly Black musical form and social scene had become decidedly more multicultural and emblematic of the hybridity at the heart of zoot culture.[49]

The aggressive cultural borrowing of these youths expressed itself in their attitudes and everyday behaviors as much as their hybrid style. A self-confident, even brash, masculinity that differed from the gentle and polite example recommended by elders and practiced by most of their peers set the boys apart. Many Asian teens modeled this masculinity from Blacks and Mexicans Americans whom they perceived as appealingly assertive. The Asians admired the Black and Mexican kids' carefree attitude, sense of style, and willingness to break rules. Lester Kimura of Boyle Heights bragged to interviewers that he "went around with a lot of Mexican guys" with whom he regularly cut school and practiced petty thievery. He credited his Mexican associates for his turn toward crime. The perception of Mexican and African-American males as audacious and strong also attracted Barry Shimizu away from a largely Nisei circle of friends and toward rebellious activities. Shimizu liked the Mexican American boys who "were rugged characters," taking "everything they wanted by force" and "being bold and daring." He joined a group of Black youths who taught him about cars, poker, and late night adventures. In comparison, Shimizu's Nisei peers in Stockton were "quiet, clean-cut," and eschewed profanity. Tommy Hamada too found the company of Black friends more enjoyable than fraternizing with the overly "Japanesey" Nisei.[50] Acting "Black" or "Mexican" gave these young Nisei men an escape from the ways of their own community. That escape was significantly different than that used by youths who lost themselves or attempted to lose themselves in White culture. Boys such as Kimura, Hamada, and Shimizu craved a way out that was consistent with their spirit of defiance, not a way up that required self-restraint and acceptance of the status quo.

The research of scholars concerning imitations of Mexican and Black cultural forms by more contemporary youths sheds light upon such mimicry in the past. Specifically, White youths who today borrow the dress, speech, and manner of Black peers have become so commonplace that they have earned a derogatory nickname, *wiggers*. Scholars observing the practice debate its significance. Some argue that White attraction to Black culture is an appropriation rather than an appreciation of difference that does little to correct racial inequalities. Others counter that taking on aspects of Black culture effectively challenges racism. The historian David Roediger disagrees with such generalized positions, insisting that the meaning of *wiggin'* depends upon the context in which it takes place. When the cultural borrowing happens as a result of specific contacts, learning it becomes less about commodification and more about understanding. But the imbalance that typically characterizes Black-White interactions often places such understanding out of reach. In the case of the minority zoot-suiters who populate this book, the copying of "Blackness" or "Mexicanness" arose out of intimate connections with Mexican and African-American individuals. Much like Maxine Hong Kingston's, theirs was an imitation grounded in regular interactions and overlapping disadvantage rather than distance and sharp discrepancies in power.[51]

Sociologists who have looked specifically at the borrowing of Black and Mexican-American culture by the children of recent immigrants have offered a different framework of explanation. In a process they describe as "segmented assimilation," immigrant teenagers within poor inner-city neighborhoods take on the behaviors and practices of native-born minority peers. At high schools in Miami, where Haitian teens rub elbows with African Americans, for example, the Haitians typically absorb from their marginalized classmates a resentment of White society and doubts about their chances of mobility. Even as these Haitians see themselves becoming more American, they separate themselves from the protection of their ethnic culture and the advantages of White Americans. Similarly, Mexican Americans in Central Valley schools, who have grown despondent over the persistence of racial prejudice, have acculturated recent Mexican immigrants in ways that limit their socioeconomic opportunities. Zoot-suiting types of the past practiced a similar kind of acculturation. Their example complicates the assumption of division between Blacks and new immigrants that many scholars have reported.[52]

Important though they were, the cultural trades of zoot-suiting proved more multidirectional and complex than merely the imitation of Mexicans and Blacks by Asian ethnics. Tommy Hamada modeled the speech of Black friends who talked "jive the best" but owed his sense of fashion to Filipinos. "I thought they were pretty snappy dressers," Hamada said, and he copied their clothes and the relaxed masculinity they exhibited inside pool halls and barbershops. Even the decidedly unhip and adult Japanese American Citizens League noticed this cultural borrowing, referring to the "Filipino haircuts" worn by Nisei zoot-suiters from Boyle Heights, Little Tokyo, and the Market District. A young man whom one sociologist identified as a pachuco because of his "poor manners, rudeness, indifference, and profound lack of self-control" also found alternative models. This Mexican-American youth had little contact with ethnic peers who described him as unlikable, but he befriended a young Nisei.[53] He learned the ways of *yogores*—chasing girls, skipping school, obsessing about cars—not from coethnics or Blacks but from his Japanese-American companion.[54] In this case and perhaps others, Asian Americans became mentors for Mexican Americans in the art of defiance.

For boys, taking on a more assertive masculinity usually meant aggressively pursuing girls of all ethnic backgrounds even as the young men fought off advances by outsiders toward women of their own ethnic group. Dismissing the convention of exclusively dating coethnics (see chapter 3), these young men pursued whomever took their fancy. Mariko, a young

Japanese-American woman who accompanied her Nisei boyfriend, George Yani, to a dance, noted the intercultural intimacies of Japanese-American zoot-suiters who arrived and fraternized with Caucasian women at a local dance. At the same party Mexican-American teens "made a great play over Maudie Yamazaki," a Nisei girl greatly enthused by their attention. The zoot-suiters likely expected, even welcomed, the disapproval of more conventional peers whose shock reinforced the boys' sense of themselves as reckless rebels. At the same time adolescents such as Maudie Yamazaki, who expressed too little disapproval of zoot-suiters, were at risk of becoming disapproved of themselves. Casually dancing and romancing across ethnic lines were scandalous acts, especially when performed in such a public venue. African-American zoots, polishing their reputations as daring young men, showed an equal willingness to proposition young women from a variety of ethnic backgrounds. "Negro youths will crack at anyone of any race who is nice looking," asserted Chester Himes of the Black zoot-suiters he observed in Los Angeles. As a self-described *yogore,* Charles Kikuchi regularly wooed girls of non-Japanese descent. Writing in his diary just before Pearl Harbor, he contemplated "going to San Francisco to chase girls tonight" with his friend Wang. Wang tried "to act like he is a man about town," Kikuchi wrote, "but he is a virgin and he really wants me to take him when Angelo and I go to Chinatown to chase girls."[55] This voracious appetite for young women of other ethnic groups set Kikuchi and his zoot-suiting partners conspicuously and deliberately apart from other male youths. The pursuit of women deemed off-limits was a central characteristic of their countercultural personas.

Although zoot-suiters sought out companions beyond their own ethnic community because they aspired to more assertive and defiant male roles, pachucas had their own ambitions. These young women were neither as numerous and notorious as their minority brothers nor as promiscuous as most press reports pretended, but they did defy and refashion gender standards. The historian Elizabeth Escobedo has argued that the pachuca persona offered young women an exciting diversion from the discrimination, poverty, and familial restrictions that marked their lives. Sporting big hair, short skirts, a sweater or tailored finger-tip coat, mesh hose or socks pulled halfway up their calves, and abundant makeup, the young women attracted plenty of uncomplimentary attention from immigrant parents, Whites, and ethnic peers. "We didn't talk to them," Rose Echeverria Mulligan, a Mexican American, insisted, referring to the pachucas. "We assumed that they would do anything that the zoot-suiters asked," a willingness she found surprising because "why would any girl dress like that or even be associated with anybody who didn't respect her?" Mary Luna agreed, refusing to become a pachuca in fact or by association. "I don't want to be seen with you like that," Luna warned her boyfriend when he appeared in the "pants and the hat and everything." Realizing how vulnerable and consequential their reputations were, these teens stood vigilant against even the smallest signs of transgression.[56]

But what these young women deemed inappropriate, others appreciated as alternatives to expected female behavior. Tommy Hamada grumbled that most Nisei girls were "afraid to be seen with me because they thought it would hurt their reputation." But other broadminded, non-Japanese girls who were looking for a little fun and adventure enjoyed young Hamada's street style and defiant attitude. Filipino and Mexican women who accepted Barry Shimizu's advances gained from their brief romances, too. None of these relationships lasted very long as Shimizu soon concluded that these women "were no good anyway and were only interested in the money I had to spend on them." Having enjoyed his spirited personality and liberal spending, they moved on to other men; these young women were less concerned about a steady boyfriend than the adventure of unconventional dating. An exasperated Japanese parent reporting on such young women claimed they went "out with anyone who can show them a good time," indifferent to whether these suitors were "Negroes, Mexicans [or] hakujins [Whites]." The chance to be shocking and unexpected in one's choice of men, to have a great time, to be treated to an evening out likely appealed to many young women.[57]

This was certainly the case for Rose Hayashi, a Nisei raised in Los Angeles. During her late teens and early twenties she dated a number of Kibei and Nisei but concluded they "were all the same," lacked "any backbone" but still "tried to make you," and "gossiped about you afterwards and spread nasty rumors." She enjoyed more satisfying treatment from other ethnic men. After dropping out of high school in 1940 to take a job in a Chinese-run gambling hall in San Diego, Hayashi found she felt "funny at first" in the company of the mostly Filipino customers. Yet she warmed to the men because "they treated me nice and whenever they won a lot of money in the gambling room, they always gave me a small share." She briefly dated a Filipino bachelor but broke off the affair to pursue a romance with her Chinese-American boss. These associations could create an appealing aura of daring and individuality for young women hoping to distinguish themselves from their ethnic peers. As a result of their cross-cultural ways, these young women enjoyed a bolder social scene and sampled new ways of being a teen.[58]

Within a larger adolescent culture zoot-suiters carved out a space for themselves marked by repeated cultural crossings. Rather than answer poverty and discrimination by adopting the norms of middle-class, White Protestants or the cosmopolitan hopes of their minority peers, these youth chose a defiant acculturation premised upon habitual, transformative ethnic crossings with many minority cultures. They may have constituted a numerically small and often estranged segment of minority youth, but these teens showcased the exciting possibilities of multicultural contacts as an alternative version of Americanization.

CONCLUSION

Thus on the eve of World War II minority youth had fashioned for themselves friendships, romances, cultural tastes, and attitudes that were truly multicultural. Having grown up in mixed neighborhoods, mixed economies, mixed churches, and mixed schools, they built identities that centered on ethnic crossing. However, youth participated in this mixed culture with different intentions and different levels of enthusiasm. Some simply enjoyed the chance to test new gender roles or familial traditions. Some embraced other minorities as part of their cosmopolitan vision and strategy for correcting the discrimination in California society. For others multiethnic lives seamlessly blended with, and helped them express their frustration with and defiance of, White society. At least in these multiethnic neighborhoods in the years leading up to World War II, these adolescents linked their lives in ways that more often expanded than constricted ethnoracial categories.

CHAPTER 3

Guess Who's Joining Us for Dinner?

When she was fourteen, a Mexican-American girl married a Filipino contract laborer in Stockton. The relationship did not last long but produced a son, Eddie Erosa, born in 1938. He grew up among similarly mixed families in the rural San Joaquin Valley. Reflecting upon the customs of his youth, Erosa explained that marriage to Mexican women "was the going thing" among Filipino men. This certainly was the case among members of his extended family; all his Mexican-American aunts chose Filipino partners, and his mother's second husband hailed from the Philippines. The valley's sizable numbers of mixed couples and single people of mixed race offered Erosa a ready-made community. But when he stepped beyond this safe circle of mestizos and encountered "unmixed" Mexican and Filipino youths, he had to "prove himself." He had little patience for both groups' airs about racial purity, given that, as he put it, "the Spaniards messed them up in the same way." After relocating to Wilmington, a city just south of Los Angeles, during junior high school, he met Gloria, whom he would marry less than a decade later. Although her Filipino parents objected to her dating a mestizo or Mexican, she recalled in a recent interview, she did not share their tastes. In fact, Gloria Erosa made it her mission early in life to find a husband of at least some Mexican heritage. She explained her romantic preference as the consequence of childhood friendships with Mexicans whose toughness she respected and depended upon in her mostly Black and White high school. Initially attracted to Mexican-American students because they could protect her, she quickly discovered other admirable traits. But her familiarity with Mexican Americans discouraged her from dating "pure" Mexican men because "they were controlling. They liked to be the boss," she asserted. Alternatively, "when you marry a 'half,' they're only half a boss so you get to be a boss, too." Eddie Erosa met her bicultural criteria, and the two married in 1954, beginning a partnership that has lasted more than fifty years.[1]

The story of Eddie and Gloria Erosa suggests the highly original intercultural choices made by minority Californians looking for love and family in the 1940s. The crisscrossing of ethnic lines by experimenting youth sometimes became more permanent and mature commitments. Certainly, the comfortable company that Gloria kept with Mexican-American teens informed her decision to marry Eddie years later. The pair's romance also highlighted how demography, work, concerns about gender, and notions of race or color informed the intimacies of non-Whites. The child of a mixed marriage, Eddie Erosa was also a member of a biethnic community built at the crossroad of skewed sex ratios, farm labor, and histories of colonialism. His impatience with existing ethnoracial categories reflected his own position. At the same time Gloria Erosa's discomfort with what she perceived as the bossiness of Mexican men showed how adults went further than experimenting youths: adults fully adopted another culture's gender roles as their own.

Scholars have long treated intimate intercultural relations such as the marriage of Eddie and Gloria Erosa as unique sites of cultural engagement and change where one can read the larger meanings of social relations. These intimacies offer a window into gender and racial mores at different times and locations. Students of European immigration typically cite high rates of intermarriage among European ethnics as evidence of their incorporation and consolidation within U.S. society. But perhaps because of legal limits, stronger social taboos, and their relative rarity, sex and marriage between Whites and non-Whites have excited the most attention. As Peggy Pascoe concluded, based upon an analysis of statutes and court cases, miscegenation laws became the ultimate "sanction for the American racial system and White supremacy" from the end of the American Civil War through the 1967 Supreme Court decision in *Loving v. Virginia* that declared these statutes unconstitutional. When a White man married to a non-White woman grew weary of and wished to end their relationship, the husband could free himself from the social and economic responsibilities of supporting an ex-wife by having the marriage annulled; men argued—an argument the courts consistently accepted—that their marriages had never been valid because they vio-

Figure 2a. Gloria Erosa, 1953.

lated state antimiscegnation statutes. Thus the intention of laws designed to protect property and patriarchy by prohibiting marriage between Whites and non-Whites (but not interracial sex) was realized. Others have concluded, perhaps optimistically, that if marriage prohibitions were intended to shore up the authority of White men, their removal, and a rising incidence of intermarriage in the late twentieth and early twenty-first century, may signify the declining significance of male authority and racial difference. The historian David Hollinger warned against romanticizing historical cases and the increasing contemporary rates of intermarriage. But he saw such mixing as potential evidence of the ability of the United States to incorporate diverse peoples despite its troubled history of racism. Renee Romano made a similar claim in her study of Black-White marriages in the second half of the twentieth century. Examining what she considered the "most tenacious of color lines," she argued that World War II produced new thinking that effectively weakened opposition to pairings between Blacks and Whites.[2]

Figure 2b. Eddie Erosa, circa 1955.

Figure 2c. Eddie and Gloria Erosa, circa 1990.

But these accounts and the larger scholarship on intermarriage to which they contribute pay little attention to the other ethnic lines that cut through and were crossed over in American society. Minorities found love and company with one another as well as with Whites, expanding and relocating ethnoracial boundaries within multiracial spaces. While marriages among European ethnics tell us about their growing affinity, and White-minority romances often highlight the longevity of White privilege, the intimacies *between minorities* reveal the bonds that increasingly connected them to one another and disconnected them from White ethnics. As Henry Yu has argued, when Whites have married Asians or Blacks or even Mexicans in the past, their transgressions have not so much eroded as reinforced standards of distinction.[3] Most cases of interracial marriage in the past were really about the preservation of White authority. In contrast the interracial intimacies between minorities—who for the most part lacked, or had fewer, privileges to protect—challenged ethnoracial boundaries more forcefully. As working-class minorities who met on relatively equal ground, partners faced contentious compromises of cultural differences. Since neither could offer the obvious advantages of White culture—the certainty of cultural acceptance and the opportunity of socioeconomic mobility—each had to and did argue for the strengths of her or his own, believing she or he could preserve her or his distinctions within a cross-cultural setting. Minority parents had to reconcile their often conflicting ideas of what constituted a healthy and tasty diet, good marriage, suitable clothes and hairstyles, appropriate work, proper education, respectful ways of communicating, and desirable leisure activities for their children. With the help of their multiracial children, such couples consolidated rather than erased racial or social bonds, coming together rather than pushing toward a monoethnic identity.

But even as non-Whites strayed from their community conventions and loved across ethnic lines, they remained attentive to certain differences. Although minority adults were less invested in existing standards, they carefully selected their cross-cultural partners, as did Whites contemplating marriage and minority youths who experimented with the opposite sex. Considerations of gender, color, ethnicity, religion, and politics determined romantic choices. The chance to escape familiar models of how men and women interacted or behaved motivated the pairings of many women. Their demographic advantage afforded them the luxury of intermarrying only when such a match appeared likely to strengthen their authority or improve their condition. For non-Whites absorbed by left-leaning political organizations, intermarriage was a natural outcome of an ideology that celebrated interracial relations. Others were drawn into uncommon relationships by the discovery of common beliefs, practices, or physical features among those outside their conventionally understood common culture. These patterns among intermarriages suggest the deliberative, if messy, ways in which California's non-Whites created new and roomier affiliations within environments of diversity. Although they and their children stretched social categories on one side of a darkening color line, they did not dispense with categories altogether.

OBSTACLES AND RESISTANCE

Close social relationships between non-Whites did not happen easily. In the second quarter of the twentieth century, legal limits and popular thinking about race and ethnicity constrained the romantic choices of all Californians. Whites expressed the fiercest opposition and directed the greatest resources to suppressing interracial dating and the marriages that might and did result. However, minorities similarly objected to romantic pairings with cultural outsiders. Prejudice, international politics, and concerns about the longevity of the ethnoracial group in a hostile American society motivated their separatism.

At the beginning of the twentieth century White Americans, persuaded by an ideology of White supremacy and fears about the state's growing heterogeneity, tried to shore up ethnoracial boundaries. Influential "scientific" studies documented the danger of intermixing and portrayed mixed-race individuals as anemic, sterile, and degenerate. White Americans for the most part accepted these views and condemned sex and love across the color line. In retreating from contact with minorities and stressing their own racial greatness, Whites believed they were defending a national identity. As primarily male minority migrants arrived in greater numbers, mixing with White women appeared more likely. To protect against this probability Whites constructed legal barriers. The California legislature pushed through a series of antimiscegenation laws prohibiting a White person from marrying "a Negro, Mulatto, or Mongolian." By 1933 the category of White had been narrowed to exclude even more groups, blocking "Malays" (Filipinos) and Japanese from legal unions with Whites.[4] Ironically, Whites had most constrained their own marital freedom. With the exceptions of North Carolina and Louisiana, where statutes prohibited long-term relationships between African Americans and Native Americans, in all other states a person of color could marry members of all ethnoracial groups, provided he or she denied a White identity.[5]

In awarding European immigrants the opportunity to intermarry with native-born Whites and one another, the law facilitated their consolidation as Whites. The steady weakening of ethnic lines, as Europeans exploited their romantic freedoms, typified a statewide trend. Throughout the

1940s marriage licenses of two counties very different in size, density, and composition—San Joaquin and Los Angeles—show how immigrants from and the descendants of Europe freely chose other European Americans as partners. In 1940 only 38 percent of Russian, 50 percent of Portuguese, and 43 percent of Italian marriages in San Joaquin County were endogamous. This pattern persisted in 1951, with only 18 percent of Portuguese and 29 percent of Italians selecting coethnic mates that year. Similar trends prevailed in Los Angeles. Based upon marriages recorded during the first few months of 1940 and 1949, European ethnics were inclined to marry descendants of Europe outside their group; for Eastern Europeans this inclination actually intensified during the 1940s. In 1940, 79 percent of Germans, 71 percent of Italians, and 56 percent of Russians, Poles, and Rumanians selected other European ethnics as spouses. Almost 10 years later the percentages were nearly unchanged for Italians and Germans but had increased to 68 percent for Russians, Poles, and Rumanians. These statistics for Euro-Americans in Los Angeles and San Joaquin counties contrast starkly with those of another legally White group: Mexicans. In San Joaquin County 75 percent of this ethnic population chose Mexican spouses between 1943 and 1946. Little had shifted by 1951 when 72 percent married within the ethnic circle. Eighty-three percent of those Mexicans who got married in Los Angeles married other Mexicans in 1940, 80 percent in 1949.[6] The differences across "White" groups suggests the uncertain status of Mexicans, who were technically White but practically colored in the eyes of many European ethnics. The increasing tendency in the 1940s for county clerks to list the "color or race" of ethnic Mexicans as "Mexican" rather than "White" on their marriage license (a substitution and mistake the clerks did not make for Europeans) further points to Mexicans' unstable position compared to others'.[7]

Minorities objected to the marital prohibitions that hurried the integration of European ethnics because the minorities feared the narrowing of already-limited civil rights. The most persistent challenges originated among Filipinos, an overwhelmingly male group that felt the restraints most acutely. By 1931 the Los Angeles Superior Court had decided four cases brought by Filipinos about the legality of their union with a White person. Black community leaders urged state government to overturn marital restrictions because such rules disrespected Black citizens, especially Black women who were made vulnerable to unscrupulous White men. Under the existing regime White men could coerce Black women to become their mistresses, discard them at will, and bear no financial responsibility since the interracial unions were not recognized by law. Japanese too chafed under antimiscegenation statutes. Marriages between Japanese men and women warranted brief but celebratory mention in widely read Japanese-American newspapers such as the *Kashu Mainichi* and *New World Sun* in the early 1930s, but the union of a Filipino man and a Japanese woman evoked longer and more poignant comment. Speculating about the racial origin of the woman's new husband—"the only chance for a Japanese to marry in this country is with Filipino, Chinese, or other Mongolian race. The gentleman in question is neither Siamese nor Chinese, so it leaves a margin for Filipino"— the article highlighted how Japanese had creatively circumvented restrictions on marriage. Based upon his research a sociologist of the period noted that despite these adaptations in marital customs, Japanese and other minorities resented what reduced them to a separate, inferior category of citizenship.[8]

Notwithstanding these principled legal challenges to and expressions of discomfort with antimiscegenation laws, most minorities preferred to pair with, and see their relatives pair with, one of their own. Concerns about ethnic longevity, inherited and learned prejudice, as well as conflicts abroad shaped these wishes. Among Chinese and Japanese immigrants, schemes for ranking and distinguishing among people that privileged Asians, disparaged Blacks, and ranked Whites somewhere between reflected popular racial views held in Asian nations. The prejudices against other groups held by Japanese and Chinese only strengthened in a California setting where social standing was so closely correlated with race and ethnicity. Chinese elders frowned upon social contacts and matches made with non-Chinese, especially with Blacks and Mexicans. The advice that George Lew offered his children—"to marry no Blacks, no Mexicans"—was the majority's opinion.[9]

Motivated by more decisive notions of racial purity, Issei objected to intimate contacts with others. They even resisted inter-Asian matches. Local economic competition compounded political tensions associated with war in Asia. As I discussed in chapter 2, Japan's aggressive expansion in the region, beginning in the early twentieth century, strained relations among Filipinos, Koreans, Chinese, and Japanese in the United States who still felt passionately about events in their countries of birth. Reaction to the elopement of Felisberto Tapia, a Filipino, and the Japanese American Alice Chiyoko exemplified the intense opposition brought to bear against inter-Asian couples. Their romance precipitated a round of kidnapping, boycotting, and protesting by the town's Filipinos and

Japanese that ultimately forced the pair's separation. However, like the Chinese, the Japanese reserved their strongest objections for pairings with Mexicans and Blacks. In a survey measuring marital expectations, more than 85 percent of this immigrant generation expressed its disapproval of marriages between Nisei and the two non-White groups. "Japanese married to [Blacks] would be looked down upon by others," offered one participant in explanation of the general ethnic sentiment.[10]

As people of mixed heritage themselves, Filipinos and Mexicans in California were usually more accepting of racial difference and mixture. The physical reality of so many mestizos in Mexico and the Philippines worked against a strict doctrine of purity. So did political events such as the Spanish-American-Filipino War (1898) and Mexican Revolution (1910), which celebrated alternatives to the Eurocentric racism of Spaniards. This common racial history and sensibility prompted Jerry Paular during a 2003 conversation to jokingly rename Filipinos in mid–twentieth century California "the Mexicans of Southeast Asia." Yet these groups were not blind to color. Mexican citizens and political officials alike often referred to the Chinese as dirty, diseased, and dangerous to Mexican womanhood, attitudes that prompted the persecution and eventual expulsion of Chinese merchants in the 1930s. Blacks and even Europeans also sometimes confronted the antipathy of mestizos. These views shaded the perceptions of Mexican immigrants to the United States. When contemplating partners, Mexican-American children and their protective parents considered factors of color and culture, privileging Mexican ancestry. Dolores Cruz's memories of her mother's color awareness suggested the attitudes of many fair-skinned Mexican Americans. The darker complexion of Dolores and her Filipino father troubled her mother's relatives, who rarely invited the mixed family to weddings and parties, a snub Cruz attributed to her own "brownness." Her mother loved her husband enough to forgive, if not forget, his coloring but continued to take pride in her own Whiteness. Filipinos drew distinctions, too. Although turn-of-the-century mestizo nationalists downplayed ethnic distinctions and stressed the essential sameness of Filipinos, ethnoracial thinking did not disappear altogether. Once in California, unmarried Filipinos tended to accept interethnic relations more readily if they included Whites or Mexicans rather than Blacks or Japanese "colonizers."[11]

Blacks and Jews favored romances and marriages with coethnics, too. Rabbis preached about religious and racial integrity, and many community members embraced a policy of discouraging branching out beyond the ethnic circle. Except in areas where few Jews resided, Jews tended to socialize with Jews. As Leo Frumkin, a Jewish American born and raised in Boyle Heights, definitively explained of customs and attitudes prevailing in the 1930s, Jews might have friends who were not Jewish, "but you wouldn't marry somebody who's not Jewish. I mean you just wouldn't." African Americans had similar preferences. Although they confronted a relatively more relaxed racial climate in California than elsewhere, persistent social prejudice and their own racial pride discouraged interethnic intimacies.[12]

The distaste that families and ethnic communities expressed about interracial relationships often brought budding romances to a sudden and premature close. As a young adult Adele Hernandez began seriously dating a Jewish coworker. "I don't think he was very good looking. He was not tall either," she said, but "I liked him quite a bit." Despite the pair's attachment, the relationship disintegrated as each felt the burden of familial and community disapproval. As she recalled, "At that time, especially with strict Jewish families, you didn't marry out of your faith." Because of these conventions and her own Mexican ancestry, she acknowledged that the affair "wasn't getting us anywhere" and ended it. The couple liked and loved one another but not enough to defy cultural norms. Harry Lem's short-lived associations with a series of Black girlfriends underscored the weight and respect afforded ethnic prejudice. According to his sister, Harry "loved Black women" and regularly brought African-American dates to family dinners, a practice his mother, like most in her Chinese community, quietly abhorred. Although this Chinese-American man pursued Black women, the relationships were always fleeting. Factors independent of external prejudice may have shaped this outcome. However, the clear disapproval of family and neighbors likely mattered. In repeatedly introducing his Black companions to his parents and sibling, Lem demonstrated the importance he gave to their opinions. When push came to shove, minorities who enjoyed intercultural dating and contemplated long-term commitments often chose the standards of their own ethnic group rather than risk ostracism.[13]

Separatist sentiments had as suffocating an effect on the creation of intercultural, even interethnic, families. As an orphan of part-Japanese, part-European descent, Jim Naritomi spent the early months of his life in several foster homes. But when a "very wealthy Chinese couple who was childless fell in love" with the child and offered to adopt him, his Japanese grandmother intervened. "She apparently would not hear of it, that I would be raised as a Chinese," Naritomi related. Although Chinese and Japanese were more willing to marry one another than they were Whites, ethnic differences still mattered and limited their crossings in the period. Naritomi's grandmother harbored an ethnic attachment and anti-Chinese feelings typical of her generation. Rather than allow an Asian-American family to form, this woman accepted the responsibility of child rearing herself.[14]

Antimiscegenation laws expressed the political will and racial prejudices of Whites, but they also reflected the social practices and views of minorities. Concerns about civil rights in the abstract gave non-Whites pause. Yet in general they promoted coethnic marriages and lobbied against interethnic ones in order to maintain familiar boundaries.

CONSENTING ADULTS

Though numerically few and frequently marginalized, some non-White adults in the period defied conventions and intermarried. In doing so, they implicitly recommended mixed-race relationships to a skeptical public and consolidated ethnic categories in much the same fashion as European ethnics. Examining their romances enables us to uncover the process by which some individuals began to fashion broader ethnoracial categories out of intimate connections and as an alternative to mono-ethnic norms. If not a majority experience, the relationships still represent some of the most private and original acts of race making in twentieth century California.

Men and women of different minority backgrounds found love and made families within a landscape of legal limits, proximity, and skewed sex ratios. Their work and leisure brought them into close contact, while a scarcity of coethnic women left men hungry for female attention. Given state restrictions and popular hostility, some of these unmarried men shied away from White women and flirted with non-White women. Physical closeness as well as a longing for intimacy and security drew minorities together.

California's peculiar demography was a matchmaker of sorts. The maleness of state residents—most pronounced in migrant communities—structured romantic choices (see table 2). An important exception to the rule, African Americans, enjoyed a sex ratio that demographers described as stable. Asians, however, suffered particularly skewed sex ratios through midcentury. Among Chinese, men outnumbered women by 27 to 1 in 1920. Through the century the difference narrowed without disappearing. In 1940 more than twice as many Chinese men as women resided in California. The Filipino community faced a similar imbalance. Between

TABLE 2. NUMBER OF MALES PER ONE
HUNDRED FEMALES BY ETHNORACIAL
GROUP, CALIFORNIA

	1940	1950	1960
All	103.7	100.1	99.4
Foreign-born White	117.0	107.4	
Black	97.0	98.4	97.0
Native American	111.0	119.5	110.0
Japanese	127.7	116.0	99.4
Chinese	223.7	161.9	127.0
Filipino			184.0
Other	746.0	303.4	131.0

SOURCE: U.S. Census Bureau.

1924 and 1929 women accounted for only 16 percent of the 24,000 Filipinos journeying to California. The gap had not closed much by 1950 when the sex ratio remained a startling 321:100. Even more male in composition than this immigrant flow were Asian Indians, 99 percent of whom were men. Comparatively, the Japanese community enjoyed a more stable demography, with women reaching roughly 42 percent of the population by 1940 and the sex ratio falling to 107.2:100 a decade later, but an inequity remained. Overall, Japanese men had the greatest reason to gripe about female companionship, but Mexican-American newcomers faced a scarcity of coethnic women, too. In Los Angeles the male-female ratio stood at 114:100 in 1930 and 107.6:100 for all Spanish speakers in 1950.[15]

One practical consequence of this abundance of male minorities was intercultural marriage. Confronted with either singleness and childlessness or family and procreation, some bucked tradition and married across cultural lines. Although scarce records make a precise accounting of interracial relationships extremely difficult, repatriation documents and interviewees' memories indicate that such marriages did occur. In surveys conducted of Chinese and Japanese Americans of California about their ethnic pasts, interviewees usually acknowledged the presence of at least one mixed minority couple in their neighborhood. Representative of such replies included William Chan's assertion that "a neighbor married a Mexican girl," Peggy Kanzawa's observation that "there were a few [Nisei] that were married to other nationalities," and Ida Lee's recollection that "a few Chinese men married colored and Mexican."

Repatriation records also pull interminority couples out from the shadows of history. In a belated corollary to an 1855 act providing that immigrant women could become U.S. citizens upon marriage to a U.S. citizen, Congress enacted 1907 legislation stipulating that American women would forfeit their citizenship upon marriage to an alien. Congress decoupled women's citizenship from that of their husbands' in 1922, but it took more than a decade and often the determined petitions of women for their citizenship to be restored. These appeals document the lasting commitment of non-White men and women. As examples, in the late 1930s two Black women, Marguerite Takeuchi and Bertia Morial, fell in love with and married immigrants from Japan and Mexico, respectively, and lived in Southern California.[16]

In one of the only published studies of intermarriage among minorities in the period, Constantine Panunzio offered more quantitative evidence of ethnoracial crossing. She calculated intermarriage rates in Los Angeles between 1924 and 1933. For Chinese men 23 of 97 marriages were exogamous; for Filipino men, 701 of 1,000. As further evidence of just how important sex ratios were to marital patterns, in the Japanese community, where women proved more numerous, intermarriages happened infrequently. Only 27 of 1,163 Japanese marriages involved non-Japanese.[17]

My own analysis of marriage records in Los Angeles is based upon a sample of months taken across a sample of years—January through early March 1940, 1949, and 1950—and confirms how the rare marriages among minorities became less rare over time. In early 1940 Blacks, Japanese, Filipinos, and Chinese married, but they did not *intermarry,* or at least did not do so according to official sources. As I have already discussed, Mexicans married non-Mexicans, specifically, foreign- and native-born Whites, but at much lower rates than Californians of European descent married European ethnics outside their ethnic circle. The greater frequency with which Russians and Poles—national-origin groups of Europe that included a predominance of Jews—married endogamously probably points to the persistent practice of Jews' marrying Jews. The only interminority marriage I discovered in my sample was the pairing of a Mexican man and a Native American woman.[18]

By the end of the decade, however, marital habits had changed. In 1950, 8 percent of Blacks selected non-Black spouses. And of that group, half of all partnerships were made with non-Whites, 25 percent with Native Americans, 12.5 percent with Mexicans, and 12.5 percent with Filipinos. Less than half of all Filipinos chose Filipino mates. While

30 percent settled down with native- or foreign-born Whites, 10 percent committed to Blacks and 20 percent to those of part-Filipino, part-White backgrounds. In 1949 Filipinos demonstrated similar preferences. Of the nine Filipinos who married during January and February, one chose a Filipino, one selected an African American, three decided upon Whites, and the remainder joined up with those of Mexican- or African-American heritage. A slightly larger number of Chinese appeared in the marriage records for early 1949. A clear majority wed other Chinese, but of those who did not, minority partners (in this case Japanese and Mexican) outnumbered Whites. At the midcentury mark Mexicans were slightly more likely to marry foreign- or native-born Whites and significantly more likely to marry Blacks, Filipinos, or even Asians than a decade before. Finally, Japanese Americans proved to be among the minorities most reluctant to make lasting bonds across ethnic lines. Of the eighty-one Japanese-American marriages in my 1949 and 1950 data, only two involved Whites and one a Chinese.[19]

Since the state chose not to bother with these marriages among non-Whites, a person of color could choose from a wide range of ethnoracial partners. The example of some Filipino-Mexican couples illustrates this opportunity. In *Gavino C. Visco v. Los Angeles County* (1931) the Superior Court initially withheld a marriage license from a Filipino man and his fiancée, Ruth Salas, because the judge construed her as White. However, the pair successfully exploited the awkward, inconsistent character of rules against miscegenation. In proving that she was partly of Native American descent, Ruth Salas gained the status of non-White and was permitted to marry Gavino Visco. The marriage records of San Joaquin County show that she was not alone in reconfiguring her ethnoracial identity for the sake of romance. In 1945 three Filipino men from Stockton married three women, each of whom described herself as Filipina to the state marriage license bureau. But the birthplaces of the women's parents revealed a more complex ethnoracial heritage. Although their fathers had roots in the Philippines, their mothers claimed Mexico or New Mexico as their place of birth. These mestizas represented themselves in more racially singular terms in order to circumvent marital restrictions. They could do so in part because officials readily accepted their self-representations. Although the one-drop rule may not have ordered relations between Whites and Asian ethnics as precisely as it ordered Black-White relations, a series of other marriage records involving individuals whose mothers hailed from the Philippines and whose fathers were born in Europe indicate that Whites were likely to classify a person of partial Filipino heritage as "Filipina" despite her father's ethnicity.[20]

This shedding or denial of White identity highlighted the more malleable racial status of Mexicans or those of partial Mexican ancestry and a willingness to sacrifice privilege for love and family. As I mentioned earlier, California law classified Mexicans as White, a distinction that many within the ethnic community dearly prized and defended because of the privileges it afforded. Unlike Asians, Mexican immigrants could naturalize and own land. Unlike Blacks, Mexican immigrants were less consistently segregated in housing and education. Thus the decision of Ruth Salas and others to step away from, rather than cling to, the security of their marginal Whiteness was a brave defense of minority rights and a challenge to White privilege. Yet authorities paid little attention to such defiant crossings. As long as minority mixing did not generate labor or political unrest, the authorities drew and policed only the color line that divided them from non-Whites. Thus minorities had good reason to select non-White rather than White partners. In fact, in Los Angeles between 1924 and 1933 more than 95 percent of Chinese intermarriages, 74 percent of Japanese, 93 percent of Black, and slightly fewer than 50 percent of Filipino intermarriages were contracted with other non-Whites.[21] The results were similar in San Joaquin County. Of the few non-Whites who intermarried there, the majority preferred other minorities. In 1948, of the ten recorded Chinese marriages, one man married a Japanese woman and one woman a Filipino man. Among Blacks the only exogamous marriage among the seventy-six recorded included a Filipino.[22]

As much as imbalanced sex ratios and the absence of state inference, the proximity of certain minority groups in the rural towns and urban neighborhoods of California immediately before the war explained not only intercultural romances but also repeated interethnic pairings. The same spaces that cultivated romances among minority youth engendered more lasting commitments. Philip Vera Cruz, a Filipino who spent much of his time moving between farm jobs in Delano, McFarland, and Wasco, California, noted the importance of shared work and location to the marriages between Mexicans and Filipinos so common in the California valleys. As Japanese and Chinese laborers became scarce after immigration restrictions were imposed, growers had increasingly recruited Mexicans and Filipinos in the 1920s and 1930s. Vera Cruz observed that many of his countrymen, "as a poor hard-working minority," married Mexican women "because they often lived in the same area." Filipinos interviewed by sociologists confirmed Vera Cruz's statement, noting that Filipinos typically befriended Mexican women in taxi-dance halls or on farms. The groups shared what the scholar called a "similar socio-occupational outlook" as overwhelmingly working-class people. In fact, unlike Chinese and Japanese men who favored Asian women when selecting mates, Filipinos favored Mexicans. In Los Angeles County between 1924 and 1933 twenty-six Filipinos chose Mexican brides but only two Japanese and one Chinese. Later studies confirmed the continuity of this preference. The sociologist Bernicio Catapusan concluded in the early 1930s that "most of the Filipino mixed unions are Filipino-Mexican; some are Filipino-White, Filipino Mulatto, and Filipino-Negro unions." Two studies, both based on Los Angeles County marriage licenses, concurred. Completed in 1954, the first determined that at least 35 percent of Filipino marriages to Whites involved Mexican women. In 1963 the second concluded that two-thirds of Filipino men who married between 1949 and 1959 had chosen Mexican-American women.[23]

In the San Fernando Valley just north of Los Angeles, a thriving community of Mexican-Filipino families set down roots. The mixed-race sons and daughters of these couples remembered how consistently Mexican women partnered with older Filipino men. During a 2002 interview Frances Marr described how her father and other Filipinos staked out the route that Mexican schoolgirls took as they walked home after classes. Marr's mother and her Mexican girlfriends eventually accepted the romantic advances of these lonely single men. After Marr's parents divorced soon after their 1931 nuptials, her mother struck up with a new Filipino man. Other interviewees from the valley described a special magnetism between the ethnic groups. Dolores Cruz's Mexican mother married three times and each time chose a Filipino husband. Another rural region of California, San Joaquin County, generated significant numbers of Mexican-Filipino couples. The legal classification of Mexicans as White concealed most of these marriages from official records until California's antimiscegenation laws were overturned in 1948. After that, marriage licenses revealed Mexican-Filipino partnerships, many of which likely formed years earlier but awaited legal recognition. From the second half of 1948 through 1949 the county documented 1,803 marriages. Among these were nine of Mexican-Filipino couples and twenty of White-Filipinos. The 480 marriages in the first half of 1950 included four Filipino-Mexican and twelve White-Filipino ones. Although numerically few, and rarer than Filipino partnerships with all European ethnicities combined, the commitments of Filipinos and Mexicans were more common than those with or between any other minority groups.

Moreover, Filipino matches with the descendants of Europeans reflected the large number and variety of European ethnics in the valley. If the "White" group was broken down into its constituent ethnic parts, Mexicans were by far the preferred and most common spouses of Filipinos.[24]

The coincidence of geography and labor produced consistent pairings and bicultural settlements of other minority groups. Toiling in the Southern California farm communities, Mexican women and Asian Indian men frequently fell in love and married. As Sikhs of peasant background, restricted from bringing wives and children to California by the tightening of immigration laws, the men sought out single young women newly arrived from Mexico. Other examples of biethnic spaces where all husbands belonged to one ethnoracial group and all wives another appeared in rural California. In the border town of Calexico, Chinese men built lives with Mexican Americans and "pretty much assimilated into the local Mexican population," a resident reported, while smaller concentrations of Mexican-Japanese families dotted the same valley.[25]

The heterogeneity of certain urban neighborhoods similarly grounded the romantic entanglements of non-Whites. Just as the fields where they labored fostered romance between Asian men and Mexican women, the work environments of cities brought sets of minorities together. In 1940s Los Angeles, Garding Liu, a local resident who chaired the city's Chinese Consolidated Benevolent Association and was an amateur historian, noted the presence of Chinese-Black couples. Black women met Chinese men while working or shopping in Chinese-owned groceries or restaurants, and Chinese men became residents of the women's boardinghouses. Everyday sightings of interracial couples in the multicultural Fillmore District, Boyle Heights, and West Oakland further illustrated the importance of place and population in interminority matches. These areas both encouraged and harbored mixed couples. Jews, Mexicans, Chinese, Japanese, Blacks, and Filipinos who grew up there looked more favorably upon and likely felt more inclined to intermarry. At the same time mixed couples who were squeezed out of familiar ethnic areas found refuge in more diverse city sections and among similar families. Dorothy Siu recalled the four interracial families in her Los Angeles neighborhood; ostracized by Chinese, they banded together and organized special picnics. Rose Mary Escobar observed a similar social dynamic in prewar Oakland. The polyglot composition of some California neighborhoods allowed support and anonymity impossible in most others.[26]

Despite and because of discrimination, demography, and diverse environments, select minorities suspended ethnoracial prejudices and

embraced local opportunities for family and connection. These heterogeneous areas, and the climate of discrimination that fostered their
economic ties and youthful friendships, nurtured intercultural romances.
Although uncommon in the period, these non-White couples were important examples of the close social ties and innovative collaborations
possible among non-Whites.

NEW AMERICAN FAMILIES, COMMON FAMILY VALUES

The matches among minorities were more than pragmatic responses to
location, laws, and prejudice. Choosing to reinterpret or associate based
upon criteria other than dominant notions of race and ethnicity—criteria
such as gender definitions, culture, and politics—non-White men and especially women defied existing standards of differentiation and adver-
tised the creative cultural, economic, and political combinations that
were happening in spaces where diversity had become an integral, accepted element of community. This involved heated negotiations and
compromises with families and one another. In the end, common principles and preferences structured the ways in which minorities looking
for love and family came together or kept their distance: women's longing for more authority, liberal political ideals, physical resemblance, and
familiar cultural traits.

Many minority women pursued and settled into relationships that offered them refuge from well-worn gender regimes and cultural expectations. In their youth they had enjoyed the freedoms of other ethnoracial
groups, but as adults who partnered with ethnic outsiders, they sought
a more permanent escape. In being swept off their feet and away from
the familiar by a minority suitor rather than a White one, these women
displayed their understanding that they might best find happiness and
stability with a man closer to them in location and social position. Their
romantic lives also demonstrated how redesigning gender was an essential dimension of remaking ethnicity and race among minorities.

In the late 1920s C. S. Machida, a Chinese American from San Francisco, married a Japanese man who took her away from a Chinese community she despised. Unlike the Japanese, whom she admired as "more
intelligent and better educated," Machida faulted Chinese in the United
States for their craftiness, disinterest in education, and conservatism.
Most important, she denounced Chinese men's treatment of women.
"They don't want them to be educated," she observed, "and when they
get to a certain point the men make [the women] stop [going to school]

because they are afraid their women will get the American idea of equality and they want to keep them nothing but chattel." Machida entered into a Japanese community whose gender relations she admired. Given ethnic preferences and sex ratios, Machida's marriage represented a particularly bold transgression and statement against Chinese norms; more than their more numerous male counterparts, minority women like Machida unsettled communities by their crossings and won more control over their lives.[27]

Like Machida, a Mrs. Chew was a woman frustrated by the conventions of her ethnic community who happily married a man from another Asian ethnic group. Unlike Machida, Chew, who was Japanese, found her refuge with a Chinese-American husband who lived and operated a small market in Oakland. In 1942 Chew said that "she didn't like Japs," had cut herself off from her Japanese family and community almost ten years earlier, and never regretted her separation. The politics of the moment, namely, growing American hostility toward Japan and its people, informed this ethnic rejection, but her marriage marked a larger dissatisfaction with things Japanese and her simultaneous attraction to another Asian culture. Chinese gender roles were just different enough to appeal.[28] Although distanced from their ethnic past, Chew and Machida did not travel far, a pattern typical among Asian women who intermarried; they showed a strong preference for Asian spouses over other minorities or Whites. No doubt, keeping their romantic choices within the Asian "family" made their decisions more palatable to their parents. William Chew Chan, for example, carefully differentiated between the marriages of Asian ethnics and Mexicans or Italians—of which he disapproved—and his Korean-American son's marriage to a woman of "the same race," a Japanese American. According to figures from Los Angeles between 1924 and 1933, 61 percent of Chinese who intermarried selected Japanese mates, while 41 percent of Japanese men and 70 percent of Japanese women found love with Chinese partners. In repeatedly finding other Asian men the best companions, these women took the lead in blurring the lines that divided distinct Asian groups, lines that would become even fuzzier in the postwar period.[29]

When explaining why they preferred Filipino men as partners, Mexican girlfriends and wives cited concerns about fair treatment, equality, and authority, issues that had also preoccupied Chinese- and Japanese-American women. These women longed for a style of masculinity or rhythm between the sexes that typically was missing from their own cultural group. This was certainly the case for Gloria Erosa, the woman whose memories opened this chapter, as well as for Dolores Arlington. Asked during a 2004 interview why Mexican women, including her mother, found Filipino men so appealing, Arlington said that Filipino husbands were kind to their wives, family oriented, and hard working. In contrast, Mexican men expected more obedience and servitude. Others speculated that the flashiness and charm of Filipino men captivated Mexican women. In the 1940s single Filipino men—"these Frenchmen with Asian faces"—impressed women with their sweet smell, fine clothes, and impeccable manners, according to Filipino Jerry Paular. A sociologist puzzled by the frequency of such marriages came to similar conclusions, based on surveys of the Mexican wives of Filipino men in 1940 Los Angeles. Benicio Catapusan commented that these wives described their Filipino partners as much better husbands overall because of their thoughtfulness, consideration, and kindness, although they were less romantic than their Mexican peers, who were "good sweethearts and lovers." While the women critiqued Mexicans as "domineering," "less concerned about personal cleanliness," quick to drink and slow to labor, they praised the work ethic, abstinence, and support of Filipinos. In an informal poll 85 percent of the wives believed they had made the right ethnic choice. A Mexican-American testimonial printed in the 24 June 1938 edition of Los Angeles's *Little Manila Times* characterized Filipino men and their romantic relations in similar terms. "My adopted people are generally sweet-natured and courteous. To those who do not know them, they may appear too solicitous and persistent. As workers they are very willing, diligent and efficient," the Mexican-American woman gushed. "They are thoughtful husbands, loving as parents, dutiful and filial, and in spite of their human faults, are builders of castles in the air, forward looking and youthful. To be with them is to be refreshed with ideas rooted in the future, of which my adopted people have a great deal." Clearly, these women believed their cross-cultural marriages had won them a financial stability, affection for family, and respect that they did not expect in a partnership with a Mexican man. If these women romanticized their husbands, their descriptions still expressed a conviction, and the courage to pursue it, that men outside the women's ethnic group made more satisfying partners.[30]

Winning more authority and independence in their romances often came at the cost of strained relations with family and friends. New brides substituted their own marital ambitions for those of in-laws and parents. Many may not have fully anticipated, but bravely accepted, the consequences of their break from ethnic tradition. According to a contemporary sociologist, the parents of a Nisei bride severed all contact with their daughter after she married a Filipino in the late 1930s. Although "quite unhappy about it," the woman resigned herself to her isolation. Even when internment aggravated that separation from her native community, she resolutely remained with her husband. She expected that she would be scooped up with other people of Japanese ancestry but "was not even able to participate in the collective punishment the Government was meting out to the Japanese," commiserated a sociologist reporting on the plight of Japanese Americans. The completeness of the woman's separation from her native community, even when that separation protected her from the misfortune of forced relocation, left her without the collective memory or support network that so many other women enjoyed.[31]

Blanche Corona weathered familial discontent and community resentment as she too realized her own desires. Corona, whose Jewish family moved to West Los Angeles soon after her birth in 1920, met and married a Mexican American, Bert Corona, in the 1930s. He shared her political interests and Los Angeles orientation. Her family readily accepted the match, but his, especially his grandmother, actively objected. His grandmother unexpectedly "confronted" Blanche Corona one day soon after her nuptials. "Although Blanche couldn't understand much Spanish," Bert Corona recounted, "she definitely knew my grandmother wasn't happy." Blanche Corona's parents then echoed the concerns of the older woman, fearing their daughter's Jewish values and those of her Mexican husband would collide and ultimately divide the pair. In disregarding parental advice and pressure, Blanche Corona expressed a different and independent understanding of marriage and cultural negotiation. So did Elaine Black Yoneda, a Jewish American who grew up in San Diego as the daughter of Russian immigrants. Elaine Black met Karl Yoneda, a Kibei from Glendale, in Los Angeles.[32] Her mother opposed the marriage to a Japanese man, insisting the relationship "wouldn't look good" and "would never work out." To prove her point she cited various cases of failed intermarriages she had learned about through gossip. By referring to local expectations and experiences, Black's mother showed the stake she put in community opinion. By marrying a Japanese man, Elaine Black Yoneda showed how little that opinion mattered. She remained true to her own affections rather than the wishes of others.[33]

For some minority women disagreements and conflicts with family were more the cause than the consequence of their romantic crossing. Frances Marr's long-plotted escape from the cultural restrictions of her family culminated in her intermarriage. After a tumultuous series of

Figure 3. Blanche Taff Corona and Bert Corona, wedding picture, Los Angeles, 1941. Source: *Memories of Chicano History: The Narrative of Bert Corona,* Mario T. Garcia, University of California Press, 1994.

events, including her parents' divorce, a custody battle, and an attempted kidnapping, she spent most of her youth in the care of her Filipino father and uncertain about her Mexican mother's whereabouts. In
a 2003 conversation she remembered him as a strict taskmaster with
overwhelming expectations. Resentful of the adult responsibilities he
commanded her to assume, she disobeyed him and sneaked off with
Mexican and White boys. Despite her ethnic heritage, she never dated
Filipinos because she assumed these men possessed the same distasteful
qualities as her father. At church she met Edmond Marr, a handsome
and kind Mexican-American man who caught her fancy. When he unexpectedly proposed and promised to "take her away from all this," she
quickly accepted. Her eagerness to break from the grip of her father explained the quickness of her decision. Against his protests she married
Edmond Marr in 1955, winning freedom from her father and the controlling masculinity she associated with his culture.[34]

These breakdowns of intergenerational controls could strengthen the
position of minority women in intercultural marriages, but so could the
equitable footing of many minority partners and their competing efforts
to perpetuate endangered minority cultures. A writer for San Francisco's
New World Sun offered a Japanese woman a recommendation that underscored the contested character and high cultural stakes of marriages
between non-Whites. In a 1936 human interest story about a Japanese
woman who had recently married a Filipino, the author urged the new
bride "to inject the culture of the Japanese and the education of American schools into your children," as if he feared the woman's husband
would win an imagined battle to influence their offspring. Recognizing
the importance of parenting to the preservation of customs and beliefs,
intermarried men aspired to be more active fathers; they lacked the com-
placency of those who married coethnic women and confidently watched
a familiar transmission to the next generation. The assertions of non-
White men, however, ran up against and wavered in the face of women's
own child-rearing strategies. Reluctant to surrender an authority assigned by ethnic communities and enhanced by the conflicted character
of intermarriage, women pressed their views and sometimes prevailed.[35]

The results of these marital contests highlighted the gains that women
might achieve through interminority relationships. Among Chinese-
Mexican couples of Los Angeles, disagreements about the gendered
treatment of children and the involvement of extended family upset husbands. Garding Liu said that in Los Angeles in the 1940s Chinese men
would grumble about their wives' reverence for daughters and inclusion

of parents, grandparents, uncles, aunts, and cousins in the care of off-spring. The men resented that their own preference for sons and discon-nection from in-laws was largely ignored. In the Punjabi-Mexican house-holds in the Imperial Valley studied by Karen Leonard, fathers sought to supervise and limit the dating practices of their progeny. However, backed by the children's Hispanic godmothers, the wives successfully un-dercut these controls, allowing sons and daughters more freedom in courtship. Alice Balinton, an African American, similarly flexed her ma-ternal muscle, to the relief of her daughter, Umpeylia, and the dismay of her Filipino husband, Egnacio. As a young girl growing up in the Fill-more District in the early 1940s with dreams of becoming a professional entertainer, Umpeylia hoped to hone her singing talents at local nightspots and talent shows. Yet Egnacio ruled that such public performances were unseemly and prohibited his daughter's participation. Luckily for Umpeylia and future fans of "Sugar Pie De Santo" (Umpeylia's eventual stage name), her mother disagreed. A classically trained pianist, Alice Balinton shared Umpeylia's affection for music and helped sneak her into clubs and choir practices without Egnacio's knowledge. This subterfuge was only one example that Umpeylia remembered of her mother's defy-ing his wishes. As a consequence Umpeylia and her siblings reported feel-ing not only much closer to their more permissive mother but also much "Blacker" in their sensibilities.[36]

Parental disagreements about child rearing as often ended in a draw, with couples deciding to blend cultural practices and bequeath a bicul-tural heritage to their offspring. For Fresno-born Clara Chin, who spent her adolescence in Boyle Heights, this meant speaking Spanish with her Chinese father and Mexican mother at home but taking Chinese-language classes after school. Although Chin's parents, Aurelia and Nuey Yuen Fong, introduced her to the Catholic faith and Mexican fiestas, they made sure that she was exposed to Chinese banquets and Chinese New Year fes-tivals as well. In the San Joaquin Valley Dolores Arlington's parents made compromises as well, confusing their daughter, who longed for the sta-bility of a single ethnic tradition. The Arlingtons regularly threw parties attended by Filipino and Mexican friends and served foods from their dis-tinct ethnic menus. Arlington may have wondered "What am I?" as her parents steered her down a "course between cultures," but this pathway permitted her an unusual breadth of choices and highlighted the willing-ness of mixed partners to offer a mixed education. If women did not suc-ceed in overwhelming the culture of their husbands, they maintained and communicated enough of their traditions to satisfy them.[37]

Figure 4. Alice, Egnacio, Miguel, and Martin Balinton, the older siblings and parents of Umpeylia Marsema Balinton, aka Sugar Pie De Santo, in an undated photo. Private photograph of Sugar Pie De Santo.

Figure 5. Aurelia and Nuey Yuen Fong, circa 1920. Private photograph of
Clara Chin.

A drive for new gender and generational dynamics by enterprising
women propelled interminority families and reorganized ethnoracial categories, but so did the search for and discovery of common traditions
and physical features. In finding signs of sameness even in groups believed to be dissimilar, minorities smeared the ethnoracial lines and suggested places to draw others. Their alternative schemes showed their interest in family structure and values, skin tone, and religion.

Chinese and Filipino men who married Mexican women cited the color
and familial sensibilities of their wives as most recognizable, admirable,
and fundamental to their union. According to Garding Liu, in the early
1940s Chinese businessmen who were based in Los Angeles often favored
Mexican women not only as employees but also as romantic partners.
"People from Mexico remind the Chinese of their own nationality," Liu
asserted, "the women are vivacious, are small in size, have black hair, and
remind in other ways of people from the Orient." These single men saw
Chinese-like qualities in the bodies and behaviors of Mexican women,
seeking out the familiar rather than the exotic. Clara Chin observed

complementarities between the Mexican and Chinese cultures of her parents. A concern for and closeness to family overshadowed other differences and linked the pair. Although outsiders who were convinced of the integrity of ethnoracial categories may have puzzled at what the Chins had in common, the couple had detected and built a relationship from the similarities that these categories typically concealed.[38]

Before they could determine what and how much they shared with Mexicans, Chinese men closely studied and evaluated the many minority cultures in their midst. After his graduation from LA's Polytechnic High School in the late 1920s, Clarence Yip Yeu, a Chinese American, worked as a servant alongside other Chinese Americans and Blacks in the homes of wealthy Whites. He remarked that the two ethnic groups "got along nice," because African Americans "respected Chinese more than the White." This understanding fostered social intimacy beyond the confines of work as Chinese men visited Black nightclubs and married Black women. Yet, within the community he observed, Black-Chinese marriages were less frequent than Mexican-Chinese ones. He interpreted this pattern as evidence of color preferences among Chinese who perceived the skin tone of Mexican-American women as closer to their own. The Chinese men worried about physical likeness for the sake of their children as much as theirs. The offspring of Mexicans and Chinese "don't look so bad . . . so different," Clarence Yip Yeu insisted. Although willing to disturb established ethnic categories by intermarrying, the Chinese men proceeded with a carefulness that showed their sensitivity to community prejudices.[39] In discovering tighter overlaps between Mexican and Chinese cultures, the mixed couples thoughtfully stretched certain ethnic boundaries, even as they left others, particularly those between Chinese and Blacks, largely untouched.[40]

Filipino men and Mexican women showed the same deliberateness and interest in color and cultural traditions when contemplating marriage partners. The mixed couples, and the sociologists who observed them, often noted that similarity of color was one reason that the two ethnic groups so often partnered. Based upon fieldwork with Filipino populations in 1940, Benicio Catapusan argued that "shared shades of color" motivated the matches. "Mexican girls understand the Filipinos better," observed the anthropologist Don Gonzalo in that same year, because "they can go together in public places without being subjected to the inquisitive glances of the people." This freedom of movement resulted in fewer divorces, he believed. Based upon his own experiences in the San Fernando Valley, Eddie Erosa, who was mestizo, explained that

Filipino men who married White women entered a "no man's land." In contrast, the brown tone of Filipinos' skin afforded the partners of Mexican wives relative anonymity. Faith and a familiarity with, if not fluency in, the Spanish language—legacies of a common past as colonial subjects of Spain—attracted these men and women as well. In his study of Filipino-Mexican couples Bruno Lasker noted that many practiced or at least claimed Catholicism as their faith. This was the case for Dolores Cruz's Filipino father and Mexican mother, who attended mass and raised her in the Catholic Church. Although they spoke English at home, her father's Visayan language borrowed sounds and words from Spanish. When Dolores Arlington was growing up, her Filipino father communicated in nearly perfect Spanish. Although critics portrayed couples like these as careless and impractical, the stories of these families show how calculated and nuanced their decisions actually were.[41]

As certainly as women's desires for other gender roles, or the cultural and color concerns of minority men and women, political beliefs shaped non-White families. For many Asian ethnics the politics of the Pacific and a reluctance to transfer international conflict into the California setting encouraged intimate encounters. Alternatively, most other ethnic minorities were attracted to each other by the politics of civil rights and anti-discrimination efforts.

The heightened importance of distant political turmoil to local interethnic intimacies became apparent as Asians in the 1930s and early 1940s voiced their objections to interethnic mingling, especially when sexual in nature. As their native countries fell victim to Japan, Koreans and Chinese increasingly interpreted pairings with Japanese as acts of political and cultural surrender. The *New Korea* of Los Angeles reported the alleged plot of the Japanese government to offer a "reward to those Koreans who marry Japanese women" and reminded its readership that "we certainly do not want their blood in our future generations." Similarly, many Chinese equated intermarriage with surrender and defeat. In an article titled "150,000 Japanese Girls Will Be Married Off," the *Hawaii Chinese Journal* of Honolulu, which claimed readers on the mainland and Hawaiian Islands, reported Japan's plans to integrate conquered peoples by coupling Japanese women and select men from the Philippines, Java, Thailand, Korea, and China. These news reports exposed the ways in which war had worsened the distrust among Asian ethnics.[42]

Although a source of anxiety for Asian communities attuned to international events and invested in existing ethnic divisions, mixed Asian couples effectively defused local interethnic tensions by committing to one another and a more American political orientation. Despite the eruption of anti-Japanese feelings and incidents in places throughout California just after the bombing of Pearl Harbor, relative calm prevailed in Pasadena. During a 1944 interview Chizu Sanada reported the persistence of peace despite the town's significant Filipino and Japanese population. She credited the good relations to "the influence of my Nisei girl-friend," who had married a Filipino. When local Japanese ostracized the young woman, she accepted the company of her husband's Filipino friends. Because "all the Filipinos knew her," they "left the rest of the Japanese alone." If love did not conquer all in Pasadena, the mixed couple's relationship did ensure the stability of the community. Moreover, their relationship rested in large part upon a shared disinterest in and distaste for Asian politics. They placed their hopes and loyalties in the United States, a conviction certainly shared by many other Asian ethnics but more dramatically and absolutely expressed by these ethnic crossers.[43]

Although fiction, a short story about a Filipino-Japanese love affair during World War II, "Mary Osaka, I Love You," suggested as well how individual romances might promote interethnic rapprochement and how a preference for American politics and identities became a source of romantic attraction. Against the backdrop of war, a Filipino bus boy, Mateo, and the daughter of his Japanese employer, Mary, fall madly in love. Mateo's Filipino friends condemn the romance as a disgrace to the Filipino nation, propose dates with a more suitable Chinese girl, and even go so far as to rough him up. Mary encounters similar resistance from her father, who tosses her boyfriend out the door. Yet Mary and Mateo eventually ease hostilities between their ethnic groups. The leader of local Filipinos realizes that "the girl is not Japanese, but an American of Japanese descent," a distinction that transforms her from enemy to friend. At the same time Mary's father warms to his Filipino son-in-law after the bombing of Pearl Harbor, begging Mateo to forgive the cruelties that Japanese have inflicted upon Filipinos and supporting Mateo's decision to enlist in the U.S. Army. In this story, which was intended as morality play, interethnic romance blurred ethnic difference and created patriots. The couple found love despite the prejudices and allegiances of friends and families, staking out a mutual claim as Americans.[44]

Although a politics that jettisoned loyalties to nations other than the United States brought distinct Asian ethnics together, many minorities met as a result of their civil rights activism. In the 1930s and 1940s progressive circles included those of diverse backgrounds who mingled comfortably, shared a frustration with the status quo, and embraced tolerance as a social ideal. In the mixed environment of labor unions and civil rights organizations, interracial marriages appeared more acceptable and customary. If one's friends and political allies were Mexican, Chinese, Jewish, and Black, why not contemplate marriage with other minorities? Certainly, more progressive political positions did not break down traditional ethnic allegiances altogether, but they did loosen and refashion these loyalties into more interethnic and panethnic forms.

The union of the minority activists Bert and Blanche Corona exemplified the powerful pull of common politics and the subversive implications of minority marriages. A prominent Mexican American, Bert Corona fought to improve the conditions of workers and immigrants. Growing up in Boyle Heights, he knew many Jewish families. In the late 1930s he met his future wife, Blanche, while both were picketing outside the North American Aviation Plant in Los Angeles. She belonged to the Democratic Youth Federation and generally involved herself in progressive politics of the era. The couple soon fell in love and eloped. To Bert Corona his marriage to a Jewish American seemed unremarkable, a logical result of the company he kept and ideas he espoused. "In the labor and radical circles I was a part of, there was a good deal of interaction, both political and social, among people of different racial and ethnic backgrounds. Our common commitments and struggles brought us together," he explained. Racism and conflict took a backseat to the young people's struggle in the popular front.[45]

Progressive politics grounded the marriage of Elaine Black and Karl Yoneda. They fell in love as they jointly pursued "labor, civil rights, and anti-fascist" activities and married in 1935.[46] Even during Karl Yoneda's military service, Elaine Yoneda carefully maintained their ties to minority activists, demonstrating how much the couple valued the connections. In her almost daily letters to her husband, she reported conversations with prominent African-American activist Paul Robeson and Jewish liberals such as Joe Hittleman and Sydney Rogers, as well as Chinese-American seamen. Her presence at meetings of the Japanese American Citizens League and county-based groups dedicated to tackling anti-Semitism and "the Negro question" during World War II were further reflections of the multicultural world the Yonedas inhabited. Against this backdrop of interethnic mingling, their mixed marriage likely felt secure.[47]

Many minorities rejected existing ethnoracial rules about marriage and child rearing. They chose spouses who complemented their own traditions, political ideals, color, and history or, for women especially, liberated them from confining cultural mores. Whatever their reasons, these interminority couples blended or combined cultural differences as well as redistributed power between wives and husbands, girlfriends and boyfriends. These unconventional families not only realigned ethnoracial lines to accommodate their similarities but also undermined the very notion that ethnoracial groups in environments of diversity did and could reliably contain sameness.

WHAT ABOUT THE CHILDREN?

As those who literally embodied ethnic crossing, mixed-minority children became active participants in the redesign of American families. Social scientists have noted the ability of bicultural individuals to select or join parental cultures in contemporary America. Even though mixed-race youngsters in the second quarter of the twentieth century faced a more rigid racial climate and blatant discrimination, they still aspired to more fluid and multiple affiliations. Because their own bodies and experiences supported more flexible notions of race, they easily left behind their singular ethnic traditions and moved toward more blended ones. In doing so, they often became mediators not simply between cultures, as the pioneering 1930s sociologist Robert Park observed, but between parents and the relatives or ethnic communities from which they had become estranged. These children made permanent their parents' defiant statement about the varied cultural unions possible on one side of a strengthening color line.[48]

Mixed-race children of all ethnoracial combinations were not without their critics. By reminding communities and families of ethnic crossings that many preferred to forget, the children invited hostility. Mary Matsuno, an orphan and resident of the Manzanar internment camp's Children's Village (see chapter 4), recalled how administrators struggled to find foster families for the less popular, less wanted "mixed bloods." Unlike full-blooded Japanese, who found a supportive environment within the camps, mixed-race children were bullied and called cruel names. Camp supervisors expressed alarm at the mistreatment of Celeste Loi, a young girl picked on by her Japanese peers because of her Chinese surname. During his site inspection in January 1943, Dr. Tetsuya Ishimaru found the abuse of mixed children like Celeste so pronounced that he urged camp officials to intervene on the youngsters' behalf.[49]

Most children were aware of and disoriented by discrimination. Looking back upon their prewar childhoods in the Imperial Valley,

Punjabi-Mexicans recalled the bitter prejudices of teachers and students. The majority Mexican population at their non-White school pushed, shoved, mocked, and generally made their lives unpleasant. Sociologists investigating Peter, a young boy of Mexican-Japanese descent, described the heavy burden of prejudice he bore in the late 1920s. Mexican, and especially Japanese, peers bullied and called Peter "half-breed." His school principal confirmed that "Peter was isolated in a certain sense," an isolation that extended beyond the campus. A local minister reported that the Japanese, who typically felt a sense of responsibility for fellow ethnics, deemed Peter an outcast because of his mixed status and denied him protection or support. The biracial offspring of Mexican women and Filipino men in rural California found easy comfort in the company of one another but had to fight for acceptance among Filipinos and Mexicans. Called "Flip," "Monkey," or "half breed," mestizos felt the antipathy of their peers. But by playing tough, many managed to quiet the taunting and teasing. As examples, the majority of Frances Marr's closest friends were exactly those Mexicans who had first spoken to her in pejorative terms. Her resilience and regular contacts persuaded them that she was one of them, that she belonged even though she was part-Filipina. During his adolescence in the San Fernando Valley, Eddie Erosa said he had to win the trust of Filipino and Mexican youths, who were at first suspicious of him because of his mixed background. As anxious family and friends had feared, multiethnic children met misunderstanding and antagonism.[50]

However, rather than being tragic victims of ethnoracial prejudice, these sons and daughters sometimes softened community resistance to ethnic crossing, repairing the social position of their parents and championing mixed families among minorities as inventive expressions of love and connection in truly diverse spaces. In part, the relatively more relaxed ethnoracial views of minority groups made such reconciliation and promotion possible. Born in 1930, Peter Jamero spent his childhood and adolescence in the farm area of Livingston, where Filipino men regularly partnered and parented with Mexican-, Japanese-, and African-American women. The spouses and mixed-race children were easily folded into the community, not ostracized. Residents did not "quibble about whether you were one third or one quarter Filipino, you were just Filipino," Jamero emphasized. Filipina "queen" pageants, in which young girls raised money and competed for the honor of becoming "Miss Philippines," provide evidence for Jamero's claims. In these popularity contests run by prominent Filipino men, young women solicited donations from community members to support their candidacy. The event culminated after distinct factions of Filipinos lobbied, cajoled, and finally voted in a winner. As public displays of power, these queen contests expressed prevailing views about race and gender. Wearing traditional dress and assuming polite manners, as prescribed by pageant etiquette, the entrants represented old-fashioned versions of womanhood that had been packaged to appeal to lonely young men. However, the presence of mestiza contestants suggested that racial mixture was consistent with public ideals of femininity. Former winner Dolores Cruz explained that she and other mestizas smiled, performed, and asked for donations alongside "pure" Filipinas. The name of the game was making money, added Gloria Quan, and as long as "you had some Filipino in you," you became eligible regardless of your mother's racial heritage. In fact, many of the voting single men preferred the "untraditional look" of mixed-race girls, Cruz reported. The success of these mestiza contestants demonstrated how relatively tolerant of mixing the California Filipinos were. Language, religion, and foodways rather than blood assured one's membership in the community.[51]

Even the more racially homogeneous Chinese population, especially those in the younger generation, demonstrated a limited acceptance of mixture. Students at one Chinese-language school in Los Angeles in the decade before World War II remembered classmates who were part Chinese and part Black or Mexican. Their Chinese fathers wished to impart some of their culture to their multiethnic offspring. According to Allen Mock, these children blended easily among their peers and gained the begrudging acceptance of local Chinese. "Anybody that even has an eighth or sixteenth blood of Chinese is considered Chinese," Allen explained. "Chinese are more accepting." At the outset Chinese Americans might oppose intermarriages, but such views could mellow after children came along. In Los Angeles Clara Chin, who was Chinese and Mexican, related how warmly the Chinese-American community had welcomed her Mexican mother. Friends taught her to cook Chinese food and invited her to Chinese social functions. Although more concerned about racial purity than were most Filipinos, Chinese still considered cultural as well as biological criteria when defining group membership. Thus, more than Whites, they could perceive the "Chineseness" of bicultural offspring. In allowing that these progeny could learn ethnic ways, the community lightened the pressures on interminority couples.[52]

Mixed-race children eased bruised feelings between generations of the same family as well, wounds first inflicted when couples chose to become long-term partners. After San Francisco–born Marshall Hoo, of Chinese

Figure 6. Miss Philippines Queen Pageant, 1954. Dolores Cruz in center.
Private photograph of Dolores Cruz.

descent, married a Korean American in 1939, both sets of parents de-
spaired. They feared their children were betraying their past and weakening the ethnic cohesion necessary to survive discrimination. Yet the
parents' resistance soon weakened. The rising number of intermarriages
through the 1940s, common Asian ancestry, and the passage of time
helped, but more important were the births of cute grandchildren. The
grandparents learned to accept their children's spouses as the parents of

their grandsons and granddaughters. Even when members of the older generation had been relatively receptive to ethnoracial crossing, their tolerance deepened with the arrival of mixed-race children. Dorothy Siu did not openly object when her son chose a Japanese-American bride in mid-1940s Los Angeles, but she acknowledged that she felt much closer to her daughter-in-law after the birth of three grandchildren. Lovable kids improved relations with extended family, reducing the stresses upon partners and increasing the likelihood of a lasting relationship.[53]

The mere presence of these children defused tensions between parents and their families or ethnic communities, but so did the youngsters' more deliberate challenges. As members by birth or adoption of mixed families, these offspring frequently became informal ambassadors of cross-cultural relationships and multicultural identities. In September 1944 the supervisor of the State Charities Aid Association, which collaborated with the War Relocation Authority, reported a surprise meeting with a young Chinese-American boy, Alva, who was in the foster care of a Nisei couple, Mr. and Mrs. Mori. The boy marched unannounced into the supervisor's office to defend his new family, particularly their ambitions to adopt a Japanese baby. Alva had overheard the Moris express their fears that the welfare service "would not want to place a Japanese child with them," because "they were Japanese" and Alva was Chinese. Hoping to correct the organization's bias against mixed families, the boy insisted his caregivers "would love a Japanese child and that it would make no difference to him": in fact, he eagerly anticipated a baby sister. Alva occupied a unique position from which he could explain the health and happiness of a family that most Californians suspected because of its blended form. He could make a case as well for the advantages of living within two cultural traditions rather than squeezing into one. An official's assertion that "the Moris are devoted to Alva and certainly have done a good job bringing him up" suggested that the young boy had been persuasive.[54]

As a surrogate son of Japanese Americans, Guy Gabaldon championed the advantages and legitimacy of mixed families. Born in 1926 to Mexican-American parents, Gabaldon spent most of his early youth in the neighborhood streets of Boyle Heights, running errands for bar girls, grabbing beers, and getting into trouble. When he was twelve, he met and became fast friends with two Nisei brothers, Lyle and Lane Nakano, whom he admired for their honesty, studiousness, and respect for the law. "Fascinated by [Japanese] tradition and customs," an interviewer noted, Gabaldon began spending a lot of time at the Nakano home, learned the Japanese language, and eventually moved in with the family, remaining for seven years until the Nakanos were interned. His parents supported his closeness to the Nakanos, hoping they would have a positive influence on their unruly son. Indeed, the Japanese Americans reshaped the young Mexican-American's life. He admired and followed in the military footsteps of Lyle and Lane, serving valiantly in the South Pacific, where he used his language skills to capture enemy troops. The thoroughness of his cultural voyage further expressed itself in his transnational residence and intermarriage. After World War II Gabaldon married a Mexican woman of Japanese descent and split his time between Modesto, California, and Saipan, Japan. In becoming a member of another family that changed his life for the better, Guy Gabaldon promoted the possibilities inherent in intimate cultural mixing.[55]

When they matured and married, mixed-race children further validated the commitment to cultural crossovers among minorities. As individuals who embodied at least two distinct cultures, they traversed ethnic lines. These men and women might search out spouses with a similarly mixed background, but these matches proved difficult to make. More important, few considered ethnoracial heritage a critical variable in calculations about marriage. To see ethnicity and race as stable and meaningful categories defied the reality of their own lives. Dolores Cruz remembered dating Filipino, Mexican, and White boys indifferent to their ethnic backgrounds before she found her lifelong mate, Louis Cruz. That his parents were born in the Philippines made little difference to a woman of Filipina-Mexican heritage who evaluated men based strictly upon their personalities. Clara Chin was similarly unconcerned with ethnic background of her chosen partner. The daughter of a Mexican-Chinese couple, she dated Mexican and Chinese boys, relishing what she generalized as the fun of the former and reserve of the latter. When she was eighteen, she married a Chinese man at her father's insistence but divorced him and years later, when she no longer felt beholden to paternal wishes, she selected George, an African American, as her second husband. Again, her choice expressed her active disinterest in ethnicity or race as romantic criteria; George's thoughtfulness and perseverance won her over.[56]

The marriage of Avery Diaz and Nami Nakashima also highlighted the dynamics by which intercultural children perpetuated mixed families. Although it was a "no-no to marry out of the race," Nakashima reported in a mid-1990s interview, her Mexican-American mother and the Japanese immigrant to whom she had become engaged in Los Angeles, slipped across the border o Mexico where the pair exchanged wedding vows. Growing up in then-rural Long Beach, the Japanese-Mexican girl

Figure 7. Louis and Dolores Cruz, wedding picture, circa 1955. Private photograph of Dolores Cruz.

observed firsthand the trials of a mixed marriage: her mother surrendered her U.S. citizenship and the support of her ethnic community when
she married an Asian alien. But rather than seek a partner who matched
her ethnic background, Nami Nakashima chose Avery Diaz, a Mexican
American, in 1939, a selection based upon mutual attraction and values
rather than a consideration of racial pedigree. Local Japanese certainly
looked upon this pairing as unusual, but the couple did not. "I just loved
her," Diaz stated simply, a sentiment that Nakashima echoed. Her unique
perspective and ancestry subverted conventional marital practices and
definitions of exogamy. With little effort or self-consciousness, she entered what outsiders tried to label a cross-cultural romance.[57]

Rather than being perpetually mixed up and miserable, as families,

ethnic communities, and even many social scientists of the period pre-
dicted, bi- or multiracial offspring of minorities could enjoy and promote
blended affiliations. Taking advantage of more flexible ethnoracial ideas
in their communities and multiethnic neighborhoods, they drew marginalized couples back into familial and ethnic networks. With their own
marriages these children committed still further to the promise of interethnic families as original responses to discrimination and diversity.

CONCLUSION

In the years immediately before World War II, only the boldest of non-
Whites established intercultural families. Even more than the friendships
of youth, their relationships expressed a willingness to defy the convention that one should remain within the ethnic group. Such a convention,
they believed, reflected awkward and antiquated notions of what constituted family and community, notions discredited by their own experience of living among multiple ethnoracial groups. These mavericks who
chose outsiders as partners often confronted greater difficulties than
most homogeneous couples did: sharper cultural and gendered differences, as well as hostile friends, relatives, and communities. Yet these
challenges did not necessarily produce weaker, more fragile families. In
the years leading up to World War II, a small number discovered and
drew together because of common values and traits that transcended traditional cultural divisions. Rather than being random, these pairings
happened in repeated ways that expressed continued concerns about
color, history, and politics, as well as the balance between genders and
generations. The thoughtful ways in which minorities of multiethnic
spaces fell in love and had children did not interrupt the color line that
increasingly divided them from White ethnics. However, their romantic
transgressions did display their ability, despite that color line, to influence California's ethnoracial structure by breaking down and creating
boundaries between one another.

CHAPTER 4

Banding Together in Crisis

"The black boy was named Clovis Scott. He for whatever reason moved around with the Japanese crowd so when I went to Santa Anita camp, he was the only visitor I ever had. And he brought me a mirror because we were not able to bring mirrors to camp. But apparently I had written him and said I didn't even have a mirror. And to tell you how limited my circle of friends were. . . . During camp when we were asked to make applications for leave, we had to make a list of friends on the outside who would testify for you—he was one." Almost forty years later Mei Nakano still remembered her childhood companion's kindness as a rare relief from the cruelty of internment. The two had met and become friends in prewar Los Angeles. Their story suggests how the coming of war tested but did not break the intercultural relations and multiethnic identities that minority adolescents, adults, and families had built in California. At this juncture new and certain old interethnic tensions intensified, especially among Asian ethnics. Yet, rather than fracture the connectedness of non-Whites, in many cases wartime strains actually strengthened them. Against a backdrop of crisis the shared misfortunes of minorities stood out.

Violence against zoot-suiters and the internment of Japanese Americans shook up minority communities. These dramatic acts of injustice at a time of pronounced democratic rhetoric startled minorities into reconsidering their own social place and interethnic relationships. For Japanese Americans internment eroded a sense of security and distinction from other non-Whites. For the others, who could so easily imagine themselves in the position of the Japanese, it inspired sympathy. For mixed families with Japanese members, internment generated more painful choices and more visible defenses of ethnic crossing. Despite government orders to split such families up, many struggled to remain together and challenge prevailing ethnoracial categories. Injustices suffered by zoot-suiters fostered solidarity among minorities, too. The distinctive subculture of youth gained in popularity during the war even as the zoot-suiters evoked hatred and violence. Although Japanese internment had a more dramatic and unifying effect upon multiple, minority communities, the willingness of minorities to put on or defend the zoot suit suggested how committed many felt to multiethnic expressions defiant of the mainstream. Both events persuaded, or at least predisposed, minorities to close ranks and to contemplate the widening gap between themselves and European ethnics. Many Whites privately condemned and publicly organized against the internment of Japanese and violence against zoot-suiters, but the origins and stakes of their White opposition were rarely as personal or as urgent as the resistance of minorities.

MIGRATIONS AND SUCCESSIONS

The removal of the Japanese and attacks against young zoot-suiters occurred in a state disoriented by new peoples and economic prospects. Opportunities in California's defense industries and on its farms attracted Native Americans, Mexicans, southern Whites, and especially Blacks to the mobilized state and added to its already-impressive diversity (see chapter 1).[1] California's success in securing defense contracts and military installations made it a national center of wartime production almost overnight. The new shipbuilding and aircraft manufacturers had trouble satisfying their labor demands within the state and began recruiting Americans from other parts of the country. The arrival of new groups changed the color of neighborhoods and businesses without altering the fundamental pattern of clustering and interdependence among minorities. As Japanese hastily packed their belongings, left their homes, and gave up their jobs, Filipinos, Mexicans, Koreans, and African Americans replaced them. The persistence of housing and employment discrimination, as well as the dramatic increase in the wartime population, meant that minorities seized any vacancies available.

African Americans had made their way to California long before wartime, but the population remained proportionately small (2 percent of the state's 1940 total) until the economic changes brought about by World War II. Thousands of Blacks from Texas, Arkansas, Louisiana, and Oklahoma answered the call of defense work. In the Bay Area of San Francisco alone the Black population increased 227 percent between 1940 and 1945. San Diego and Los Angeles witnessed similarly impressive gains. These men and women hoped for better wages, more skilled jobs, a chance to vote, and an escape from the more virulent prejudice of their home region.[2]

In slightly smaller numbers Jews and Mexicans joined Blacks as new California residents. In Los Angeles the Jewish population grew from 130,000 in the early 1940s to 300,000 by 1951. The freshly arrived included discharged servicemen and easterners lured by the promise of better jobs and a more leisurely lifestyle. These Jews typically settled in older communities like Boyle Heights before moving to the suburbs. Mexicans too came in sizable numbers. Despite Depression-era efforts to drive them from the state, Mexicans responded to the very different economic incentives of the mid-1940s and crossed the border. As American workers joined the military or entered defense work, shortages in the agricultural sector instigated intensified labor recruitment. With the cooperation of Mexico the U.S. government arranged for the importation of 150,000 braceros, or temporary fieldhands, many of them to California. Other Mexicans left familiar locales in Mexico and southwestern states for jobs in California canneries, railroads, fields, and military manufacturers. Cities like Oakland and San Jose, which possessed relatively small, prewar Mexican-origin populations, still experienced noticeable increases in the number of Latino residents.[3]

Even Native Americans headed to booming California. While the 1930s had witnessed federal policies and Native American actions that privileged tribal sovereignty over assimilation, opportunities in military service and defense plants strained the integrity of tribes and their reservations. Like African, Mexican, and Jewish Americans, Native Americans eagerly seized positions in defense industries, especially those of Los Angeles. Their makeshift quarters, thrown up around shipyards and aircraft plants, displayed their new urban existence. While 46 percent settled in central Los Angeles, the remainder scattered along the city's outskirts. Between 1940 and 1945 approximately forty thousand left their reservations with the hope of better lives in California. By the close of the war one-fifth of all Native American women and one-half of all civilian Native American men had left their tribal lands.[4]

Native-born Whites from Arkansas, Louisiana, and Oklahoma contributed to the population boom. Like their Depression-era predecessors, they hoped the Golden State would relieve them of southern-style poverty. In Los Angeles White families from southern states overflowed working-class suburbs occupied by the economic refugees of earlier decades. In the Bay Area such migrants constituted the largest percentage of new urban dwellers by 1944. Established residents typically greeted the pejoratively labeled "Okies" with contempt, stereotyping them as uneducated and unrefined.[5]

Although length of residence mattered to social status in wartime communities, race often mattered most of all. A drastic shortage of housing for workers invited government intervention. A guest worker program urged Bay Area homeowners to take in boarders. Working-class Irish, Italian, and eastern European immigrants, who were less put off by the customs of rural southerners than their native born, middle-class counterparts, usually responded. In participating in the program the immigrants not only gained income, but, as the historian Marilyn Johnson has argued, they may have also improved their socioeconomic position by inverting the typical relationship between immigrant and native born. In other words, the European ethnics could whiten themselves by suggesting their parity to, even advantage over, White migrants. The housing problem also prompted the Federal Housing Administration to extend favorable loans to private contractors. However, the resulting subdivisions restricted residence to those of "the Caucasian race." Thus White ethnics enjoyed the space and security of homes in emerging suburbs, while African Americans crowded into central districts long designated for Blacks or foreigners. Similar race-based favoritism shaped housing practices in Southern California, initiating a pattern of segregated suburbs that would continue in the postwar era. If newcomers to California of all colors faced discrimination, they did not do so in equal amounts or for equal lengths of time.[6]

Along with established residents these newcomers gained from the sudden evacuation of Japanese. They moved into the internees' former residences, changing the precise complexion but not the fundamentally mixed character of so many prewar neighborhoods. Into the newly emptied Little Tokyos rushed minorities of all colors, but especially African Americans. In Los Angeles "jitterbugs, hep-cats and just plain hardworking war workers have replaced the nervous Nisei, the shrinking Issei and intolerant Kibei. The loud familiarity of the share cropping South now reigns in a section of the city once given over to the ever polite and reserved manner of the Sons of Heaven," reported the *Negro Digest*. In 1942 the *(Sacramento) Pacific Citizen* observed that the city's "Nihon-machi [Japanese neighborhood] was quickly populated in turn by Mexicans and Negroes" whose "honky-tonks and tortilla houses" marked the place as their own. Demographic changes were as striking in San Francisco. "As the Japanese disappeared," recalled Maya Angelou of San Francisco's Fillmore District, "soundlessly and without protest, the Negroes entered with their loud jukeboxes, their just released animosities and the relief of escape from southern bonds." So too in Oakland did Blacks and other non-Whites transform once-Japanese neighborhoods.[7]

Internment created commercial opportunities for non-Whites, preserving the multiethnic, interdependent character of business as well as residence in minority districts. As the war tore holes in the economic web spun by non-Whites in the prewar period, many took advantage of the openings. They bought the shops, farms, and smaller possessions of the displaced Japanese. Items as random as "a chop suey palace," "newspaper press," and hog farm, "together with a garbage contract that provided for their feed," passed between minorities.[8] So did the more conventional cars, furniture, and groceries. Chinese buyers quickly snapped up the Japanese-owned restaurants and curio shops lining Grant Avenue in San Francisco's Chinatown, while Filipinos in the city pooled their resources and converted a Japanese building into a recreation center. These Asians likely enjoyed a familiarity with Japanese goods and services that facilitated these shifts, but African Americans also leased hotels and cafes from internees in San Francisco, Los Angeles, and Oakland.[9]

In rural parts of the state property also changed hands in these ways. The army's wartime Civilian Control Administration observed that "up and down the West Coast, Chinese, Mexicans and Filipinos took over various holdings frequently receiving special Farm Security Administration (FSA) loans."[10] The FSA described its role as that of middleman between Japanese evacuees and interested operators. "If a Negro farmer is qualified to operate the land," the agency explained, "we will assist him." In this capacity it arranged for Yahei Kato, an Issei farmer, not only to turn his land over to a Chinese organization but also to "teach the art of truck gardening" to his replacement.[11] Acquisitions made in rural and urban areas alike brought many non-Whites unprecedented financial gains. A Korean's success at reselling Japanese groceries at prices twenty times what he had paid, and a Chinese man's rise from rags to riches of $100,000, exemplified the dramatic shift in minority fortunes. Although White ethnics gained from the sudden exile of Japanese

Americans, their physical and often material distance made them less common beneficiaries.[12]

If minorities felt guilty about the economic gains they had made thanks to the losses of Japanese Americans, few expressed such feelings publicly and fewer offered payments matching the real value of property transferred. Looking back, Cesar Chavez recognized that "it was an awful thing" that Mexican farmworkers in Oxnard celebrated the removal of their Japanese employers. However, at the time Japanese growers worked their employees so hard, Chavez explained, that to the workers "it was liberation." The National Negro Business League even went so far as to advise Black Californians to "take the place of these alien farmers and fisherman," not only because such succession would "contribute to urgent defense needs" but also because it would allow Black "entrenchment in a manner not previously granted." The organization's assertion that Japanese had monopolized agriculture and displaced Blacks from domestic positions highlighted the sense of promise that African Americans discerned in the current environment. More starkly, the statement conveyed the competition and distrust of Japanese stirred up by wartime conditions.[13]

In many instances minorities stepped softly into the evacuees' place, but in others they leaped. The alacrity with which they acquired vacated businesses, houses, and miscellaneous property suggested the spatial and socioeconomic closeness of California minorities. Although they found opportunity in the misfortune of the Japanese, they did not instigate that misfortune. In fact, the continued concentration of non-Whites in residence and commerce reflected the persistent privilege of Whites, who did not need or want what Japanese Americans had left behind. Ethnic successions in wartime did not alter the underlying reality of California: the congregation of disadvantaged ethnoracial groups. This economic and residential landscape shaped minorities' reactions to civil rights abuses during the war.

INTERNMENT AND ITS DISCONTENTS

The fortunes of many minorities may have improved during World War II, but their financial gains did not insulate them from anxieties about the internment of the Japanese community. These concerns sometimes precipitated organized public protests on behalf of the evacuees. More often, a sense of vulnerability limited collective action. Historians and contemporary activists have faulted non-White groups for this response, for not answering the evacuation noisily enough, for being as passive in their position as White progressives and conservatives were. However, if these critics listened hard enough, they would hear the faint but clear sounds of sympathy emanating from mixed, non-White neighborhoods. These utterances typically came from individuals whose personal connections to Japanese Americans, as much as an abstract sense of injustice, motivated their expression. These small, often highly personal, gestures of support suggested the depth of minorities' discontent and the breadth of their connections to other non-Whites. Though too subtle and incomplete to prevent or shorten internment, non-Whites' support for Japanese and disapproval of the removal highlighted a dramatic shift in how minorities understood their own position in the United States and their relationship to other disadvantaged groups. For adolescents, adults, and mixed families alike, internment emphasized the common situation of minorities subject to the vicissitudes of a discriminatory society. If they did not represent these views in very public or formal ways during the war, their changing awareness opened the door for more active coordination in the postwar era.[14]

Organized, sustained opposition to internment was more the exception than the rule, especially in the beginning of the war and especially at the national level. Groups long active in civil rights such as the American Jewish Congress, National Association for the Advancement of Colored People (NAACP), National Urban League, American Jewish Council, National Council for Negro Women, and Chinese American Citizens Association responded with uncharacteristic timidity. In most cases muted or nonexistent resistance from non-Whites betrayed a sense of danger in the wartime climate rather than agreement with the executive order that set internment in motion. Ellen Eisenberg has argued that, for Jewish agencies in Los Angeles and San Francisco, the primary goal of eradicating anti-Semitism required hearty expressions of support for the war, expressions that many Jews worried were incompatible with support for the evacuees. Outsiders could too easily construe a public challenge to internment as unpatriotic. The subdued reaction of Black organizations and the Black press to the misfortune of the Japanese (even as these groups heatedly spoke out against the mistreatment of Black GIs and workers) also reflected a strategy shaped by self-interest and fear. The NAACP, National Urban League, and others concluded that strong criticism of the war would feed rumors of a Black fifth column and jeopardize their efforts to win legal equality. These civil rights organizations had made it their business to challenge racism before the war, but wartime conditions made them narrow the scope of their efforts.[15]

Within this constrained context of war, select minority organizations still defended the rights of Japanese Americans. Even though it did so inconsistently and weakly, the NAACP criticized the placement of Japanese Americans in relocation centers. In a letter dated 1945 to a Japanese American who had expressed interest in the history and mission of the NAACP, the regional director, Noah W. Griffin, referenced a 1942 conference in Los Angeles where the NAACP had issued a statement against internment.[16] Specifically, it resolved to "protest vigorously the use of race or color as the sole basis for any arbitrary classification by which the fundamental rights of any group of American citizens is infringed." Although not the strongest of condemnations, the organization was publicly opposing the executive order at a time when most others were not. Walter White, chief secretary of the NAACP, offered a more specific and forceful comment. Pointing to the preferential treatment given Americans of German and Italian descent, who retained their civil rights, he labeled internment a racist act. The NAACP's official publication, *Crisis,* questioned the government's policy in that same year. It said the Nisei were "hapless citizens who had been deprived of their constitutional rights and constitutional protection" because they suffered the misfortune of having non-White ancestors. The writer concluded that what had happened to the Japanese was of "direct concern to the American Negro, for the barbarous treatment of these Americans is the result of the color line," and African Americans and Jews had reason to fear loss of their own citizenship and property.[17]

The quickness and decisiveness with which Black, Jewish, and Chinese-American civil rights groups criticized internment as soon as the war was over suggests that their opposition may have originated *during* the war. At a conference on interracial cooperation convened by the Pacific Coast Committee on American Principles and Fair Play in 1948, Black, Korean, and Filipino delegates pledged to "safeguard the rights and liberties of the returning evacuees" and warned that "any attempt to make capital for their own racial groups at the expense of the Japanese Americans would be sawing off the limb on which they themselves sat." Filipino and Korean spokesmen additionally promised that "indignation over atrocities by the Japanese military" would not lead them to take "revenge on innocent and unfortunate persons of Japanese descent here." In that same year the American Jewish Congress and the National Council of Jewish women supported the right of citizenship for Japanese immigrants. Even the organized Chinese community broke its wartime silence. In a 1950 editorial the San Francisco–based *Chinese Press* defined evacuation as "the tragedy of 1941, when for the sake of 'security' thousands of loyal Japanese were sent to internment camps." Minority organizations were not alone in reenvisioning the removal of Nisei and Issei after the fact; Whites of liberal and conservative political stripes did, too. But non-White organizations stated their regret so assertively, so soon after the war and in terms so related to their own fortunes, that it seems likely that the sentiment preceded its public expression.[18]

Although the most established and visible minority organizations— often those national in scale—saved a forceful defense of Japanese Americans until after the war, minority individuals extended their sympathy during the conflict. This shift toward a quasi-cosmopolitan sensibility that privileged the connectedness of minorities was perhaps most pronounced within the group most directly affected—the Japanese. The sudden, painful uprooting of Japanese immigrants and their children transformed their lives and their attitudes about American society. Many had believed education, hard work, and good relations with Whites would bring them greater acceptance and integration into California society. As I discussed in earlier chapters, Japanese immigrants and their children eschewed contact with Filipinos, Mexicans, Blacks, Native Americans, and even Chinese for fear of losing status through association with groups ranked lower in the nation's racial hierarchy. In interviews conducted in the mid-1940s, Issei and Nisei alike confessed how recently they had harbored these prejudices, especially toward Blacks. In a 1944 interview Richard Moto, a Nisei, acknowledged his displeasure upon learning at the start of his internment that "colored people" rather than Whites would rent his family's home in California. He believed most Nisei shared "the idea that the Negroes were inferior" and never realized that they "were applying the same discrimination" against Blacks as so many Whites "directed at us."[19]

Yet after days, weeks, and months spent inside the camps, many Japanese began to realize that racial prejudice disregarded the distinctions they had painstakingly drawn between themselves and other non-Whites. When Robert Sakai overheard other internees express surprise that Whites were treating them like "Mexicans or Jews or Negroes," he reminded them of how damaging their own cultural prejudices could be. Another internee confessed that he had held "some funny ideas about Negroes and Jews" but learned "now what they have to 'buck'" and would "work for fair play for every minority group once released." Even Richard Moto, who had similarly disparaged Blacks and Jews—describing the former as "dirty" and the latter as "money grubbers"—credited internment for changing his mind. "My attitude has become much more liberal," he stated from the distance of 1944 Chicago, "and I now feel more sympathetic towards these other groups. I feel that one of the biggest problems of this country is the color line." Another Nisei summed up the affect of internment on the racial consciousness of so many Japanese when he explained in 1948 that "the shock of evacuation and the hectic years of resettlement taught most of us firsthand what can happen to minority groups in wartime America." The realization led "Japanese Americans together with other minority groups" to collectively criticize the nation's failings.[20]

The ethnic disguises of Nisei determined to avoid evacuation further underscored their changing notions of ethnoracial identity during wartime. For those Japanese Americans brave enough or incensed enough, assuming the identity of another minority, oftentimes a Chinese, Filipino, or Korean American, offered the chance to stay out of the camps. Posers included Kumahichi Yoshida, a Japanese man and San Francisco resident who represented himself as Korean, and Rose Hayashi, a frequent performer in Chinatown clubs who feigned Chinese ancestry. The FBI eventually discovered and interned them both. The most famous of these pretenders was Fred Korematsu, who would eventually file a lawsuit challenging the constitutionality of internment. When he learned of the order to intern individuals of Japanese descent, the Northern Californian Nisei scratched the words *enemy alien* off his draft card and changed his printed name to the ethnically ambiguous "Clyde Syrah." To further his charade he underwent mild plastic surgery. Korematsu told those who asked about his background that he had Spanish and Hawaiian ancestors. Until local police and the FBI discovered him, he lived and worked comfortably in Oakland. By passing themselves off as members of other minority groups, Korematsu and others learned both the value of ethnic crossing and the arbitrariness of U.S. racial categories. California minorities had played these games of masquerade in the prewar period. Such crossings expressed the appeal of other cultures and the experimental instincts of youth. However, when performed by Japanese Americans in the context of war, passing acquired a subversively political meaning.[21]

Even more than the Issei, Japanese youth trapped behind barbed wire fences rethought their social attitudes and relations with other minorities. In doing so, they committed or recommitted to the multiethnic youth culture that had developed in mixed neighborhoods before the war. The camp experience deepened and broadened their sense of themselves as disadvantaged minorities, and many found an outlet for their frustration in the attire and spirit of the zoot-suiters. Mary Oyama reported that at the weekly "jam sessions," young men arrived "wearing their jerk hats and 'zootu suits' with the 'reat pleats,'" looking more like the Oriental version of Good Ole Siwash than the smiling, bespectacled, buck-toothed fascist of the cartoons." Groups organized as "pachuco gangs . . . crashed social affairs" and settled "all personal grudges with physical assault," inspiring resentment among other youth. Many of these disapproving young men and women portrayed the zoot-suiters as belligerent and ill mannered. They objected in particular to the aggressive sexual personas of the young men who arrived at dances dateless, drunken, and expectant. To protect their boyfriends and preempt potential fights, young women reportedly consented to the dance requests of *yogores*. In copying the assertive masculinity of Mexican, Filipino, and Black youngsters that they remembered from prewar settings, the young male internees found a way to vent their anger. At times the zoot suits offered another kind of relief: an escape from the monotony of camp life. At Tulare Tamie Ihara and her friends led an informal recreational program at the Tulare Assembly Center. As part of a July Fourth celebration, she "dressed as a Negro zoot suiter" and strutted around the stage. She described her performance as "a lot of fun," and it likely amused her audience. But her daring gender- and racial-bending act had the flavor of a minstrelsy show. Unlike the zoot-suiting Nisei, who implicitly respected Black teens through their cultural borrowing, Tamie Ihara's was a stylized impersonation intended as entertainment rather than personal statement.[22]

Even Ihara and other Japanese Americans who mocked or rejected the zoot suit as an extreme expression of discontent found that their forced removal encouraged a reevaluation of American society and recognition of new links with non-Whites. "Experiencing evacuation made on a racial basis and seeing discriminatory actions against other ethnic groups as he resettles, he begins to make legitimate inquiries," commented one Nisei in 1944. He further hypothesized that "being a color 'in-between,'" Chinese, Korean, Native American, and Filipino Americans could act as "a wedge for the darker minority [African Americans]." In improving their own status Japanese Americans could open "the eyes and heart" of the nation to "the more complex Negro problem." Here, the speaker recognized the intertwining of Black and Asian lives and urged Nisei to challenge prejudice far and wide. Tommy Yoneda, who was a young boy when he was interned, acted upon such appeals. The son of an interracial couple who were political activists, he sent a small donation to the United China Relief to support the agency's work with suffering Chinese. "I'm sorry it is only a dollar," he apologized in the accompanying note, "but I am an evacuee here with my parents." Despite or because of his own predicament, he could imagine a larger community of the disadvantaged.[23]

Internment brought still other Japanese-American youths to a new state of political consciousness. During a 1944 interview Bill Katayama acknowledged that "there has been many a time when I wished I were a White person" because "it's a handicap to have a Jap face." Yet his longing to be White faded as he left the camps and realized that "this racial discrimination is not too bad when I know that there are many other racial groups in the same fix like the Negroes, Jews, Chinese, and Filipinos." His eventual involvement in postwar Oakland's Young Democratic Club suggested this sentiment had real staying power. For Chohei Sakamoto the experience of removal crystallized the difference in racial positions between White ethnics and non-Whites as well. In 1943 she fumed to a sociologist that "lots of Italians and Germans have sympathies in their heads for their country, but they have become loyal citizens here now" because "White Americans say that they are equal to them." Sakamoto did not understand why Whites "will not do this for the Japanese and Chinese." Italians and Germans may have been among the playmates of Nisei in mixed, working-class neighborhoods, but the very different experience of Asian ethnics during World War II distanced them from these former friends. As the color line became more vivid, Japanese Americans remembered and turned toward minority neighbors who appeared to be as unprotected and vulnerable as they. The trauma of internment redefined the ethnoracial views of Issei parents and especially their children. For many this redefinition was not about downplaying ethnicity and playing White but about seeing other minorities as comrades in misfortune.[24]

DESERT ENCOUNTERS

Japanese Americans' changing notions of power, place, and race were most visible under the bright rays of the Arizona sun. Californians removed to Arizona camps built on the Colorado River Indian Reservation encountered a startling new landscape and people. Many could not help but observe the parallels between their own displacement and containment and that of local Native Americans. Such observations encouraged and accompanied a larger shift in Japanese Americans' understanding of U.S. history: they increasingly highlighted discrimination against minorities in their narrative of the nation's past.[25]

Long before the government issued its internment orders, Japanese Americans in California had shared experiences of discrimination and crossed paths with Native Americans. American Indians were numerically few and scattered throughout the state, but they appeared at many of the same neighborhoods, schools, playing fields, and stores frequented by Japanese Americans. As I related in chapter 2, Nisei like Kisako Yasuda of Long Beach came to believe that she too was Native American and expressed surprise when her parents failed to comprehend the language she had learned so speak. The thoroughness of her cultural immersion set her experiences apart from most of her ethnic counterparts and suggested that at least some Japanese were not strangers to Native Americans before their relocation.[26]

Beyond the personal connections created among individuals, the lives of the ethnic groups overlapped as similarly categorized and disadvantaged minorities. As the historian Michael Bottoms explained of mid–nineteenth century efforts to codify racial distinctions, Whites limited the civil rights of Chinese by lumping them together with Native Americans. In a case determining the limits of testimony laws, the California justices denied Chinese the power to testify in court on the grounds that they were biologically and historically related to Native Americans, a group already determined to be ineligible for the privilege. The decision rested upon the scientific notion of the day that stressed the physical and spatial closeness of Asian ethnics and Native Americans. Given the still relative rarity of Japanese immigrants in California at that time, the justices did not specifically associate them with Native Americans. However, the shared racial status of Japanese and Chinese as "Mongolians" in state law implied the connection. Even when Whites did not explicitly conflate Asian and Native American groups, they did so implicitly by subjecting them to the same kinds of abuses through the first four decades of the twentieth century. Discrimination in housing, education, and employment constrained both groups.[27]

The relocation of California's ethnic Japanese to reservation lands in Arizona would more completely, intimately, and self-consciously connect them to Native American peoples. Despite the objections of Pima and Colorado River tribes that almost unanimously opposed the plan of the War Relocation Authority (WRA), nearly twenty-five thousand, or one-quarter of all Japanese evacuees, found themselves in a barren, dusty, intermittently scorching-hot or freezing-cold stretch of Arizona desert. Specifically, the WRA distributed them between two sites—the Pima-held Gila Reservation immediately outside Phoenix, and the Colorado River Reservation in Poston, Arizona. Despite the protests of Pima, Chemehuevi, Navajo, and Mojave, the Office of Indian Affairs, which was supposed to manage the reservations in the groups' interest, reasoned that the tribes would benefit from the construction of new barracks and improvements that Japanese Americans would likely make to the land. Moreover, the agency argued that its experience in managing one minority community prepared it to oversee another. That the government had overruled the tribes' objections came as no surprise to their governments, which viewed it as one more example in a long history of abuse and false promises.[28]

Although federal administrators concluded that the construction of internment camps in Arizona was smart policy, they feared the possibility of commiseration and collaboration between Native Americans and Japanese Americans. As high-profile and liberal an individual as Eleanor Roosevelt linked the two groups when she warned in 1943 of "another Indian problem" if Japanese were released to coastal rather than inland communities; presumably, she was referring to the struggle of recently urbanized Native Americans to adjust to life outside reservations. This tendency to equate minority populations underwrote official efforts to separate them. If Japanese were the "new Indians," the logic went, they might join together with the "old Indians." Thus the WRA tried to keep Japanese and Native Americans apart. According to the historian Alison Bernstein, the WRA director, Dillon Myer, viewed the evacuees as "transients" who should not be permitted to "develop ties to their temporary surroundings." Indeed, regular and intimate contacts between the two peoples never became the norm.[29]

The U.S. government may have anticipated what Agnes Savilla, a Pima, described as "a crop of Mojave-Japanese or Chemehuevi-Japanese" children, but the reality was quite different. "Our people, they're satisfied to be with their own; they don't bother anyone," she said, "so even if they met [Japanese Americans] and talked with them, they liked them and were friends, but they didn't seek them out." Simon Lewis, also a Pima, and Iver Sunna, a Hopi, concurred. Japanese, Pima, and Hopi labored alongside one another to make camouflage nets—a camp-based operation that drew workers from the three ethnic populations—but they did not always develop close ties. In a 1993 interview Lewis recalled that "they work and we work, and I don't know if we were allowed to talk to them or what." As far as Sunna could remember, Japanese Americans "were friendly," "hard workers," and "just like any other people," but "we didn't have much contact with them because "they would come and go back." These statements suggested the active hands of government officials in segregating the groups.[30]

When the WRA did permit encounters between internees and locals, the contacts were closely supervised and designed to accentuate their differences. According to the *Gila News-Courier,* the camp newspaper put out by the Japanese American Citizens League, Indians regularly performed traditional dances and songs for the amusement of bored internees. The sight of "Chief Big Buffalo" and "Chief Blue Eagle" in "full ceremonial costume," the "two squaws," or nine Choctaw entertainers taught Japanese Americans little about the current lives of Arizona Indians. These displays of so-called Native American culture glossed over their everyday struggles and history of oppression. Camp officials likely believed such sanitized representations might dissuade evacuees from seeing or making common cause with Native Americans.[31]

Camp officials counted upon, often correctly, the ignorance of arriving ethnic Japanese. A Nisei born in Gardena and removed to Pasadena confessed his surprise on discovering that "real" Indians looked so different from those he had seen in "magazines, you know, where they are tall." The people he encountered one warm day when he eluded camp guards and stole beyond camp grounds were short and squat, he said, prompting him to wonder, "Are they Indians or are they Mexicans?" A short-lived section of the youth newspaper *Kampus Krier* revealed similarly flat and superficial cultural impressions. Accompanied by the image of a smiling Native American child, the gossip column, titled "Chi Wee Checks," expressed its juicy tidbits in the pidgin English stereotypically ascribed to Native Americans: "Let's see what big talk, Chiwee givem today," one edition opened. Without more personal, regular interactions, Japanese Americans might have consumed "Indianness" much like their White counterparts and much as the WRA preferred—in ways that distanced and exoticized Native Americans.[32]

Yet despite and perhaps even because of their clichéd understanding, Japanese Americans clamored for a more complete education about native peoples and the surrounding environment, one that went deeper than the government-sanctioned versions. Robert Spencer, a prominent anthropologist who was studying camp life as part of the University of

California's Evacuation and Resettlement Study, commented that "the Japanese are extremely interested in the Indians," so much so that one group begged him "to give a series of lectures on Indian life."[33] Curiosity led other Nisei to conduct investigations of their own. A Poston publication of adolescent writings printed Kazue Tsuchiyama's thoughtful, relatively balanced account of Native Americans in Gila River. His essay depicted them as resourceful and artistic, as those who "dug shallow pits and roofed them over with bark from the cedars and pines for houses" and "wove such beautiful baskets." Tsuchiyama also acknowledged episodes of violence among Native Americans. However, his conclusion— that the Japanese Americans who occupied territory "formerly known only by the Mojave and Chimewawa Indians" shared a "heritage" with the tribes and "were bound to win, as we huddle together here"—most suggested his learned sensitivity to the history of Native Americans and the place of Japanese Americans within that history.[34]

When they visited one another's schools and performed dances, Nisei youth further educated themselves about Native American culture, inverting the government-introduced stereotypes. Ishimi Tagawa, a Los Angeles–born Nisei, remembered her dance troupe's excursion beyond the barbed wire to the city of Sacaton, where the dancers entertained a group of Native Americans. Weeks later the Native Americans reciprocated, demonstrating their own dances before an appreciative Tagawa and her friends, "who never forgot that time." This exchange of places by Native Americans and Nisei as performers and audience members allowed each culture to have a more intimate understanding of the other. Within this context of reciprocity both sets of youngsters learned more about one another than they did when the WRA sponsored Native Americans to entertain evacuees. Japanese Americans' efforts to educate themselves communicated not only their longing to understand their immediate circumstances but also the instinct that they were not alone in their misfortune.[35]

Learning about and interacting in limited, but sometimes intimate, ways with Gila River residents lifted Nisei sensibilities beyond curiosity to anxiety and empathy. Japanese Americans traded with willing Native Americans to supplement food supplies and obtain other longed-for materials. They labored alongside one another in the manufacture of camouflage nets and the management of local cattle, competed against each other in high school sports, and even shared lessons with the few Native Americans who attended camp-based schools. These associations likely underscored the tendency of evacuees to use Native American history as a framework for their own experience. Spencer noted not only regular interethnic interplay but also that "the Indians and Japanese both feel that they are persecuted minority groups," a conviction he attributed to their awareness of common conditions and "Mongolian antecedents." Spencer may have exaggerated the racial underpinnings of the relationship, but camp administrators confirmed the explicitness of the interethnic connection that the groups had drawn. Japanese-American inmates repeatedly asked Richard Leighton of the Bureau of Indian Affairs, and the WRA "if they would be kept all the rest of their lives on 'reservations like the Indians.'" In seeking to comprehend the dizzying set of events that culminated in their desert confinement, Japanese Americans reached for a historic precedent and found the discomfiting one of Native Americans. Using the Native American past to contextualize their lives, Japanese Americans came to appreciate another group's suffering.[36]

Rather than reject this analogy as a misappropriation of their history, local Native Americans confirmed it, reciprocating the sense of relatedness. Although the Native Americans resented the intrusion of outsiders, most distinguished between the decision makers and the subjects of those decisions. In a 1978 interview Agnes Savilla, a Mojave born on the reservation and connected to the Indian Tribal Council, encapsulated this distinction. Tribal leaders were "sore—not at the Japanese," she explained, "but at the authorities for getting them in here." Concluding that "the White man is treating them just like he treated us," council members interpreted relocation in highly personal terms. This did not preclude moments of disapproval. Savilla resented what she deemed the wastefulness of Japanese who would periodically toss "boiled ham sandwiches" over camp fences. "We couldn't buy bacon or ham or whatnot," she explained, a poverty that made the internees' actions seem selfish. Her observation suggested that even as the government contained Japanese Americans, it did so in kinder, gentler ways than it treated Native Americans. The subtly preferential treatment might have divided the communities, but Savilla gave the internees the benefit of the doubt, proposing that "maybe they threw" the food out, "thinking an Indian would grab and eat it." Though sometimes conflicted, the feelings that she and most Native Americans had toward the Japanese contrasted with those of White Arizonans. Residents of nearby Parker, Arizona, resented the placement of a population they deemed enemies of the United States and did little to disguise their displeasure. Angry looks, refused service, and signs that read "No Japs Allowed" clearly stated their feelings. Although

Native Americans warmed to Japanese newcomers as fellow victims of injustice, no such recognition dulled the hostility of most local Whites.[37]

Native Americans like Albert Cooley and his daughter, Ruth, Pimas who had intimate, daily contacts with the evacuees, expressed this sense of kinship most poignantly. While Albert Cooley labored as a paid wrangler at one of the camps, training Nisei to ride and maneuver cattle, his daughter attended the camp school. Work relationships spilled over into social life as Albert Cooley and the men played cards, listened to the radio, and consumed chocolate cake together. He remembered how passionately the Nisei hated the camp's White employees but "treated [him] right." "I got along good with all of them," he insisted. Despite his authority over internees and affiliation with the camp's administration, Albert Cooley was close to Japanese Americans in ways out of reach and perhaps unappealing to his White counterparts. The common status of Japanese and Native Americans as minorities facilitated interethnic friendships.[38]

Ruth Cooley created even tighter ties and felt a keener camaraderie with Nisei. The Japanese children she met at school became her best friends. She visited their Buddhist churches, ate meals with their families, and listened to their elders' stories of life before relocation. On one occasion she organized the temporary escape of Nisei pals to her aunt's home, where they enjoyed Indian corn and a swim in a nearby canal; a few burritos assured a camp guard's silence. Out of these social interactions she gained a respect for and deep understanding of the evacuees. She admired the agricultural skills, generosity, and industry of Japanese Americans, who "worked hard at everything" and woke "before the sun would be up." As important, she knew and pitied their misfortune. Witnessing the tears of older Issei, who "would be sitting on the beds in their house and crying," she "felt sorry for them." From the vantage point of 1993 Cooley believed she "got along so good" with the Nisei children precisely because she had felt such empathy. An awareness of Pima misfortune prepared her to appreciate the mistreatment of Japanese Americans. "They [Japanese Americans] are the ones who had to suffer up there," she related, "we went through the Trail of Tears and all of that stuff." In connecting the two episodes of injustice, she emphasized the essential similarities in the histories of the minority communities. The passage of time may have helped her articulate this linkage, but even as a young child she felt it.[39]

Revisions in Japanese Americans' thinking about their history and relationships with other minorities that were occurring in internment camps throughout the American West were quickened in Arizona. The experiences of Native Americans offered language and structure through which the displaced Japanese could explain their own circumstances. When World War II ended, their new ethnic narrative would inform many Niseis' more inclusive civil rights efforts, which considered the grievances of other minorities as well as their own.

ON THE OTHER SIDE OF THE BARBED WIRE

Although they did not experience internment with the immediacy of Japanese Americans or the proximity of Native Americans in Arizona, other minorities reconsidered and spoke out against the American racial system because of it. These Californians quickly realized removal's unpleasant and unpredictable implications for all non-Whites. Jews, Mexicans, and Asians who knew individual Japanese Americans professed their solidarity and confessed fears that they might be the next group singled out for discriminatory treatment. Because many minority adults felt as vulnerable as the Japanese, they articulated their opposition in more reserved and private ways. Though heartfelt, their protests generally moved through less visible and public channels.[40]

African-American individuals and groups objected most vociferously to evacuation, connecting Black and Japanese fortunes in the United States. Their personal contacts with Japanese Americans in the years before the war informed their largely empathetic reactions. In a 1984 interview Ruth Washington described the Black-Japanese couple with whom she worked at a Los Angeles photography studio. She spoke affectionately of the pair and their "fine children." During the war she had not objected to internment, believing the decision was the "government's business." However, her acceptance was never an endorsement. "Because [of] me being close to" the Williams family, "they didn't seem a threat." A contemporaneous journalist from the Baltimore-based *Afro-American,* Vincent Tubbs, insisted that Washington's thinking was the norm rather than the exception. Dispatched to San Francisco during the war to take the pulse of the city's Black residents, Tubbs discovered a gap between the near indifference of easterners to Japanese internment and the genuine sorrow expressed by their California counterparts. Black San Franciscans, Tubbs reported, considered Japanese Americans their "good friends" and reminded him of what most African Americans elsewhere failed to recognize: the misfortune of Japanese Americans might one day become their own.[41]

Literary and legal challenges to internment further exemplified Black individuals' interested opposition to evacuation. In the novel *If He Hollers, Let Him Go,* written and set in World War II California, Chester Himes's Black protagonist, Bob Jones, eloquently states the impact of removal upon his racial community. After witnessing the pathetic sight of Japanese Americans who had been uprooted and locked up "without a chance," Jones notes that he is "the same colour as the Japanese" and as likely to be named "a yeller-bellied Jap by Anglo Americans." This character's unease captured the fear of many Blacks in California who interpreted internment in personal terms. The mistreatment of Japanese deepened their sense of vulnerability in a society that discriminated so broadly.[42]

In more literal ways Blacks in Los Angeles lashed out against injustice. Hugh MacBeth, an African-American attorney, not only defended the rights of Japanese Americans in public forums but also visited internees at the camp near Granada, Colorado. There, he insisted, Blacks and Japanese shared the status of slaves and recommended "a comprehensive alliance of colored peoples." Such proclamations motivated his legal practice during the war. In a case testing the constitutionality of Executive Order 9066, which authorized the camps, MacBeth appeared as a friend of the court. His statement reiterated his earlier theme: the compatibility of Black and Japanese interests. "Thirteen million Negroes were interested in these cases, because if citizens of Japanese ancestry could be evacuated," he reasoned, "the next group might be Negroes and the next Jews. If persons can be discriminated against because of their race alone, the whole structure of living in this country would have to be revised." His level of advocacy may not have been typical, but it suggested how heavily internment weighed on the thoughts of some African Americans.[43]

Other minority groups added their voices to the chorus of opposition to internment. Generally, Asian groups remained quieter or adopted a more cautious tone in their protests than African Americans because of international politics and fears of misidentification. Feeling endangered as racial minorities, many of these Asian Americans concluded that evacuation was, in the words of Kim Fong Tom of Los Angeles, "none of our business," even as they feared its implications. Yet other Chinese, Koreans, and Filipinos overcame fears and enmities to empathize with the internees. In her autobiography Patricia Justiniani, a Norwegian-Filipino who grew up in Los Angeles, recalled her Filipino father's disapproval of Japanese evacuation. Jose Justiniani was never a polite progressive; he

stereotyped Jews as money grubbing, Mexicans as peasants, and the English as pompous. However, when White Americans confiscated the lives
of Japanese who "had been living and working hard at peace for years,"
Justiniani shouted that "it wasn't right." In West Oakland Vangie Buell
had a vivid memory of how "terribly upset" her Filipina grandmother
was when the Japanese friends with whom she had socialized and whose
grocery stores she had patronized departed for the camps.[44]

Asian ethnics supported Japanese Americans in more active and defiant ways. The ethnic disguises that Nisei fashioned to fool government
officials and avoid internment typically depended upon the complicity
of Chinese and Koreans. It was their physical features that Japanese
Americans appeared to possess and within their communities that Japanese Americans hid. Even before the formal removal of Japanese,
Charles Kikuchi borrowed an "I am Chinese" button from a Chinese-
American friend so that he could stay out past the San Francisco cur-
few. "It did not bother the Chinese," he explained. Without the resources of his companion or the willingness of the larger community of
Chinese Americans to accept the button at face value, Kikuchi could not
have circumvented government restrictions. Rose Hayashi, the performer who remained in San Francisco's Chinatown long after Kikuchi
and others had entered the camps, found that her Chinese contacts po-
litely avoided the topic of ethnicity and internment. "They never said
anything to me about the Japanese and they did not talk to me about
the war when I was around," she said. "I guess they kept quiet because
I was Japanese and they did not want to hurt my feelings." In protecting Rose Hayashi, her Chinese acquaintances and friends put themselves at considerable risk. Betty Lem's parents had warmly welcomed
their daughter's friend Rose into their home. But the law against con-
cealing Japanese made them increasingly nervous. Sensitive to their danger, Hayashi eventually packed her bags and turned herself in to the authorities. Ben Loo found the Chinese community less welcoming than
Betty had, but he too gained safety in its midst. Representing himself as
a Korean, he entertained at a Chinese night club until the owner of a
rival establishment, who suspected Loo's Japanese background, betrayed him. However, since the authorities had never been called, three
weeks later Loo landed a gig at the nearby Club Shanghai. The proprietor likely knew about, but chose to ignore, Loo's ethnicity. On discovering his identity, other entertainers expressed surprise, along with
tolerance and sympathy. In playing along with the masquerades of
Nisei, Chinese and Koreans became coconspirators. They expanded

ethnic boundaries to temporarily enfold Nisei, challenging the ethnoracial status quo as they did so.[45]

The possibilities and perils of ethnic misidentification did not structure the reactions of Mexican Americans, yet those with intimate connections to Japanese also felt keenly discomfited by internment. Dionicio Morales, who would become a professional educator, political
activist, and founder of the Mexican American Opportunity Foundation,
tasted the bitterness of prejudice as he was growing up in 1920s and
1930s California. Morales remembered the humiliation of eating food
on the back steps of an Imperial Valley cafe after its owners refused him
service indoors. Memories of discrimination as a college student still
darkened his mind. At Santa Barbara College he became a close friend
of "Tack" Takahashi's. A 1942 telephone call from Takahashi left
Morales angry and perplexed. In a "shaky voice" Takahashi informed
Morales that he and his family were being sent away to a relocation
camp in Northern California. Years later Morales referred to his friend's
misfortune as an example of "the extremes to which color bias can go
when people who know better remain silent." As a minority at the moment of internment, Morales was one of those people who knew better
but did not act upon that knowledge. However, his efforts to comfort
Takahashi communicated his grief and sense of injustice. Similarly,
Daniel Luevano, who would become a civil rights activist and politician,
regretted but did not actively challenge the government's decision. Fresh
out of high school in 1940, Luevano got a job at a Japanese-owned hardware store in Little Tokyo. He may not have made "judgments that it [in-
ternment] was wrong" or burned with moral outrage in 1942, as he did
years later. Yet even then, Luevano recollected, "I knew I was sorry
about it. I knew I was sorry for the people who were standing in front of
me who were going to be leaving."[46]

These statements of support paled in comparison with the bold act of
Ralph Lazo. This Mexican American and Boyle Heights native chose to
register as Japanese and suffer internment alongside his Nisei friends.
"Who can say I haven't got Japanese blood in me? Who knows what
kind of blood runs in their veins?" Lazo said when the government discovered his ruse and ousted him from the camp. Thus for Lazo and less
dramatically inclined California minorities, internment, more than previous discrimination, made clear the ubiquitous and inescapable character of racial prejudice.[47]

Just as evacuation had left a deeper imprint upon Japanese youth than
upon their elders, so did internment more noticeably change the views

of minority teens and push them closer together. Many Nisei, swayed by the general political opinion of the day, opposed the aggressive expansion of Japan. At the same time few minority youth viewed the American-born Japanese as connected to the imperialist power, and even fewer implicated them in Japan's war making. Personal connections with Japanese discouraged feelings of hatred and raised doubts about the rightfulness of internment. I have already described how the Pacific war built tension into local inter-Asian relations, but American-born Asians tended to trust Japanese Americans and carefully distinguished their views from those of older relatives.[48]

Non-White youngsters and interned Japanese Americans, such as the pair whose story opened this chapter, maintained friendships during the war, signaling the value of and ultimately cementing their cross-cultural ties. Regular visits, letters, and small gifts reminded the evacuees that minority friends had not forgotten them. Miné Okubo recollected the patient visits of a Chinese-American friend who waited hours to pass through security and deliver Okubo's favorite egg-flower soup. The diligent, intimate correspondence between Mollie Murphy, who was African American, and a handful of her Nisei friends from Boyle Heights perhaps best captures the durability of ties among certain non-White youth. Penned over the entire period of internment, the letters of Chiyeko, June, Violet, and Sadie speak about their situation with an honesty and vulnerability reserved for very close friends. Days after her arrival Chiyeko cheerfully described Manzanar in a note to Mollie as "just 'swell.'" "I just eat, sleep, and play everyday," she continued, "As there are no schools as yet, this is just a long vacation to us here." But her feelings and those of other evacuees shifted quickly, and they did not hesitate to express their discontent. "Man, camp life is really drab—don't see how I'm enduring it! It's so stale," Chiyeko moaned a year after her rosy first report. Sadie Saito poured her heart out to Mollie as well. Frustrated by government efforts to recruit teens for work in camouflage factories, Sadie screamed her resentment, "Man! They could go somewhere if they think I'm going to work in that hot sun and break my back. What do they think we are anyway?" Behind her anger lay the disappointment that she also shared with her Boyle Heights confidante: "All my plans of going to college are all gone. All I could think of now is to be a dumb ox and not ever graduate high school!"[49]

Beyond their candid depictions of camp life, holiday greetings and queries about family members and old acquaintances from the neighborhood exposed the emotional closeness of the Nisei girls and their

African-American friend. At times the internees stated this affection explicitly. "Mollie you can be sure that I'll never forget you," wrote Violet from Chicago in 1945. "You were so kind to me while I was in camp,
and that kindness will never be forgotten." In a note composed a year
earlier Chiyeko also thanked Mollie "a million for your kindness again.
Your friendship's enuff, honestly!" As the war's end drew closer and the
young women contemplated a return to Los Angeles, they looked to
Mollie for a candid assessment of circumstances there. "Can you tell me
how the conditions are out there? I know Mayor Bowron is still dead set
against our returning," June wondered in July 1944. Despite the passage
of time and physical distance, they continued to trust their friend. The
strength and longevity of the attachments of these young women may
not have been typical, but they suggest the quiet, highly private ways in
which minorities could and did preserve their prewar connections. In
doing so, they communicated the significance of cross-cultural relations
to their personal identities.[50]

In reaching out to and realizing how their lives intersected with the
Japanese, minority youth felt anxiety as much as concern. They breathed
sighs of relief about retaining their own freedom but were anxious about
their futures. Sadness gripped Rose Echeverria Mulligan after she lost
Japanese friends to distant camps, but she never answered their epistles
for fear "they'd [the government] read my letter or something." Patricia
McReynolds, a Filipina, shared her father's troubled thoughts about internment. She responded fearfully to the sudden removal of her Nisei
companions, including "John, the skinny, quietly smiling math genius,
and Choiye, my round-faced, sensitive friend, whose only sin I knew of
was that she didn't believe the Mikado truly Japanese." Recognizing that
she "wasn't much different from them [the Nisei]," McReynolds viewed
internment as a danger she had only narrowly escaped. Charles Kikuchi
corroborated this strengthened awareness of linked lives, observing that
his Chinese, Black, and Jewish friends believed internment set a "dangerous precedent . . . which could easily include them later." Conspicuously absent from Kikuchi's list of concerned friends were most European ethnics. They may have had misgivings about internment, but
self-interest did not drive or intensify those misgivings as they did for minority youths. The singling-out of one minority not only raised concerns
among others but also tightened the bonds of youth.[51]

In more public and collective ways minority teens sympathized with
Nisei and articulated their attachment to multicultural identities. The
students at Boyle Heights's Roosevelt High who had prided themselves

on their cosmopolitan character mourned the departure of Nisei and made clear their continued commitment to ethnoracial tolerance. In 1939, when war heated up overseas, Masamori Kojima, the president of the senior class, had urged open political discussions that respected the competing opinions about the war held by the mixed student body.[52] Despite the school's success in maintaining a tolerant environment, larger social prejudices intruded upon the campus. When the government announced its decision to intern the Japanese, Harry Rosenberg, a Jewish American, eloquently expressed the regret of his classmates: "This action will affect all of us here at Roosevelt. Many of our school officers and friends are of Japanese lineage. There is nothing that can be done to remedy the situation. I'm sure that our Japanese students realize the necessity of this action. That we shall miss them, should they leave, can go without saying. They have done many fine things here at Roosevelt."[53] This homage to Nisei internees displayed the depth of respect they had earned among their classmates.

At the Los Angeles institution where so many Roosevelt alumni and other minority youth advanced their education, students openly fretted about the internment and its significance for other minorities. As the relocation began, the Los Angeles City College newspaper, the *Collegian,* printed the report of former student Paul Ichino. From the Owens Valley Reception Center he asked for news about those Nisei remaining at LACC, described camp conditions "as not so bad," and thanked "each and every one of you for what you have done." Printed in such a public forum, the letter displayed not only the longing of one individual for his old friends but also how much those feelings were reciprocated by the campus community.[54]

During the war repeated conversations about the role of minorities in the postwar period exposed the anxiety and solidarity that evacuation had precipitated. On October 12, 1942, the *Collegian,* the student newspaper at Los Angeles City College (LACC), chronicled the visit and lecture of the Reverend Baxter Carrol Duke, a Black minister and founder of Avalon Church in Los Angeles. The minister spoke about the responsibility among minority groups—"Negroes, Mexicans, Filipinos, and Jews"—to the development of the country. "Many people do not realize that the majority of the population in the world is non-White and this is an important factor," he concluded. His definition of minority, one that deliberately excluded European ethnics other than Jews and assumed a clear color line, was becoming the convention during the war and would be the convention after it. The minister crafted his message to inspire the diverse students of LACC who were concerned about their fates in a world of war and discrimination. A campus gathering a year later to discuss the "role of minority groups in establishing Post-War Reconstruction" showed how much that message had struck a chord. A collection of mostly minority students expressed the special responsibilities and need for collaboration among non-Whites. While Charles Kopp urged minorities to "act as balance wheels to bring public spirit back to an even keel when hatred and mass hysteria threaten," Lincoln Haynes and Emma Tom tasked them to work "with the majority in order to obtain successful rehabilitation." Using different metaphors but communicating like ideas, George Acevedo, senior class president, "defined the duties of minority groups as instigators and checks." All these students agreed that minorities were a set of distinct people with distinct interests. The wartime setting in general and Japanese internment in particular sharpened this sense of difference.[55]

Outside the environment of schools, certain minority youth more harshly and directly criticized the policy of evacuation. Such protests positioned them as political advocates of ethnic crossing. Young Chinese Americans from throughout the state gathered at the 1944 Chinese Christian Youth conference at Lake Tahoe. Organized by the Chinese Christian Youth movement of America, this thirteenth annual event spotlighted faith and social justice. The 153 West Coast participants spent days in prayer and discussions of interracial tensions, housing shortages, jobs, and returning vets. Pledging themselves broadly to end "discrimination and segregation" for all racial minorities whose "problems of recognition and integration are essentially the same," they focused special attention that year upon the fate of Japanese Americans. In addition to sending a letter of sympathy to the relocated Nisei, Chinese-American youth condemned evacuation and asserted the fundamental similarities of Asians in America. Paul Louie, a prominent member of the youth movement, captured the thoughts of his peers: "The Nisei are identical with us in their oriental ancestry and are nurtured within an atmosphere of Western culture. They are familiar with the traditional American history of life, liberty and the pursuit of happiness. They understand the workings of democracy at its best and at its worst."[56] As internment highlighted what they shared, these Asian ethnic youths leaned more closely together.

In exposing the depths of American ethnoracial prejudice, internment invited minorities to look with fresh eyes upon California society and their place within it. What they saw was not only the precariousness of their own lives but also how much misfortune connected their lives to certain groups and not to others. As they felt and shared this sensibility, they were recognizing a sharpening color line that separated them from long-established Whites and more recent European ethnics.

INTERNMENT AND ITS FIGHTING FAMILIES

Intercultural families forged in the prewar period were as stressed and ultimately strengthened by internment as the more casual relationships connecting minority adults and youth. Executive Order 9066 strained mixed couples already pressed by the prejudices of family and community. Within this wartime environment they fought to preserve their relationships and the very possibility of permanent ethnic crossing in a nation insistent upon ethnoracial segregation. As the crises of the era made intercultural marriages and children more public, ethnic communities felt new stress to acknowledge, if not condone, these crossings. Thus personal struggles promoted even greater acceptance of ethnic mingling among non-Whites in postwar California.

Even more than the escalated tensions between Asian nations, internment stressed and changed mixed families. The War Relocation Authority (WRA) ordered that all people of even partial Japanese ancestry living on the West Coast abandon their homes for remote camps in more interior parts of the West. This policy did not originally consider the non-Japanese spouses of evacuees or their mixed children, an early oversight that added confusion to the anxiety already felt by mixed-race families. A Japanese minister assigned to a U.S. congregation chronicled the uncertainty of a Filipino-Japanese couple he met days before evacuating. In his autobiography he explained that "neither she nor her husband knew for sure whether she and their children were entitled to stay where they were or, if they had to be evacuated, whether her husband was entitled to accompany them to camp." Couples such as these challenged the WRA's assumption that families were racially singular and prompted an elaboration of government rules. Non-Japanese wives and husbands could choose to enter camps or remain outside. More complicated and shifting regulations governed the offspring of such couples. Part-Japanese children with non-Japanese fathers could return to their homes, but those with Japanese fathers had to stay. The gendered distinction reflected the WRA's conviction that fathers rather than mothers determined the political and cultural loyalties of the next generation.[57]

The existence of orphaned or abandoned part-Japanese offspring forced even more policy contortions. The Japanese community supported three major orphanages before World War II: Maryknoll and Shonien (Japanese Children's Home) in Los Angeles, as well as the Salvation Army Home in San Francisco. Consistent with the U.S. government's belief that even the smallest fraction of Japanese blood compromised one's loyalty to the United States, authorities closed these establishments. Those responsible answered the plea of Father Lavery, the head of Maryknoll and pastor of the affiliated St. Francis Xavier Church, for the exemption of certain children by explaining, "They have one drop of blood in them," so they "must all go to camp." Thus residents of these homes entered Children's Village, a specially created division of Manzanar. To ensure no youth slipped through the cracks and violated the rules, officials investigated orphanage records for signs of Japanese ancestry and invited non-Japanese foster parents to turn over their charges.[58]

The reality of internment tested and focused new attention upon the progeny of and relationships between Japanese and non-Japanese; couples had to surrender their romances and families or make unprecedented sacrifices to maintain them. Some broke apart under the weight of internment, but many survived. Mixed-race children faced new uncertainties and hostilities as well. For the families who chose to stay together despite wartime pressures, their varied, periodically dangerous, strategies highlighted the injustice of internment and the arbitrariness of the American ethnoracial system.[59]

The government's decision to relocate Japanese proved too sudden and severe for some couples and families. Mio Jean Ikebuchi, a Japanese American, called off her wedding to a Chinese American, Leonard Wan. Although she acknowledged loving him as fervently as before the war, she feared his mistreatment by the thousands of Japanese at Santa Anita. "I love Leonard too much to allow him to figure in anything that might prove painful," she explained. Internment tore apart established families as well. Rather than risk prosecution or the loss of personal freedom, a Mexican foster mother in San Jose surrendered her Nisei children. In another case authorities puzzled over how to handle Ronald Yamamoto, the six-month-old baby of a Japanese internee and his Mexican-American wife. Police had arrested the woman, Rael Yamamoto, after she abandoned the child on San Diego streets. Although they considered placing Ronald in camp with his father, in the end they concluded that "the man wasn't reliable" and sent the baby to Children's Village.[60]

Other couples risked social ostracism, protecting the form and principle of mixed families. Miyo Joan Kobuchi won approval to temporarily leave Santa Anita Assembly Center to marry her Chinese-American boyfriend. Despite the obstacles of removal and separation that the youths confronted, they chose to formalize their courtship rather than end it. A Filipino-Japanese pair made a similarly loving but painful decision to maintain their marriage at a distance. In 1943 Tamie Tahara told an interviewer about the Filipino man's faithful visits from Los Angeles. "He really loved [his wife] and was most considerate," she observed. "He bought Japanese foods to her mother so that they accepted him more." When his wife finally secured permission to move east, her devoted spouse quit his job and followed her.[61] Braving internment and the prejudice of Japanese evacuees, the partners preserved their relationship.

Although non-Japanese partners were under no legal obligation to do so, some protected their cross-cultural families by entering the camps. A University of California study of the Tule Lake Internment Camp concluded that Japanese Americans often teased and tormented the Japanese partners of mixed marriages. Having disapproved of and avoided such couples before the war, they were dismayed to live in such close contact with them during it. Justly concerned about the hostilities of fellow evacuees, intermarried wives and husbands periodically disguised their identities. In an act of ethnic passing as ingenious as those practiced by Nisei defying the evacuation order, a wife pretended to be Japanese. Jeanne Wakatsuki Houston noticed that one of her neighbors at Manzanar "was a tall, broad woman, taller than anyone in camp," who "walked erectly and wore an Aunt Jemima scarf around her head." Houston used to play with the adopted Japanese daughter of this distinctive woman and her Japanese husband. Only later did she realize that the woman was actually "half-black, with light mulatto skin, passing as Japanese in order to remain with her husband." Avery Diaz, who was Mexican, and Nami Nakashima, a Japanese Mexican, may not have altered their appearances, but they "mainly stayed together" once evacuated, because they "stuck out like a sore thumb" within the "sea of Japanese faces." The couple sensed the depth of disapproval beneath the other internees' superficial politeness.[62]

By accompanying loved ones, waiting patiently for their release, or committing more absolutely to intercultural relations outside the camps, minorities rejected the government's preference for ethnically homogeneous units. And minorities were not alone in their dedication to loved ones and defiance of law. Whites married to Japanese put family first, too. As the historian Paul Spickard discovered, these intermarried spouses petitioned the courts, left the coast for the interior, hid out from authorities, entered camps together, and risked living temporarily apart.[63] But the implications of their transgressions were different. White-Japanese marriages suggested the artificial and awkward position of a darkening color line that defined and divided Whites from others. Additionally and distinctively, the marriages among minorities highlighted the consolidation and compromise that was happening because of and on one side of that color line. In the prewar period Milicio and Treba Jacoban, Filipino Americans, became deeply attached to their Nisei foster child. In the face of internment, rather than surrender the boy and dissolve their mixed family, they successfully undertook adoption proceedings and negotiated his permanent exemption from the camps. Lacking these legal loopholes, Elaine Black Yoneda joined her Kibei husband and their son, Tommy, at Manzanar. When Karl Yoneda enlisted in the Military Intelligence Service, Elaine Black Yoneda secured her and her son's release but not before first defending interracial families. The U.S. Army stipulated that Tommy remain only in the company of Caucasians, to which Elaine retorted, "If Tommy was to spend weekends or what have you with any of our Chinese, Filipino or Negro friends, would he be in violation of his right to be in Military Area No. 1?" In a similar case Avery Diaz denounced the injustice of internment but followed his wife, Nami, out of the Western Defense Zone. "I didn't feel sorry for my wife, I just loved her," Diaz explained. Even for those men and women who opted to live apart and hoped that interment would be brief, keeping children with their mothers preserved a semblance of family unity. Kim Fong Tom remembered at least two Japanese women who cared for their part-Chinese, part-Japanese kids inside the camps while their husbands waited at home.[64]

Other families used riskier, extralegal means for preserving family unity that testified to the importance of their bonds. At times Japanese partners violated Executive Order 9066, continuing to live with their non-Japanese spouses in California. This path defied the removal policy and its disregard for intermarriages. In 1942 police arrested Ida Esteban, the young Nisei bride of a Filipino, on their farm in Sunnyvale. She faced criminal charges as a woman of Japanese descent for remaining in a prohibited zone. Authorities also uncovered the attempt by Liwa Chew to conceal herself in her husband's ethnic community. The *Hawaii Chinese Journal* noted her arrest in Oakland as the first Bay Area case in which

Figure 8. Yoneda family at Manzanar Internment Camp. Karl G. Yoneda Collection, collection 1592, Department of Special Collections, Charles E. Young Research Library, University of California, Los Angeles.

"alien restrictions" caused marital troubles.[65] The struggle of mixed couples for family preservation defied conventions of ethnoracial conformity and homogeneity, though not always deliberately or directly; they implicitly defended the right to cross ethnic lines, creating more capacious and varied categories of affiliation along the "colored" stretch of the ethnoracial spectrum.

Internment and general wartime anxieties shook up mixed-race progeny as forcefully as their parents, pushing questions of identity to the fore. Internment taught Dennis Baumbauer new lessons about his heritage. After scrutinizing files kept by orphanages for Japanese children, authorities concluded that Dennis's mother was part Japanese. They delivered Dennis, who had only recently been placed in Shonien Orphanage by his non-Japanese caregiver, to Manzanar, where he grappled with his new ethnic designation and the surname Tojo that had been suddenly thrust upon him. Although the government had revealed him as a person of partial Japanese descent, he had no understanding of what it meant to be Nisei. The teasing of the other Children's Village residents only reinforced his sense of disconnection and disorientation. Tommy Yoneda had long known of his varied background, but it seemed to matter more during the war years. Once released from Manzanar, Elaine Black Yoneda worried "whether[,] attacked for his Japanese ancestry or for his Jewish ancestry," her son could protect himself in their new hometown of Petaluma. Given the wartime hostility toward Jews and Japanese, Tommy Yoneda's background made him doubly vulnerable. However, he used his defensive skills not in response to anti-Semitic or anti-Japanese slurs but because some of his classmates "were just terrible as far as the Negroes are concerned."[66] Tommy Yoneda's challenge to the boys' racism likely reflected his own heightened preparedness for or awareness of discrimination.

As wartime made mixed couples reluctant activists or mediators, and exacerbated the identity issues of mixed-race children, it simultaneously forced ethnic communities to confront the phenomenon of intercultural families. As I related in chapter 2, mixed couples who felt the disapproval of their relatives and friends often moved to places and socialized in ways that hid them from view. In keeping low profiles, they permitted their ethnic groups of origin to deny or forget their existence. But internment forced many of these couples into the public's line of vision. As a result community opinion slowly shifted.

The pages of the Japanese-American press recast mixed families from social outcasts into compelling victims of injustice. Throughout 1942 and 1943 Los Angeles's Japanese community continued to avidly read the *Pacific Citizen,* which continued publication during the war thanks to its inland location in Salt Lake City. The newspaper empathetically depicted the struggles of Chinese, Blacks, and Filipinos who were married or related to Japanese. Among the stories shared were those of a Japanese-American woman arrested when she attempted an unauthorized reunion with her Filipino husband, and an ebullient Nisei girl granted permission to marry her Chinese-American beau. The sudden prominence of these people in the newspaper contrasted sharply with their near invisibility in the prewar years. Their plight now served to dramatize the suffering of Japanese unfairly pushed from the West Coast.[67]

Internment brought mixed marriages to the attention of San Francisco's Filipinos as well. Miguel Ignacio, the secretary of the Filipino Community of San Francisco, Inc., joined forces with Ernest Besig of the American Civil Liberties Union to consider the fate of Japanese partners of Filipinos. The men acknowledged surprise at learning about such unions in the middle of a war. Together, they demanded a separate location for the Japanese wives of Filipino men, arguing that marriage effectively changed the ethnic status of these women. They were "no longer Japanese in the sight of Hirohito" and thus deserved special treatment.[68] In addition, the long history of inter-Asian tension made Besig and Ignacio fear for the safety of the women. All this interest in the fate of Filipino-Japanese couples marked a noticeable transition in awareness from the prewar period. Rather than dismiss or disregard these men and women, as the Filipino community had done before the crisis of evacuation, it moved slowly toward accepting responsibility for them.

The Chinese-American community similarly took note of and appeared to soften its opposition to intercultural couples. In a case that also displayed their implicit opposition to Japanese internment, Chinese Americans of Los Angeles protected an interethnic marriage. As Allen Mock recalled in 1983, a Chinese-American man and his Japanese-American wife operated a small barbershop in wartime Chinatown, where they served an almost exclusively Chinese clientele. Although authorities sought to locate and intern the wife, they failed in their endeavor. When a FBI agent arrived at the barbershop and asked about her whereabouts, customers unanimously denied knowing the woman. The duped official walked away, unaware that the couple had stood before him cutting hair. The willingness of Chinatown residents to encircle the couple underscored war's success in changing community attitudes about ethnicity and race, especially among Asian groups.[69]

Intercultural couples who remained together rejected the assumption implicit in internment that ethnic distinctions could be neatly drawn. Their defiance brought them unprecedented public exposure and ever so gradually changed attitudes. Confronted with the reality of these committed and sentimental ethnic crossers, non-White communities moved grudgingly to support them. As an example of intimate and sustained interracial relations, these minorities expanded ethnic sensibilities.

FRIENDS OF THE ZOOT

Witnessing the Zoot Suit Riots in June 1943, minorities did not express the same depths of sorrow and sharpness of disapproval that they had in response to Japanese internment. However, this violence, by White servicemen against mostly Latino zoot-suiters, did fuel criticism by minority communities and deepened their sense of interdependence. Adults and especially adolescents more clearly articulated and committed themselves to the idea of multiethnic community. Those youth who wished to retain the hybrid identity of the pachuco even in the wake of intense wartime scrutiny demonstrated the strength of their involvement in an alternative culture. Theirs was not a flimsy statement about the value of ethnic crossing and the problem of ethnoracial discrimination that collapsed quickly when tested. In defending themselves against violent assaults and the criticism of media, government, and social scientists, these teens were standing up for their own blended lives. At the same time nonwearers who stepped forward in support of zoot clothes and attitudes—most assertively, African Americans—were declaring their common interests.

During the infamous Sleepy Lagoon murder case and Zoot Suit Riots, minority youth fought to protect their carefully crafted identities (see chapter 2). Ironically, the legal abuse and physical violence reflected the very success of the challenge manifested in their unique style and behavior. As war intensified, so did negative reports circulated by police and media about the look and activities of zoot-suiters. According to popular opinion, these pachucos and their female counterparts were uneducated, dirty, dangerous, and, perhaps worst of all, unpatriotic. Steeped in these prejudices, police in Los Angeles charged a group of Mexican-American teens with the murder of José Díaz. Authorities had found Díaz lying dead in the dirt near a gravel pit called Sleepy Lagoon that was commonly used as a swimming hole. Despite irregularities in the trial, and the absence of concrete evidence, the vehement anti-Mexican and antipachuco rhetoric of the press helped bring about the boys' conviction in 1942. A year later, buoyed by antipachuco sentiment, White sailors on leave began patrolling primarily Mexican neighborhoods and attacking youth they encountered. Days of fighting ensued, with authorities intervening only when Mexican-American youth fought back or gained an advantage. Other non-Whites became the targets of attack almost as often as ethnic Mexicans. "Street cars were halted while Mexicans, and some Filipinos and Negroes, were jerked out of their seats, pushed into the streets, and beaten with sadistic frenzy," Carey McWilliams reported.[70] The defiance of zoot-suiters provoked the ire of many Whites, who understood such a crossing of ethnic lines as a breach of the system upon which their authority rested.

Because Californians associated zoot-suiters with hybridity and challenge, the youth frequently felt themselves more deeply invested in these characteristics. Suddenly, their challenge had a wide and interested audience. Among the Sleepy Lagoon defendants, a few came to understand the much broader implications of their personal plight. "I can see now that this would not only be a victory for all the boys now at San Quentin but for all the minority races and different people who are fighting against race discrimination," acknowledged Ysmael "Smiles" Parra from the prison cell where he awaited retrial. The outpouring of support from other minorities further connected young adults to a multicultural world. Although still locked inside the camps, some Japanese stated their support for Mexican-American zoot-suiters. A select group of young adults held at Manzanar signed and sent a petition to California Attorney General Robert Kenny calling the trial's outcome an example of racial prejudice. More indirectly, select Nisei teens endorsed the zoots by being zoots themselves. They tried to establish legitimacy for the look and call attention to the injustice of White reactions by continuing to wear the baggy clothes and practice the assertive manner. Black teens added to this critique. Members of the NAACP's junior council joined forces with the Mexican Youth Defense Committee in the wake of the riots. The resulting working group dedicated itself to ending prejudicial treatment of minorities.[71]

Older members of minority groups rallied around the zoot-suiters as well. As they had been during internment, African Americans were frequently the most visible and vocal supporters. They had good reason to be. A document prepared by the multiethnic Sleepy Lagoon Defense Committee made clear how much Blacks and Mexicans had in common. Members of these groups, the committee reported, suffered arrest almost the moment they ventured beyond "Mexican and Negro areas." "So in riots, the same logic is applied in practice," the report continued. "First attack the Mexican—then the Negroes." In the midst and the aftermath of the Zoot Suit Riots, the Black community, as represented in the pages of the *California Eagle,* largely interpreted the riots as part of a sustained and shared pattern of abuse against Mexican and Black youths. Jeannette Cohen obtained and chose to reproduce in her *Eagle* column one of the many letters that Mexican workers had sent to the Los Angeles mayor denouncing discrimination against Mexicans who wore zoot suits. The letter's author, a war worker named Dolores Figueroa, related how two Mexican coworkers were innocently shopping for records during their lunch break one day when the police arrested them "because they were Mexicans." Alarmed, Figueroa asked, "Does the way a person dresses necessarily mean he is a criminal?" She ended her epistle by highlighting the essential contribution made by Mexican-American men serving in the U.S. Army. Cohen believed that Figueroa's definitions of unfairness and patriotism were so consistent with her own and those of the Black community that she decided to reprint the woman's words free of editorial comment. Two weeks later, as riots reached a fever pitch, the *California Eagle* challenged the mainstream press's conclusion "that the Mexican and Negro communities [are] dens of corruption, vice, murder and sabotage." It promised and encouraged its readers to counter such mischaracterizations at every opportunity.[72]

No longer willing to accept the mistreatment of Mexican and Black youths, African Americans called for partnership with Mexican Americans. More than fifteen hundred people gathered at the Peoples Independent Church in Los Angeles with the hope of preempting what the NAACP, Mexican Defense, Negro Victory Committee, and Congress of Industrial Organizations feared were the efforts of "powerful interests in Los Angeles . . . to provoke a mass race clash in the city through piling grievance after grievance upon the Negro and Mexican community on the one hand, and smearing Mexicans and Negroes as 'zoot suit killers' on the other." Rather than take what they saw as the bait of violent protest, the gathered parties urged peaceful cooperation between Mexicans and Blacks. In a full-page advertisement purchased by the "People's Victory Market," a commercial establishment at the heart of the Central Avenue district, Blacks were asked to share their long political experience in fighting oppression. The ad implored, "Because we in the Negro community are more unified and have greater political power, we must lead in the demand for full police protection of the Mexican community," and concluded, "We must say to our great United Nations neighbor,

Mexico—Saludos Amigos!" As the historian Josh Sides has noted, the local NAACP agreed; chapter president Thomas L. Griffith urged President Roosevelt and Governor Earl Warren to end the violence against the Mexican community.[73]

Like their elders, Mexican and Black youths saw their fate as intertwined following the Zoot Suit Riots. The Mexican Youth Defense Committee and Junior Council of the NAACP sponsored a large-scale youth meeting in June 1943. Jeanette Slavis of the Mexican Youth Defense Council explained that after the crisis of recent weeks, youth needed to take on more responsibility, "striking at every form of race discrimination." "This unification of city-wide youth," another council member argued, was "the best way of fighting." In another effort at interracial solidarity Mexican and Black youths, together with members of the Jewish Community Council, gathered and prepared an antidiscrimination statement. Intended for the Los Angeles mayor, the document called for an end to segregation in restaurants, dance halls, and other public facilities. Although zoot-suiting was portrayed in the mainstream press as a problem of Mexican youth, the Black and Mexican communities of Los Angeles regarded zoot-suiting as a multicultural expression of disenchanted minorities. The effort highlighted the particular vulnerability of Mexicans and Blacks and implied the kinship these groups shared more than other minorities.[74]

Following the Sleepy Lagoon murder and Zoot Suit Riots, local Jews expressed solidarity with Mexican Americans as well. While the American Jewish Congress demanded an investigation, Al Waxman of the *Jewish Voice* equated violence against zoot-suiters with Nazi mistreatment of European Jews. To support his provocative analogy he published a damning firsthand account of police abuse. While standing on a corner in early July 1943, Waxman had witnessed four boys wearing zoot suits emerge from a local pool hall. Police intercepted the group and announced they were under arrest. When one asked, "Why am I being arrested?" 'Waxman related, an officer "answered with three swift blows of the nightstick across the boy's head and the boy went down. As he sprawled he was kicked in the face." Waxman concluded the piece by describing the Mexican mother who cried out in the background, "Don't take my boy, he didn't do nothing." The editor's positive portrait of Mexican-American youths and a distraught mother expressed not only his personal sympathies but also his desire to stir the outrage of his readership.[75]

Among the Anglos, Irish, Mexicans, Asians, and Blacks who made up the Sleepy Lagoon Defense Committee (SLDC), Alice McGrath was perhaps the most prominent. Although she could claim a long history of activism for minority causes, this woman gained greatest attention as a defender of Mexican Americans. A Yiddish-speaking daughter of Russian immigrants, she grew up in 1930s and early 1940s Los Angeles. McGrath remembered anti-Semitism as whispered and indirect but sufficiently noticeable to make her "recognize the pattern of discrimination as being against 'the others' of whom I was mysteriously a part." Her sensitivity to prejudice and diversity of associations broadened while she was in high school and college, culminating in her active involvement in the Communist Party and the SLDC. Her concern for the wrongly accused boys was rooted in her personal observations and experiences of injustice as a working-class Jew in Los Angeles. Her close—many even speculated, romantic—relationship with one of the defendants, Henry Reyna, demonstrated how McGrath's contacts with other minorities inspired her political commitment on their behalf.[76]

As conspicuous minorities on the margins, zoot-suiters simultaneously inspired the opposition of many Californians bent on order and stability and the support of non-Whites who understood and appreciated zoot-suiting as a multiethnic statement of discontent. As White sailors lashed out against minorities and police stood idly by, non-Whites stepped forward to acknowledge their shared disadvantages and work together to change them.

REMEMBERING INTERETHNIC CONNECTIONS

The willingness, even urgency, with which Native, Japanese, Mexican, and African Americans spoke about their relatedness decades after internment and the Zoot Suit Riots suggests the significance of the interethnic connections they had realized during World War II. In a 1950 article the *Pacific Citizen* reported the opposition of the Japanese American Citizens League to the U.S. government's recent acquisition of Native American lands. The organization launched its objection from the position of a minority that understood injustice firsthand. "Having been evicted once from our own homes, and confined to relocation centers," the journalist reminded his readers, "we persons of Japanese ancestry fully realize the degradation, indignity, and terrible enervation that results from such treatment of an entire ethnic group." Even with internment safely behind them, Japanese Americans did not forget how closely their lives had resembled those of Native Americans. Moreover, although their endorsement risked the displeasure of government authorities,

Japanese Americans chose to publicly support the interests of Native Americans.[77]

More recent efforts by former internees and Gila River Indians to memorialize the Arizona camps and the shared interest of African- and Mexican-Americans youths in the Zoot Suit Riots demonstrates a collective confidence in the connectedness of minority histories. Certainly, this belief in intersecting lives tells us as much about present-day sensibilities and desires as past ones. Americans have a new appreciation for the conditions and history of minorities and a willingness to reflect upon past injustices. In addition, Mexican Americans and Blacks in urban California, whose current relations are often strained, even combative, seek out strategies for getting along.

However, the 1998 collaborative campaign, "Transforming Barbed Wire," led by the Arizona Humanities Council, could not have gained support from Native and Japanese American communities if the interethnic relationships it celebrates were not real and meaningful to so many who lived through the war. The project, a reminder and reconsideration of Japanese internment in Arizona, brought together former internees and members of the Gila River Indian Community. At a formal presentation Mary Thomas, the Gila River governor, shed tears as she took the hands of Japanese Americans and acknowledged that "babies were born on our land and some of your people died here. You are part of our community and we apologize for what happened."[78]

Similarly, African Americans and Mexican Americans have taken up a dramatic historical moment—the Zoot Suit Riots—and made it central to their respective ethnic communities' understanding of a common past. In the late 1970s, when the Zoot Suit Riots were brought to the stage by the playwright Luiz Valdez in *Zoot Suit,* Black and Mexican youths from Los Angeles high schools attended. The young theatergoers expressed their surprise and dismay upon learning about the discrimination that Mexicans and Blacks had both suffered. "Blacks are not the only ones who have been done wrong. The Mexicans have been done wrong too," commented a young Black woman after viewing the performance. Another Black student agreed that "history ignores the Mexicans Americans." In particular, members of Edison High School's Rainbow Club, a group committed to bringing their largely segregated and antagonistic Mexican and Black classmates together, hoped the play would advance their mission. In using the past to serve their contemporary ambitions of interethnic peace, the students necessarily changed that past, much like Japanese Americans and Native Americans had with "Transforming

Barbed Wire." But their choice of the Zoot Suit Riots as a history capable of inspiring present-day collaboration also testified to the essential significance of that history for multiple minority groups. If the relationships among Japanese and Native Americans or Mexicans and African Americans faded over time, the desire to revisit—and the emotional intensity of those returns—emphasizes their significance in the mid-1940s as much as the late 1970s and the first decade of the twenty-first century.[79]

CONCLUSION

World War II has often figured in historical works as a period of remarkable transition, even transformation. Scholars have pointed to new industries, an enlarged government, expanded population, hurried urbanization, and an enlivened civil rights movement as evidence of a postwar America very different from its prewar version. For minority relations this thesis largely holds true. The experiences of zoot-suiting, and especially internment, dramatized the discriminations that non-Whites suffered and advanced a collective sensibility. Ethnic lines that had blurred in mixed neighborhoods of the 1930s and 1940s began to dissolve during World War II. At the same time the lines separating European ethnics from other ethnoracial groups thickened. As chapter 5 explores, the journeys of minority soldiers beyond the physical borders of California challenged minorities to further expand their emotional and mental borders.[80]

Minority Brothers in Arms

> The sergeant didn't even look at me; he called over to a cop by the door in a bored, indifferent voice, "Here's another soldier."
>
> "Come on, boy," the cop said.
>
> The two Mexican youths he had with him grinned a welcome.
>
> "Let's go, man, the war's waiting," one of them cracked.
>
> "Don't rush the man," the other said. "The man's not doing well"; and when I came closer he said, "Not doing well at all. Looks like this man has had a war. How you doing, man?"
>
> They were both brown-skinned, about my colour, slender and slightly stooped, with Indian features and thick curly hair. Both wore bagged drapes that looked about to fall down from their waists, and grayish dirty T-shirts. They talked in the melodious Mexican lilt.
>
> "I'm still here," I lisped painfully.
>
> They fell in beside me and we went out and started up the hill toward the induction centre, the three of us abreast and the cop in the rear.
>
> Two hours later I was in the Army.[1]

By the time readers get to this final scene in Chester Himes's 1945 novel, *If He Hollers, Let Him Go*, Bob Jones, an African-American defense plant worker in Los Angeles, has been beaten up, betrayed by his girlfriend, chased by police, arrested, and falsely charged with rape. A local judge settles the case by arranging for Jones's enlistment in the army. Jones sees the decision for what it is: a punishment no better than a prison term for a crime he did not commit. Two Mexican-American youths dressed in the distinguishing garb of zoot-suiters will share

Jones's misfortune of mandatory induction. By ending the novel with the image of three minority men solemnly and resentfully marching off to war, Himes inverts the more conventional picture of enthusiastic, if idealistic, volunteers. This denouement demonstrates the dilemma of military service for minorities—why should they risk their lives to defend a political and ideological system that more often than not mistreated them? many wondered. The common fate of Jones and the Mexican-American youths also suggests the sense of kinship that non-Whites carried into the armed forces. For minorities who remembered the common spaces and discriminations that they left behind in California, the experience of military service made those spaces and discriminations all the more poignant. And military service raised new concerns among those who had overlooked or ignored what they shared with other minorities.

During training and tours of duty beyond the borders of California, these young men encountered new peoples and ethnoracial etiquettes that altered their views of other minorities and made them sharper critics of California's ethnoracial system. From these distant vantage points many customs that they had endured back in California and thought permanent now seemed worthy of challenge and susceptible to change. A pervasive notion of brotherhood in the military complemented and at other times compromised the notion of togetherness among minorities. Official calls for unity across ethnic lines of all kinds and the necessity of cooperation in warfare brought many European ethnics, Asian ethnics, Blacks, and Mexicans into closer, and ultimately more comfortable, company. Yet cosmopolitanism and the amiable relations that it promoted between Whites and minorities faltered in the face of stubborn prejudices and structural limits. Non-Whites responded by putting their faith in one another and a more qualified, cautionary cosmopolitanism, much as they had been doing on the home front. Certainly, minority women joined and felt deep attachments to one another in the armed forces. But they enlisted in such small numbers and in such restricted ways that this book focuses upon their male counterparts.[2] The very scarcity of minority women left a space in which GIs fashioned an idea of multiethnic community that was distinctly masculine.

These Native, Asian-, Mexican-, and African-American men increasingly saw parallels in their histories and contemporary circumstances. Black enlistees both welcomed the relative tolerance shown toward, and articulated a sense of kinship with, darker-skinned peoples in the Pacific Islands; closer to home Black GIs noticed how Asian Americans, American Indians, and Mexican Americans were mistreated in surprisingly familiar ways. At the same time Asian ethnics training in the South and South-west gained a new appreciation for the plight of minorities who lived in those regions. Combat against enemy Japanese, whose complexions but not political loyalties resembled their own, shifted understandings of Asian ethnicity as well. Japanese-, Korean-, and Chinese-American soldiers felt a new connection as fellow descendents of Asian countries and fellow victims of anti-Asian attitudes.

MINORITY BROTHERS IN ARMS

Many of the same motives, aspirations, and outcomes linked the military service of Californians regardless of ethnoracial background. A taste for adventure, a desire to conform, and pangs of patriotism propelled enlistment. Many of these soldiers rallied behind official explanations of the conflict: that the United States was fighting to spread democracy abroad and to ensure its survival at home. Whites and non-Whites alike developed feelings of camaraderie that in part reflected their successful integration into American military culture. In the midst of war fighting men felt an almost familial responsibility to one another, an identification that contributed to the efficiency and success of military operations.[3]

This cohesion developed despite the vast differences and localized identities that divided the recruits. At midcentury young Americans of all colors rarely journeyed beyond the confines of their hometowns, let alone home regions. This parochialism, historians have noted, generated strong, locally oriented loyalties. In the rush to establish stable identities amid the confusion and constant motion of the military, soldiers reported their hometowns and home states as readily as their surnames. More so than the generations that followed, Californians in World War II were acutely aware of being from California. In moving enlistees out of familiar scenes and into strange ones, where individuals dressed, acted, spoke, worshipped, and looked different, the armed forces intensified this awareness. This localism played out in the meeting of Japanese Americans from Hawaii and the mainland. Nisei Californians commented not upon the islanders' common Japanese ancestry but their discomfiting looks, uneducated speech, and brusque manner. Conversely, the Hawaiians viewed their cousins across the Pacific as arrogant and overly individualistic. These location-based rivalries, sometimes good natured and sometimes not, built tensions into Japanese American units. Thus, as much as a notion of brotherhood, non-Whites and Whites shared a sense of disorienting newness and difference.[4]

To a large extent California soldiers agreed that prejudice of any kind had no place in the military. This conviction, that ethnoracial difference ceased to matter in the face of battle, was not simply the wishful thinking of European ethnics. Many non-White soldiers described a military culture that came close to an uncompromised cosmopolitanism. Sergeant Ben Kuroki related that he flew alongside a Native American pilot and Polish-American tunner gunner, worked with a German-American bombardier, and was helped by a Jewish American soldier. "What difference did it make?" he said. "We had a job to do, and we did it with a kind of comradeship that was the finest thing in the world." Ernest Chavez believed as firmly that ethnoracial and regional distinctions did not get in the way of duty. From a desert training center in California, Chavez wrote a letter to the political progressive Carey McWilliams explaining that, rather than argue and segregate, "the boys here in my outfit are from all over the country. Yet we live together like one was still at home. We don't have fights with each other. We all treat each other the very same."[5]

But in other ways the expectations, experiences, and solidarity of minority soldiers set them apart from their White peers and demonstrated how incomplete and limited cosmopolitanism was. The reluctance to enlist displayed by Chester Himes's protagonist, Bob Jones, was not unusual among minorities whose experiences of discrimination complicated the meaning of patriotism. Cesar Chavez articulated this ambivalence in his autobiography. Recalling his 1944 induction into the navy, he said, "I suppose my views were pretty much the views of most members of a minority group. They really don't want to serve, but they feel this awesome power above them that's forcing them to do it." While frustration about persistent prejudice in California made military service feel more coerced than voluntary to some, others signed up eagerly because they believed that fighting for democracy overseas would win them greater participation in American society. In serving their country, these men reasoned, their country would serve them, extending long-withheld political rights and socioeconomic opportunities. The very involvement of these racial minorities in the U.S. armed forces came about only after artful persuasion and a reassessment of manpower needs. Black leaders successfully lobbied to place African Americans in the combat settings for which they had trained, and Filipino Americans convinced President Roosevelt to revise the Selective Service Act, reclassifying them as citizens eligible for enlistment. Even many Japanese Americans, whose enthusiasm for conflict one might doubt, given the injustice of internment, argued for and won the chance to fight.[6]

As much as early resistance to their inclusion, their mistreatment as soldiers threatened minorities' ambitions for change. Although Chinese Americans and Filipino Americans fought within both ethnically exclusive and integrated divisions, Japanese Americans and African Americans, with very few exceptions, were assigned to segregated regiments. Jewish and Mexican Americans fought alongside European ethnics but expressed self-consciousness about their integration. Moreover, isolated quarters, controlled access to leisure activities and local populations, the hostility of White soldiers, and frequent confinement to the lowliest, noncombatant positions reminded Asian, African, and Native Americans in particular that, in leaving civilian society, they had not left larger structures of injustice.

These men quickly discovered that military policy restricted the patriotic endeavors of multiple ethnoracial groups. Bert Corona, the prominent political activist from East Los Angeles (see chapter 3), joined the Army Air Corps. Soon after his arrival at Buckley Airfield near Denver, Corona realized that Anglo sergeants were blocking the promotion of Jewish and Mexican-American airmen by unfairly awarding them lower grades on tests of intelligence and physical conditioning. The military's consciousness and abuse of ethnic differences also troubled Jim Williams, an African American.[7] In an unusually diverse squad of officer candidates in Barclay, Texas, Williams trained alongside a "Japanese American, two Whites, one Jew." When the men attempted to leave the base for a lively evening on the town, Williams told the historian Maggi Morehouse years later, a local official broke up the party, directing the Nisei back to camp, Williams to the "other side of town," and the Whites to wherever they pleased. Rather than face disciplinary action, the group grudgingly complied. Despite his early idealism Kiyoshi Kagawa observed army practices that opened his eyes as wide as Corona's and Williams's to the common troubles of minority GIs. During a conversation with the Nisei sociologist Tom Sasaki in 1946, Kagawa stated that, along with "Mexicans, Negroes, and Kibeis," at Fort Riley, Texas, he cleaned horse stables as commanded by a superior officer. With a mixture of irony and despair the soldiers nicknamed themselves "the prisoners of Bataan." Long before many enlistees traveled overseas and engaged foreign enemies, they had already begun to question the armed forces' commitment to equal treatment.[8]

Ethnoracial minorities with whiter complexions and legal privileges learned about not only the discriminations others suffered but also the instability of their own status. Luis Sanchez, who grew up among a mix of ethnoracial groups in East Los Angeles, had little experience with discrimination until his enlistment. Days after donning his uniform, he was asked by a sergeant to name his "nationality." When Sanchez nervously answered, "Catholic" and then "Mexican," the officer shouted that if he were born in the United States, he was "a Caucasian," a "White." Sanchez accepted the racial designation, even though his tentative answers betrayed an uncertainty about his White identity. But his superior officer's insistence that Sanchez's ethnicity, religion, and color were irrelevant points of difference, that Sanchez belonged, was not a reassurance that other minorities often received. So when that reassurance came, as it did for Mexicans-American soldiers like Raul Morin, they welcomed it. In repeating an often-used wartime slogan—"Okies, Mexicans, Polaks, and Wops, that's all you'll find in the infantry"—Morin celebrated how military service could blur the perception of difference between Mexicans and European ethnics. Although Mexican Americans could not always depend upon such acceptance, the very possibility made eventual attachments with Asians or Blacks less obvious choices.[9]

At the same time dramatic reminders that they were not quite White kept Mexicans from forgetting their place among minorities. The interethnic tensions that built up and spilled over between White sailors and young Mexican-American civilians during World War II spoiled the relations between servicemen, too. News of the Zoot Suit Riots traveled all the way to Kodiak, Alaska, where Frank Lares was stationed. Lares, Los Angeles native, recollected the dirty looks and embarrassing questions that other artillerymen shot in his direction. "What kind of citizens are those Mexican Zoot-Zooters that would beat up on our own Navy men?" they asked. Only when these men learned of Private Jose P. Martinez's heroic efforts to secure a strategic pass in the Aleutians, an act of bravery for which he would posthumously receive the Congressional Medal of Honor, did they ease up on Lares. Martinez's ethnic example emphasized what Lares had known all along: not all Mexican Americans were gang members. Yet the quickness with which White sailors equated Mexican-American seamen—whose patriotism was visible and conventional—and Mexican-American pachucos spoke to the precariousness of the ethnoracial status of Mexicans and how "colored" they still were. In a letter to Eduardo Quevedo, a prominent activist who defended Latino youngsters, Rudy Sanchez puzzled over this persistent tendency to malign the loyalties of Mexican-American youths. Sanchez, who was a sailor, had discovered the plans of White sailors to attack zoot-suiters and had attempted to preempt the violence, without success.

Furious about what the White sailors' actions implied about the unity and place of minorities in the armed forces, Sanchez declared that Mexican Americans "eat, live, fight, and die fighting for our country just like everyone else." Wearing zoot suits did not make men "killers, gangsters or hoodlums." In fact, "thousands of former 'zoot suiters' are fighting for Uncle Sam" and intended to win the war. Sanchez concluded his letter with the provocative query: "Who's side is the Navy on anyway, Uncle Sam or Hitler?"[10]

Bert Corona was as troubled by the readiness of White sailors to label Mexicans as zoot-suiting traitors. He recalled the fears and resentment of Mexican sailors stationed at Santa Ana, California: "We had some similar incidents in which some of our Anglo servicemen beat up on local Chicanos. It caused much concern among the fairly large number of Mexican-Americans soldiers in our camp and in surrounding camps also." Mexican Americans in the military learned that despite putting on government-issue uniforms and putting their lives at risk, they had not put off the stereotype of the baggy pants–wearing rebel. The inequalities and ethnoracial uncertainties of their civilian lives followed them into the armed forces. And some of these Mexican-American soldiers began to question inequalities, a habit to which they would commit more intensively when the war ended. Although his family had "been challenging the growers for some time," Cesar Chavez's first, distinctive, and public act of defiance occurred while he was on leave from the navy. Entering a Delano, California, movie theater with a group of military buddies dressed in civilian clothes, Chavez chose not to sit in the section reserved for Mexicans, Blacks, and Filipinos. "I decided to challenge the rule," he said in his autobiography, "even though I was very frightened." Like the multiethnic civil rights activism in which so many other minorities were engaged after World War II, Chavez's career as an organizer of farmworkers was seeded during his military service.[11]

COLORED LIKE US: AFRICAN-AMERICAN SOLDIERS

Shared frustrations with military-style discrimination and shared, if qualified, hopes for a more perfect American democracy pulled minority soldiers closer. This proved especially the case for Blacks, whose contact with other societies and cultures threw into sharp relief the depth of American discrimination. For some their racial education began even before they journeyed overseas. Although unhappy with the segregation of the Jim Crow South, African Americans raised below the Mason-Dixon

Line were at least accustomed to the restrictions that governed the southern towns hosting most military bases. As reported by the U.S. Army,
Black northerners and westerners expressed almost universal dismay and
suffered adjustment difficulties when assigned to southern training
camps. Among the most disappointed and ill equipped were Californians such as Arthur Holmes and Atoy Rudolph Wilson. Shipped from his
hometown of Los Angeles to Camp Shelby, Mississippi, in 1943, Holmes
soon discovered how little he understood the state's racial rules. Following the customs of Los Angeles, he waited in line with Whites for a
public bus and returned the admiring gaze of a White woman. Almost
instantly, a Black man begged him to quit his behavior, lest he "get us
all killed." Holmes learned the surprising thickness of the South's color
line again when he unexpectedly ran into and hugged a White friend
from Los Angeles, only to have a superior officer order him "get over
there with your people." Wilson, an African American who grew up in
Boyle Heights, was similarly ill prepared for the racial restrictions elsewhere in America. As a draftee sent to West Virginia, he fought a driver
who ordered him to the back of a streetcar, and Wilson complained
about the exclusion of Blacks from the performance of a famous entertainer even though Italian prisoners-of-war were permitted to attend.
"Not being brought up under it [Jim Crow]," he told an interviewer, "to
me down South seemed like an isolated situation."[12]

The rigidly divided, biracial environment of the South disturbed
African-American oriented to relatively more tolerant and multiethnic
environments, but so did the differently complexioned Southwest. The
region's mix of peoples may have more closely resembled California's
own, but the relative absence of Asians, presence of Native Americans,
and different migration histories had created a distinct racial order.
Blacks often felt themselves strangers and evolved new interethnic sympathies among the region's unique mix of Mexicans, Native Americans,
Anglos, and Blacks. A Black soldier named Al, stationed in Abilene,
Texas, related his misadventures in a letter to his sister. Two military police officers arrested him while he was standing outside a local bus depot
in 1943. Presuming him to be Mexican, the MPs imprisoned and beat
him nearly unconscious. The case of mistaken identity demonstrated to
Al the violence and injustice that connected his life and that of other
Blacks with those of Mexicans in the United States.[13]

The efforts of the U.S. government to conceal the historical coexistence of Native Americans and Blacks in Arizona encouraged African
Americans to contemplate the region's second-largest minority group,

Native Americans. In a gesture that conveyed the same fear of minority insurrection that would slow the deployment of Black troops overseas, the U.S. government whitewashed murals at Fort Huachuca, Arizona, removing signs that Black troops had been stationed in the area at the same time as the Geronimo campaign. The army substituted a more sanitized, monoracial version of western history for the African Americans stationed there during World War II. As Arnett Hartsfield, a long-time resident of Los Angeles, recalled for Maggi Morehouse, during the unveiling of the repainted mural White officers sang rounds of cowboy songs while Native Americans hired for the event danced. Unmoved by a narrative of the region's past that hid Blacks and their potential links to Native Americans, Arnett dismissed the War Department's "Wild West Show."[14]

Certainly, their relocation to unfamiliar areas of the United States shook up the ethnoracial assumptions of African Americans, but their movement overseas proved more profoundly disconcerting and relevant to their changing ethnoracial affiliations. During their tours of duty Blacks repeatedly found themselves in relatively more tolerant racial environments. Within Western Europe, parts of Asia, the Caribbean, and even Hawaii, locals looked upon them with curiosity but not the disdain to which they had grown accustomed in many parts of America. In the United Kingdom Black Americans celebrated while White Americans seethed at the warm welcome that most Brits extended to the "Tan Yanks." The proliferation of romances between African Americans and local ladies confirmed in the minds of many that the racial views of the Allied nations were as far apart as the ocean between them. As Beth Bailey and David Farber reported of World War II Oahu, ethnoracial prejudices existed, especially among locals who accepted the racial prejudices imported and disseminated by White southerners. But these prejudices were rarely as severe and certainly not as widespread as those on the mainland. That so many African Americans chose to remain in Hawaii long after World War II ended demonstrated how much they preferred its ethnoracial rules.[15]

On other Pacific Islands, especially the Philippines, Black sailors not only encountered a refreshingly new social system but also began to identify with other oppressed groups. Interactions with native Filipinos, especially sexual encounters with Filipinas, heightened the Black sailors' awareness. In his memoir Adolph Newton, a Black sailor stationed in the Philippines during World War II, remembered the early efforts of White servicemen "to put the idea in their [Filipinos'] minds that Negroes were bad and should be avoided." High-ranking military officials agreed with Newton that White soldiers imported and disseminated prejudice among foreign populations. The civilian aide to the secretary of war concluded in 1946 that a Filipino's shooting of a Black sentry on duty "was brought about by White American soldiers" whose goal was to "extend their racial credo to an area hitherto relatively free of color prejudices." According to Newton, Whites were determined to teach racial prejudice to Filipinos because White soldiers resented the attention that African Americans directed toward local women. Whites "were really captivated" and "fascinated by the color" of these Filipinas even though these "Dixie boys" would never have pursued or risked getting caught with these brown-skinned women back home. Admittedly, "Negro sailors went for these girls, but they weren't as fascinated by their color the way I believe the white guys were," Newton concluded; the Black Americans viewed Filipinas in more equitable terms. Despite the objections of members of the "Dixie Division [who] couldn't stand the Filipino girls going for the Negro soldiers," as Walter Green, another Black soldier of the Ninety-third Division, observed, Black soldiers repeatedly won out in their competition with White men for local women.[16]

Black soldiers likely exaggerated their magnetism and dismissed their capacity to exoticize foreign women as they battled White racism in the armed forces, but the similar skin color of African Americans and Pacific Islanders did generate similar sensibilities and experiences. In 1944 Bill Downey and the rest of the Fifty-first Defense Battalion, one of the only Black units in the Marine Corps, landed on the Funatati Atoll. Beyond the attractiveness of the women and rampant rumors of their accessibility, Downey, who was from Harlem, immediately noticed that "we had quite a bit in common in some respects" with the local population because they too "came in all colors from light to dark." Elsewhere in the Pacific, Californian Howard Hickerson experienced relations more intimate and affectionate between Blacks and Filipinos, who treated African Americans "like kings" and threw parties "with the girls."[17]

Albert Newton's account of his harrowing escape from an angry White patrol conveyed the same themes of interethnic fondness and the ability of Blacks to claim masculinity by accessing the bodies of darker-skinned women. While he was sleeping at the home of his girlfriend one night, Newton was startled awake by a patrol outside that was shouting its intention "to shoot 'any niggers' it sees." Immediately, he leaned nearer the Filipina and spread her hair across his face, attempting to pass as a slumbering Filipino. The ruse depended upon, and succeeded because of, the common color of the couple. In joking that "one time my color paid off," Newton acknowledged not only a closeness between Filipinos and Blacks but also the possibility of collaboration against injustices delivered by Whites. In continuing relations with Filipinas despite White objections and even after the war's close, Black soldiers used interracial romance as a protest, a confident assertion of themselves as American men.[18]

At times native populations returned and reinforced the good feelings of African-American GIs. This reciprocity reinforced the idea increasingly accepted by African Americans during World War II of a global network of colored peoples. Nelson Peery's account of his stint in the Philippines with the all-Black Ninety-third Division communicated the ways in which Filipinos reached out to and expected solidarity with Blacks.[19] Disturbed by native poverty and the U.S. failure to help, Peery organized a food drive of sorts within his unit; the men donated one, sometimes two, of their government-issued meals to hungry Filipinos. Recipients expressed their thanks with complimentary shoe shines and huge smiles. However, the generosity of Black soldiers evoked more than gratitude; it encouraged Filipinos to consider African Americans as potential allies. "They were very aware that they were colored and we were colored," Peery related. Stories that Filipinos shared of the Aguinaldo-led rebellion in 1900 "never failed to include heroic tales of Corporal David Fagen, who with five other Black soldiers, deserted the invading U.S. Army and went on the side of the revolution." Beyond the principled defection of these men, the refusal of Black soldiers to "fight their black Filipino brothers" when sent to crush the Moro Rebellion in 1914 was widely remembered by Filipinos and emboldened them to solicit support from the World War II generation of Black GIs. As a communist sympathizer and passionate believer in the common misfortune of non-Whites—he argued that they "gotta stop fightin' one another for the White man"— Peery probably articulated the ties between Filipinos and African Americans more explicitly and with more political intention than most of his cohort, but they too appreciated these ties.[20]

Anthropologists who observed the responses of Pacific Islanders to American GIs during World War II often reported the natives' close identification with African Americans on the basis of skin color. Melanasians celebrated the status of American Blacks, who appeared to enjoy privileges akin to those of Whites. As reproduced by Gerald Smith, Jonathan Fif'i related his and other Solomon Islanders' impressions: "We saw the black soldiers there, and they all wore shirts, and they wore trousers. And their

job was to work just like the White soldiers. . . . They were really great
people! Any kind of thing that the Whites did, they could do it too." Tan-
nese workers laboring alongside members of the Black Twenty-fourth Infantry Regiment shared these positive views. "The Negroes . . . they
were good men," commented a villager in 1943. "When they called out,
they didn't say—they called us 'brother.' Brother, their brothers. They
didn't say that we were no good. They liked us, and because of this our
hearts were happy with them." Social scientists uncovered evidence of islanders' discomfort with Black soldiers too, but more frequently their
studies reinforced that Pacific Islanders were heartened by the presence
of Black men in uniform.[21]

The U.S. military feared the consequences of and actively worked to
repress this cross-cultural identification. Its manpower policy for Black
troops at best delayed their deployment and at worst directed them to
less strategically important locales. Condemning the practice as discriminatory, the Black press argued that the army had "hatched the plan
of confinement of colored units" in order to prevent "colored personnel
from being observed" by local peoples as enjoying relatively greater advantages and equity with Whites. But such a program betrayed more
than American prejudice. Foreign governments, including many in Western Europe, Australia, the Caribbean, and East Asia, implored the United
States not to station Black troops within their borders for fear they
would inspire civil unrest among local peoples with whom Blacks shared
darker complexions and histories of repression. Even on U.S. soil White
leaders worried that African-American soldiers might upset the racial
status quo. Although four Black regiments of engineers helped build
Alaska's famed Alcan Highway, they did so against the protests of the
state's governor, who expected "the mixing of Negroes with the native
Indians and Eskimos would be highly undesirable," the historian Ulysses
Lee wrote in his authoritative work on the use of Black troops in World
War II.[22] Presumably, contact with African Americans would remind
Native Americans of their own discontent and encourage resistance.

Such opposition and suspicion angered Black troops and encouraged
their developing sense of themselves as members of a global community
of colored peoples. A few went so far as to seriously contemplate defection from the U.S. military. The disdain of "the warrior for the civilian,"
as Richard Welch put it, made such a complete transfer of loyalty unlikely.[23] But many African Americans demonstrated a propensity to construe the war in the racial terms that were designed to separate them
from White compatriots. The Black GIs' perspective reflected that of

many Black intellectuals who had embraced internationalism as an ideology of world affairs soon after the United States had begun to extend
itself overseas at the turn of the century. Specifying ethnoracial prejudice
as a major source of international conflict, they correlated the demise of
racism with the onset of peace. To achieve the peace the Black leaders
recommended a global alliance of oppressed colored peoples. By World
War II these largely elite notions had gained currency among the Black
rank-and-file, including GIs whose contacts with non-White peoples
seemed to confirm the wisdom of the position. Well into the 1930s Black
internationalists celebrated Japan, whose record against Western powers, they reasoned, made it the most suitable to lead a nascent union of
what they had coined the "darker races." Even as Black reverence for the
island nation weakened during the 1930s and into the 1940s, Black
media and Black organizations reported Japan's aggression with more
ambivalence than their White counterparts.[24]

Nelson Peery of the all-Black Ninety-third communicated this sensibility when he chastised U.S. Marines who arrogantly underestimated
the Japanese, dismissing them as "monkey men' and a "colored people"
who would quickly fall to American superior might. In contrast, Peery
spoke of Japanese as "excellent soldiers" who "had been fighting in the
Pacific for a long time, swallowing up bits and pieces." Rather than evidence of disloyalty, Perry's admiration for the enemy suggested how
racialized was the patriotism of U.S. soldiers and how war enlarged the
backdrop against which they viewed their own difficulties.[25]

Other Black leaders and soldiers made uncomfortable by Japan's
expansion redirected their affections to China, constructing this other
Asian nation as a worthy, substitute ally in the worldwide struggle of colored peoples. The NAACP, prominent Black commentators, and ordinary
citizens alike actively courted China during the war years, raising money
for its relief, supporting efforts to overturn the Chinese Exclusion Act,
and publishing positive analyses of Chinese affairs. Black army engineers
and truck drivers who helped build the Burma Road to China articulated
an early sense of kinship with the Chinese. One Black GI interviewed in
1942 depicted locals as "fine fellows who have treated us like brothers."
Such positive encounters among individuals, another GI believed, symbolized the friendship between the two nations and assured that "our
racial group has not been forgotten." Although faith in the bond between
Blacks and Chinese as fellow non-White peoples was shaken when Black
troops learned that the Chinese leader Chiang Kai-shek had arranged for
their exclusion, Black GIs retained some confidence in the tolerance and

amity of the Chinese population as a whole. A Black journalist reporting from China reinforced and echoed this view. In a column published in the *Horizon,* he chastised China for failing "to give the aid and comfort it could to its natural allies in this world-wide struggle" and for ignoring "the common relationship between problems of these masses and other masses throughout the world." But the reporter acknowledged that "people in general, especially those in rural areas, proved to be quite congenial." Even as the action of Chinese officials through the mid-1940s belied their interest in an alliance with African Americans, the sustained hopefulness of Blacks showed how deeply many had come to believe in the idea of a "colored people."[26]

Black soldiers created and imagined links with oppressed, darker-skinned peoples, but they simultaneously rejected other ethnic attachments, thereby complicating notions of cosmopolitanism and multiethnic community. Adolph Newton felt a kinship with Filipinos, but when a Jewish GI stationed in the Philippines told Newton that "we are in the same boat, you know. My people have been persecuted for over two thousand years," Newton dismissed the connection: "All you have to do is change your religion and you have ended your problem. . . . I cannot change anything to get this shit off my back." The notion that Jews enjoyed advantages that set them above Blacks inflected the thinking of other African-American enlistees. Resenting the cold shoulders his mostly White and Jewish unit turned toward him, Senior Master Sergeant Felix Goodwin challenged his colonel at a base in Indiantown Gap, Pennsylvania: "Sir, since everyone around here is Jewish why can't you accept me?" "That was the wrong thing to say," Goodwin soon concluded, as "they were all over me." Goodwin's plea for inclusion rested upon the presumption that Blacks and Jews were similarly positioned minorities, a presumption flatly rejected by other soldiers. The failure of his ethnic analogy and Newton's uneasy relations with Jewish GIs highlighted the uncertain, in-between status of Jewish Americans of the period. As in the multiracial neighborhoods of prewar California, historical and contemporary discriminations encouraged Jews to reach out to Asians, Mexicans, and Blacks. Yet the Jews' European heritage and relatively greater socioeconomic advantages meant that even in the context of shared military service, these other groups sometimes slapped them away. Confusion and contest over what constituted a minority shaped its emergence as a larger category of affiliation.[27]

Witnessing injustices against colored peoples abroad and in other regions of the United States prompted Blacks to demand improvements for non-White Americans even before the war ended. As I discussed in chapter 4, while battles blazed beyond U.S. borders, conflict erupted within them. Upon limited and prejudicial evidence a group of Mexican-American teens was imprisoned for the beating and death of another. The Sleepy Lagoon Defense Committee—civil rights activists convinced of the young men's innocence—fought for their release. Learning of the defense campaign, sympathetic Americans penned letters of support. Among them were African Americans in the military. A Corporal Samuel, a Black GI who learned of the case while on duty in Hawaii, wrote that "we members of the colored race are sympathetic to your worthwhile and moral fight to free the Mexican boys." And Dolores Figueroa, whose letter denouncing violence against pachucos was reprinted in the *California Eagle,* received a thank-you note from a sub-scriber and army man who appreciated "her stand against discrimina-tion." Another act of injustice on American soil evoked the protests of soldiers far away. Moments before an important mission members of the nation's first all-Black paratrooper unit reflected upon the "fear, preju-dice, and hatred" that had sent Japanese Americans to concentration camps but conspicuously left German Americans and Italian Americans free. Even on the brink of battle, they recognized the plight of another minority and the emerging color line that protected European ethnics. Such a critical, racialized perspective on the war emphasized the gap be-tween wartime democratic rhetoric and the discrimination suffered by African Americans and others.[28]

Closer to home, Black soldiers training at Fort Huachuca, Arizona, celebrated Negro History Week in 1944 by reaching out to nearby in-ternees. As a young Nisei reporter explained, the African Americans were not so much advocating for themselves as expressing "the need for a closer relationship among various groups" and bringing "a better un-derstanding toward interracial unity." Blacks, politicized by their ser-vice, promoted these ideals by recruiting Black entertainers to perform at the Gila River Relocation Center. In still another case of interethnic allegiance and assertiveness, Black soldiers rallied around Chinese Amer-icans. The all–Chinese American 407th Air Service Squadron trained in aircraft manufacture at Patterson Field in Ohio. As the former squadron member Chor Y. Law remembered, a few of his cohort befriended White women on base, much to the chagrin of White soldiers. When verbal al-tercations between Chinese-American and White soldiers broke out, African Americans working at Patterson stepped quickly to the Chinese Americans' defense. African Americans' willingness to choose the side of fellow minorities, even though the allegiance would likely bring down upon them the wrath of White soldiers, demonstrated how a military context could create cross-cultural loyalties. As in the Pacific, Whites fought for exclusive access to local women. However, non-White men defied such proprietary claims (in this case collaboratively); in doing so, they declared confidence and boldness, as well as the crossing of ethnic and color lines, as defining features of their male identities.[29]

FACES OF THE ENEMY AND FACES OF FRIENDS: ASIAN-AMERICAN SOLDIERS

Conflict in the Pacific had strained relations among Asian ethnics, especially Asian immigrants, through the 1930s, but Japan's accelerated expansion and the uncertain neutrality of the United States exacerbated these strains in the 1940s. However, Asian ethnics serving in the U.S. armed forces had little appreciation and even less use for these intercultural tensions. California's Asian ethnics, unfamiliar with the character of racial prejudice in other regions, expressed similar surprise on discovering the predicaments of African Americans and Native Americans. Training for the U.S. military in the American South and fighting for the United States abroad also encouraged new understandings among Asian soldiers and new articulations of their identities as ethnic Americans. As those whose faces most resembled, or were most often confused with, those of the Japanese enemy, these men felt a particular need to prove they were loyal Americans.

Certainly African-American soldiers chafed under the severe restrictions of the Jim Crow South, but the region's racial climate proved particularly perplexing to Chinese and Japanese Americans who had neither direct experiences with nor education from friends and family to prepare them. The historian Peter Phan described as a "gray area" the ethnoracial location of Chinese-American soldiers who traveled beyond ethnic enclaves of California. Chinese-American members of the Fourteenth Air Service Group training in the South expressed unease at the biracial division of society. Accustomed to a different kind of racism in California, they wondered about their appropriate social place. Where they should sit on buses, from which water fountains they should drink, and how they should interact with Whites puzzled them.[30]

Japanese Americans were similarly confused by local racial customs. On their arrival at Camp Shelby, Mississippi, where the 442nd Regimental Combat Team and 100th Infantry Battalion trained—both were all-Nisei units—the men were given a crash course in the region's racial rules. The company commander told his charges to observe the ways of Mississippi: "You may not like it, but that's the way they do things here and that's the way it's going to be. . . . Much of this will rub you the wrong way but I am asking that you abide by it." Nisei found themselves unexpectedly shoehorned into the category of "White"; most expressed ambivalence about this new racial status. Mike Masaoka explained that "the race problem posed a delicate problem for most of us. Most of the officers—at least those who counted—insisted that we Nisei act and be treated as Whites." Being White in this southern context meant "using the White latrines, sitting in [the] front of streetcars and buses when we went to town, eating in the restaurants instead of being handed our food out in back," a set of privileges that Nisei accepted even though they were uncomfortable. When initially confronted with the choice of being Black or White, most Nisei presumed that they were Black and accordingly positioned themselves in the back of buses and used Black facilities until angry drivers or officers told them otherwise.[31]

Immersed within this new regime, Nisei expressed surprise and opposition to the prejudices that Blacks suffered on a daily basis. Masaoka confessed that "discrimination became the subject of many intense discussions" among Nisei soldiers in Mississippi who "gained a sense of social justice involving others as well as ourselves." Noting racial injustices in the South, Takeo Kaneshiro wondered in a 1945 diary entry whether there would ever be "another great president like" Lincoln who would correct both the continued discriminations against Blacks as well as recognize that Japanese "are good citizens like the rest of us Americans." Another young Nisei, newly released from the camps and enlisted in the military, similarly explained how his encounter with southern society pressed him to make a reappraisal of his own racial attitudes. "I never thought about it before but we Japanese are still lucky," he acknowledged in a 1947 letter excerpted in the *Los Angeles Tribune*, "because colored people" in Louisiana are not allowed to "even ride to certain part on bus or street car."[32]

At times the simmering sense of injustice that Nisei felt on behalf of Black civilians and soldiers boiled over. Much of the resistance seemed to take place in the awkwardly segregated space of public buses. George Goto and fellow Nisei soldiers who were already seated watched with disappointment as a bus driver ordered a boarding Black GI to the back of the vehicle. The Japanese Americans pleaded with the driver, "Awww, let him alone he's a solider," to which the driver stubbornly responded,

"This bus doesn't move until that nigger gets in the back." In a similar case a member of the 442nd Regimental Combat Team, emboldened by a bit of beer, answered southern segregation by assaulting a driver who had forced an African-American serviceman off his bus. In raising their voices and fists against the region's discrimination, the Nisei communicated a concern for the civil rights of minorities other than themselves.[33]

In regions of the United States where Native Americans were more numerous, Japanese Americans gained new insight into the lives of another minority group. A member of the 100th Army Infantry Battalion, which was training at Camp McCoy, Wisconsin, Raymond Nosaka visited the nearby towns of Sparta and La Crosse on his weekend leaves. Bartenders at local establishments assumed he and his Nisei pals were Native Americans and refused them liquor as federal law prescribed. Surprised, because he "didn't know" about the restrictions—much like Japanese-American internees at Poston didn't know the past and present conditions of Colorado River Indians—he tried to convince the establishment that he was Japanese, not Native American. Seen by others as men of the same color as Native Americans, Japanese began to see themselves in a different light. The ability of an outsider's gaze to change the perceived and actual identifications of minorities had most affected (and would continue to affect) the descendants of Asian immigrants, but here it blurred the ethnicity of Asians and Native Americans. Harry Kukuhara had a similar experience. When Kukuhara, an officer in the Military Intelligence Service, joined the 158th Marine Corps, he "got along real good" with the Italians in his unit because they "had a lot of things in common, like in things we eat, and the family situation." Yet he formed faster friendships and found even more in common with Native Americans, who first mistook him for an Indian. Kukuhara and fellow Nisei translators hung out with these non-Whites "because they were minority groups, so we kinda sorta tended to mix real well with them." Speculating that the company he kept, the shape of his nose, and the darkness of his suntanned skin explained his passing as Native American, Kukuhara accepted the ethnic confusion as helpful to his work. He was less conspicuous as a Native American than he was as an "Oriental," and he gained entry into an ethnic group with whom he had no association in the prewar era. Being mistaken for or blending in among other minority soldiers taught non-Whites the breadth and particularities of prejudice in the United States.[34]

However, World War II brought Asian ethnics into contact and responsibilities that most profoundly changed how they thought about one another. At home and abroad bewilderment about ethnic membership and the serious consequences of that bewilderment helped expand the ethnoracial notions of Japanese-, Filipino-, and Chinese-American soldiers. Precise ethnic identifications became all the more important in California after the bombing of Pearl Harbor, when already-heated anti-Japanese sentiments got even hotter. Japanese, as well as Chinese and Filipinos, feared for their livelihoods and lives. Few Whites bothered to or succeeded in differentiating those of distinct Asian heritage. Chinese Americans, Filipino Americans, and some Korean Americans strove to disidentify themselves. They wore large buttons proclaiming their ethnicity and posted similar signs in their storefront windows to inform their customers. Sometimes the desire to disidentify and wartime resentments went well beyond such peaceful statements of ethnicity. Even though Japanese Americans and their newspapers may have exaggerated the violence and the real threat of Filipinos, the accounts clearly reflect how much interethnic interactions had deteriorated. Throughout 1942 the Japanese-American press reported crimes in various California locales. In El Centro Japanese-American owners shut down their shops after Filipinos fired at two Japanese exiting a pool hall. A few days later a Filipino gunman shot an elderly Japanese couple in the same town. San Francisco police questioned Filipinos armed with knives and brass knuckles, while Los Angles law enforcement arrested Filipinos and charged them with robbing and beating a Japanese hotel porter. The Nisei press reported other violent incidents, including a drive-by shooting in Costa Mesa, a kidnapping in Gilroy, and the breaking of shop windows in Stockton. All were allegedly perpetrated by Filipinos.[35] Meanwhile ethnic Chinese made clear their politically fueled anger. During an event to raise money for war relief in January 1942, a Chinese-American woman attacked a Japanese interloper "by whirling her arms," and Lim Dum Dong shot a Japanese-American ticket collector, Susie Yamagama, outside a Sacramento theater. Investigators could find no motive for the latter crime until a witness testified that the defendant often "brooded about the war which is now in progress between China and Japan" and objected to paying "a Japanese girl for admission to the picture show."[36] Signs posted, buttons worn, knives drawn, bullets shot, and insults hurled were forceful, defensive gestures of ethnic difference that betrayed the common insecurity of Asians in America.

Sometimes Asian-American soldiers were as susceptible to this sense of insecurity and as determined to assert a more specific ethnicity as civilians. For Sunao Ishio, a Nisei soldier strolling along the streets of San Francisco during a brief R&R in 1945, being mistaken for "something other than a Nisei" bothered him immensely. Perhaps like many of his generation he hoped his enlistment would prove the loyalty of Japanese Americans, a statement lost on a public unable to recognize his ancestry. His position suggested how the special burden of proof that Nisei GIs felt themselves to bear could drag against an Asian-American affiliation. But the importance of this example was not the hostility toward Chinese-, Filipino-, or Korean-American soldiers that fed the ethnic pride of Japanese but the ethnoracial confusion of White outsiders.[37]

However, most Asian Americans in the military made ethnic distinctions the basis for commonality and camaraderie. Chinese-American and Japanese-American soldiers began to feel a kinship as fellow victims of anti-Asian attitudes even before they left American soil. Four Japanese-American language instructors at the Military Intelligence Language School (MISLS) were traveling through Pocatello, Idaho, in the company of two Chinese-American escorts, who presumably were assigned to protect the quartet from the anti-Japanese feelings of the civilian population. While dining at a restaurant, the group was interrupted by Pocatello's sheriff. Determined to discern the purpose of these men in military uniform whose appearance had unnerved local diners, he rigorously questions the two Chinese-American officers. The Nisei instructors were left alone, an irony both bodyguards and teachers laughed about afterward.[38] Outside their civilian California routines, Asian ethnics felt a new connection. As one of the few Asian faces among a sea of White engineers, Stanley Mu instinctively reached out to the rare Japanese, Korean, or Filipino he encountered in the Army Corps of Engineers. When the paths of Asian ethnics crossed at the Virginia base to which he was assigned, they inevitably exchanged smiles, handshakes, and invitations to hang out at a local bar, Mu recalled. These cases suggest how linked the fortunes of Asian Americans had become during the war years and their recognition of this development.[39]

In the Pacific theater, where explications of ethnicity and nationality were matters of life and death, Asian Americans quickly learned the frustration and danger of mistaken identity. Hoping to avoid costly confusions, the U.S. military distributed a pamphlet titled "How to Spot a Jap" to its Asia-based troops. The literature had only modest success, prompting Chinese-American servicemen such as a medic at the Twenty-third Field Hospital in New Guinea to print "Chinese" in bold letters across the top of his helmet. Yet fellow Americans and their reductive ethnic understanding were not the only threats that Asian-American soldiers faced, as Won-loy Chan explained. The California native and senior member of the special language program of the Military Intelligence Service (MIS)—the program responsible for translating intercepted enemy messages and for bringing Japanese and Chinese Americans into closer, more regular contact than any other military division—explained in his memoir that "to the Chinese we often resembled Japanese, while to the Japanese we often looked like Chinese." Such confusion put Asian Americans at even greater risk than other American combatants. Once, while emerging from the jungle with a Nisei and fellow officer of the MIS, a unit of approximately twenty Chinese surrounded and nervously pointed their weapons at the translators. Although Chan could not comprehend their words, from their tone he understood his own danger and that "this Japanese American GI was about to meet his Japanese ancestors." Luckily, at that moment an American officer appeared and explained in fluent Chinese that Chan "was on their side."[40]

A Nisei in the Philippines was nearly killed in a similarly harrowing incident. While driving a senior army staff member in Manila, Harvey Watanabe was startled by a local Filipino, who reached through the car window, grabbed the steering wheel, and threatened him with a huge bolo knife. "I thought he figured he caught a Japanese soldier making an escape," Watanabe reasoned and defused the situation by calmly stating his nationality. The Filipino released the car and waved a good-natured good-bye. Life-endangering and consciousness-raising cases of mistaken identity prompted protests by other Nisei stationed in the Philippines. According to an overseas publication in 1946, sixty Nisei graduates of the Military Intelligence Service, angered by the hostile attitude of Filipinos who stared at them and hollered the pejorative 'hap-pan' or 'Croix,' meaning get the hell out," had demanded transfers. As dedicated members of the U.S. armed forces, the Japanese Americans resented that they were not seen as the equals of or treated with the same respect as White GIs. In requesting transfers, they were calling upon the U.S. government to take responsibility for and correct this injustice; more than the ignorance of the local population was at fault, they reasoned.[41]

Ethnic confusions and prejudices that originated from within the U.S. Army as well as outside it forced Chinese Americans to reflect upon racial categories and foreign legacies. In 1942 Jim Fung, a Chinese American, joined the U.S. Navy and soon thereafter journeyed to the Pacific. While pulling into a local harbor, Fung caught a glimpse of a sign posted by American sailors that read: "Kill Japanese, Kill Japanese, Kill the Yellow Race." Fung objected to the racial construction of a war he understood as a struggle to safeguard democracy. He identified himself as a member of the "yellow race" as well as an American. The implicit, war-inspired empathy for Japanese Americans that one could infer from Fung's notion of "yellowness" was more explicitly expressed by two Chinese-American soldiers. The statement of a Captain Liu appeared in an official 1944 publication of the Committee on American Principles and Fair Play, "Fighting Men Speak Out," which was intended to communicate the patriotism and fairmindedness of those in the armed forces. In the pamphlet Liu dismissed claims that "returning soldiers would desire to slit the throats of loyal Japanese at home" and explained that "we'll do our fighting on the battlefields against our country's enemies, and not on the streets at home against our country's friends." In his letter to a Nisei soldier, which was reprinted in the *Pacific Citizen,* an unnamed Chinese-American GI reassured his friend that he "had no ill feelings for the Japanese Americans" and was "glad you agree with me that they are just as loyal as you or I." Though probably chosen because these firsthand accounts fit the intended message of the political committee and the Nisei newspaper, the statements were not a fabrication and probably not exceptional. They conveyed a faith in national over ethnic differences that was rooted in military experience. Their identities challenged, Japanese-American and Chinese-American soldiers reached for larger categories of affiliation as Americans and Asian Americans.[42]

Indeed, in the face of a common enemy, many of the cultural, economic, and political disagreements that separated Asian ethnics in the prewar period faded among World War II servicemen, permitting a tentative, collective awareness to surface. The military careers of Young Oak Kim and Won-loy Chan best illustrate the shifting interethnic dynamic. Ranked as a colonel, Young Oak Kim took charge of an all-Nisei regiment because, as the Korean American explained in a 1995 conversation, the War Department "really didn't know what to do with me" and felt "reluctant to send me to a regular American outfit and have an Asian command a platoon or whatever." Kim accepted leadership and effectively minimized Japanese-Korean tensions by invoking a common Asian ancestry. Kim's impassioned articulation of an identity shared by both Korean and Japanese soldiers as Americans of Asian descent successfully united the soldiers on the battlefield. The *Korean Independence* marveled at the cooperation between Kim and a Japanese-American private, when they "crawled into enemy territory near Cisterna" and captured two German soldiers while the German army remained completely unaware.[43]

Won-loy Chan mentored and depended upon the Japanese-American linguists with whom he collaborated as part of the U.S. military's intelligence efforts. When the Nisei officers Yasuharu Koike and Toichi Ishimura first arrived in China, Chan struggled to convince skeptical Chinese allies that "the two Nisei were on our side—were in fact, valuable human assets to be protected." In the high-stress setting of war Chan came to trust and respect his Nisei companions. "Without the presence of the MISLS-trained Japanese Americans in Burma and in the Pacific, winning World War II would have been much more difficult." These men, he insisted, "served gallantly" and the "full story of this outstanding group of Japanese Americans would fill a book." Japanese and Chinese Americans closed ethnic ranks as they discovered mutual patriotism and bravery. But these warriors also put aside ethnic distinctions because they realized the limits and learned to manipulate the possibilities of their common Asian ancestry and color. Tasked to break the silence of four battle-hardened veterans from Japan's Eighteenth Division, Chan and Ishimura got creative. Chan confessed that he was a captain in the U.S. Army, but "as you can see, my skin is the same color as yours. I'm a Chinese American and the sergeant here is a Japanese American." By eliminating "a few samurai Japanese generals and admirals of the Imperial Command who have deluded the Emperor and got Japan into a war she can never hope to win," Chan explained to the expectant captives, "you and other soldiers of whatever nationality [would] be able to go home and live in peace." Swayed by Chan's words and the linguists' "yellow race," the prisoners began sharing secrets. Even as Asian-American soldiers proved impeccable American patriots, their encounters with Asian enemies made them aware of genuine and presumed commonalities of color, history, and culture that connected the lives of Asian ethnics in the United States.[44]

MORE MULTIETHNIC THAN EVER

Military service broadened ethnic definitions and political aspirations of those who had been indifferent or unaware of how their lives overlapped with other minorities', but it also reinforced and stretched the ambitions of those already accustomed to the problems and possibilities of multiethnic communities. Not coincidentally, many minorities who advocated multiethnic approaches to civil rights in the postwar era—Fred Ross, Bert Corona, and Ed Roybal, to name a prominent few—not only had grown up in diverse spaces but also had served in the military. The stories of Raul Morin, Karl Yoneda, and Guy Gabaldon exemplify the influence of multiethnic homes upon experiences of service. Raul Morin and his Mexican-American buddies from East Los Angeles felt immediately at

ease with the diversity of their units because they had lived, worked, and
played amid diversity. However, as Morin related, those "who came
from various and different types of sectors of the United States where minority groups were kept segregated or where minority groups were small
in number," struggled to adapt to demographic conditions for which the
Californians were already prepared. Karl Yoneda's multiethnic roots (the
Japanese-American activist was married to the Jewish American Elaine
Black) not only eased his transition to military life but also reconfirmed
his commitment to civil rights. Through the 1930s and early 1940s he
had fought to improve conditions for all minorities. He carried his discontent and defiance into the army when he became a member of the
MIS in 1943. His political perspective colored his understanding of his
wartime experience. He was quick to see and criticize unfair military
practices. On his way to basic training at Camp Shelby, Mississippi,
Yoneda found the military police urging him to move forward into the
"Whites Only" section, an order he obeyed only after arguing that he
was not White and that such segregation was the worst form of racism.[45]
For Yoneda the world he encountered as a member of the army did not
so much awaken him to the breadth of racial injustices as intensify his
belief that such injustices existed and should be challenged through
multiethnic protest.

A comfort and familiarity with diverse minority cultures, strengthened by the obligations of military service, proved a strategic asset for
some non-Whites. Guy Gabaldon, the Mexican-American resident of
Boyle Heights whose Nisei friends, Lyle and Lane Nakano, taught him
Japanese, enthusiastically joined the Marine Corps when war broke
out. During a battle over Japanese-occupied Saipan, he stole quietly to
the edge of a nearby cliff and, using a combination of fluent Japanese
and firepower, managed to capture enemy Japanese. Gabaldon's multicultural skills and associations made his heroism possible. In publicizing the ways in which cultural crossing benefited the war effort,
these men provided examples of the value of diversity for peacetime
America.[46]

CONCLUSION

For minority soldiers from California, home looked different from a distance. As World War II drew to an end, many anticipated their return to
California with mixed feelings. They longed to escape from the discomforts and dangers of military service, but wartime encounters made the

familiar less comfortable. Among the souvenirs of their journeys non-Whites brought back both a heightened frustration with the status quo and a conviction that other minorities had reason to share their frustration. And it became clear that military service and the cosmopolitan pronouncements of World War II gave to European ethnics what was still withheld from Blacks, Asians, Mexicans, and Jews: equal treatment. Through what Roger Lotchin called "the crucible of patriotism," Italian Americans, Polish Americans, Portuguese Americans, and most others of eastern and southern European heritage were increasingly integrated into California society just after World War II.

Minority soldiers may not have cohered as a colored brotherhood, but as they entered into peacetime California, they were more willing to challenge discriminations collectively. Historians have long highlighted the heightened political assertiveness of minority GIs in the years following their service but have attributed that assertiveness to ethnically particular trials and tribulations of military service. In fact, their interactions with other non-White civilians and soldiers were as fundamental to their changed consciousness and directed them, as chapter 6 will explore, toward multiethnic rather than strictly monoethnic, civil rights action.[47]

Panethnic Politics Arising from the Everyday

"Brotherhood is not easy. . . . It means living next to a Jew, eating next to a Negro, sitting next to an American of Japanese descent, working next to an American of Mexican descent," argued Homer Jack in the *Los Angeles Tribune,* one of Los Angeles's two Black newspapers, in 1946. Though arduous and painful to realize, Jack continued, minorities had no choice but to "live as brothers or perish." He urged non-Whites to move beyond more superficial, intercultural activities such as visiting Little Tokyos or "slumming it in Negro nightclubs" and begin "reading pamphlets, distributing literature, organizing meetings, and protesting discriminatory institutions."[1] This editorialist acknowledged both the discomforts and possibilities of political coalition in multiethnic spaces. In the wake of World War II minority Californians increasingly saw themselves as a group set apart from European ethnics and capable of coalition even as they struggled with the often-difficult realities of integrated living. The Zoot Suit Riots, internment, and military service strengthened and sanctioned the intimate relations that minorities had created before the war. By the mid- to late 1940s this heightened awareness of interdependence and discrimination motivated political action.

Asian-, Mexican-, African-, and Jewish-American residents of mixed California neighborhoods selectively collaborated in the postwar period. Through individual gestures of support, multiethnic political organizations, and localized campaigns, these frequent neighbors sought to free themselves from constraints in housing, marriage, education, and citizenship. Neither their interests nor strategies for realizing these interests were perfectly complementary. Just as concerns about color, culture, and class framed minorities' choices of friends, lovers, and spouses, so did they influence their selection of political partners. Thus, through interethnic political as well as social relationships, non-Whites made new ethnoracial categories even as they broke down older ones. While Asian ethnics rallied around a common frustration with restrictive immigration and the perception of being perpetually foreign, Mexican Americans debated joining African Americans, with whom they shared a problem of school segregation, if not the privilege of legal Whiteness. Even when minorities were at odds about the particularities of their civil rights objectives, many accepted the credo that discrimination against one ultimately hurt them all. For example, Japanese Americans and Jewish Americans cared more about limits on citizenship than educational discrimination, but this did not discourage their working with Mexican and African Americans to desegregate California schools. This more inclusive vision of civil rights, as much as the groups' immediate self-interests, shaped coalitions and exemplified a mode of panethnic politics that was unitary but not totalizing. Minorities respected differences even as they stressed and acted upon their situational commonalities to advance their positions.

In this chapter I place interminority relations within the larger context of postwar politics while focusing on the interplay of non-Whites' everyday social and cultural encounters with political forms. The panethnic politics of the period did not develop from a detached set of activists and agendas but out of the neighborhoods, schools, work districts, and wartime relocations of non-White Californians. Veterans and other adults took the lead in civil rights efforts. But youth of mixed spaces also tested their political voices and claimed responsibility for future ethnoracial relations, intensifying their earlier expressions of cosmopolitanism. Certainly, a national mood favoring reform energized the civil rights program of minorities and helped ensure their successes of the late 1940s; many Americans during and after the global conflict determined that domestic conditions should more closely match democratic promises. Activists of all colors subscribed to and often organized around the idea that positive intergroup relations could bring about a more equitable society. This notion carried minorities into civil rights activities with sympathetic White liberals. However, it was their collaboration with one another that often had an intensity and intimacy reflective of shared misfortune. More decisively than ever before, they excluded European ethnics from their definition of minority. Such exclusion illustrated the very different sociopolitical place at which European ethnics had arrived, or nearly arrived, by the late 1940s. For non-Whites political inspiration derived most immediately and persuasively from personal histories of intermingling.

POSTWAR JOSTLING

With World War II behind them, minorities faced new difficulties of demobilization and readjustment. A cooling economy raised unemployment and slowed construction of new housing. Meanwhile the arrival of Black migrants from the South and return of Japanese from the camps heightened competition for property and jobs. This changed demography and economy introduced new tensions and uncertainties into minority lives. However, their dedicated efforts to manage these conditions, to comfortably coexist in integrated spaces, became a kind of panethnic politics arising from the everyday. This continued experience of and commitment to intercultural living would also support more formal, coordinated demands for equal rights.

In the mid- to late 1940s minorities suffered the pains of a postboom state. The rapid increase in California's population had strained its physical infrastructure and resulted in crowded commutes, food shortages, and scarce housing. Conditions only worsened after 1945 as once-flourishing shipbuilding and aircraft manufacturers closed or reduced production. Concurrently, military bases shut down or laid off thousands of workers. All residents felt the negative effects of this recession and congestion, but minorities were the most inconvenienced. As those last hired, they generally lost their jobs first. Mexican, Asian, and especially African Americans saw their gains in defense employment quickly evaporate. By 1950 African-American men in the Bay Area experienced a 25 percent unemployment rate, nearly twice that of their White counterparts. Besides loss of work, non-Whites had trouble finding housing. The slowdown in new building exacerbated the artificial scarcity created by restrictive covenants and discriminatory real estate practices. The basics of solid shelter and a steady job remained elusive for these Californians.[2]

The return of Japanese Americans from internment camps only compounded the problems of other non-Whites in the mid 1940s. As these evacuees filtered slowly back into their former neighborhoods, farms, and businesses, they confronted a new ethnic tableau but one still defined by the clustering of non-Whites. Evacuees and the minorities who had replaced them in businesses and neighborhoods anticipated a tense, conflict-ridden transition. With space already scarce and the economy flagging, they had good reason to worry. While Nisei felt "anxious above everything else to avoid any friction," one survey reported, other minorities were torn between their fear of "losing hard-won improvements gained during the war and evacuation" and "losing all rights eventually if they did not unite with other minorities to defend the evacuated minority." The *Pacific Citizen* corroborated the anxieties stirred up as non-Whites awaited the Japanese homecoming. Reportedly fearing that "the returnees will furnish further competition to them in their already difficult search for housing and the better class of jobs," Blacks and Filipinos resisted changes to their neighborhoods. Politicians like G. Vernon Bennett, an LA city councilman, attempted to capitalize on such worries, courting Mexicans and Blacks in Los Angeles's Fourteenth District by promising to defend them against any loss of employment caused by the return of Japanese.[3]

As these non-Whites expected, Japanese reentered California society with difficulty. A tight housing market accounted for much of the resulting tension. At least initially, crowded conditions forced many families to accept lodging at churches, temples, community centers, trailer camps, and army barracks. The Sanos even resorted to living with the Black family to whom they had rented their house in Berkeley until the tenants agreed to move. Others resorted to more aggressive measures, pressuring current Black residents to vacate. Art Takemoto remembered one incident in which a harried Japanese landlord asked him to intercede in a dispute with African Americans. Such disagreements became typical as Japanese owners ordered evictions or bought up leases. Most Nisei viewed these practices as fair and necessary for reestablishing themselves and had "no intention of restoring [a] segregated enclave," as Japanese leaders insisted. However, many Blacks saw things differently. "It's pretty rough some times," one boy said of Blacks' housing problems in Los Angeles. He believed Japanese were "trying to drive the negroes out," even though "the negroes are the best friends the Japanese have."[4]

As much as finding a place to live, repositioning themselves in the local economy created intercultural friction. Japanese expressed despair at finding their businesses now run by other minorities. The success of these others reminded Japanese Americans how much internment had cost them. "Before the war, the Japanese gardeners would pick up Mexican labor on Third and La Brea every morning as helpers," remembered one Japanese man in 1946, but now "these Mexicans have moved into the neighborhood and continued to do the work that the Japanese used to contract." He confessed that "it hurts" that Mexicans and Blacks held the positions once occupied by Japanese. Similarly nostalgic for prewar economic roles, a man identified in archival records only as "Dr. K." hoped that an imminent depression would allow "the Japanese to gradually take over" because "the Mexicans and Filipinos will not stay when the going gets tough." A former nursery operator expressed less optimism about the ability of Japanese to reclaim the places they filled before the war. A new set of confusing economic interconnections seemed to tie minorities together. While strolling through the market at Ninth Street and San Pedro, the Issei found "most of the names changed to other more Caucasian sounding names plus names such as Gomez, Sung, Lee, etc." and noted how little of the produce was now supplied by Japanese farmers. Convinced that "if it weren't for the evacuation, the Japanese would have made all the money that all the Chinese, Mexicans, and Caucasians made," he also realized the daunting task of regaining these markets from those who "want prices so high that it isn't worth it at half the price."[5]

Eventually, and begrudgingly, minorities made room for the evacuees in their former neighborhoods and economic networks. Japanese bought back or bought new businesses. Yet the pattern of non-White interactions differed from the early 1940s. Issei and Nisei increasingly owned businesses whose customers were African Americans. This community had constituted an important, but much smaller portion, of their clientele before the war when Japanese Americans had largely served European immigrants and coethnics. A Mr. Sugiro's admission after the war that he had "lots of colored trade" and Tom Tiara's, that "I have all negro people living in the hotel," represented the changed situation of many Japanese in Little Tokyo. Another small businessman, who had purchased his drugstore from a Black family, offered a more quantitative analysis of the local economy, explaining that "75% of my business now is with the colored people who are good spenders and they don't quibble so much."[6]

As Japanese Americans reintroduced themselves into the local economy, misunderstandings and anger arose. Other minority businesses resented being displaced. Citing Japanese boycotts and a more generalized campaign "to push the Negro back to Central Avenue and up to Fifth," African Americans watched their establishments go under. Other non-Whites used violence to protect their interests. In Los Angeles Filipinos and Mexicans loathe to surrender lucrative gardening contracts lashed out against their Nisei competitors. Customers and employees had objections of their own. Discourteous treatment and job discrimination at the hands of Japanese Americans frustrated them. According to one disgruntled Black, we are "coldly received as if our trade was not wanted" at Nisei shops. Adding insult to injury, the local Japanese newspaper refused to print his classified advertisement. Making matters even worse, more and more Japanese store owners moved their residences out of the neighborhood. African Americans interpreted this choice, to live in one place and work in another, as disrespectful to, even destructive of, the immediate community.[7]

From the perspective of Japanese owners, however, they were simply pursuing good business practices and taking advantage of new housing options adjacent to downtown. When asked to justify a style of customer service that many non-Japanese deemed unfriendly, they cited cases of criminal activity. Burglaries and muggings that were attributed to young African Americans deepened the Japanese community's suspicions and encouraged defensive measures. Inspired by these concerns, Los Angeles's Japanese American Business Association hired a security detail to patrol the area. Entrepreneurs felt more at ease, but African Americans viewed the measure as a slap in the face.[8]

But compromise and cooperation steadied these mixed postwar neighborhoods. Rather than devolve into places of constant conflict, these districts achieved cordial and workable, if not always friendly, intercultural relations. Despite the surface tensions, many minorities worked for community peace, aware of what they had in common and that they needed to get along within close environs. In doing so, they practiced cooperation and reinforced the ideal of intergroup relations that would facilitate joint civil rights activities.

During the days and weeks immediately following internment's end, influential Blacks and Japanese united in promoting the cause of successful integration. In part they were responding to expectations of racial conflict expressed in the mainstream press. *Ebony* magazine noted "the glum predictions of both social scientists and Hearst headline writers" who "huffed and puffed for a race war" and shrieked about "Japs reinvading Little Tokyo." Ethnic presses were only too happy to counter these reports. The *Pacific Citizen* and *Ebony* described positive interactions between African Americans who were "not scared by skin color [and] felt a strong brother-bond towards discriminated against Japanese" and Nisei who "were glad to share crowded quarters with Negroes." The articles went on to note the absence of violent incidents in

Bronzeville (formerly, Little Tokyo) as well as the opening of interracial, religiously affiliated institutions such as Pilgrim House and the First Street Clinic. Pilgrim House, a medical clinic and source of employment for local Chinese, Mexican, Japanese, Jews, and Anglos, opened in 1943 in a former Buddhist Temple, and at first served the Black community until the return of evacuees prompted a shift in focus. A Nisei sociologist corroborated evidence of interracial peace, insisting that "relations between the Japanese and Negroes were good with small attempts to break the harmony." In discovering and publicizing positive interactions, Blacks and Japanese dismissed or at least downplayed stories of confrontation that could themselves sew discord. As significant, by blaming Whites for inventing or exaggerating interracial animosity, they offered new reasons for collaboration among minorities.[9]

Critical to the rhetoric and reality of interethnic stability were Nisei and Black veterans. Their experiences beyond state borders encouraged a more critical, panethnic view of social conditions. As a group minority soldiers regularly put themselves on the front lines of skirmishes to end restrictions in the postwar period. Their patriotism made them compelling spokesman for reform and unity among minorities and compelled them to become involved. In 1946 Los Angeles's Little Tokyo/Bronzeville section, Japanese-American soldiers formed the Nisei Veterans Association and pledged to extend the fight begun on the battlefields of Europe and Asia to the United States. "Unless we fight for ourselves," they explained in the organization's manifesto, "no one is going to fight for us." Their definition of *us,* however, comprised groups other than Japanese Americans. We will "work with any and all organizations that are working for the welfare of minorities," the manifesto concluded.[10]

Black GIs of the district echoed these inclusive notions of rights and responsibilities. In an interview with the sociologist Tom Sasaki in 1946, a Black soldier expressed his fondness for Japanese Americans and the hope that Black-Japanese amity would prevail in Bronzeville. In a story he related to Sasaki, he communicated how much wartime encounters with Japanese nationals and Nisei troops had shaped his ethnoracial thinking:

> I was in Tokyo last October and I saw the Japanese. They aren't our enemies. The whites hate their guts, but we don't feel that way. We're all colored. Of course we look mighty funny to them because not many of them have seen a colored man. . . . Another time we were looking around for something hard to drink. We had one helluva time. Then some of the Nisei officers said that they would fix us up. They took us to a beer parlor and we had a good time, but it wasn't strong enough.[11]

This moment of cross-cultural camaraderie in Asia convinced the African American GI "that there is no reason in the world why we shouldn't get along" here in Los Angeles. "After the Japanese know what kind of people we are, they like us, they like [our] easy ways and easy money." Another Black veteran whom Sasaki interviewed explained that his empathy for local Japanese Americans drew upon his years in the armed forces. After declaring his opposition to the bombing of Japan and willingness to "go down there and shoot about a hundred of those Whites," the Black veteran endorsed the position of Clayton Russell, the Black pastor of People's Independent Church who stressed helping Japanese get resettled. Without guaranteeing the peaceful coexistence of Blacks and Japanese in the Los Angeles district, the attitudes and statements of Black and Nisei GIs did contribute to that objective.[12]

As time passed, daily struggles for jobs and homes began to chip away at minority resolutions to cooperate, but few abandoned this objective altogether. Los Angeles's Pilgrim House organized a series of meetings to "promote good relations," and local residents attended.[13] One of its most memorable featured an appearance by W. E. B. DuBois and attracted a large crowd of Blacks, Japanese, and Mexicans. DuBois advocated the revival of American democracy through more popular political participation and centrally planned economic production. At this particular gathering he spoke about "getting acquainted" and the problem of minorities' not knowing each other, "except through the hysteria of the majority." The estrangement of non-Whites, he argued, served to fragment the nation and shore up the authority of Whites. Only by "knowing each other" could minorities win back power. In addition to providing a forum for interracial discussion, Pilgrim House educated participants about successful interracial ventures, including the peaceful mixing of Nisei and Black children at its nursery school. San Francisco's Booker T. Washington Community Center (the preinternment site of a Japanese-language school) did the same. Its director gathered Black and Nisei adults for a discussion titled "Test of Democracy" in 1945. Representatives from the NAACP, Japanese American Citizens League (JACL), and Black newspapers spoke about strains and gains in the mixed Western Addition neighborhood. The importance of bridging gaps between non-Whites was a message often communicated as Japanese settled back into their neighborhoods. Reminding returnees that reparations made "at the expense of other minorities" weakened "the whole structure of the democratic plea," the Los Angeles Tribune urged all minorities to "be sympathetic toward one another" and recognize their "interest in justice and the triumph of conscience."[14]

Compromises concerning the fates of neighborhood institutions further underscored a dedication to intercultural peace. At the Buchanan YMCA in San Francisco's Fillmore District, which Japanese Americans had controlled before the war, they initially balked about having to share the facility with the area's new African American residents. At the same time Black newcomers had grown accustomed to monopolizing the YMCA. Yet gradually the organization designed a program of activities, ranging from language classes to bridge games, that brought both racial groups inside and together. A grudging but solid acceptance of the Y as a multicultural space emerged among residents of the Fillmore. Similarly, a conflict about a house of worship ended peacefully in Los Angeles. The space, originally occupied by a Japanese Buddhist Temple, was rented by the Black Providence Baptist Association during internment. When the Baptists attempted to renew the lease, a representative of the temple refused, explaining that he expected the imminent end of evacuation. With the hope of retaining possession of their new home, the Baptists first sued the Buddhists. Yet they quickly and graciously accepted as inevitable the Japanese Americans' return and surrender of the building. Because "the Japanese were a minority people like themselves, they had no wish to deprive them of their own property," one of the association's leaders testified. This respect for the suffering of another minority averted a crisis between the Black Baptists and Japanese Buddhists.[15]

Japanese and Blacks were not the only groups that competed, compromised, and committed to intercultural living just after World War II. In Los Angeles's Watts section local Mexicans tussled with an expanded population of African Americans.[16] In his late 1940s study of the district Eshref Shevky, a sociologist associated with the Haynes Foundation, a social science research organization, discovered that established Mexican Americans often stereotyped Black migrants as rowdy, aggressive, and promiscuous. In other contexts minority veterans frequently promoted interracial work, but in Watts a few Mexican-American veterans publicly vowed "to band together and run the newcomers out of the community." Blacks in turn hypothesized that a Sinarquista organization was actively promoting racism among Mexican inhabitants.[17] At neighborhood-based institutions tempers flared because of the near-exclusion of Blacks from the activities of the Catholic Youth Organization and the proposal by ministers of Mexican descent to divide a prospective summer camp into Black and Mexican branches since "Mexicans and Negroes would be happier by themselves."[18]

Yet beneath these currents of discontent ran a belief in interconnection. Black and Mexican residents alike agreed that the city police and sheriff's departments were openly "antagonistic toward the minority group." As the Zoot Suit Riots had dramatically demonstrated, African and Mexican Americans more often felt the injustices of municipal law enforcement than did Asian Americans or Jews. Thus African and Mexican Americans more regularly, if inconsistently, identified with one another and collaborated as victims of racist authorities. A 1946 editorial in the *Los Angeles Tribune* demanded the appointment of a minority representative to the city's police commission to escape the "scornful, accusing finger of Negro and Mexican communities." Acknowledging that the poverty of both groups made them more vulnerable to police errors, the writer portrayed their predicament as common and undifferentiated by ethnoracial background. A year later an opinion piece in the same newspaper chastised Los Angeles police for targeting neighborhoods "where Negroes and Mexicans would be likely to congregate," and labeled such practices as scapegoating.[19]

The ethnic groups of Watts acted out their shared frustration in spontaneous ways. In 1946 Mexican and Black teenage boys gathered at a local joint called the "Hideout," where they exchanged unfriendly remarks with White teens from neighboring Lynwood. The hostile words escalated into physical violence. Three days of so-called border battles pitted the Lynwood kids against the minority teens of Watts and ended only after a favorite coach intervened. Unfair practices of the Watts Merchant Bank sparked more moderate interethnic action. At a town meeting neighbors swapped tales about discrimination practiced by the establishment. Although minorities constituted the majority of the financial institution's customers, it refused to hire them. Outraged Mexican and Black residents organized a telephone campaign with the intention of changing the bank manager's practices.[20] Much like the Zoot Suit Riots, these incidents displayed how quickly the common experience of disadvantage and integrated living could precipitate pragmatic alliances among Blacks and Mexican Americans.

Minorities negotiated the difficulties of integrated living in other segregated postwar spaces. In the Hollenbeck section of Los Angeles Mexicans had moved into the homes of evacuated Japanese, sharing the neighborhood with Jewish Americans. Initially, the two groups felt more displeasure than pleasure at their proximity. According to another district study conducted by Eshref Shevky, Jewish adults reported significant tensions with Mexicans. In 1945, after being assaulted by a young Mexican teen, a Jewish American businessman called an interethnic meeting to discuss the issues of unruly youths and neighborhood stability. The poor attendance of Mexican-American parents only confirmed Jewish impressions of Mexican indifference and disorderliness. But Jewish prejudices gave Mexicans good reason to stay clear of the meeting. According to field researchers, the exclusion of Mexican-American teens from Jewish-supported community centers and the widely practiced parental policy of prohibiting Jewish children from playing with their Mexican peers fed a distrust and dislike of Jewish neighbors. When one center relaxed its rules and organized a dance of Mexican and Jewish youngsters, its leaders were so disappointed by the results that they quickly reintroduced the restrictions. Mexican youths who attended supposedly drank, talked, and fought too much. At the same time a woman in charge of one of the Brooklyn Avenue playgrounds described the prejudices of Jewish children. They were taught by their mothers to tell Mexican youngsters looking for friendship, "You're dirty, you have a disease. I can't play with you."[21]

Amid all this tension and animosity, the ethnic groups demonstrated an acceptance of their interethnic space and commitment to amicable local relations. Mexican and Jewish businessmen agreed to request more police protection and establish a permanent citizens' committee to discuss the concerns of neighbors. In Hollenbeck's Aliso Village sociologists credited peaceful intercultural relations at the public housing project "in no small part because of the successful management and creation of an elected council of residents who address issues of juvenile delinquency and other conflicts." "There is no real reason why people can't live together," proclaimed one Jewish member. "This is my first experience in living together with people of many national and racial origins. At first I was shocked by all the things I heard and saw. It is much more than just throwing people together. All situations where differences and trouble may begin must be met with intelligence and foresight. The question goes farther than just an intellectual acceptance in principle of the equality of peoples."[22] This practical, experiential understanding of what it took to live amid different minorities informed the hesitant cooperation of Mexican, Jewish, and Black youths of the Aliso Village project. When a Mexican girl and her Black friend had a falling out that brought them to blows, the fight expanded into a massive interracial brawl. Once it was brought under control by law enforcement, community members organized a youth rally at the Soto Center with the hope of building a lasting interracial peace. Hundreds of youths participated. On a panel of Jewish, Black, and Mexican young people—many of whom had actively joined in the fighting—the adolescents preached against interethnic conflict and urged those involved to "forget all about it." A Japanese-American sergeant recently returned from three years' service overseas applied lessons learned in battle to the local situation. He urged teens to choose compromise over the cowardice of conflict. Still another speaker, the sociologist Shevky observed, pointed out "that the majority group likes to see minorities fighting each other and stressed the importance of lifting the level of living until no man needs to go hungry." These events reminded minorities of the space and interests they had in common and how they might comfortably inhabit that common ground.[23]

In these years immediately after World War II, non-Whites faced unemployment, relocation, and displacement. As they struggled to find places for themselves in a society in which discrimination persisted, they periodically ran into and up against one another. Daily struggles to find shelter in constrained multicultural spaces prompted them to work together, often grudgingly. This cooperation, born of necessity and proximity, informed an intercultural and panethnic approach to civil rights in the postwar years.

YOUTHFUL AMBASSADORS OF THE INTERCULTURAL

Youths in these multiethnic spaces joined parents in promoting the possibility of peaceful integrated living and the value of intercultural relations. They elaborated upon those themes of cosmopolitanism that many had articulated in the 1930s and early 1940s. Wartime stresses and the era's rhetoric of freedom and inclusiveness strengthened their attachment to the practice and idea of ethnic crossing. Non-White youngsters tapped into and advanced this discourse about democracy, offering up their own interethnic connections—primarily with one another—as a national model. A vision still inclusive of White ethnics guided their activities and statements, yet cultural borrowings and diverse relations with non-Whites most directly informed and lent credibility to that vision. The youths made sure that cosmopolitanism meant more than Whites' deigning to discover the variety of minority cultures. Frequently, the young people worked through or under the auspices of educational and religious institutions where they had grown up and regularly encountered people of other ethnicities. Personal experiences of intermixing inspired their activism.

Youth instigated and participated in a bevy of new postwar programs designed to build amity among different ethnoracial groups. Six California girls, who identified themselves as "a Negro, Mexican, Chinese, Jew, Protestant, Catholic," embarked on a three-month nationwide speaking tour in 1946. Seeking to "personify an American ideal," these young adults discussed their own cultural similarities and differences with high school students around the country. The young women intended to create better interethnic relations and promote an image of Americans as racial and religious composites. After returning to Pasadena from an internment camp, Esther Nishio also acted as a kind of cultural ambassador. She attended potluck suppers at African-American homes, where she shared her experiences of forced relocation, and she later joined an interracial traveling panel of Latinos, Blacks, and some Caucasians.[24]

Closer to home non-White youth educated themselves and their local communities about the value of tolerance and interethnic camaraderie. As part of a "race relations workshop" a group of diverse young teens from the United Christian Youth Fellowship visited LA's Black and Mexican neighborhoods and Japanese hostels. They also listened to speakers from the NAACP and the city's race commission. Young Nisei from a Palo Alto church quizzed a prominent Chinese minister about his role at the Topaz Relocation Center in Utah before discussing their common interests with Chinese-American Christians. In East Los Angeles youths drawn from "a cross-section of the city's racial and religious groups" formed the Eastside Council for Brotherhood, an organization dedicated to the promotion and appreciation of diverse cultures through discussions, activities, and sports competitions. Other young residents of East LA, representing "20 distinct racial, national or religious groups," tried to spread a cosmopolitan spirit through a musical production with the hopeful title "Harmony in A-Flat." According to observers, the program "brought a significant increase in friendship and understanding among these youth" and proved "to be one of the most effective means of bringing harmony and peace in multicultural neighborhoods in these troubled times."[25]

Discussions at California's mixed, largely non-White high schools further reflected the earnestness with which many adolescents approached ethnoracial peace. They saw themselves as diplomats best positioned to bring about a true democracy. In their newspapers and yearbooks teens emphasized tolerance, even as they recognized that students often strayed from this principle in their daily interactions. Oakland Technical High

School's newspaper, the *Campus Crier,* explained, "Different races are here and will continue to be here for a long time. Intolerance can't change that," however, school "could become a lot nicer place" if "all of us [would] pitch in and do our share," especially by refraining "from any cracks or actions against . . . schoolmates." The paper went on to chastise those students who had burned an African American in effigy, despairing that "if such is the real reflection of their opinion," there was little reason to "speak well of American youth." The notion that this generation had an important role to play in improving race relations surfaced again and again. "This is the land of opportunity and equality where one man has the same chance as another," one teenager proudly wrote but warned, "greatest responsibility falls upon us. We are the ones who will mold our country in the future. And, unless we learn tolerance now, we might lose the right to live as a free people."[26]

Across the San Francisco Bay in the heterogeneous Fillmore District, students at local Girls High made even stronger statements and took more regular action to forward good interethnic relations. Between 1931 and 1946 the school's population and philosophy shifted dramatically. Few faces looking out from the pages of yearbooks in the 1930s belonged to minorities, but by 1946 the student body could claim a remarkable diversity: Chinese, Mexican, Japanese, and African Americans now attended. As the people changed, so did the direction of the institution. Multicultural learning permeated the school. A senior noted that the most important lesson that she and the other graduates had learned was getting along harmoniously and "successfully with other people." "Understanding and cooperating are keynotes and are plainly practiced" here, said another, underscoring just how thoroughly tolerance was woven into the lives of students. At "Intercultural Assemblies" the young women confirmed their dedication to ethnic mixing. Latin dances, Chinese poetry readings, Black spirituals, and discussions of famous minority women both entertained and educated the students. Given the school's general philosophy of inclusiveness, these performances were more than superficial representations of distinct cultures. Instead, they reinforced what the young women took away from their everyday interactions.[27]

These multiethnic schools nurtured more radical demonstrations of intercultural ideals. The planned 1945 visit of the openly anti-Semitic and anti-Black Gerald L. K. Smith galvanized left-leaning and minority communities in Los Angeles. This polarizing figure vowed to return the nation to its Christian foundations, a promise explicitly hostile to other religious traditions. Jews were the first to sound the alarm, but Black organizations and the Black press soon followed. The scathing criticisms and rallies by these minorities did not deter Gerald Smith. In October 1945 he requested and received, despite the complaints of civil rights groups, a permit from the board of education to speak at Polytechnic High School. Fifteen to twenty thousand Angelenos, many of them students, turned out for one of the largest demonstrations in the city's history. Among the youthful activists was Leo Frumkin. Born in 1928 in Boyle Heights to Russian immigrants, he grew up among politically savvy Jewish and Mexican Americans who schooled him in socialist ideas. Although he embraced those beliefs, he described the politics of his youth in a 2001 interview as inspired by "what I saw around me," rather than the writings of Karl Marx or Frederick Engels. Frumkin practiced his principles by organizing the Socialist Youth Club at Polytechnic High School and campaigning against Gerald Smith. Among Frumkin's supporters were African Americans at neighboring Jefferson High School whom he mobilized with an impassioned speech. "If you want to ride in the back of buses like they do in the South, then don't do anything," he shouted from atop the lunchroom table he had turned into a stage, "but if you're opposed to that, then come out with us and protest this guy who wants to put you on the back of buses and is anti-Black." Frumkin's pitch had its desired effect. He and many other students, including Blacks from Jefferson High, marched through East Los Angeles shouting their disapproval and eventually settling outside the offices of the board of education. Later in the week the *Los Angeles Times* reported the growth of a student picket line outside Polytechnic High as more and more youngsters gathered in solidarity. Police arrived and ordered the students to disperse. Most complied peacefully, but some lingered and were arrested or were treated for injuries. The confrontational character of this youthful politics distinguished it from the more indirect expressions of most minority youths, but it had roots in the same multiethnic soil of discontent and desire for change.[28]

Daring experiments in cosmopolitan living highlighted the willingness of youth to comprehend and speak out for one another as well. After answering a classified ad placed in a Nisei newspaper by the *Los Angeles Tribune,* the Black newspaper, Hisaye Yamamoto became an unlikely reporter. She threw herself into LA's African-American community, where she befriended Black youth, attended Black clubs, shopped at Black stores, and wrote a column for the Black newspaper. Certainly, zoot-suiting youths who aggressively engaged with other cultures implicitly

critiqued established ethnoracial lines. But Hisaye's cross-cultural journey was a more intentionally political one. Writing nine months into her
stint at the *Tribune,* she discussed both the gains and the limits of her
multicultural learning. In 1946 she knew "that K. B. Williams is always
a favorite in the annual drag hall at Club Alabam, that when you stay
awhile on the Avenue, you be got by the life." Expressed in the cadence
of local African Americans, Yamamoto's statement displayed her awareness not only of Black speech patterns but also of the rhythms of the
Black social scene. She was privy to information once reserved for cultural insiders. But despite this knowledge, she felt she imperfectly understood the African-American experience. At one time she had read the
work of Richard Wright and judged him too harsh in his views of Blacks,
believing he "was too close for perspective." Now she realized that her
own closeness to the Black community clouded her vision.[29] At the end
of her internship, Yamamoto's intercultural education was incomplete,
but not unlike many other young non-Whites, she had chosen to reach
outward in the postwar era.

These activities and discussions may not have purged California of
discrimination, but youth involvement in and enthusiasm for a multicultural society was important in itself. Drawing from their own experiences, these youngsters could imagine the state as a place of active and
peaceful mixing. This perspective likely influenced their elders and mainstream society to at least revisit their own assumptions. Furthermore, the
thoroughness and longevity of youth's own multiethnic relationships
supported an ideal of intergroup harmony that was rooted as much in
their interactions with other minorities as with Whites.

THE VOGUE OF INTERCULTURAL ORGANIZATION

During, but especially after, World War II civil rights groups made the
interracial relations that were so central to the everyday lives of minority youths and adults central to the structures and strategies of these organizations. Along with newly built organizations designed to be interracial, older ethnic organizations remodeled themselves to accommodate
the concerns of other minorities. And these organizations defined *minorities* more narrowly than they had before the war. An consensus of
sorts emerged that Jews, Asians, Blacks, Mexicans, and Native Americans were troubled and unfairly treated groups but southern or eastern
Europeans were not. Although the activism of political moderates and
progressives was nurtured by the fresh postwar consensus that positive

interracial relations could cure social ills, the social and cultural mixing of the organizations' minority members also played a role.

World War II ushered in a period of civil rights optimism, as Americans shifted their fight for democracy to the home front. Most conceived of the global conflict as a fight against religious and racial intolerance that could strengthen the nation's foundation. In emphasizing values of equality, the government inadvertently made injustices suffered by minorities more visible and encouraged postwar efforts of reform and redress. A multitude of new and established civil rights organizations seized the moment to demand change. Most of these referenced wartime goals and the disenchantment of minorities to justify their endeavors. "The apparent impatience of minority groups to achieve these ends has been sharpened by the war," observed leaders of the Urban League, "when, in the face of repeated affirmations of our democratic form of life, freedom and equality for all, and other clichés, there were increased and widespread evidences of discrimination." As an expanding group of historical works has documented, these groups also took advantage of international politics to advance domestic causes. Examples include the mid-1940s efforts of Black groups, including the more conservative NAACP, to link the liberation of African peoples to the struggles of African Americans. Leaders demanded that the U.S. government oppose colonialism along with Jim Crow. In 1945, before a scheduled conference of the United Nations in San Francisco, the city's Civic Unity League urged the governor to be on guard against acts of racial intolerance because "how we here in San Francisco and our neighbors in outlying counties conduct ourselves toward yellow men and Black men will be news to more than a billion colored men from other parts of the world." The league's ability to make such arguments underscored how amenable to civil rights the political climate had become.[30]

This enlivened civil rights movement embraced interculturalism as the best strategy for achieving social change. Certainly, Californians had practiced interracial cooperation in the past, but this approach achieved much greater acceptance in the postwar period. Harvard Sitkoff has characterized the interracial orientation as a sudden, almost faddish, effort of liberal groups to solve the nation's racial problems at midcentury. Government officials proved as eager as private individuals to sponsor interracial organizations. By the close of 1943, Sitkoff noted, more than one hundred state, local, and national commissions dedicated to improving race relations had appeared. Among the newcomers in California were branches of the Chicago-based American Council for Race

Relations, the Bay Area Council Against Discrimination, the Los Angeles County Committee for Interracial Progress, Commission on Interracial Progress (later renamed Committee on Human Relations), and California Federation for Civic Unity. Despite subtle differences in structure
and memberships, these boards, birthed between 1943 and 1944, similarly advocated an "integrated, mixed race approach" to build "better
understanding between the races." Emphasizing the distinctiveness of
California as what the executive director of the California Federation of
Civic Unity called "the most multiracial state in the union," they aspired
to "establish out here the most advanced democracy in the world."[31]

Officials hoped that they could stave off racial conflict by creating a
forum in which minorities joined Whites in a discussion of current social
problems. Serving as representatives on the Human Relations Committee of Los Angeles, for example, were Manuel Ruiz, a Mexican American; the Reverend Clayton Powell, an African American, and Rabbi
Edgar Magnin. It is important to note that this commission and others
defined race and interracial problems in ways that confirmed the consolidation and commonality of most European ethnics. In a statement of
its mission the LA committee dedicated itself to promoting racial unity
within the city by focusing upon problems among "Negroes, Japanese,
Mexicans, Filipinos, and Chinese. . . . We shall not at present concern
ourselves with the Europeans." This selection of groups worthy of as-
sistance, sometimes modified to include Jews, was the standard of the
time.[32]

Despite the elite, mostly White, founders and top-down perspective of
such organizations, non-Whites recognized their potential and selectively
supported the government-appointed commissions. The NAACP, National Negro Congress, and Japanese American Citizens League backed
voter registration drives in minority neighborhoods and political campaigns for like-minded candidates. Along with the League of United
Latin American Citizens and the American Jewish Committee, they
spoke about the problems of their respective ethnic groups to commission members eager to listen. Ethnic newspapers, including the *Chinese
Press,* endorsed the multiracial activities of the Civic Unity Council, encouraging "Chinese Americans interested in the welfare of minority
groups" to get involved.[33]

Minorities hesitantly signed up with less moderate organizations, ,
even the Communist Party, that were marching to the interracial beat of
mid-1940s California. As part of its larger class struggle, the party championed the rights of minorities, becoming a dominant voice in campaigns

about housing, employment, and police protection. According to the historian Mark Wild, as early as the 1930s the Communist Party attracted diverse residents of the central districts of Los Angeles with its inclusive and street-based message. Its emotional rhetoric and radical ideas were particularly persuasive in a time of economic depression. The party shifted the emphasis of its organization away from the streets and toward factory floors by 1935—a move that undercut the possibility of a broad-based, neighborhood coalition sympathetic to communist ideals—and was weakened nationally by the fragmentation of the popular front. However, by the mid-1940s the party had begun to rebound. It played a prominent role in the organization of the Sleepy Lagoon Defense Committee and the education of Californians about racism against Mexican Americans. By the end of the war the party had reconstituted itself, becoming a more influential voice for change. As the decade wore on and anticommunist sentiments intensified, minorities grew more wary of associations with the Communist Party. However, between 1944 and 1945 the party was vital, and Los Angeles—responsible for 10 percent of the party's national membership by 1949—was central to its vitality. Jews and Blacks in particular embraced its message of racial equality. Although detractors portrayed the Communist Party's interest in minorities as self-serving, minority members and sympathizers disagreed. African Americans in Los Angeles found little appeal in the organization's abstract critique of global capitalism but plenty to like in its direct action campaigns against local incidents of discrimination. In East Los Angeles a sizable number of Jews associated with communists, while three hundred to four hundred Mexicans became party members in the early 1940s.[34]

Whether sponsored by independent political leftists or moderate government officials, interracial coalitions received the support of minorities, even at the expense of the autonomy and localism enjoyed by single ethnic organizations—a signal that they deeply valued intercultural work. This turn toward interculturalism inspired active coordination across minority organizations as much as support for White-instigated or -dominated ones. These groups shared not only an ideal of ethnoracial equality but also specific interests. This commonality invested allegiances between minorities with a concreteness and stability most likely absent from loyalties forged with Whites on more abstract, purely ideological, grounds. Minorities were guided by a history of neighborhood mixing and discrimination. A 1947 conversation between Hisaye Yamamoto and Fred Fertig across the pages of the *Los Angeles Tribune* spoke to the special chemistry that bonded non-Whites. "Will every Negro or every minority deny to the White his best intentions and expect the worst? . . . Can Hisaye or you or I do nothing to change the bias of Whites and the counterbias of minorities?" moaned Fertig. Yamamoto's decisive response to the Fertig, who was White, was, "I don't think I have ever had to struggle to clear my mind and heart of the anti-Negro obsession," which dismissed the possibility of effective White-minority coalitions and unbiased White liberalism. Many non-Whites in the period agreed that liaisons among them made sense. They viewed collective activity as an honest and strategically powerful expression of shared interests, even as they struggled with the difficult details of collaboration.[35]

With the hope of giving minorities a stronger voice in the political process and healing racial tensions following the race riots of 1943, Los Angeles officials formed almost 170 Unity Leagues. The ethnic sensitivities expressed by minority members of s the Unity Leagues and of the Human Relations Committee demonstrated how this postwar proclivity to work together was maintained amid ethnoracial differences. As the historian Mark Brilliant has reported, cooperation among minority participants happened slowly and uncertainly. Small differences of opinion that members of more homogeneous organizations easily negotiated became more enduring points of controversy. Fred Ross, a lead organizer, recalled one meeting at which Mexican Americans became "frantically fidgety at times over the long-windedness and repetition on the part of the two Negro members." While Blacks and Japanese Americans complained about the "organizational naivete" of Mexicans Americans, Blacks and Mexicans grew frustrated at "periodical memory lapses of some of the Nisei during discussions of minority-wide discrimination." Such disagreements and misperceptions, Ross explained, mandated post-meeting conversations "to smooth things over." Despite the aches and pains of interethnic organization, though, minorities continued to see it as a viable means of achieving change.[36]

Minority members of the Human Relations Committee wrestled with distinctions and decided upon commonalities, too. On September 11, 1944, a Mr. Torrez of the Mexican Chamber of Commerce and Mexican Affairs Coordinating Committee asked the group to classify Mexicans as a nationality, not a race. He acknowledged that "the American citizen of Mexican background is justly proud of his heritage" but believed social and economic background, not race, should be the basis from which Mexicans attempted fuller adjustment and integration in American society. Although this reluctance to identify as something other than White set conditions on alliances with minorities—a consistent theme in the civil rights approach of many middle-class, fairer-skinned Mexicans—it did not prohibit these connections altogether. Even moderate activists like Torrez still sought out the benefits of an organization that linked the misfortunes of Blacks, Mexicans, and Asians in California. Three years later, when asked at a Human Relations Committee meeting to describe the contributions another minority group had made to American culture, representatives of the JACL, *Los Angeles Sentinel,* and Jewish Labor Committee responded with thoughtfulness and empathy. Frank Chuman, president of the city's JACL chapter, stressed the "Americanness" of Blacks who "stood in a different situation from the Jewish, Mexican, and Japanese American." He continued: "It is our responsibility as Americans to work for and with them to see that they attain their full rights as citizens and that the bitter rancor and discrimination against them is eliminated." In response Le Roy S. Hard, editor of the *Los Angeles Sentinel,* depicted Japanese Americans as "the highest type of American citizen." He countered criticism that Japanese cloistered themselves in "Little Tokyos" in the United States by explaining their isolation as a condition "forced upon them as the result of the American social conditions and laws of the general American public. This same American racial policy is still forcing the American Negro into ghettos." The practice, Hard explained, "retards the contributions this largest minority can take to the general culture of the nation by developing their own latent potentialities." He complimented Japanese Americans as "tolerant of other racial minorities" and believed any antipathy they felt toward "Nordic Americans" was well deserved. For Hard and so many minorities who cooperated politically in the postwar era, "minorities, themselves, are tiring of our government making a mockery of our much-wanted 'democratic way of life' and being laughed at by other nations of the world." Deliberately omitted from the program of poignant presentations were discussions of the troubles and interests of Polish or Italian or even Catholic Californians. By the calculations of those most active in the state's postwar civil rights movements, these groups did not belong within the ranks of minorities.[37]

Putting this perspective into practice, the JACL, NAACP, Chinese American Citizens' Alliance, Community Services Organization, American Jewish Congress, and American Jewish Committee all increased their activism and cooperative endeavors after the war. In doing so, they drifted from their more ethnically particular foundations. Many of these groups were originally conceived as advocates for specific minority communities. For example, in its bylaws the Chinese American Citizens' Alliance limited its membership to men of Chinese descent and committed itself to advancing the interests of Chinese Americans. An editorialist's critique of the alliance's reluctance to cooperate with non-Chinese as late as 1950 testified to the strength of barriers between minorities. Although perhaps more adamant and long lasting, the Chinese alliance's ingroup preferences were not unique.[38]

Wariness about a political strategy that required crossing cultural lines also shaped the decisions of other ethnic organizations. In its beginning stages the JACL had focused primarily upon planning social activities for Japanese immigrants and their children. This ethnocentric intent was reinforced at the annual conference in 1929. There, two Chinese Americans spoke about the many commonalities of Chinese and Japanese. They encouraged a Sino-Japanese friendship in the United States and abroad to ensure world peace and domestic harmony. Despite their eloquent appeal for tighter relations between the ethnic communities, the Japanese audience responded unenthusiastically.[39]

Minority organizations did not discount opportunities to affiliate with politically progressive Whites, but an acceptance of an intercultural ideal did draw them into new alliances with one another. The JACL perhaps made the clearest, most explicit turn toward intercultural coordination. By 1947, following the political rise to leadership of a second generation, the JACL had become a more inclusive, collaborative organization and would remain so into the next decade. In 1944 the organization expanded its membership criteria so that Americans of any ethnicity could join. The following year Saburo Kido of the JACL negotiated with leaders of the African-American migrants who had settled in former Japanese neighborhoods to ensure the peaceful reentry of the evacuees.[40]

The JACL boasted of its success and gained confidence in its multiethnic approach as the 1940s advanced. "This incidence of intergroup cooperation stands as a classic example of what can be done when the proper public relations program is instituted," one official insisted. In 1946 the JACL's president acknowledged the debt that Japanese Americans owed to other minorities "in view of their splendid support and effort during the years" and promised "to recognize that the problems of other minorities are also our problems." Four years later at the annual conference one member's proposal to dissolve ethnically singular civil rights campaigns showed just how far the thinking of some of the organization's members had come.[41]

Groups representing other minorities made a similar postwar turn toward interethnic activity. Filipinos, who had primarily expressed their
frustration with the status quo through labor collectives, established
groups such as the Filipino American Citizens League and the Filipino
Inter-Community Council that more broadly dedicated themselves to
civil rights and minority outreach.[42] Concurrently, the NAACP, especially its western chapters, expanded dramatically in membership and
visibility in the second half of the 1940s. Although interracial at its 1909
inception—bringing together Black and White intellectuals worried
about race relations generally and the position of Black Americans
specifically—the NAACP diversified its membership rolls and causes by
midcentury. In California in 1946 Los Angeles counted 14,012 members;
San Francisco, 2,911; and Oakland, 3,000. The Los Angeles Urban
League, originally conceived to advance the interests of African Americans, broadened its focus. In a 1940 report its director, Floyd Covington, acknowledged that "the problems affecting Mexican, Oriental, Filipino, and Negro populations" were not always identical but in most
instances were parallel. These problems had gotten worse, he noted, and
were so bad that he believed California was well on its way to "reliving
almost identically the same experiences that imprinted themselves upon
the historical South during the slave period." This alarming comparison
conveyed the league's intention to aggressively champion the concerns of
minorities.[43]

Mexican-American political groups gained size and energy and
crossed cultural lines after World War II. Founded in 1947 with the help
of the practiced organizers Saul Alinsky and Fred Ross, as well as the
Jewish community of Los Angeles, the Community Services Organization grounded its activity in the barrio of East Los Angeles. Reflecting its
grassroots orientation and the participation of men like Daniel Luevano,
the civil rights activist and politician, the organization focused on narrower, neighborhood-specific issues such as the absence of streetlights,
poor drainage, and infrequent garbage collection. Later it organized
voter registration drives and fought discrimination in education and
housing. Often misrepresented as a Mexican-American organization, the
Community Services Organization actually attended to the problems of
and worked with African, Jewish, and Asian Americans.[44]

Like other ethnic organizations, Jewish agencies made alliances with
other minorities after World War II. In the early twentieth century
groups such as the American Jewish Congress, American Jewish Committee, and the Community Relations Committee maintained relatively

low profiles for fear of provoking anti-Semitism. They primarily relied upon education programs and public relations techniques to change American attitudes about Jews. However, World War II broadened their approach to civil rights. Jews' heightened sense of insecurity in a world where anti-Semitism was ascendant helped them appreciate the connections they shared with other American minorities. Seeing White racism, anti-Jewish sentiment, and other forms of bigotry as parts of the same whole, the American Jewish Committee, American Jewish Congress, and Community Relations Committee adopted a more aggressive posture on civil rights issues, taking to the courts to challenge discriminatory practices. After World War II pragmatism as much as ideology pushed Jews toward universalism. Fears that demands for reform couched in ethnically particular terms would be dismissed as divisive encouraged this more multiethnic and universalistic orientation. With greater regularity Jewish groups filed amicus briefs and sued to challenge discrimination in housing, education, and employment. In 1947 the American Jewish Committee convened Mexican, Black, and Jewish leaders to discuss "a permanent liaison among minority groups." Attendees praised the group for its attention to "restrictive covenants, segregation, and discrimination." As the historian Shana Bernstein has noted, the Community Relations Committee made interracial work a priority, becoming the first Los Angeles Jewish agency dedicated almost entirely to bridging the gaps among ethnoracial communities. The group worked with the Community Services Organization, for example, reaching out to residents of the poorer East Los Angeles and concluding that Jews, Mexicans, and other minorities had much in common despite class- and color-based tensions. Once social service agencies for the Jewish community, these ethnic organizations became leading forces for the civil rights of Jews and other minorities.[45]

The trajectory of the Chinese American Citizens' Alliance may best represent exactly how multicultural the civil rights of minority groups had become by 1945. Ironically, although it remained one of the most self-contained, ethnically particular agencies in its philosophy and membership, it regularly found itself working alongside other ethnic organizations. Non-White interests had become so intertwined that addressing issues important to Chinese Americans necessarily brought the group face to face with forces such as the NAACP. Sustained interracial living, poverty, and the remembered violence of the Zoot Suit Riots focused various ethnic communities on the common goals of peace and relief.

Civil rights organizations favored ethnic crossing as a political strategy in large part because their members reported such positive social experiences with other minorities. Members had faith in the power of mixing because they had successfully shared military battlefields, neighborhoods, workplaces, and schools with other non-Whites. This intimacy made them appreciate cultural differences as well as common interests. Rather than being strange or awkward, then, joining forces with other non-Whites to achieve reform seemed a natural extension of their everyday lives. Vangie Buell chose to do more than regret the racial discrimination she observed in her diverse neighborhood; she challenged it as a member of the NAACP. As a devotee of Black music and friend of many African Americans', the Filipina felt a deep sense of connection with West Oakland Blacks. This empathy and familiarity were the basis of her decision to join a predominantly Black civil rights group. Similarly, Danny Kim, a Chinese American, became an NAACP member out of affection for Black music and clubs of San Francisco. Perhaps because he had spent so many evenings as one of the few non-Blacks at local jazz joints, Kim felt at ease as the sole Chinese American of his Northern California chapter. He embraced the group's political programs and complimented it for leading Chinese and other minorities toward equality.[46]

Asian Americans were not the only non-Whites whose social and cultural mixing made them advocates of interethnic political activity. A Mexican American identified by a reporter only as "Mrs. Maldonado" of Riverside knew little about the NAACP and its civil rights program until she battled alongside Black parents to desegregate the local school system. As I explain later in this chapter, this collaboration brought both political results and drew once-estranged Blacks and Mexicans closer within the community. Most likely, Maldonado learned about the NAACP from some of her new African-American friends. Thus, when local officials refused to address her complaints, she called upon the organization. Pleased by its representation of her interests, Maldonado urged other Mexican Americans to join and became an unofficial spokesperson for the virtues of interethnic politics. Even Tarea Hall Pittman, an African-American woman raised in the San Joaquin Valley who became the first director of the NAACP's West Coast regional office, credited her membership to multicultural rather than Black sensibilities. The haunting memory that her mother had shared, of Mexican bodies twisting from the tree branches where they had been hung by Whites in Bakersfield, informed the political activism of Pittman's adult years.[47]

Multicultural environments informed the thinking of other civil rights activists. An early comfort with cross-ethnic relations surely grounded the politics of Daniel Luevano. Born and raised in a West Los Angeles neighborhood where few Mexicans resided, Luevano, who would become a major supporter of the Community Services Organization, learned about other cultures and peoples at school and work. He built solid friendships with the half-dozen Nisei at his high school and later credited this closeness for his positive ideas about Japanese Americans. Luevano also was employed at a Japanese-owned hardware store in Little Tokyo, following in the footsteps of his father. It seems probable that these casual but meaningful early relations contributed to the man's later dedication to a broad civil rights program, one that encompassed Japanese Americans. Although he chastised himself for his early silence regarding internment, he was openly expressing his outrage as early as 1944.[48]

Like Luevano, Bert Corona was steered toward minority-centered politics by his formative experiences on military bases and neighborhoods streets. After leaving his home state of Texas to attend the University of Southern California, Corona spent years in Boyle Heights, easily mixing with Blacks, Mexicans, and Jews. During his service in the U.S. military the discrimination he witnessed against Jews and Mexicans reinforced his broad understanding of injustice and his determination to reform society. In his postwar political career Corona chose to associate with those who shared his intercultural ideals. Recalling that period, he explained his openness to other peoples as typical of those in the "labor and radical circles," where "racism or ethnic conflict was not a part, or at least not a significant part, of those interactions." Corona's experiences highlight the way in which political mixing fostered social closeness. After a few African Americans gained leadership positions in local unions, Luevano threw a party both "for strategy sessions and for socializing" and ignored the racist complaints of his landlord, who feared integration of the neighborhood. "Many of our Black friends" attended, Corona reported.[49]

While minorities expressed their panethnic interests through civil rights organizations, they also sought representation through electoral politics. Candidates they could agree upon had firsthand knowledge of the dynamics of multiethnic neighborhoods. The career of Edward Roybal perhaps best illustrates the nexus of interethnic social and political relations. Born in Albuquerque in 1912, Roybal and his family moved to Boyle Heights eight years later. There, he grew up among a rich collection of minorities: Jews, Mexicans, Japanese, and Blacks. As a young man he served in World War II, returning like many of his generation with a sharpened awareness of injustice in California. His growing desire for change only intensified during a postwar stint with the California Tuberculosis Association. In his capacity as inspector he visited the state's poorest, typically minority, communities and learned their complaints.[50]

Given this background, running for office on a multicultural platform designed to capture the attention of the diverse groups of Los Angeles appeared a logical next step to Roybal. He successfully gained the votes of African, Asian, and Jewish Americans as well as those of his own ethnic community, winning the right to represent the Ninth District on the city council. Beatrice Griffith, a contemporary sociologist, noted that "various nationality groups combined their forces to work unanimously for a councilman election." Ethnic newspapers praised Roybal in their pages, while important Black leaders such as Gus Hawkins, the state assemblyman, endorsed him. Joe Kovner, editor of the Jewish newspaper the *Sun,* explained why local Jews backed this Catholic, Mexican-American candidate. "Eddie was the best man," he said. "What's good for Boyle Heights is good for the Jews. . . . We keep pounding away on the theme of sticking together. An injury to one is an injury to all."[51]

Japanese Americans of Boyle Heights climbed onto Roybal's multiethnic bandwagon more slowly but with eventual confidence. Prominent Nisei such as Art Takei had initially fronted a coethnic candidate for a seat on the city council. When they realized the individual lacked the stamina to continue with "the rough and tumble campaigning," they decided to support Roybal. Takei downplayed the tension between the Mexican and Japanese communities generated during the brief period when both had candidates in the local race. Instead, he stressed the way in which Mexicans and Nisei came together against Roybal's more conservative rival. Like Roybal, Takei had grown up mingling with cultural outsiders in Boyle Heights. These connections likely conditioned his acceptance of a mixed politics, too. At a critical juncture in the campaign Takei chose to cross ethnic lines and endorse Roybal rather than preserve borders and insist that a Japanese American pursue the council seat.[52]

Remaining true to the interests of his varied constituents once he was elected, Roybal demonstrated the potential of multicultural politics. He helped introduce legislation that mandated new hiring practices in local companies, demanded an improvement in city services for minority neighborhoods, and challenged restrictive housing covenants. More

indirectly, Roybal countered prejudice by offering an example of the political heights to which minorities could rise. Leaders of the African-
American community took heart from Roybal's success, concluding
that his "victory proves that the growing demand for election of a
Negro Congressman can succeed next year." In the years that followed,
minorities—among them, Frank Mankiewicz and Richard Ibanez—
gained office throughout the state by imitating Roybal's interethnic political style.[53]

The intercultural intimacies and ideals of minorities became more
than customs of their multiethnic neighborhoods. In the postwar period
Californians hurried to realize domestically the democratic promises that
the nation made internationally. To do so they created new and endorsed
old organizations dedicated to peaceful race relations. Minorities took
advantage of these groups and the energy directed at minority problems.
Concerns about discrimination that they shared in close spaces now had
a broader audience and stronger institutional support. Panethnic connections rooted in everyday encounters flowered into the politics of collective action.

EVERYDAY POLITICS WRIT LARGE

The multiethnic ethos, institutions, and personal experiences of minorities underwrote their postwar campaigns to correct injustices. They selectively collaborated around issues that bore the imprint of local concerns and relationships: housing, education, marriage, and citizenship.[54]
Even as their combined efforts exposed or opened up fissures among
them, they also realized the power of their marriages of circumstance.
Thanks in large part to their collaborations, much of the legal apparatus
supporting discrimination in California was undone: antimiscegenation
statutes, school segregation, restrictive housing covenants, and limits on
citizenship.

Acutely aware of how restrictive covenants and discriminatory real estate practices made a difficult postwar housing market even worse, minorities began their first organized challenges. As when pursuing other
causes, they carefully delineated which groups suffered from housing
discrimination and which did not, acknowledging the appearance of a
clearer, postwar color line between Whites and minorities. In reporting
the creation of a local group dedicated to "put[ting] an end to restrictive
covenants," the California Eagle listed only "the Negro, Japanese, Chinese, Korean, Mexican, and Jewish" as interested and invested parties.

Among those who joined the fight were veterans who focused upon a variety of civil rights abuses but were particularly distressed by and determined to fight unfair housing practices. Certainly, some men lent their patriotism to ethnically specific efforts. Anthony Perez reiterated the hesitancy of Mexican Americans contemplating alliances with other minorities when he urged Councilman Edward Roybal to expand housing opportunities because "we must learn to live with our non-Latin fellowmen. As members of the White race there are many of us who would make fine neighbors." However, many others also championed the right of all minorities to live where they pleased. "You know as we know that minority groups have already earned the rights to live like the next fellows in this democratic nation during the last war," a veteran, J. Chinn, wrote Governor Earl Warren in 1947. "The Caucasian must have imagination to realize how hurt the non-Caucasian veterans feel about racial intolerance when they fought against the same thing overseas, returning home with the same problems staring at them wherever they go to seek the right to live freedom from this and that." These men's individual misfortunes in the housing market offered other Asian, Mexican, and Black Angelenos the chance to vent their long-simmering frustrations about spatial segregation.[55]

Tom Amer and Yin Kim, Asian-American veterans, also stated their claim in ways that implied racial inclusiveness, not exclusiveness. Minority Americans rallied around and publicized the trouble that these men had finding housing in Southern California. Ethnic newspapers, including the *Philippines Mail, California Eagle, Pacific Citizen,* and *Los Angeles Sentinel,* publicized their support for the veterans. The *Pacific Citizen* called the "prohibition on occupancy" a "viciously undemocratic practice" that hurt not only Amer and Kim but also "all Americans who are not of Caucasian ancestry." The paper reported that Japanese Americans, especially GIs, eagerly awaited the case's outcome. It is notable that the minority press couched its critique in language that suggested the linked fortunes of non-Whites. Similarly, the left-leaning African-American newspaper the *Los Angeles Sentinel* endorsed the veterans' efforts, praising their postwar courage: "Amer is not afraid of a fight. He proved this in the three and half years he volunteered. . . . And he is prepared to fight for his rights here in Los Angeles." Across the street from Amer's home, the *Sentinel* noted, a Black family awoke to find a cross burning upon the lawn. Amer, however, remained steadfast in his fight. This account cast the Chinese American not as an ethnically specific hero but one furthering, and worthy of representing, the interests of the Black community.[56]

Civil rights organizations threw their support behind these and other minorities kept out of neighborhoods to which they wished to move and succeeded in overturning housing restrictions. Along with community newspapers, the JACL, American Civil Liberties Union, and NAACP joined forces in their defense of Amer and Kim. The JACL explained its participation as consistent with efforts to address "the issues [that] arise merely because such persons were born or not born of a particular race." When Whites opposing the integration of their Redwood City neighborhood burned the home of an African-American veteran in 1946, Jewish and Black groups condemned the violence. A year later the JACL, NAACP, and American Jewish Congress all filed suit against the City of Pasadena on behalf of Ernest Chamberlain and his wife, who had been denied housing because of their race. The Los Angeles chapter of the NAACP was particularly tireless in its legal challenges, filing more suits to overturn legal covenants than any other organization in the nation between 1945 and 1948. Indeed, two defendants with NAACP backing saw their cases make it all the way to the U.S. Supreme Court in 1948. The JACL had championed a sizable number of suits too and filed an amicus brief in the NAACP case eventually selected for review. In its momentous decision in *Shelley v. Kraemer* the Court ruled against the enforcement of those covenants. In the follow-up case of 1953, *Barrows v. Jackson,* the Court declared the covenants themselves unconstitutional. The end of covenants did not cleanse the housing market of discrimination. Whites reluctant to integrate their neighborhoods used financial and social pressure, harassment, and sympathetic Realtors to limit the consequences of *Shelley*. But the decision at least gave minorities opportunities to push the spatial boundaries, in California and across the country.[57]

Concerns about school segregation and the narrowed opportunities it offered their children brought minorities together in strategic coalition. The issue, and the campaigns they mounted to address it, underscored their years of mingling and interethnic familiarity. Although Jewish Americans typically attended integrated schools, African-American, Mexican-American, and in some places even Asian-American students learned in segregated environments. In part, the composition of schools simply reflected the character of neighborhoods. But more direct forces of discrimination shaped education and frustrated minority elders. Frequently, school districts drew their boundaries and distributed their resources in ways designed to benefit White pupils and hinder minorities.

Mexican and African Americans in Riverside's rural Bell Town allied to challenge school segregation and in doing so made social and cultural crossing a more integral and regular part of the town's relations. Black migrants had joined the predominantly White and Mexican community of the farm region in the 1930s. Although their entry initially troubled Mexican adults, who competed with the newcomers for agricultural jobs and housing, Black and Mexican children mingled easily at the town's "colored" school. While these non-White children attended an aging, four-room, wooden schoolhouse in Bell Town, a few miles away White children of the community enjoyed the modern structure, impressive facilities, and strong faculty of the West Riverside School.[58]

When Mexican- and African-American parents learned that bond money approved during the recent election would be spent exclusively on White schools, they overcame earlier differences and joined together in protest. With the help of the American Council on Race Relations these two groups created interracial committees and voted into office a multiethnic leadership. Observers reported that though this "was the first instance of joint action of any kind involving both Negro and Mexican-American residents of Bell Town . . . without exception Mexican-American officers were nominated by Negroes, and Negro officers by Mexican Americans." The parents sent representatives to Los Angeles to register a legal complaint against the West Riverside School board and the county superintendent of schools, charging them with violating the California State School Code and the Fourteenth Amendment.[59]

A shared frustration with the status quo not only brought two ethnic groups together in unprecedented collaboration but also altered their perceptions of and long-term interactions with one another. One Mexican parent acknowledged that her work with Blacks had made her realize "that the only way one group of us will ever get any place is to join with all the other groups that get stepped on, and work it out together." This faith in intercultural cooperation as a political strategy best suited to challenge White power knit together the everyday lives of Bell Town's Blacks and Mexicans. Although their children had fraternized regularly, the parents rarely mingled, regarding one another with suspicion and mistrust. However, after banding together to fight school segregation, the dynamic changed. Mexican and African Americans met for community-wide picnics and pie suppers whose proceeds underwrote their protests. For the first time Black families began to attend Sunday afternoon gatherings at the invitation of their Mexican neighbors. Home visits between members of the two groups, initially motivated by political concerns, evolved into more social calls. Mrs. Maldonado's insistence that "with all this new business here in Bell Town and the new friends we are making with the Negro people, my whole life is changed," spoke to the social transition brought about by collective political activity. What happened in this community may not have been widespread in California, but it revealed the opportunity for greater social interaction presented by intercultural organization. Political and social dimensions of interethnic relations were reinforcing.[60]

A sense of connection and mutual responsibility among non-Whites was behind a more expansive effort to end school segregation. In 1945 Mexican-American parents filed a class action suit, *Gonzalo Méndez v. Westminster School District of Orange County,* on behalf of their children who attended segregated schools in the El Modena, Garden Grove, Westminster, and Santa Ana districts of Orange County. They charged administrators with violating their children's Fifth and Fourteenth Amendment rights. Stark segregation shaped the community's educational system; White children attended Lincoln High School, while minorities enrolled at Roosevelt. Though the institutions stood a mere one hundred yards apart, they differed dramatically in quality. Lincoln students faced ill-prepared teachers, outdated materials, and a curriculum heavy with vocational courses. No wonder fathers like Lorenzo Ramirez asked to transfer his sons to Roosevelt. However, the principals of both institutions refused Ramirez's request, prompting the disgruntled parent to take legal action. Explaining his participation in the class action suit, Ramirez argued that he was defending the rights of minorities broadly, not merely those of Mexican Americans. "The days will come when the Japanese, Filipinos, and Negroes [will] be together again," he insisted. This father's words suggested not only an awareness of, but also a willingness to, publicly articulate the links between minority experiences.[61]

Minority civil rights groups echoed this conviction as they assigned their lawyers and publicists to the case. The JACL, NAACP, and American Jewish Congress all filed amicus briefs, claiming school segregation as more than a "Mexican" issue. The emphases of their arguments differed. The NAACP made racial discrimination the central concern in its brief. It pointed out that segregated schools violated the guarantees of equal protection before the law and expressed its hope that *Méndez v. Westminster* would bring "the American courts closer to a decision on the whole question of segregation" and liberate not only "one particular minority" but also "any group subjected to the practices of racial segregation—be that group Negro, Mexican, Latin American, or Japanese in its origins." In its brief the American Jewish Congress was similarly inclusive of non-Whites. It defined Jewish interests as "inseparable from those of injustices" and declared that those interests were threatened whenever "persecution, discrimination, or humiliation is inflicted upon any human being because of his race, creed, color, language or ancestry." The JACL's brief emphasized that the preeminent legal issue was arbitrary discrimination due to ancestry or national origin rather than race. Mexican Americans tended to dismiss the relevance of racial difference altogether for fear of losing their current classification as White. Despite these variations Mexicans Americans still welcomed the support of other groups, and all parties contested the fairness of the educational system. By endorsing the challenges of Mexican-American parents in Orange County, the American Jewish Congress, NAACP, and JACL articulated their understanding that minority issues were interdependent. They also helped guarantee that the decision of the U.S. District Court would be upheld on appeal, overturning segregation.[62] A collective minority assault had ended in victory.

Personal experiences of mingling sparked collaborative efforts by minorities to free themselves from still another form of discrimination: marital restrictions. As I argued in chapter 4, internment pressed minority couples and their children to defend alternative forms of family. Their defenses led to greater acceptance of mixture in the postwar period. In addition, the return of African-American soldiers with Asian war brides, and more numerous cases of interethnic adoption, dampened resistance to those who loved outside their own cultural group. In the years immediately following World War II, sociologists, as well as the ethnic and mainstream presses, noted a new social phenomenon: a considerable increase in mixed marriages. They were referring to the hundreds of minority servicemen who brought brides, many of them from Asia, home to the United States. Mixed-race clubs like Los Angeles's Club Miscegenation sprouted up in the period to accommodate these unusual couples. Marriages to ethnic insiders remained the preferred and commonplace arrangement through the late 1940s, but this standard began to weaken. This gradual but definitive shift in social practice and attitudes grounded political action.[63]

These newlyweds confronted significant barriers as they settled into postwar neighborhoods. Often ostracized by Whites and non-Whites alike, they socialized together while struggling to establish wider circles of acquaintances. In a study of Black-Japanese spouses settled in Indianapolis, sociologists observed relationships and community dynamics that most likely characterized the California scene as well. Japanese war brides received chilly welcomes from established Blacks and Japanese of the city who resented them. Different understandings of appropriate marital relations in part fed the bad feelings. According to the researchers, Black women criticized the way Japanese women spoiled their men, and envied the kind treatment the foreign brides received. However, the stresses of adjustment for these wartime lovers went beyond community disapproval. Following his tour of duty a Mr. Reyes of Mexican descent brought his Japanese wife home to San Francisco, only to suffer humiliation and the collapse of their relationship. Allegedly, his wife became sexually promiscuous with several men, including the local grocer and a neighbor who was teaching her how to drive. The dissolution of the marriage demonstrated the cultural strains inherent in the peacetime setting. The early bloom of romance faded as couples of strikingly different backgrounds faced the real, severe strains of everyday life in California.[64]

Despite these tensions many Japanese women made successful matches and gained gradual acceptance by minority communities. Through common attendance at church and conversations begun in adjacent backyards, interracial friendships slowly formed. The ability of Black servicemen to draw upon their own experiences of discrimination helped them relate to the troubles their wives faced. White GIs lacked the same sources for empathy and advice.[65]

Never accepted unequivocally within minority communities, war brides and their husbands still raised the profile of mixed marriages and helped erode some of the opposition to them. The *Los Angeles Sentinel* reported that foreign wives of Black GIs faced obstacles in their married lives but fared "better than war brides of Whites," who were more often "jilted and divorced." The newspaper suggested the normality and health of these pairs, who "are having no more or less trouble than any other young couple." *Ebony* magazine treated the marriage of Woodrow Strode, an African American, and Luukialuanna, a Native Hawaiian, with similar respect. In the article Strode discussed his strong, happy, six-year marriage to Luukialuanna. The caption under a photo of the frolicking duo, "Woody Strode and his lovely Hawaiian wife, Luukialuanna, peel clothes in hot weather and play cards on the floor," depicted the ordinariness and strength of their relationship. As crossers of oceans as well as ethnoracial lines, these couples confronted challenges distinct from those of American minorities who intermarried. However, the positive, regular coverage of such matches revealed the local ethnic community's interest in and changed thinking about outmarriage generally.[66]

Like these marriages, an increase in intercultural children and adoptions, or at least heightened discussions about their existence or likelihood in the immediate postwar era, chipped away at resistance to mixed families. An apparent increase in the population of part-Japanese children marked the war's disorienting effects on Nisei Californians. Of those 101 children of Japanese descent relocated from community-run homes to Children's Village at Manzanar in 1943 and then taken in by biological or foster families after the war, about 19 percent were of mixed race (defined as one-half Japanese or less), a much higher percentage than in the population at large. Sociologists studying the group noted "there were more very young than older of biracial ancestry," a pattern credited to "the strain of the months between the beginning of the war against Japan and the evacuation." The researchers further conjectured that the "greater acceptance of other races by sansei and nisei," and an acute desire to "overcome the limitations of race" at a time when race seemed so determinative, motivated their mixing.[67] Whatever the reasons, the ethnic boundaries of the Japanese community had been breached, and the breaches had become more visible by the mid- and late 1940s.

The ethnic press's heightened coverage of intercultural adoptions exposed these changing trends in sexual behavior and forced the Japanese and even the Chinese community to recognize mixing within their midst. The *Pacific Citizen* depicted the longing of a Japanese man separated from the Chinese children whom he had adopted as orphans years before.[68] Using the story as further evidence of the injustice of internment, the paper also implied the legitimacy of such interethnic families.

Even when the media portrayed intercultural adoptions more problematically, their accounts made clear the postwar weakening of ethnoracial boundaries. Orphanages in Los Angeles listed the Nisei children needing foster homes in the area. Perhaps, in the interests of truthful advertising, they specified the racial background of the orphans: twelve pure Japanese, and six part Japanese. Many of these kids then were living in Black and Caucasian homes, even though the placement agencies preferred to match the race of the adoptees and their adoptive parents. The Alameda County Welfare Commission announced the availability of "two full-blooded Japanese babies" and one "Chinese-Japanese girl." These orphans had places in White foster homes, but the organization desired an "Oriental family" to become their permanent guardians. Cases of ethnic mixture confounded efforts to maintain racial purity.[69]

The clash between a desire for racial uniformity in families and the growing reality of mixture also shaped the postwar Chinese community. The *Chinese Press* referred to "the tragedy of Chinatown": the failure of Chinese to take care of coethnic orphans. Histrionically, it depicted the fates of "Eugene who must live in a Negro home because his own people do not care" and "Rosie, who for the want of a home is forced to live with Caucasians."[70] Even as the community attempted to preserve its ethnic homogeneity, real cases of mixed families showed the futility of such efforts. Chinese Americans could no longer deny the changed composition of their group in postwar California.

The more liberal marital practices of the second generation wore away miscegenation fears, too. These young adults still favored marriages with cultural insiders, but this preference was less strongly felt and practiced. By the mid-1930s some in the second generation were already criticizing prohibitions to intermarriage. In the *New World Sun* an editorialist claiming to speak for the second generation insisted that "the unsuccessful marriage is not caused by intermarriage itself" and proposed a policy of considering it "as an individual problem" rather than "condemning it generally" for fear of "practically welcoming racial discrimination."[71]

Such attitudes about romance hastened the thawing of tensions between Asian communities in California. With peace between Asian nations domestic disagreements weakened. A short story by Hisaye Yamamoto, "Wilshire Bus," first published in 1950, emphasized this theme of growing closeness among different Asian ethnics. In this tale, which unfolds during a bus ride through Los Angeles, Esther Kuroiwa, a young Nisei, observes, with a mixture of relief and discomfort, the harassment of an elderly Chinese couple. "Go back to China, where you can be coolies working in your bare feet," a drunken passenger shouts at the pair, prompting Kuroiwa to wonder "whether the man meant her in his exclusion order or whether she was identifiably Japanese." Initially relieved that the man has only specified Chinese as unwanted, she soon chastises herself for her "moral shabbiness" and attempts to express empathy for the couple by "smiling and shaking her head." But Kuroiwa feels her "kindness rebuked or unaccepted," a response that leaves her sobbing hysterically at the close of the story. Even as "Wilshire Bus" makes clear the continued space separating Japanese and Chinese Americans, it suggests in important ways how the trauma of wartime California created a greater willingness to narrow the interethnic gap.[72]

Asian ethnics took advantage of this sensitivity to interethnic relations, including marriages. Marge Ong recalled her Chinese-American brother's marriage to a Korean as the first of its kind in Los Angeles. Ong confessed that her parents "would have disowned her" if she had attempted such a crossing, but because her sister was younger, "by then" her father "didn't mind so much," explaining to his wife that "she's oriental, we're Chinese, what's the difference?" A Japanese father who embraced his two Chinese-American sons-in-law did not seem to mind inter-Asian matches, either. At a birthday party for one of his seven Chinese-Japanese grandchildren, he appeared assured and contented. The relative ease with which Asian ethnics contemplated inter-Asian matches shaped the romantic choices of Gloria Quan as well. During a 2004 interview the American-born Filipina who then lived in Venice, California, recalled dating Filipino, Chinese, Japanese, and White Americans, her choices dictated only by "whom she liked." As a college student at Los Angeles City College she palled around with a group of "Orientals" through whom she met Al Wah, the Chinese American she married in 1956. Cases such as these supported Allen Mock's assertion that "the color line started to break and the Japanese girls were just as acceptable and pretty" to Chinese Americans after World War II. These men increasingly married Nisei and in doing so mellowed the objections of their parents. Mock recalled that the growing sentiment of the community was, "What the heck at least it's an Oriental."[73]

These seemingly subtle changes in how non-Whites thought about intercultural marriages crystallized as legal challenges to antimiscegenation laws. Interethnic marriages between leftist activists such as the Yonedas and Coronas (see chapter 3) highlighted how complementary were personal and political views; those committed to racial equality and multiethnic organizing often enacted those principles when choosing romantic partners. But in 1948 one couple's affection had more far-reaching political implications. The pair, whose case rose through the court system and ultimately ensured full marital rights for non-Whites, were of African and Mexican descent. The daughter of Mexican immigrants, Andrea Perez grew up among Chinese, Mexican, and European ethnics in a section of downtown Los Angeles. Her husband-to-be, Sylvester Davis, the son of southern migrants, lived in the city's Central Avenue district where he too mingled with diverse ethnoracial groups. Later he graduated from the eclectic Los Angeles City College. After a few years of dating their courtship was interrupted by the wartime draft. While Davis battled overseas, Perez served the war effort as a worker at Lockheed. After the war the pair reunited and planned to marry. Although Davis identified Perez as Mexican, state law described her as White and prohibited the pair's formal union. This racial understanding, inscribed in statutes, was shared by many Californians, including Perez's father. He accepted his poverty, and Mexican roots, but rejected contacts with

Blacks for fear such associations would erode his family's status still further. Despite these familial and institutional obstacles Perez and Davis married in St. Patrick's Church in Los Angeles. Approached by Dan Marshall of the Catholic Interracial Council, a group organized in 1944 by Catholics concerned with social justice, Perez and Davis agreed to make their relationship a test case for the constitutionality of the law. In 1948 the California Supreme Court ruled in their favor, striking down the antimiscegenation statute as a violation of the equal protection clause.[74]

The man and woman who guaranteed freedom of marriage for minorities were themselves minorities. As a woman of Mexican heritage, Perez likely had mixed ancestors, yet she consistently described herself on marriage licenses and legal petitions as "unmixed." In classifying herself the way she did, she left the court no doubt about the applicability of the antimiscegenation statute to her relationship; she used her privilege as a marginal White to challenge American racism. Perez and Davis's case suggests the willingness and ability of those on the border of racial privileges and familiar with other minorities to pull closer those positioned at a distance. More than a decade earlier Ruth Salas, a woman of Mexican descent, had exploited the flexibility afforded Mexicans within the American racial system; in 1932 she denied a White identity so that she could marry a Filipino (see chapter 3).[75] Perez's self-designation—a more broadly political act than Salas's and one more deliberately intended to advance the interests of other minorities—suggested her personal courage. It also spoke to the changed climate of opinion and practice in late 1940s California that nurtured such a direct and ultimately effective challenge. Mexican Americans continued to express ambivalence about their racial positions and political strategy in the postwar period, but for those like Andrea Perez, who knew minorities intimately, the choice to affiliate as non-White made sense.

Although minority organizations did not throw their weight behind the couple during the case, non-Whites responded enthusiastically to the decision. The number who took advantage of their new freedom remained modest but significant all the same. In San Joaquin County minorities and Whites hurried to formalize their relationships. Roughly from June 1948 until the close of 1949, 51 of the 1,803 recorded marriages involved interethnic pairs whom the county clerk would have turned away a year earlier. Between January and July 1950 about 4 percent of total marriages owed their legality to the recent changes in the marriage statute. Typical of these newly minted California partners were Los Angeles–based Ulysses Livingston and Henrietta Rosenthall, a

Black-Jewish couple who had married in Mexico four years earlier and had a son but wanted to make their match official in the United States.[76]

Ethnic presses reported *Perez v. Lippold* as grounds for celebration. "Few members of the minority racial groups have been affected by the law or are likely to be in the immediate future," the *Pacific Citizen* acknowledged, yet "its existence on the statute books of California has been a blow at the dignity of the non-Caucasian population." The *California Eagle* and *Los Angeles Tribune* echoed this sentiment. The papers condemned as racist a brief issued by the Los Angeles Board of Supervisors supporting the miscegenation statute, while the board praised the Catholic Church for its participation in the suit. More indirectly, the *Chinese Press* in 1949 supported the case's denouement by uncritically acknowledging eleven interracial marriages of Los Angeles County Chinese that it made possible. *La Opinion* and the *Los Angeles Sentinel* also depicted the decision as a moral and political victory for minorities.[77]

Postdecision coverage of interracial couples in *Ebony* sustained this theme of legal, if not social, triumph. An article about the formation of "miscegenation clubs" in three U.S. cities spotlighted Los Angeles, which boasted the biggest and most successful club, "ironically, enough," it noted, because "until two yeas ago mixed marriage was illegal." A friendly description of club members and their activities—picnics, card parties, and Sunday afternoon meetings—demonstrated the magazine's approval of families of all racial combinations. However, it also revealed a particular sensitivity to the practical troubles that intermarrying Mexicans and Blacks might face. Gloria Jackson, a woman whom *Ebony* identified as Mexican, and her husband, Frank, described as a Negro, related the unfortunate experience of their daughter, whom a White classmate had called "nigger." "We've got to teach our children Negro history and White history and Mexican history," offered a Black member of the Los Angeles club identified only as "Clarence," to which Frank Jackson added, "We teach our children they are members of the human race. We try to make them realize all people are one—White, Black, or brown." These men's proposed solutions to the problems of prejudice that intermarried couples and mixed-race children would continue to face communicated not only a confidence in their relationships but also the same racial understanding that informed the romance of Perez and Davis and their lawsuit: that Mexicans were a distinct minority. Although the decision had overturned only the legal hurdles to their intimacies, it inspired Mexicans and Blacks to topple ones sustained in practice. Non-Whites celebrated the dismantling of discrimination that had begun from their own ranks. Political success born of common social experiences pointed the way toward future collaborations among non-Whites and greater consciousness of interlocking lives.[78]

Minorities challenged restrictions on citizenship too but with less dramatic results and more dramatic conflicts. As those most personally pained by limits on immigration and naturalization, Jews and Asian ethnics took the lead in campaigns for reforms. Blacks and Mexicans backed them up. At a meeting of LA's Human Relations Committee as early as 1941, participants advised soliciting the support of both Chinese and Japanese as "aliens ineligible for citizenship" in "the push for naturalization." This proposed pan-Asian alliance gained momentum in a campaign against the long-standing Chinese Exclusion Act. In 1943 the *Pacific Citizen* endorsed efforts to repeal the legislation, arguing that "if Congress can do what is right on the Chinese question," it would "do the same to American citizens of Japanese ancestry." As fellow immigrants or descendants of immigrants from Asia, Japanese Americans understood the frustrations of Chinese in very direct, personal terms, but other minorities cooperated. In 1943 the *California Eagle* framed the issue in international and cross-racial terms when it reproduced a section of a speech delivered by a spokesperson for the National Negro Congress. Thelma Dale called the act's repeal a source of "hope and encouragement to hundreds of millions of colored peoples throughout the world." She then urged "all organizations of the Negro people to express their solidarity with the four hundred million peoples of China." Invoking the U.S. government's own wartime rhetoric months later in the pages of the *Eagle,* Clare Luce described the Exclusion Act as a "gross insult to the Chinese people" and an unsustainable position for a nation "fighting for and with the Chinese for freedom and human dignity." These regional critiques of the Exclusion Act were echoed nationally. As the historian Marc Gallicchio discussed, Black leaders like W. E. B. Du Bois publicly attacked the legislation as an example of egregious racism. By portraying the battle against the Chinese Exclusion Act as a critical skirmish in the longer, larger war against discrimination, African-American leaders made the issue relevant. Their support and that of other minorities was rewarded in 1944 when Congress finally lifted the heavy restrictions on Chinese immigration.[79]

That Japanese and Chinese acknowledged and sometimes acted upon their common stake in immigration reform did not mean that they or Jews, Mexicans, and Blacks consistently saw eye to eye when it came to ways to achieve that reform. In 1952 minorities split over the McCarren-Walter

Act, a split that expressed the limits and opportunities of minority coalitions in the period. The legislation was proposed and passed as part of a series of conservative laws that reflected growing concerns about the spread of communism and the reputation of the United States overseas. Although it opened up immigration from particular Asian nations for the first time, the act set such restrictive and racially determined quotas that it effectively confirmed rather than challenged the preferential treatment that northern and Western Europeans had long received. In addition, it tightened exclusions directed against potential subversives. Chinese and Korean Americans sided with Jewish, Mexican, and African Americans in opposition to the law's provisions. Jewish Americans became the most vocal of critics, denouncing the act's ban against "subversives" as a racist opportunity to exclude thousands of peaceful World War II refugees, many of them Jewish. African Americans objected to limits on Black migrants from the West Indies. Mexican Americans remained outside the system of racial quotas, but they too spoke out against the McCarren Walter Act. They resented the prohibitions it placed on their chances to suspend deportation proceedings. During a hearing of President Truman's Commission on Immigration and Naturalization held in Los Angeles just after the act's passage, representatives from these groups angrily pointed out the discriminations it left intact.[80]

Conspicuously disagreeing with the testimony of these minorities were Japanese Americans represented by the JACL. The organization emphasized progressive elements of the bill that permitted the naturalization of residents of Japanese origin and the extension of immigration quotas to Japanese, Koreans, and Southeast Asians for the first time. Although an imperfect revision, Japanese believed it was a step in the right direction, better encouraged than blocked. The case certainly demonstrated the absence of a unitary minority interest, an absence that interrupted other cooperative efforts in the period. The JACL's stance put strategic distance between Japanese and other minorities, including Chinese Americans, with whom they had the most in common. Despite its different, controversial approach the organization fundamentally accepted the ideological closeness of minorities struggling for the respect and freedom long afforded so many European immigrants.[81]

As non-Whites voiced their opposition to California injustices, they spoke in local accents. Sharing lives, they knew shared troubles firsthand. Thus non-Whites felt emboldened to act in the postwar period. Doing so was no easy task. The discriminations that minorities tackled weighed unevenly across their shoulders, an imbalance that created differences of approach and commitment. Yet a record of joint statements and legislative victories of commonality announced the entry of panethnic, neighborhood-based relations into the realm of formal politics. Banding together in political units, minorities translated their grievances into real social reform. Although Whites had become a more clearly differentiated group and retained many of their privileges by 1950, their advantages were stripped of most legal protections. Minorities had their own intercultural efforts to thank.

CONCLUSION

With war behind them, minorities reshaped long-emerging social and cultural connections into political relationships. Until this period their ties remained largely informal and apolitical. But the shocks of wartime and a hospitable climate for reform encouraged them to challenge prevailing discriminations. Drawing from current and past experiences of integrated living, these minorities fashioned a politics expressive of personal, everyday concerns. As they did so, the possibilities and complexities of panethnic affiliations became clearer. Carefully constructed minority coalitions helped collapse the legal barricades that separated them from the spaces of citizenship that so many White ethnics occupied. By the early 1950s, as discrimination persisted in practice, if not in law, and the particular physical and political foundations that supported their collective action began to crumble, minorities could celebrate the select gains that they had cooperatively achieved.

Conclusion

Amid rapid ethnoracial change, twenty-first century Americans oscillate between doubts and determination that we can all get along. Will we blur as we notice the many ethnoracial lines that run through the United States? Which ones will fade and which ones will hold their color? Californians of multiethnic, segregated spaces in the past wrestled with these questions. They got along quite intimately, if not quite easily, forming relationships and families that crossed and faded ethnoracial divisions. Rather than intuitive tolerance, their interactions reflected a pragmatic and discriminating approach to living in a society of true diversity. Considerations of gender, class, generation, politics, religion, work, and color shaped their choices of associations. They married, befriended, conspired, and eventually banded together politically, broadening without dissolving the ethnoracial communities to which they already belonged. In other words, panethnic affiliations were as much about disconnecting from certain groups as connecting with others.

With an eye toward the implications for the contemporary United States, I have traced the gradual, tentative, and often messy evolution of these panethnic relations in 1930s, 1940s, and early 1950s California. In these decades the confluence of shared geography, legally codified discriminations, and dislocations of wartime supported creative attachments among minorities looking for affection and greater authority. Their affiliations gave rise to collective, organized challenges to social injustices in the immediate postwar period. Such collaborations effectively removed the most obvious obstacles to marriage, citizenship, military service, housing, and education that had blocked their paths.

Yet despite these legal triumphs, minorities walked with hesitation into the mid-1950s. Discriminations once sustained in law still had the stubborn support of practice. Many European ethnics, feeling more secure in their privileges, became intransigent and limited the meaning of freedoms won by others. Incentives for collaboration remained, but the more private and informal character of prejudice left minorities uncertain about their targets and strategies going forward. Other changes shook up the particular physical and political foundations upon which minorities had made connections. Fears of, and official campaigns against, communism gained momentum after 1947 and forced civil rights groups to retract, regroup, and moderate their activities through the 1950s. Meanwhile suburbanization and urban renewal reconfigured the multiethnic spaces that had given rise to the political grievances and cooperation of non-Whites.

The unique multicultural environments shared by non-Whites began to dissolve as the postwar era wore on. During the 1950s and early 1960s suburbanization, downtown reconstruction projects, and the end of housing covenants tore apart neighborhoods that once had been very mixed. Boyle Heights, the Fillmore District, and West Oakland were among the casualties. Historians of suburbia have described the redistribution of people as the end of "heterogeneous industrial cities" and noted the tightening of racial lines within communities where length of residence had been the most salient distinction among their varied inhabitants.[1]

Urban redevelopment projects loomed large among the forces responsible for the loss of mixed, mostly minority, communities. City planners targeted low-income, multiethnic neighborhoods as worthy of renewal. But their programs for rehabilitation mandated the razing of homes without providing compensation or relief for current residents. Non-Whites would have to fend for themselves. In San Francisco a commission catalogued local decay, pointing to the Western Addition as "the largest single area of blight" and Chinatown as a section with "some of the worst housing in the city." Not coincidentally, areas defined as dilapidated and unlivable were disproportionately inhabited by non-White groups. Chinese, African, and Japanese Americans protested. According to Deborah Sullivan, the NAACP called plans for redevelopment first proposed in 1948 undemocratic and inadequate because they made no provision for displaced residents. The Japanese American Citizens League (JACL) agreed, asking for promises of nonsegregation, nondiscrimination, and low-cost housing from city officials so that minorities might return to the neighborhood that had been their own. Yet these demands did little good. By the late 1950s and early 1960s, into the Western Addition had come highways and tall office building; out had gone most minorities.[2]

Similarly, residents of Boyle Heights and West Oakland found their familiar neighborhoods transformed by eager developers. Boyle Heights lost 10 percent of its land and 10,000 of its people following the construction of five highways and three public housing projects between 1943 and 1960. The Mexican American population grew to more than 40,000—half of the section's total—while the number of Jews declined to 14,000 and people of Japanese descent to 6,500. Two decades after World War II, Boyle Heights had become a classic Mexican barrio. Meanwhile in West Oakland revitalization efforts and Asian flight created a much blacker, poorer neighborhood than had existed in the second quarter of the twentieth century.[3]

The legal demise of restrictive housing covenants and newly realized prosperity carried some non-White groups away from inner cities and, like redevelopment, contributed to the dissolution of heterogeneous neighborhoods. Asian and Jewish Americans, who more commonly won the resources and the acceptance of Whites, suburbanized much faster than Blacks and Mexicans. The affluent and secular Jews of Los Angeles began moving out of Boyle Heights and South Central as early as the 1920s, but not until the 1950s did the majority abandon these areas for parts west and north: West Adams, the Fairfax District, and the Wilshire area. Chinese, Japanese, and Filipinos also established new homes outside the center of Los Angeles. A few years after their release from the camps, many Japanese moved into or toward suburbs. Crenshaw, Monterey Park, Montebello, Long Beach, and especially Gardena, where the Japanese-American population increased 480 percent between 1950 and 1960, were popular destinations. Following a similar trajectory, Chinese increasingly left older settlements for homes in Crenshaw, West Adams, and especially Monterey Park. Even Filipinos joined this flow of Asian ethnics, moving from Bunker Hill and Temple Street into Silver Lake, Highland Park, and Carson by the early 1960s.[4]

In the Bay Area, Asian Americans suburbanized as well. Observers reported that by the late 1950s Chinatown had "burst its seams" and families had relocated to the Richmond District and Bay View. Chinatown held only 40 percent of the city's Chinese population in 1950, a figure that dropped steadily through the decade. Jim Fung, a Chinese American, remembered purchasing a San Francisco home soon after the war in a once exclusively Italian neighborhood. He was not alone. The city's Council of Civic Unity noted in 1960 that in the preceding decade Chinese Americans had steadily bought up homes and businesses in the North Beach section adjacent to Chinatown. At the same time Nisei had left the Fillmore for Pacific Heights, Hunter's Point, and especially the nearby Richmond District. Only a handful of minority families called the Richmond area home in 1950, but seven years later a real estate agent estimated that 15 to 20 percent of the residents were minorities, primarily of Asian descent.[5]

Meanwhile middle-class Mexican and African Americans established residence in the suburbs, but did so more rarely than their Jewish or Asian peers. The majority stayed in older downtown neighborhoods that became more homogeneous ethnoracial clusters, or what Albert Camarillo has called "color line borderlands"—areas marked by persistent racial homogeneity. As examples, once-diverse West Oakland, South Central, and Watts became noticeably blacker and browner. Between 1950 and 1960 established Black settlements along Central Avenue and in East Los Angeles pushed westward and southward, creating a much larger and contiguous area of African-American residence. In fact, the Black population of the fourteen census tracts south of Exposition and west of Broadway increased 554 percent by 1960. While Black expansion happened along distinct spatial corridors, Mexicans "exploded around multiple nodes" within the downtown region. An almost identical trend reshaped the Bay Area. A 1963 study confirmed the segregation of Mexicans and Blacks that characterized the region after 1950. It observed that as Asian groups entered the middle class and exited old ghettos, they had become virtual strangers to Mexican and African Americans.[6] All these changes marked the passing of a unique moment in which so many distinctive non-White groups lived and worked in proximity.

The regime of discrimination against which non-Whites had first rallied changed, much like the spaces in which they lived. By the midcentury minorities had helped overturn much of the legal apparatus supporting inequalities: housing covenants, bars to Asian naturalization, school segregation, antimiscegenation statutes, and military segregation. Essentially, the distinction between who was White and who was *definitely* not White was written out of the state's legal system. Ethnoracial injustices assumed less conspicuous and legal forms, mandating new strategies.

At the same time, as the nation shifted its attention from a hot war against fascism to a cold war against communism, the struggles for social justice lost their popular stamp of approval. Organizations such as the NAACP, for example, which expanded its ranks and leaned leftward in 1947, began to bleed members and shift rightward by the early 1950s. Interracial efforts did not fade away, as new scholarship on the intersection of the Cold War and the domestic civil rights movement demonstrates. However, these relationships and political agendas did moderate. Panethnic affiliations survived into the second half of the twentieth century, but the unique social, cultural, and political context of 1930s and early 1940s California, as well as the wartime enthusiasm that first gave birth to these larger sensibilities, had changed.[7]

Although the particular constellation of ethnoracial groups that came together in shared spaces to challenge shared discrimination did not last, their example of coalition did. Diverse Californians who jointly demanded fair housing and fair employment practices later in the twentieth century drew upon this legacy of multiethnic cooperation. Such efforts brought together an even wider cross-section of Californians committed to ideals of equality. Their ethnoracial composition and orientation departed from the arrangement conceived by the multiple minority groups chronicled in this book but stuck close to its principles of interdependence and interracial harmony. Newly created in the early 1950s to address the frustrating job prospects of many minorities, the California Committee for Fair Employment Practices enjoyed the support of the NAACP, the Community Services Organization, Jewish civil rights groups, and the state's Irish governor, Pat Brown. Such a combined effort paid off in 1959 when the state legislature established the Division of Fair Employment Practices. Although it eventually was effectively disabled by Proposition 14, the Rumford Fair Housing Act, a moderate bill that outlawed racial discrimination in sections of the housing market a few years later, owed its successful passage to the work of diverse activists. Among others, the NAACP, Catholic Interracial Council, Council for Civic Unity, and Western Christian Leadership Conference collectively fought for the legislation. If not quite a habit of California society and politics, multiethnic activities, varied in intention and participants though they were, had become a practical option.[8]

This book has focused on a multiethnic past not conjured up out of imagination or exotic longings but grounded in the intimate experiences of specific spaces. At its heart it argues that minorities have drawn and redrawn ethnoracial borders to create more capacious affiliations in the past. My hope is that tracking these combinations contributes to our understanding of how ethnicity and race operate in societies of pronounced diversity.

Notes

INTRODUCTION

1. A panethnic affiliation develops as several ethnic groups come to perceive themselves and be perceived by others as sharing some kind of kinship. Even as they imagine themselves as members of a more expansive community, however, members hold on to narrower identities. This generalization of ethnic solidarity and identity is distinct from what social scientists have called ethnogenesis, in which individuals lose touch with former allegiances. Whereas in the United States such terms as *German American* and *African American* reflect ethnogenesis, the terms *Native American* and *Asian American* embody panethnicity. See Yen Espiritu and Wilbur Zelinsky, *The Enigma of Ethnicity: Another American Dilemma* (Iowa City: University of Iowa Press, 2002), 28–41.

2. Young Oak Kim, interview, 100th Infantry/442nd Regimental Combat Team, box 2, Oral History Project, National Japanese American Historical Society, San Francisco; Young Oak Kim, interview by Karen Ishizuka and Robert Nakamura, 28 August 1995, Veterans Oral History Project, Japanese American National Museum, Los Angeles; Young Oak Kim, interview, Korean American Museum Oral History Series, Korean American Digital Archive, University of Southern California Digital Archive, Los Angeles; *Korean Independence,* 12 July 1944.

3. Alexander Saxton, *The Indispensable Enemy: Labor and the Anti-Chinese Movement in California* (Berkeley: University of California Press, 1971); Karen Brodkin, *How the Jews Became White Folks* (New Brunswick: Rutgers University Press, 1998); Berge Bulbulian, *The Fresno Armenians: History of a Diaspora Community* (Fresno: Press at California State University, 2000). For the Americanization of Italian immigrants in early twentieth century San Francisco, see Dino Cinel, *From Italy to San Francisco: The Immigrant Experience* (Stanford: Stanford University Press, 1982). Thomas Guglielmo pays closer attention to the

racialization of Italians in his Chicago-based study, *White on Arrival: Italians, Race, Color, and Power in Chicago, 1890–1945* (New York: Oxford University Press, 2003). For a more sweeping account of the fate of European ethnics, see Matthew Frye Jacobson, *Whiteness of a Different Color: European Immigrants and the Alchemy of Race* (Cambridge: Harvard University Press, 1998); Erika Lee, "The Chinese Exclusion Example: Race, Immigration, and American Gate-keeping, 1882–1924," *Journal of American Ethnic History* 21, no. 3 (Spring 2002): 49–50.

4. Here, and throughout the book, I use *Mexican American,* and *Mexican*—terms that have slightly different, sometimes contested, meanings but are often used interchangeably—to refer to people of Mexican descent living in the United States regardless of citizenship. Because of its more recent origins and associa-tion with the civil rights struggles of the late 1960s and early 1970s, I do not use the term *Chicano.* For fuller discussions of terminology see Sarah Deutsch, *No Separate Refuge: Culture, Class, and Gender on an Anglo-Hispanic Frontier in the American Southwest, 1880–1940* (New York: Oxford University Press, 1987), 1, and Christopher Arriola, "Knocking on the Schoolhouse Door: *Mendez v. Westminster,* Equal Protection, Public Education, and Mexican Americans in the 1940s," *La Raza Law Journal* 8 (1995): 166–207.

5. Jacobson, *Whiteness of a Different Color.* I subscribe to the near con-sensus among scientists and social scientists alike, a consensus expressed in the writings of such historians as Michael Winant, Howard Omi, Barbara Fields, and David Hollinger, that race and ethnicity are socially determined rather than biologically fixed concepts. See Hollinger, *Postethnic America;* Barbara Fields, "Ideology and Race in American History," in *Region, Race, and Reconstruction: Essays in Honor of C. Vann Woodward,* ed. Moran Kousser and James McPher-son (New York: Oxford University Press, 1982); Michael Omi and Howard Winant, *Racial Formation in the United States: From the 1960s to the 1990s* (New York: Routledge and Kegan Paul, 1994).

6. For the most influential and carefully produced examples of this prolifer-ating scholarship on Whiteness, see David Roediger's *The Wages of Whiteness: The Making of the American Working Class* (London: Verso, 1991); Jacobson, *Whiteness of a Different Color;* Linda Gordon, *The Great Arizona Orphan Ab-duction* (Cambridge: Harvard University Press, 1999); Thomas Guglielmo's *White on Arrival.* On the promises and pitfalls of Whiteness studies, see Peter Kolchin, "Whiteness Studies: The New History of Race in America," *Journal of American History* (June 2002): 154–73, and a symposium by six historians: "Scholarly Controversy: Whiteness and the Historian's Imagination," *Interna-tional Labor and Working Class History* no. 60 (Fall 2001): 1–92.

7. Russell A. Kazal, "Revisiting Assimilation: The Rise, Fall, and Reappear-ance of a Concept in American Ethnic History," *American Historical Review* 100 (April 1995): 438–71.

8. Works such as those of George Sanchez and Judy Yung depict the complex process of cultural adjustment by which Mexican and Chinese Americans, re-spectively, blended familiar, inherited traditions with those of the American mainstream. Bicultural identities resulted. Mexican-American teens in Los An-geles drew closer to a white American culture as these youngsters expressed

themselves by purchasing products and attending movies unavailable in the small home villages of their parents. American-born daughters also defied their Chinese parents by acculturating to the American mainstream: dating men of their own choosing, pursuing higher levels of education, and wanting independent careers. See George Sanchez, *Becoming Mexican American: Ethnicity, Culture, and Identity in Chicano Los Angeles, 1900–1945* (New York: Oxford University Press, 1993); Judy Yung, *Unbound Feet: A Social History of Chinese Women in San Francisco* (Berkeley: University of California Press, 1995).

9. David Gutiérrez, *Walls and Mirrors: Mexican Americans, Mexican Immigrants and the Politics of Ethnicity* (Berkeley: University of California Press, 1993), 76–80; Gloria Miranda, "The Mexican Immigrant Family: Economic and Cultural Survival in Los Angeles, 1900–1945," in *Twentieth Century Los Angeles: Power, Promotion and Social Conflict,* ed. Norman Klein and Martin Schiesel (Claremont, CA: Regina Books, 1990), 41–42; Marilyn Johnson, *The Second Gold Rush: Oakland and the East Bay in World War II* (Berkeley: University of California Press, 1993), 151–63; Shirley Ann Moore, *To Place Our Deeds: The African American Community in Richmond, California, 1910–1963* (Berkeley: University of California Press, 2000), 81; Sucheng Chan, *Asian Americans: An Interpretive History* (Boston: Twayne, 1991); Yuji Ichioka, *Issei: The World of the First Generation Japanese Immigrants, 1885–1924* (New York: Free Press, 1998)

10. Peggy Pascoe discussed the efforts of middle-class women reformers in San Francisco to "rescue" Chinese prostitutes and introduce them to Christianity. Many Chinese women used these services to their own advantage, breaking free of abusive marriages and unpleasant labor. Both sides benefited from and directed outcomes. See Peggy Pascoe, "Gender Systems in Conflict: The Marriages of Mission-Educated Chinese American Women, 1874–1939," *Journal of Social History* (1989): 631–53. Tomás Almaguer traced how the separate relationships of whites with African Americans, Asian Americans, Native Americans, and Mexican Americans similarly supported white power in the West. Whites racialized each group in distinct ways, a historical process conditioned by the different material and cultural circumstances in which they encountered "the other." See Tomás Almaguer, *Racial Fault Lines: The Historical Origins of White Supremacy in California* (Berkeley: University of California Press, 1991).

11. Roger Lotchin bemoaned historians' neglect of western intergroup relations in favor of single ethnic groups and their relations with the "majority." See Roger Lotchin, "The Impending Western Urban Past: An Essay on the Twentieth Century West," in *Researching Western History: Topics of the Twentieth Century,* ed. Gerald Nash and Richard W. Etulain (Albuquerque: University of New Mexico, 1997), 67. Among the earliest works to address the historiographical gap are Beth Bailey and David Farber, *The First Strange Place: The Alchemy of Race and Sex in World War II Hawaii* (New York: Free Press, 1992); Eiichiro Azuma, "Racial Struggle, Immigrant Nationalism, and Ethnic Identity: Japanese and Filipinos in the California Delta," *Pacific Historical Review* 67 (March 1999): 163–200; Daniel Liestman, "Horizontal Interethnic Relations: Chinese and American Indians in the Nineteenth Century West," *Western Historical Quarterly* 30 (Autumn 1999): 327–49. More recent scholarship

has sustained the interethnic and multiethnic focus. See Shana Beth Bernstein, *California Dreaming in a Divided World, Building Multiracial Bridges in World War II and Cold War Los Angeles,* forthcoming; Mark Brilliant, "Color Lines: Civil Rights Struggles on America's 'Racial Frontier,' 1945–1975" (PhD diss., Stanford University, 2002; forthcoming from Oxford University Press); Elisabeth Orr, "Living along the Fault Line: Community, Suburbia, and Multiethnicity in Garden Grove and Westminster, California, 1900–1995" (PhD diss., Indiana University, 1999); Mark Wild, *Street Meeting: Multiethnic Neighborhoods in Early Twentieth-Century Los Angeles* (Berkeley: University of California Press, 2005).

12. Gary Gerstle, *American Crucible: Race and Nation in the Twentieth Century* (Princeton: Princeton University Press, 2001), and "Immigration Restriction, Racial Nationalism, and the Making of Modern America," unpublished paper presented to U.S. History Colloquium, University of California, Los Angeles, 2002; George Sanchez, "Race, Nation, and Culture in Recent Immigration Studies," *Journal of American Ethnic History* 18 (Summer 1999): 66–84; Omi and Winant, *Racial Formation in the United States*; David Hollinger, *Postethnic America: Beyond Multiculturalism* (New York: Basic Books, 1995).

13. Ernesto Galarza, *Barrio Boy: The Story of a Boy's Acculturation* (Notre Dame: University of Notre Dame Press, 1971), 198–99.

I. CALIFORNIA CROSSROADS

1. Ernesto Galarza, *Barrio Boy: The Story of a Boy's Acculturation* (Notre Dame: University of Notre Dame Press, 1971), 3, 198.

2. U.S. Census Bureau, *Sixteenth Census of the United States: 1940, Population: Characteristics of the Non-White Population by Race* (Washington, DC: GPO, 1942). The racial breakdown of other large states: Florida, 72.1 percent White, 27.1 percent Black, 0.1 percent all others; Michigan, 95.8 percent White, 4.0 percent Black, 0.2 percent all others.

3. U.S. Census Bureau, *Sixteenth Census: 1940, Population: Characteristics of the Non-White Population by Race.* In descending order the sex ratios of states with more pronounced imbalances: Nevada, 125.4:100; Montana, 114.8:100; Idaho, 111.4:100; Michigan, 105.2:100; North Dakota, 109.4:100; Washington, 109.1:100; South Dakota, 107.1:100; Arizona, 107.1:100; Oregon, 106.8:100; Minnesota, 104.6:100; New Mexico, 104.6:100; Wisconsin, 104.1:100; West Virginia, 103.8:100.

4. George Sanchez, *Becoming Mexican American: Ethnicity, Culture, and Identity in Chicano Los Angeles, 1900–1945* (New York: Oxford University Press, 1993), 22; Camille Guerin-Gonzales, *Mexican Workers and Americans Dreams: Immigration, Repatriation and California Farm Labor, 1930–1939* (New Brunswick: Rutgers University Press, 1994), 22, 27–28.

5. Sanchez, *Becoming Mexican American,* 20; Guerin-Gonzales, *Mexican Workers,* 55; David Gutiérrez, ed., *Between Two Worlds: Mexican Immigrants in the United States* (Wilmington, DE: Scholarly Press, 1996), 41.

6. Sanchez, *Becoming Mexican American,* 41, 66, 133; Gutiérrez, *Between Two Worlds,* 66; Walter Nugent, *Into the West: The Story of Its People* (New

York: Alfred A. Knopf, 1999), 206; Phil Ethington, "Segregated Diversity: Race, Ethnicity, Space and Political Fragmentation in Los Angeles County, 1940–1994," Final Report to the John Randolph Haynes and Dora Haynes Foundation, 13 September 2000.

7. Sucheng Chan, *This Bittersweet Soil: The Origins of Chinese Immigration to the United States, 1848–1882* (Berkeley: University of California Press, 1986), 18–20; Yong Chen, "The Internal Origins to Chinese Emigration Reconsidered," *Western Historical Quarterly* (Winter 1997): 540–46; Erika Lee, *At America's Gates: Chinese Immigration during the Exclusion Era, 1883–1943* (Chapel Hill: University of North Carolina, 2003).

8. Sucheng Chan, *Asian Americans: An Interpretive History* (Boston: Twayne, 1991), 10–14; Judy Yung, *Unbound Feet : A Social History of Chinese Women in San Francisco* (Berkeley: University of California Press, 1995), 296.

9. Chan, *Asian Americans,* 10–14; Nugent, *Into the West,* 166–67.

10. Chan, *Asian Americans,* 17–18; Nugent, *Into the West,* 217; Dawn Mabalon, "Life in Little Manila: Filipinas/os in Stockton, California, 1917–1972" (PhD diss., Stanford University, 2004), 47.

11. Eui-Young Yu, *East to America: Korean Life Stories* (New York: New Press, 1996), 5.

12. Chan, *Asian Americans,* 18–23.

13. Mark Wild, *Street Meeting: Multiethnic Neighborhoods in Early Twentieth-Century Los Angeles* (Berkeley: University of California Press, 2005), 29–30; Donna Gabaccia and Fraser Ottanelli, *Italian Workers of the World: Labor Migration and the Formation of Multiethnic States* (Urbana: University of Illinois Press, 2001); Raymond Stevenson Dondero, "The Italian Settlement of San Francisco" (master's thesis, University of California, 1950); Gary Morimoto and George Pozetta, "Ethnics at War: Italians and Americans in California during World War II," in *The Way We Really Were: The Golden State in the Second Great War,* ed. Roger Lotchin (Urbana: University of Illinois Press, 2000), 144.

14. Max Vorspan and Lloyd Gartner, *History of Jews in Los Angeles* (Philadelphia: Jewish Publication Society of America, 1970), 109; Nugent, *Into the West,* 211.

15. Nugent, *Into the West,* 212; Josh Sides, *L.A. City Limits: African American Los Angeles from the Great Depression to the Present* (Berkeley: University of California Press, 2003), 15.

16. James Gregory, *American Exodus: The Dust Bowl Migration and Okie Culture in California* (New York: Oxford University Press, 1989), 11, 40–42, 251. Gregory noted that whites from Oklahoma, Arkansas, Texas, and Missouri constituted a majority of the San Joaquin Valley agricultural labor force until the 1950s, when Mexicans reentered the country in large numbers.

17. Kevin Kenny, "Diaspora and Comparison: The Global Irish as Case Study," *Journal of American History* (June 2003): 134—62. For more on the meanings of transnationlism and how migrants simultaneously participate in the making of multiple nation-states, see Linda Basch, Nina Schiller, and Cristina Blanc, eds., *Nations Unbound: Transnational Projects, Postcolonial Predicaments, and Deterritorialized Nation-States* (Australia: Gordon and Breach, 1994).

18. Thomas Guglielmo, *White on Arrival: Italians, Race, Color, and Power in Chicago, 1895–1945* (New York: Oxford University Press, 2003); Mae Ngai, *Impossible Subjects: Illegal Aliens and the Making of Modern America* (Princeton: Princeton University Press, 2004), 25–55.

19. Using a comparative framework, Malcolm Campbell affirmed what most historians have come to argue: Irish Californians were more successful and fortunate than Irish immigrants back East. Among the reasons he offered was the cosmopolitan character of the state: "Where California's Irish were from mid-century viewed within an assimilatory frame, as English-speaking and considered to have much in common with other new arrivals from the British Isles, the substantial Chinese population was not" (Malcolm Campbell, "Ireland's Furthest Shores: Irish Immigrant Settlement in Nineteenth-Century California and Eastern Australia," *Pacific Historical Review* 71 [2002]: 88).

20. Samuel Francis Vitone, "Community, Identity and Schools: Education Experiences of Italians in San Francisco from the Gold Rush to the Second World War" (PhD diss., University of California, Berkeley, 1981), 188.

21. Joe Cruciano and Teresa Angeluzzi, interviews by Micaela Di Leonardo, in *The Varieties of Ethnic Experience: Kinship, Class, and Gender among California Italian-Americans* (Ithaca: Cornell University Press, 1984), 173–74.

22. Mabalon, "Life in Little Manila."

23. Paul Spickard, *Mixed Blood: Intermarriage and Ethnic Identity in Twentieth-Century America* (Madison: University of Wisconsin Press, 1989), 42; David Goodman, "Anti-Semitism in Japan," in *The Construction of Racial Identities in China and Japan,* ed. Frank Dikotter (London: Hurst, 1997), 177–86; Michael Wiener, "The Invention of Identity: Race and Nation in Pre-War Japan," in Dikotter, *Construction of Racial Identities,* 110–35. In Hisaye Yamamoto's short story "Yoneka's Earthquake," Japanese characters accept the "irrefutable fact" promoted by their ethnic community that Filipinos are lazy and gaudy (Yamamoto, "Yoneka's Earthquake," *Seventeen Syllables and Other Stories,* [New York: Kitchen Table–Women of Color Press, 1988]), 47–53; See also Eiichiro Azuma, "The Politics of Transnational History Making: Japanese Immigrants on the Western 'Frontier,' 1927–1941," *Journal of American History* 89, no. 4 (March 2003): 1401–30.

24. Eiichiro Azuma, "Racial Struggle, Immigrant Nationalism, and Ethnic Identity: Japanese and Filipinos in the California Delta, 1939–1941," *Pacific Historical Review* 67 (1998): 172.

25. Once an innocuous term used to describe those from Oklahoma, *Okie* took on a crueler, wider meaning in California during the 1930s. *Okie* expressed the popular assumption that poor, White southwesterners were uneducated, dishonest, dirty, and ignorant.

26. Gregory, *American Exodus,* 102, 165–68.

27. Ngai, *Impossible Subjects,* 25–55.

28. Al Camarillo, "Comparing Ethnic and Racial Borderlands in American Cities: Urbanization and Community Formation among African Americans, European Americans, and Mexican Americans between the World Wars," paper presented at the annual meeting of the Organization of American Historians,

Washington, DC, April 1996; Sanchez, *Becoming Mexican American*, 77; *Shelley v. Kraemer*, 334 U.S. 1 (1948).

29. Connie Tirona is quoted in Yen Le Espiritu, *Filipino American Lives* (Philadelphia: Temple University Press, 1995), 70; the ticket taker is quoted in Patricia Justiniani McReynolds, *Almost Americans: A Quest for Dignity* (Santa Fe: Red Crane Books, 1997), 270. Espiritu, McReynolds, and these authors discuss patterns of segregation: John Modell, *The Economics and Politics of Racial Accommodation: The Japanese of Los Angeles, 1900–1942* (Urbana: University of Illinois Press, 1977), 74; Scott Kurashige, "Transforming Los Angeles: Black and Japanese American Struggles for Racial Equality in the Twentieth Century" (PhD diss., University of California, Los Angeles, 2000), 55; David Mas Masumoto, *Country Voices: The Oral History of a Japanese American Family Farm Community* (Del Rey, CA: Inaka Countryside Publications, 1987), 61.

30. "In Furtherance of Unity," *Now: The War Worker,* May 1944; Japanese-American minister, interview, August 1943, reel 74, Japanese American Evacuation and Resettlement Records (hereafter JAERR), Bancroft Library, University of California, Berkeley; Edwin B. Almirol, "Church Life among Filipinos in Central California," in *Religion and Society in the American West,* ed. Carl Guarneri and David Alvarez (Lanham, MD: University Press of America, 1987), 306; Fred Cordova, *Filipinos, Forgotten Asian Americans: A Pictorial Essay, 1763–circa 1963* (Dubuque, IA: Kendall/Hunt, 1983); Gaston Espinosa, "Borderland Religion: Los Angeles and the Origins of the Latino Pentecostal Movement in the U.S., Mexico, and Puerto Rico, 1900–1945" (PhD diss., University of California, Santa Barbara, 1999), 29. Charles Wollenberg offered the most thorough account of school segregation in California. San Francisco's Chinese families challenged late nineteenth century laws that segregated their schoolage children. By 1927 poor enforcement of the restrictions led one legislator to propose their removal. The concentration of Chinese in Chinatown, however, meant that high schools such as Commodore Stockton enrolled Chinese students almost exclusively. In 1921 the state added Japanese to the list of groups subject to segregation. Yet only four Sacramento counties bothered to place Nisei in special "Oriental schools." Nisei in other parts of California attended more integrated institutions. Although never formally segregated, Filipinos remembered principals who encouraged them to enroll in mostly Asian schools. Mexican students became more segregated, especially in Southern California, as the Mexican population increased during the first decades of the twentieth century. "Colored schools" for Black children appeared in San Francisco as early as 1854. Districts throughout the state soon followed suit. Even after the discriminatory statute was struck down in San Francisco in 1875, de facto separation of Blacks persisted. In 1939, for example, Los Angeles had nine mostly Black schools, a figure that rose steadily through the 1940s. See Charles Wollenberg, *All Deliberate Speed: Segregation and Exclusion in California Schools, 1855–1975* (Berkeley: University of California Press, 1976), 27, 44–45, 73, 112.

31. Quintard Taylor, *In Search of the Racial Frontier: African Americans in the American West, 1528–1990* (New York: W. W. Norton, 1998), 226–27;

Garding Liu, *Inside Los Angeles Chinatown* (Los Angeles: n.p., 1948), 155–56; Daniel Luevano, interview by Carlos Vasquez, 1988, Oral History Program, University of California, Los Angeles; Marshall Hoo, interview by Beverly Chan, 24 May 1980, Southern California Chinese American Oral History Project, collection 1688, Department of Special Collections, Charles E. Young Research Library, University of California, Los Angeles; Espiritu, *Filipino American Lives,* 70–74; Tarao "Pat" Neishi, interview by Sheryl Narahara, Summer 1992, box 8, Military Intelligence Service Biography Project Oral History Transcripts, National Japanese American Historical Society, San Francisco.

32. Charles Spaulding, "Housing Problems of Minority Groups in Los Angeles," *Annals of the American Academy of Political and Social Science* (1946): 248; Eshref Shevky and Marilyn Williams, *The Social Areas of Los Angeles: Analysis and Typology* (Berkeley: University of California Press, 1949), 53; Los Angeles Housing Authority, *Digest of Final Report: Housing Survey, City of Los Angeles* (1940), 19.

33. San Francisco Department of City Planning, *The Population of San Francisco: A Half Century of Change, 1900–1950* (1954), 17–19; Bryce Young, *Oakland's Changing Community Patterns* (Oakland City Planning Department, 1961), 3; Gregory, *American Exodus,* 52.

34. James Allen and Eugene Turner, *The Ethnic Quilt: Population Diversity in Southern California* (Northridge: Center for Geographical Studies, California State University, 1997), 94–95.

35. Sanchez, *Becoming Mexican American,* 77; Marilyn Johnson, *The Second Gold Rush: Oakland and the East Bay in World War II* (Berkeley: University of California Press, 1993), 93.

36. Based upon Phil Ethington's census compilation in "Segregated Diversity," the category of "White" excludes those born in Mexico and/or those with Hispanic surnames.

37. Allen and Turner, *Ethnic Quilt,* 125–27; Shevky and Williams, *Social Areas of Los Angeles,* 49; Alonzo Smith, "Blacks and the Los Angeles Municipal Transit System," *Urbanism Past and Present* (Winter/Spring 1981): 26; Earl Hansen and Paul Beckett, *Los Angeles: Its Peoples and Its Homes* (Los Angeles: Haynes Foundation, 1944), 12.

38. Davis McEntire, *Residence and Race: Final and Comprehensive Report to the Commission on Race and Housing* (Berkeley: University of California Press, 1960), 48; Allen and Turner, *Ethnic Quilt,* 125–27; Hansen and Beckett, *Los Angeles: Its Peoples,* 40.

39. Allen and Turner, *Ethnic Quilt,* 120; Hansen and Beckett, *Los Angeles,* 40; Marshall Hoo, interview by Beverly Chan, 24 May 1980, SCCAOHP.

40. Harry Honda, interview by Cynthia Togami and Sojin Kim, 1 April 1998, REgenerations Oral History Project (hereafter ROHP), Japanese American National Museum, Los Angeles; Art Takei, interview by Tim Carpenter, 22 November 1995, ROHP. The breadth and relative balance of minority populations in Boyle Heights were fleeting. Between 1940 and 1950 the district's Mexican-origin population rose from 7 to 15 percent to 46 to 59 percent. The homogenization of the area only increased during the next decade. By 1960 Mexican Americans comprised 59 to 79 percent of the relevant census tracts.

41. William Woodman, interview in Clora Bryant et al., eds., *Central Avenue Sounds: Jazz in Los Angeles* (Berkeley: University of California Press, 1998), 109.

42. As in the case of Boyle Heights, Watts would lose its multiethnic character, becoming predominantly Black, almost 95 percent, by 1958 (Sides, *L.A. City Limits,* 19, 109).

43. Thelma Gorham, "Negroes and Japanese Evacuees," *Crisis,* November 1945; Sugar Pie De Santo, interview by author, Oakland, 16 February 2001; Jerry Flamm, *Good Life in Hard Times: San Francisco's '20s and '30s* (San Francisco: Chronicle Books, 1977), 73; Far West Surveys, *San Francisco–Oakland Metropolitan Area: Population Report of White, Negro, and Other Races* (San Francisco: Far West Surveys, 1961); Leonard Austin, *Around the World in San Francisco: A Guide to Unexplored San Francisco* (San Francisco: Fearon, 1955), 63. The censuses of 1940 and 1950 categorized all Asian ethnics as "other races." Thus it is likely that the 2,503 to 4,189 members of "other races" counted as living inside or adjacent to Chinatown (78–99 percent of tract totals) included Koreans, Filipinos, and Japanese.

44. Neishi interview; Rose Hum Lee, quoted in Judy Yung, ed., *Unbound Voices: A Documentary History of Chinese Women in San Francisco* (Berkeley: University of California Press, 1999), 44; article in *China Digest* quoted in Roger Lotchin, ed., *The Way We Really Were: The Golden State in the Second Great War* (Urbana: University of Illinois Press, 2000), 170.

45. Sebastian Fichera, "The Meaning of Community: The History of the Italians of San Francisco" (PhD diss., University of California, Los Angeles, 1981); Di Leonardo, *Varieties of Ethnic Experience,* 176.

46. City of Oakland, California, *Housing Authority Annual Report* (1940–63); Lotchin, *Way We Really Were,* 192; Johnson, *Second Gold Rush,* 93; Rose Mary Escobar, interview by author, Oakland, 8 March 2001.

47. Delores Naso McBroome, *Parallel Communities: African Americans in California's East Bay, 1850–1963* (New York: Garland, 1993), 98; U.S. Census Bureau, *Sixteenth Census of the United States: 1940, Population and Housing: Statistics for Census Tracts, San Francisco–Oakland, California* (Washington, DC: GPO, 1942).

48. The reporter is quoted in B. Shrieke, *Alien Americans: A Study of Race Relations* (New York: Viking, 1936), 23; Carol Hemminger, "Little Manila: The Filipinos in Stockton prior to World War II," *Pacific Historian* 25 (1980): 212. Figures for 1940 are unavailable at the census tract level for Sacramento.

49. Duncan Chin, *Growing Up on Grove Street, 1931–1946: Sketches and Memories of a Chinese American Boyhood* (Capitola, CA: Capitola Book, 1995), 57–67.

50. Galarza, *Barrio Boy,* 198–99; Return of Japanese to Imperial Valley Community, reel 107, JAERR; Karen Leonard, *Making Ethnic Choices: California's Punjabi Mexican Americans* (Philadelphia: Temple University Press, 1992), 33; Mabalon, "Life in Little Manila," 56–57; Ruth Alexander, "Racial Characteristics and Conditions at Watsonville Union High School" (master's thesis, Stanford University, 1940), 15; Kathryn Cramp, *Study of the Mexican Population in Imperial County* (New York: Committee on Farm and Cannery Migrants, 1926), 15; Harold Wise, *Characteristics of the Low Rent Housing*

Market in Brawley, Holtville, Calexico, Imperial and Westwood, California (Planning and Housing Research Associates, 1950), 23.

2. YOUNG TRAVELERS

1. Soo Young Chin, *Doing What Had to Be Done: The Life Narrative of Dora Yum Kim* (Philadelphia: Temple University Press, 1999), 43.

2. Ibid., 49.

3. Pardee Lowe, *Father and Glorious Descendant* (Boston: Little, Brown, 1943), 95; Yori Wada, interview by Frances Linsley and Gabrielle Morris, 1983 and 1990, History of Bay Area Philanthropy Series, BANC MSS 921770c, Bancroft Library, University of California, Berkeley. Lowe and Wada were two examples of the many minorities who recounted the ease of their childhood mixing. Others included Allen Chan, interview by George Yee, 22 February 1980, Southern California Chinese American Oral History Collection (SCCAOHC), collection 1688, Department of Special Collections, Charles E. Young Research Library, University of California, Los Angeles; Vangie Buell, interview by author, Oakland, 24 May 2000; Hana Shiozama, interview by Charles Kikuchi, May 1944, reel 77, Japanese American Evacuation and Resettlement Records (hereafter JAERR), BANC MSS 67/14c, Bancroft Library; Peter Jamero, interview by author, San Jose, 10 August 2000; Patricia West, interview by Woodrow Odanaka, 16 July 1973, Japanese American Project, Center for Oral and Public History, California State University, Fullerton; Clora Bryant et al., eds., *Central Avenue Sounds: Jazz in Los Angeles* (Berkeley: University of California Press, 1998), 103–109; Margarita Salazar McSweyn, interview by Sherna Berger Gluck, 1983, "Rosie the Riveter Revisited: Women and the World War II Experience," Oral History Resource Center, California State University, Long Beach; "Adventure in Brotherhood," *War Worker*, April 1944.

4. Sucheng Chan, *Asian Americans: An Interpretive History* (Boston: Twayne, 1991), 103; David Yoo, *Growing Up Nisei: Race, Generation, and Culture among Japanese Americans of California, 1924–49* (Urbana: University of Illinois Press, 2000); K. Scott Wong and Suchen Chan, eds., *Claiming America: Constructing Chinese American Identities during the Exclusion Era* (Philadelphia: Temple University Press, 1998); John Modell, *The Economics and Politics of Racial Accommodation: The Japanese of Los Angeles, 1900–1942* (Urbana: University of Illinois Press, 1977), 154; K. Scott Wong, "War Comes to Chinatown: Social Transformation and the Chinese of California," in *The Way We Really Were: The Golden State in the Second Great War*, ed. Roger Lotchin (Urbana: University of Illinois Press, 2000), 183.

5. George Sanchez, *Becoming Mexican American: Ethnicity, Culture, and Identity in Chicano Los Angeles, 1900–1945* (New York: Oxford University Press, 1993), 254; Edward Escobar, *Race, Police and the Making of a Political Identity: Mexican Americans and the Los Angeles Police Department, 1900–1945* (Berkeley: University of California Press, 1999), 166–67.

6. *People v. Pascual Bergasol,* 22 Cal. App. 2d 327 (1937); *People v. Cabaltero,* 31 Cal. App. 2d 52 (1939); Charles Kikuchi, *The Kikuchi Diary: Chronicle from an American Concentration Camp: The Tanforan Journals of*

Charles Kikuchi, ed. John Modell (Urbana: University of Illinois Press, 1973), 20–21.

7. Judy Yung, *Unbound Feet: A Social History of Chinese Women in San Francisco* (Berkeley: University of California Press, 1995), 229.

8. Monica Sone, *Nisei Daughter* (Boston: Little, Brown, 1953), 119; Lorena How, interview by Judy Yung, in *Unbound Voices: A Documentary History of Chinese Women in San Francisco,* ed. Judy Yung (Berkeley: University of California Press, 1999), 46. Although set in Seattle, Monica Sone's description of Chinese-Japanese tensions was true of California locales.

9. Jeanne Wakatsuki Houston and James D. Houston, *Farewell to Manzanar: A True Story of Japanese American Experience during and after the World War II Internment* (Boston: Houghton Mifflin, 1973), 10.

10. Yuri Kosamoto, interview by Charles Kikuchi, 12 October 1943, box 47, Charles Kikuchi Papers, collection 1259, Department of Special Collections, Charles E. Young Research Library; Mary Lew Shepard, interview by Judy Yung, *Unbound Voices,* 48.

11. Mary Odem, *Delinquent Daughters: Protecting and Policing Adolescent Female Sexuality in the United States, 1885–1920* (Chapel Hill: University of North Carolina Press, 1995). Valerie Matsumoto depicted differences between boys and girls in the rural community of Cortez, California. Boys had greater freedom than girls who handled domestic tasks, field labor, and care of younger siblings. See Valerie Matsumoto, "Redefining Expectations: Nisei Women in the 1930s," *California History* 73, no. 1 (Spring 1994): 63–65. Dawn Mabalon discussed how a tradition of chaperonage circumscribed the social activities of young Filipinas in Stockton before the war. Dawn Mabalon, "Life in Little Manila: Filipinas/os in Stockton, California, 1917–1972" (PhD diss., Stanford, 2004), 139.

12. Duncan Chin, *Growing Up on Grove Street, 1931–1946: Sketches and Memories of a Chinese American Boyhood* (Capitola: Capitola Book, 1995), 57–67; Frank Nishio, reminiscences, 16 July 1996, box 9, Military Intelligence Service Oral History Project Transcripts, National Japanese American Historical Society (hereafter NJAHS), San Francisco.

13. Ernesto Galarza, *Barrio Boy: The Story of a Boy's Acculturation* (Notre Dame: University of Notre Dame, 1971), 198–99; Bill Sorro, "A Pickle in the Sun," in Helen C. Toribio, ed., *Seven Card Stud with Seven Manangs Wild: Writings on Filipino Americans* (San Francisco: Eastbay Filipino American National Historical Society, 2002), 170.

14. Chin, *Growing Up on Grove Street,* 53.

15. Kazuo Inouye, interview by Leslie Ito, 13 December 1997, REgenerations Oral History Project (hereafter ROHP), Japanese American National Museum, Los Angeles.

16. Jamero, "Maeda's Place," 46.

17. Roberto Vallangca, *Pinoy: The First Wave* (San Francisco: Strawberry Hill Press, 1977), 63–66; Allen Ihara, Chicago Case Histories, Kikuchi Papers.

18. Chizu Kitano Iiyama, interview by Lisa Tsuchitani, 27 October 1998, "Women Oral History," Oral History Project (OHP), NJAHS.

19. Motoko Shimosaki, interview by Charles Kikuchi, 22 September 1944, and Yone Mizuno, interview by Charles Kikuchi, 1 May 1944, reel 78, JAERR.

20. Nikki Bridges, interview by Eric Saul, 23 November 1985, "Women Oral History," OHP, NJAHS.

21. Frances Nishimoto, interview by Charles Kikuchi, 13 December 1943, reel 78, JAEER; a Nisei, Ch Am (the name is reproduced as it appears in the record), also held herself aloof from the Filipino customers who borrowed money from her father at an Oakland gambling establishment. She had trouble explaining the source of her anti-Filipino feelings but maintained them through much of her life (Ch Am, interview by Charles Kikuchi, 1943, reel 74, JAERR).

22. *People v. Henderson,* 4 Cal. 2d 188 (August 1935).

23. Tamie Ihara, interview by Charles Kikuchi, July 1943, reel 74, JAERR; Jane Kim, interview by author, Los Angeles, 6 December 2003; Rose Mary Escobar, interview by author, Oakland, 8 March 2001.

24. Galarza, *Barrio Boy,* 209–12; Kimbo Kurihara, interview by Charles Kikuchi, 17 November 1944, reel 78, JAEER; Marge Ong, interview by Beverly Chan, 11 December 1979, SCCAOHC.

25. Doris Ihara, interview by Charles Kikuchi, May 1944, reel 77, JAERR; Richard Moto, interview by Charles Kikuchi, 29 February 1944, Chicago Case Histories, box 47, Kikuchi Papers.

26. Tadashi "Blackie" Najima, interview by Charles Kikuchi, 7 March 1944, Kikuchi Papers; Ellen Tanna, "East of West," *Kashu Mainichi,* 2 October 1932; Jerry Paular, interview by author, 14 October 2003.

27. "Negroes Prove Worth despite Historical Tale of Opposition," *Mexican Voice,* Spring 1938.

28. James Alex Tolmasov, interview by Sojin Kim, 2 and 17 April 2001, Boyle Heights Oral History Project (hereafter BHOHP), Japanese American National Museum; Marshall Royal, interview by Steven Isoardi, 1996, "Central Avenue Sounds," Oral History Program, University of California, Los Angeles; Leo Frumkin, interview by Kenneth Burt and Sojin Kim, 19 December 2001, BHOHP.

29. Mark Wild, "'So Many Children at Once and So Many Kinds': Schools and Ethno-racial Boundaries in Early Twentieth-Century Los Angeles," *Western Historical Quarterly* 33, no. 4 (Winter 2002): 460; Galarza, *Barrio Boy,* 211; Sue Kunitomi Embrey, interview by Al Hansen, Japanese American Project, Center for Oral and Public History, California State University, Fullerton; Paula Fass, "Creating New Identities: Youth and Ethnicity in New York City High Schools in the 1930s and 1940s," in *Generations of Youth: Youth Cultures and History in Twentieth-Century America,* ed. Joe Austin and Michael Nevin Willard (New York: New York University Press, 1998), 95–117. Vangie Buell complimented her teacher in West Oakland for introducing the class to a wide range of musical styles, including the works of Black artists Marion Anderson and Paul Robeson (Buell interview).

30. See, for example, *Olla Podrida* (Berkeley High School); *Lincolnian* and the *Railsplitter* (Lincoln High School); *Campus Crier* (Oakland Technical High School); *Junior Campus* (Los Angeles City College); and *Campanile* (Belmont High School). For specific coverage of Roosevelt High School's International Days, see the following stories in the student newspaper, the *Rough Rider:* "Fiesta Group Performs at World Friendship Program," 20 June 1940; "Students

Plan International Dress-up Day," 18 April 1940; "Students and Faculty to Don Racial Clothes," 11 April 1940; "International Dress-up Day to Be Observed May 5," 3 April 1940; "International Dress-up Day Combined with Cinco de Mayo," 1 May 1940.

31. "Commentary," September 1939, and "Brotherhood at Roosevelt," 26 March 1942, *Rough Rider;* Atoy Rudolph Wilson, interview by Sojin Kim, 2000, BHOHP; Frumkin interview.

32. *Lincolnian* (1940).

33. *Junior Campus* (1934).

34. Freda Ginsberg Maddow, interview by Paul Spitzzeri, 27 June 2000, BHOHP.

35. "Aims of Mikado Club," *Railsplitter,* 7 June 1940; "Negro Culture Group Presents Alpha Dance" and "Misled Minority Flays Negroes in Demonstration," *Los Angeles Collegian,* 4 March 1941; *Junior Campus* (1936).

36. Again, respondents might have preferred to remember harmony rather than conflict, but the large number of interviewees who responded similarly strengthened their accounts. A sampling: Paul Skenazy and Tera Martin, eds., *Conversations with Maxine Hong Kingston* (Jackson: University of Mississippi, 1998), 114–15; Shiozama interview; Young Oak Kim, interview by Karen Ishizuka and Robert Nakamura, 28 August 1995, Veterans Oral History Project, Japanese American National Museum.

37. Young Oak Kim interview.

38. Buell interview; Ruth Takahashi Voorhies, interview by Debra Kodama, 18 November 1997, ROHP; George Yoshida, interview by Darcie Iki, 23 July 2001, BHOHP. In her work on the Nisei of Cortez, Valerie Matsumoto also concluded that Japanese families rarely celebrated the birthdays of individuals. See Matsumoto, *Farming the Home Place: A Japanese American Community in California, 1919–1982* (Ithaca: Cornell University Press, 1993), 76.

39. Maya Angelou, *I Know Why the Caged Bird Sings* (New York: Random House, 1969), 198; Gloria Quan, interview by author, Orange County, California, 10 November 2003; Lisa Tsuchitani, interview by Chizu Kitano Iiyama, 27 October 1998, "Women Oral History," OHP, NJAHS; Eddie Ramirez, interview by Raul Vasquez and Sojin Kim, 11 January 2002, BHOHP. Many of the interviews consulted for this book made vivid reference to food. For histories of how food shapes ethnic identity, see Donna Gabaccia, *We Are What We Eat: Ethnic Food and the Making of Americans* (Cambridge: Harvard University Press, 1998), and Hasia Diner, *Italian, Irish and Jewish Foodways in the Age of Migration* (Cambridge: Harvard University Press, 2001).

40. Maxine Hong Kingston, *The Woman Warrior: Memoirs of a Girlhood among Ghosts* (New York: Vintage, 1989), 176.

41. Ruben Leon, interview by Steven L. Isoardi, 1996, "Central Avenue Sounds"; Nel King, ed., *Beneath the Underdog: His World as Composed by Mingus* (New York: Alfred A. Knopf, 1971), 50–52.

42. Kisako Yasuda, interview by Charles Kikuchi, 31 October 1944, reel 78, JAERR; Tom Kawaguchi, interview by John Tateishi, in *And Justice for All: An Oral History of the Japanese American Detention Camps,* ed. John Tateishi (Seattle: University of Washington Press, 1984), 176.

43. Hazel Nishi, interview by Charles Kikuchi, April 1943, reel 74, JAERR.

44. Barry Shimizu, interview by Charles Kikuchi, August 1944, reel 78, JAERR; Jerry Paular interview; Britt Woodman, interview in Clora Bryant et al., eds., *Central Avenue Sounds: Jazz in Los Angeles* (Berkeley: University of California Press, 1998), 4. According to one Mexican American, pachucos "were carrying on habits and traditions of their land of origin" (unsigned statement, folder 10, box 4, Sleepy Lagoon Defense Committee Papers, collection 107, Department of Special Collections, Charles E. Young Research Library. Cecil Wan remembered the presence of Chinese zoot-suiters on San Francisco street corners (Cecil Wan, interview by author, tape recording, San Francisco, 19 April 2000). Chester Himes, Carey McWilliams, and Emory Bogardus emphasized the diverse participation in zoot culture. See Chester Himes, *Black on Black: Baby Sister and Selected Writings* (New York: Doubleday, 1973), 220–21; Carey McWilliams, "Blood on the Pavement," in George E. Frankes and Curtis B. Solberg, eds., *Minorities in California History* (New York: Random House, 1971), 95–97; Emory Bogardus, "Gangs of Mexican-American Youth," *Sociology and Social Research* (September 1943): 55, 58.

45. Jerry Paular interview; Eduardo Obregón Pagán, *Murder at the Sleepy Lagoon: Zoot Suits, Race, and Riot in Wartime L.A.* (Chapel Hill: University of North Carolina Press, 2003), 39.

46. Summary Judgment, 1937, Preston School of Industry, Inmate Records, Inmate Histories, Youth Authority Records, California State Archives, Office of the Secretary of State, Sacramento. Unfortunately, this citation is incomplete.

47. Kikuchi, *Kikuchi Diary*, 126–28; Beatrice Griffith, "The Pachuco Patois," *Common Ground* (Summer 1947): 81.

48. The young Mexican-American woman is quoted in Bruce Tyler, "Zoot Suit Culture and the Black Press," *Journal of American Culture* (Summer 1994): 25; Pagán, *Murder at the Sleepy Lagoon*, 53–54; Manuel Ruiz reported the meeting of Mexican and Black youngsters at dance clubs as a common California phenomenon (Minutes of Meeting of Council of Latin American Youth, folder 9, box 3, Manuel Ruiz Jr. Papers, M295, Special Collections, Stanford University Libraries). The following works also point to the hybrid character of jazz and boogie-woogie music and their connection to zoot-suiting: Quintard Taylor, *In Search of the Racial Frontier: African Americans in the American West, 1528–1990* (New York: W. W. Norton, 1998), 249; "Zoot-Suit Culture and the Black Press," *Journal of American Culture* 17, no. 2 (Summer 1994): 23–27.

49. Anthony Ortega, interview by Steven L. Isoardi, September 1997, "Central Avenue Sounds"; Tote Takao, interview by Tom Susaki, October 1946, JAERR; Paul Banni, interview by Enid Hart Douglass, 1989, Earl Warren Oral History Project, Regional Oral History Office, Bancroft Library. Natividad Ramos reported that Ben Watkins's band of Black musicians shared the stage at Sweet's Hall, the popular dance hall in West Oakland, with Merced Gallegos, a Latino (Natividad Ramos, interview by Aurora Morales, 28 June 2000, "The History of Latinos in West Oakland: Community Narratives," Latino History Project, Oakland Museum of California). Corey Woodman remembered gigs in Montebello where "we played Mexican." Britt Woodman recalled the many

Mexican dances and weddings at which the group performed (Bryant et al., *Central Avenue Sounds,* 98, 120).

50. Lester Kimura, interview by Charles Kikuchi, September 1944, reel 78, JAERR; Shimizu interview; Tommy Hamada, interview by Charles Kikuchi, October 1944, JAERR.

51. David Roediger, "What to Make of Wiggers: A Work in Progress," in *Generations of Youth: Youth Cultures and History in Twentieth Century America,* ed. Joe Austin and Michael Nevin Willard (New York: New York University Press, 1998), 358–66.

52. Carl Bankston and Min Zhou, "The Social Adjustment of Vietnamese American Adolescents: Evidence for a Segmented Assimilation Approach," *Social Science Quarterly* 78 (June 1997): 509–15; Alejandro Portes and Min Zhou, "The New Second Generation: Segmented Assimilation and Its Variants," *Annals of the American Academy of Political and Social Science* 530 (November 1993): 81–96; George Sanchez, "Face the Nation: Race, Immigration and the Rise of Nativism in Late Twentieth-Century America," *International Migration Review* 31 (1997): 1009–30; Shelly Fisher Fishkin, review of *Playing in the Dark: Whiteness and the American Literary Imagination,* by Toni Morrison, *Journal of American History* 80 (1993): 629.

53. Hamada interview; "JACL's National Emergency Report," 1942, reel 84, JAERR. See also Bert Corona, "A Study of the Adjustment and Interpersonal Relations of Adolescents of Mexican Descent" (master's thesis, University of California, Los Angeles, 1955).

54. *Yogore* was the pejorative but widely used Japanese term for rebellious youth. It derives from the Japanese verb *yogoreru,* meaning "to get dirty."

55. Mariko's experience is related by George Yani, interview by Charles Kikuchi, November 1943, reel 77, JAERR (Yani identified her only as Mariko); Himes, *Black on Black,* 224; Kikuchi, *Kikuchi Diary,* 44. Zoot-suiters bragged about their success with girls, and most observers described them as dogged pursuers. "Every week a new wisa [a presumptuous, disrespectful term for a female date]. He gives them a present of a kiss—all girls, lots girls," reported one boy of his pachuco pal (Beatrice Griffith, "The Things of Life," *Common Ground* [Summer 1948]: 61). Chester Himes described the characteristic activities of pachucos as fighting, stealing automobile parts, and jostling over girls. He even speculated that violence between White sailors and zoot-suiters in Los Angeles and other California cities was precipitated by the two groups' competition over women (221–23).

56. Daring, interethnic flirtations were the custom at popular dance halls such as Sweet's Hall. Catherine Ramirez, "Crimes of Fashion: The Pachuca and Chicana-Style Politics," *Meridians: Feminism, Race, Transnationalism* (2002): 15; Rose Echeverria Mulligan and Mary Luna, interviews by Gluck, 1983, "Rosie the Riveter Revisited." According to Elizabeth Escobedo, many Mexican-American women aimed to prove their respectability, morality, and patriotism in response to stereotypes to the contrary. See Elizabeth Escobedo, "Mexican American Home Front: The Politics of Gender, Culture, and Community in World War II Los Angeles" (PhD diss., University of Washington, 2004), 71, 83, 106.

57. Hamada interview; Shimizu interview; Anonymous, interview by Tom Sasaki, October 1946, "Observations of Wholesale Market, Los Angeles," reel 108, JAERR.

58. Rose Kazuko Hayashi, interview by Harry Ando, 10 December 1943, Chicago Case Histories, box 47, Kikuchi Papers.

3. GUESS WHO'S JOINING US FOR DINNER?

1. Gloria and Eddie Erosa, interview by author, Gardena, California, 6 December 2003.

2. Peggy Pascoe, "Miscegenation Law, Court Cases, and Ideologies of 'Race,'" in *Sex, Love, Race: Crossing Boundaries in North American History,* ed. Martha Hodes (New York: New York University press, 1999); *Loving v. Virginia,* 388 U.S. 1 (1967); David Hollinger, "Amalgamation and Hypodescent: The Question of Ethnoracial Mixture in the History of the United States," *American Historical Review* 108, no. 5 (December 2003): 1363–90; Renee Romano, *Race Mixing: Black-White Marriage in Postwar America* (Cambridge: Harvard University Press, 2003). In her history of interracial intimacy Rachel Moran explored how White privilege defined the marital relations and parental strategies of mixed couples. The Whiteness of White women, she argued, was put at risk by their associations with non-Whites. At the same time the very longing for such associations reinforced their White privilege. See Rachel Moran, *Interracial Intimacy: The Regulation of Race and Romance* (Chicago: University of Chicago Press, 2001), 56, 67, 116. In her study of contemporary pairings of White women and Black men, Ruth Frankenberg noted that racial dynamics of the larger society influenced personal relationships. White women married to Black men typically became more socially conscious but never fully departed from their own position of privilege. See Ruth Frankenberg, *White Women, Race Matters: The Social Construction of Whiteness* (Minneapolis: University of Minnesota Press, 1993), 110–15. Analyzing divorce records, Peggy Pascoe discovered the ease with which White men disentangled themselves from long-term relations with non-White women. Denied the protections of a legalized marriage, these women's claims to joint property and resources were ignored. See Peggy Pascoe, "Miscegenation Law, Court Cases, and Ideologies of 'Race' in Twentieth-Century America," *Journal of American History* 83 (1996): 44–70.

3. Henry Yu, *Thinking Orientals: Migration, Contact, and Exoticism in Modern America* (New York: Oxford University Press, 2000), 56–63; Henry Yu, "Tiger Woods Is Not the End of History: Or Why Sex across the Color Line Won't Save Us All," *American Historical Review* 108, no. 5 (December 2003): 1406–14. Yu argued that intermarriage offers an opportunity to discuss broad social trends and constitutes "the most focused example of what interracial and intercultural relations mean." He linked the early preoccupations of 1930s sociologists to our own contemporary fascination with intimate relations between the races. Yu also talked about intermarriage as a mode of assimilation and the role of exoticism in White-Oriental interactions. See Henry Yu, "Mixing Bodies and Cultures: The Meaning of America's Fascination with Sex between 'Orientals' and 'Whites,'" in Hodes, *Sex, Love, Race,* 446–58.

4. Pascoe, "Miscegenation Law," in Hodes, *Sex, Love, Race,* 467; Gary Nash, "The Hidden History of Mestizo America," *Journal of American History* 82 (December 1995): 941; Yu, "Mixing Bodies and Cultures," 458; Yu, *Thinking Orientals,* 58. For a comprehensive account of the construction and eventual collapse of the antimiscegenation regime in the United Sates, see Peter Wallenstein, *Tell the Court I Love My Wife: Race, Marriage and Law—An American History* (New York: Palgrave Macmillan, 2002).

5. Louisiana Constitution (1920), art. 220; North Carolina *Consolidated Statutes* (1927), sec. 2495; John D'Emilio and Estelle Freedman, *Intimate Matters: A History of Sexuality in America* (New York: Harper and Row, 1988), 93. In the 1948 opinion that finally overturned California's antimiscegenation law, state Supreme Court justice Roger J. Traynor cleverly extended the logic of the statute to challenge White privilege: "It might be concluded therefore that section 60 is based upon the theory that the progeny of a white person and a Mongolian or Negro or Malay are inferior or undesirable, while the progeny of members of other different races are not. . . . Furthermore there is not a ban on illicit sexual relations between Caucasians and members of the proscribed races. Indeed it is covertly encouraged by race restrictions on marriage" (*Perez v. Lippold,* 32 Cal. 2d 711, 712 [1948]; this case is also known as *Perez v. Sharp*).

6. The calculations are based upon my review of approximately thirty-five hundred marriage licenses filed in Los Angeles County between January and March 1940. The Los Angeles County Marriage Licenses and Certificates from 1940 are available through the Los Angeles Regional Family History Center (hereafter LARFHC).

7. Figures are based upon my analysis of marriage licenses in San Joaquin County as well as Los Angeles County. I selected San Joaquin because of its sizable but quantitatively manageable population of minorities (especially those of Mexican and Filipino descent) and because it differed from the more urban, larger Los Angeles. San Joaquin statistics are drawn from annual figures for 1940 and 1949. For Los Angeles I use the approximately three thousand to thirty-five hundred marriages recorded between January and mid-March in 1940 and 1949 as a representative sample of yearly patterns. The San Joaquin County as well as the Los Angeles County records are available through the LARFHC.

8. Nellie Foster, "Legal Status of Filipino Intermarriages in California," *Sociology and Social Research* 16 (May–June 1942): 449–50; Rachel Moran, "Interracial Intimacy," *Kashu Mainichi,* 11 December 1931; George Simpson, *Racial and Cultural Minorities: An Analysis of Prejudice and Discrimination* (New York: Harper, 1953), 503; untitled article in the *New World Sun,* 3 May 1936; Paul Spickard, *Mixed Blood: Intermarriage and Ethnic Identity in Twentieth-Century America* (Madison: University of Wisconsin Press, 1989), 229.

9. On prevailing notions of ethnicity and race in China or Japan, see Frank Dikotter, *The Discourse of Race in Modern China* (London: Hurst, 1992), 90, 131–36; Michael Weiner, "The Invention of Identity: Race and Nation in Pre-War Japan," in *The Construction of Racial Identities in China and Japan: Historical Contemporary Perspectives,* ed. Frank Dikotter (London: Hurst, 1997): 135; George Lew, interview by Beverly Chan, 18 August 1979, Southern California Chinese American Oral History Collection (hereafter SCCAOHP),

collection 1688, Department of Special Collections, Charles E. Young Research Library, University of California, Los Angeles.

10. Arleen De Vera, "The Tapia-Saiki Incident," in Valerie Matsumoto, ed., *Over the Edge: Remapping the American West* (Berkeley: University of California Press, 1999), 206–209. Conclusions about Japanese marital attitudes are based upon my analysis of 194 cases in "Issei Interview Survey," Japanese American Research Project (hereafter JARP), collection 2010, Department of Special Collections, Charles E. Young Research Library. I use the results of this survey to buttress my conclusions about racial ideas. I do not mean to suggest that Isseis' perceptions did not reflect the character of their experiences in the 1960s, but I believe Japanese ideas retained some consistency (if anything, opposition to intermarriage lessened) between 1925 and 1960.

11. Paul Paular, interview by author, Gardena, California, 21 October 2003; Jerry Paular, interview by author, 14 October 2003; George Sanchez, *Becoming Mexican American: Ethnicity, Culture and Identity in Chicano Los Angeles, 1900–1945* (New York: Oxford University Press, 1993), 30; Spickard, *Mixed Blood,* 42, 353; Alan Knight, "Racism, Revolution, and Indigenismo: Mexico, 1910–1940," in *Idea of Race in Latin America, 1870–1940,* ed. Richard Graham (Austin: University of Texas, 1990), 95; Dolores Cruz, interview by author, Monterey Park, California, 22 November 2003; Barbara Posades, "Mestiza Girlhood," in *Making Waves: An Anthology by and about Asian American Women,* ed. Asian Women United of California (Boston: Beacon, 1989); Barbara Posades, "Crossed Boundaries in Chicago: Pilipino American Families since 1925," in *Unequal Sisters: A Multicultural Reader in U.S. Women's History,* ed. Ellen DuBois and Vicki Ruiz (New York: Routledge, 2000).

For more about the racial characteristics of Filipino nationalism, see John Schumacher, *The Propaganda Movement: 1880–1895, The Creators of a Filipino Consciousness, The Makers of Revolution* (Manila: Solidaridad, 1973); Michael Salman, *The Embarrassment of Slavery: The Controversies over Bondage and Nationalism in the American Colonial Philippines* (Berkeley: University of California Press, 2001), 10–19; and Antonio Pido, *The Pilipinos in America: Macro/Micro Dimensions of Immigration and Integration* (New York: Center for Migration Studies, 1986). For other works that suggest the comfort of Filipino immigrants with intermixing, see Paul Spickard, "Injustice Compounded: Amerasians and Non-Japanese Americans in World War II Concentration Camps," *Journal of American Ethnic History* 5, no. 2 (Spring 1986): 5–22.

12. Spickard, *Mixed Blood,* 353; Leo Frumkin, interview by Kenneth Burt and Sojin Kim, 19 December 2001, Boyle Heights Oral History Project (hereafter BHOHP), Japanese American National Museum, Los Angeles.

13. Adele Hernandez Milligan, interview by Sherna Berner Gluck, 1983, in "Rosie the Riveter Revisited: Women and the World War II Experience," Oral History Resource Center, Special Collections, California State University, Long Beach; Betty Wong Lem, interview by Jean Wong, 5 April 1979, SCCAOHP. Harry Lem's consistent choice of *Black* women hints at the possibility that he exoticized them.

14. Jim Naritomi, interview by Daisy Satoda, 22 November 1989, box 5, Oral History Project, National Japanese American Historical Society (hereafter NJAHS), San Francisco.

15. Sucheng Chan, *Asian Americans: An Interpretive History* (Boston: Twayne, 1991), 10–14, 17–23; Karen Leonard, *Making Ethnic Choices: California's Punjabi Mexican Americans* (Philadelphia: Temple University Press, 1992), 23. Warren Thompson, *Growth and Changes in California's Population* (Los Angeles: Haynes Foundation, 1955), 85; George Anthony Peffer, *If They Don't Bring Their Women Here: Chinese Female Immigration before Exclusion* (Urbana: University of Illinois Press, 1999).

16. Other Asian-American interviewees remembered interminority marriages. For more examples see survey results 0700202, 763204, 725201, 796205, 183204, JARP; "Women Oral History," NJAHS; The interviews quoted are William Chew Chan, interview by Suellen Chung, 7 January 1980, and Ida Lee, interview by Beverly Chan, 29 July 1980, both in the SCCAOHP; Also, Peggy Kanzawa, interview by Kiku Funabiki, 8 February 1989, "Women Oral History," NJAHS. For the repatriation petitions of Marguerite Takeuchi and Bertia Morial, see "Application to Take Oath of Allegiance to United States under Act of 25 June 1936, as Amended and Form of Such Oath," 246-R1236 and 246-R1526, Repatriation Documents, National Archives, Laguna Niguel, California.

17. Constantine Panunzio, "Intermarriage in Los Angeles, 1924–1933," *American Journal of Sociology* 47 (March 1942): 690–701. Although Panunzio's work does not cover the entirety of the time period, 1925–1955, under review in this book, it indicates general patterns of intermarriage that likely persisted through midcentury. These limited statistics, as well as remembered and recorded cases of intermarriage, underscore the existence of mixed marriages and hint at the presence of others. Given the indifference of Whites to relations among minorities, mainstream sources took less note of such pairings. At the same time embarrassment about interracial intimacy in minority communities discouraged members from speaking about or publicly acknowledging known cases. The recovered evidence therefore likely understates the number of mixed marriages and progeny. If not beside the point, counting is secondary to my analysis. Even the limited sample of committed relationships in this study demonstrates the mechanisms by which minorities fashioned families that defied traditions of separatism and discrimination.

18. Los Angeles Marriage Licenses and Certificates, 1940, LARFHC.

19. Los Angeles Marriage Licenses and Certificates, 1949, 1950, LARFHC.

20. *Gavino C. Visco v. Los Angeles County State of California,* No. 319408, Superior Court (1931); San Joaquin County Marriage Licenses and Certificates, 1943–46, LARFHC.

21. Foster, "Legal Status of Filipino Intermarriages," 449; percentages calculated from Panunzio, "Intermarriage in Los Angeles," 694–99, and San Joaquin County Marriage Licenses and Certificates, 1943–46, LARFHC.

22. San Joaquin County Marriage Licenses and Certificates, 1947–49, LARFHC.

23. Craig Scharlin and Lilia V. Villanueva, *Philip Vera Cruz: A Personal History of Filipino Immigrants and the Farmworkers Movement* (Los Angeles: UCLA Labor Center, Institute of Industrial Relations, and UCLA Asian American Studies Center, 1992), 53; Lilian Galerdo and Theresa Quilenderino Mar, "Filipinos in a Farm Labor Camp," in *Letters in Exile: An Introductory Reader*

on the History of Pilipinos in America (Los Angeles: UCLA Asian American Studies Center, 1976), 53–60; Karen Leonard, "Intermarriage and Ethnicity: Punjabi Mexican Americans, Mexican Japanese, and Filipino Americans," *Explorations in Ethnic Studies* 16, no. 2 (July 1993): 149, 152; Panunzio, "Intermarriage in Los Angeles," 695; John Burma, "Interethnic Marriage in Los Angeles, 1948–1959," *Social Forces* (December 1963): 159; Benicio Catapusan, "Filipino Intermarriage Problems in the United States," *Social Forces* (January–February 1938): 267.

24. Cruz interview; Frances Marr, interview by author, 11 November 2003; San Joaquin County Marriage Licenses and Certificates,1947–49, LARFHC.

25. Leonard, "Intermarriage and Ethnicity," 152.

26. Garding Liu, *Inside Los Angeles Chinatown* (Los Angeles: n.p., 1948), 154–56; Dorothy Siu, interview by Jean Wong, 12 January 1979, SCCAOHP; Rose Mary Escobar, interview by author, Oakland, 8 March 2001.

27. C. S. Machida, interview by Chloe Holt, 2 July 1924, Survey of Race Relations Records, Hoover Institution Archives, Stanford, California. Conducted just a year before the period considered by this book, 1925–55, this interview is helpful in understanding how gender affected the intermarried couples.

28. "Japanese Wife of Oakland Chinese Arrested as Alien," *Hawaii Chinese Journal,* 16 July 1942.

29. Panunzio, "Intermarriage in Los Angeles," 694, 698; Chan interview.

30. Gloria Erosa, interview by author, 6 December 2003; Dolores Arlington, interview by author, 24 November 2004; Benicio Catapusan, "Social Adjustment of the Filipinos in the United States" (master's thesis, University of Southern California, 1940), 166–68.

31. Daily Reports from Santa Clara County, reel 108, July 1946, JAERR.

32. *Kibei* is the term for someone of Japanese descent, born in the United States and sent to Japan for his secondary education.

33. Mario T. Garcia, *Memories of Chicano History: The Life and Narrative of Bert Corona* (Berkeley: University of California Press, 1994), 130; Elaine Black Yoneda, interview by Lucy Kendall, 21 May 1977, Elaine Black Yoneda Papers, Labor Archives, San Francisco State University.

34. Marr interview.

35. Buddy Ono, "She Married a Filipino," *New World Sun,* 3 May 1936.

36. Liu, *Inside Los Angeles Chinatown,* 157; Leonard, *Making Ethnic Choices,* 149, 154–57; Sugar Pie De Santo, interview by author, Oakland, 16 February 2001. Rachel Moran noted the ability of White parents to extend their racial privileges to their mixed-race children. Non-White spouses tended to embrace this transmission. See Moran, *Interracial Intimacy,* 103–104. Leonard reported that Hispanic wives often successfully challenged the marriages that their husbands had proposed between their offspring and either local Punjabi pals or Indian women abroad. Most members of the second generation managed to choose partners that pleased them (Leonard, *Making Ethnic Choices,* 123–26).

37. Clara Chin, interview by author, Los Angeles, 14 November 2003; Arlington interview.

38. Liu, *Inside Los Angeles Chinatown,* 157.

39. Clarence Yip Yeu, interview by Suellen Cheng, 24 April 1980, SC-CAOHP.

40. Clara Chin interview.

41. Catapusan, "Social Adjustment of the Filipinos," 165; Arlington, Eddie Erosa, and Cruz interviews. The conclusions of scholars Bruno Lasker and Don Gonzales are quoted in Catapusan's master's thesis.

42. "150,000 Japanese Girls Will Be Married Off," *Hawaii Chinese Journal,* 3 June 1943; "Matrimony by Bribery," *New Korea,* 10 April 1941.

43. Chizu Sanada, interview by Charles Kikuchi, September 1944, reel 78, JAERR.

44. John Fante, "Mary Osaka, I Love You," *Good Housekeeping,* October 1942.

45. Garcia, *Memories of Chicano History,* 130.

46. The Communist Party, to which Karl Yoneda was first drawn when he witnessed its street demonstrations in downtown Los Angeles, was central to his political activism. See Mark Wild, *Street Meeting: Multiethnic Neighborhoods in Early Twentieth-Century Los Angeles* (Berkeley: University of California Press, 2005), 189.

47. Elaine Yoneda to Karl Yoneda, 11 August 1943, folder 7, box 3, Elaine Black Yoneda Papers.

48. Historians such as Paul Spickard asserted that multiracial individuals had little opportunity to choose identities for themselves until well after the civil rights movement of the 1960s. Before then, most accepted socially ascribed, monoracial identities. See Paul Spickard, "The Illogic of American Racial Categories," in *Racially Mixed People in America,* ed. Maria Root (Newbury Park, CA: Sage, 1992), 165. Echoing the early twentieth century thinking of Robert Park, who depicted biracial children as likely cosmopolitans, Lise Funderburg and Rachel Moran have noted greater tolerance and attraction to "dualism" in the desires and attitudes of mixed-race individuals. See Lise Funderburg, *Black, White, Other: Biracial Americans Talk about Race and Identity* (New York: William Morrow, 1994), 197; Moran, *Interracial Intimacy,* 158; Kathleen Odell Korgen, *From Black to Biracial: Transforming Racial Identity among Americans* (Westport, CT: Praeger, 1998), 78.

49. "Children in Residence—Japanese Children's Home," 31 March 1942, Children's Village Project Materials, compiled by Art Hansen, Center for Oral and Public History, California State University, Fullerton; Ellen Levine, *A Fence away from Freedom: Japanese Americans and World War II* (New York: G.P. Putnam's, 1995); Tetsuya G. Ishimaru, Report on the Children's Village of Manzanar Relocation Project, January 1943, Children's Village Project Materials.

50. Life History of Peter by William C. Smith, 1924, Survey of Race Relations Records, Hoover Institution Archives; Leonard, *Making Ethnic Choices,* 132; Marr and Eddie Erosa interviews.

51. Peter Jamero, interview by author, San Jose, 10 August 2000; Cruz and Clara Chin interviews; Dawn Mabalon, "Life in Little Manila: Filipinas/os in Stockton, California, 1917–1972" (PhD diss., Stanford, 2004), 119–27. Mabalon observed the participation of mestizas in the queen contests. In her study

of Seattle-based Filipino Americans, Dorothy Fugita-Rony noted the very different racial expectations for and standards applied to local queen contests. Speculating that at root was a prejudice against Native Americans, many of whom had married Filipinos, she described the contestants as universally "pure" in racial background. See Dorothy Fugita-Rony, *American Workers, Colonial Power: Philippine Seattle and the Transpacific West, 1919–1941* (Berkeley: University of California Press, 2003), 181.

52. Allen Mock, interview by Jean Wong, 13 December 1980, box 47, SCCAOHP; Clara Chin interview.

53. Marshall Hoo, interview by Beverly Chan, 24 May 1980, SCCAOHP; Siu interview.

54. Marion Brainerd to Ralph Merritt, 1 September 1944, Children's Village Project Materials.

55. Guy Gabaldon, interview by Ruchika Joshi, 25 July 2000, "U.S. Latinos and Latinas and World War II," *Narratives* 2 (Fall 2000), published by the Department of Journalism, University of Texas, Austin.

56. Cruz and Clara Chin interviews.

57. Levine, *A Fence away from Freedom*, 7.

4. BANDING TOGETHER IN CRISIS

1. In his comprehensive account of World War II California, Gerald Nash pointed to an increase in diversity as evidence of the conflict's transformative impact. See Gerald Nash, *The American West Transformed: The Impact of the Second World War* (Bloomington: Indiana University Press, 1985).

2. Josh Sides, *L.A. City Limits: African American Los Angeles from the Great Depression to the Present* (Berkeley: University of California Press, 2003); Rudolph Lapp, *Afro-Americans in California* (San Francisco: Boyd and Fraser, 1979), 39; Marilyn Johnson, *The Second Gold Rush: Oakland and the East Bay in World War II* (Berkeley: University of California Press, 1993), 53, 59.

3. Albert Camarillo, *Chicanos in California: A History of Mexican Americans in California* (San Francisco: Boyd and Fraser, 1984), 77–78; Johnson, *Second Gold Rush*, 55–57; Deborah Dash Moore, *To the Golden Cities: Pursuing the American Jewish Dream in Miami and Los Angeles* (New York: Free Press, 1994), 25–27; Stephen Pitti, *The Devil in Silicon Valley: Northern California, Race, and Mexican Americans* (Princeton: Princeton University Press, 2003), 124.

4. Alison Bernstein, *American Indians and World War II: Toward a New Era in Indian Affairs* (Norman: University of Oklahoma Press, 1979), 87; Walter Nugent, *Into the West: The Story of Its People* (New York: Alfred A. Knopf, 1999), 283.

5. James Gregory, *American Exodus: The Dust Bowl Migration and Okie Culture in California* (New York: Oxford University Press, 1989).

6. Johnson, *Second Gold Rush*, 44, 89, 93. For more on patterns of white migration and suburbanization, see Becky Nicolaides, *My Blue Heaven: Life and Politics in the Working-Class Suburbs of Los Angles, 1920–1965* (Chicago: University of Chicago Press, 2002).

7. "Little Tokio's Jumpin Now," *Negro Digest,* October 1943; "Back Home in Sacramento," *Pacific Citizen,* 21 May 1949; Maya Angelou, *I Know Why the Caged Bird Sings* (New York: Random House, 1969), 202; Shirley Ann Moore, *To Place Our Deeds: The African American Community in Richmond, California, 1910–1963* (Berkeley: University of California Press, 2000), 74–75.

8. "Japanese Property for Sale," *Eastside (Los Angeles) Journal,* 24 September 1942.

9. Hank Hiroshima, interview by Walter Tanaka, 16 October 1997, box 9, Military Intelligence Service Oral History Project Transcripts (MIS), National Japanese American Historical Society (hereafter NJAHS), San Francisco; Dr. Nakadote, interview by Tom Sasaki, 14 September 1946, reel 108, BANC MSS 67/14c, Japanese American Evacuation and Resettlement Records (hereafter JAERR), Bancroft Library, University of California, Berkeley; Mary Oyama, "A Nisei Report from Home," *Common Ground,* Winter 1946; Amy Uno Ishi, interview by Betty E. Miston and Kristen Mitchell, 9 July 1973, Japanese American Project, Center for Oral and Public History, California State University, Fullerton; *Bennett v. State Bar of California,* 27 Cal. 2d 31 (1945); anonymous interview, May 1976, Asian American Oral History Composite, BANC MSS 78/123c, Bancroft Library; Nakadote interview; Masaji Inoshita, interview by Sheryl Narahara, 14 September 1997, box 4, MIS.

10. "Japanese Farms in California Taken over by Many Operators," *Pacific Citizen,* 11 June 1942.

11. "Race Farmers Must Deal with Japs for Farm Lands," *California Eagle,* 23 April 1942.

12. "Chinese and Japs Cooperate on West Coast," *Philippines Mail,* 12 August 1942.

13. Jacques E. Levy, *Cesar Chavez: Autobiography of La Causa,* (New York: W. W. Norton, 1975), 64; "Business League Sees Negro Fisherman and Farmers as Result of War with Axis," *California Eagle,* 18 December 1941.

14. Cheryl Greenberg attributed what she deemed the failing of Black and Jewish civil rights organizations to denounce evacuation orders to a mix of factors: racism, the success of the government's rhetoric portraying internment as a military necessity, and self-interest. See Cheryl Greenberg, "Black and Japanese Responses to Japanese Internment," *Journal of American Ethnic History* 14 (Winter 1995): 3–37. Scott Kurashige cited the neglectful coverage of the liberal-leaning Black newspaper the *California Eagle* as evidence of indifference and/or subtle support for internment among African Americans in "Transforming Los Angeles: Black and Japanese American Struggles for Racial Equality in the Twentieth Century" (PhD diss., University of California, Los Angeles, 2000), 357–59. Based upon his reading of the Chinese-American newspaper *Chinese Press,* K. Scott Wong concluded that Chinese Americans implicitly condoned Japanese internment. They did so, he proposed, in order to prove their loyalty to the United States. See K. Scott Wong, *Americans First: Chinese Americans and the Second World War* (Cambridge: Harvard University Press, 2005), 84–88.

15. Even those scholars who fault minority civil rights organizations for not challenging internment acknowledge the discomfort and periodic protest made at chapters in the West where members had more intimate contact with Japanese.

For example, Cheryl Greenberg noted the concern expressed by the Alameda County chapter of the NAACP to national headquarters. See Greenberg, "Black and Japanese Responses to Japanese Internment," 15.

16. Noah W. Griffin to Mr. Y. Yoshino, 28 April 1945, National Association for the Advancement of Colored Peoples, Region I, records, 1942–1986, BANC MSS 78/180c, Bancroft Library, University of California Berkeley; Reginald Kearney, *African American Views of the Japanese: Solidarity or Sedition?* (Albany: State University of New York Press, 1998), 168.

17. Harry Paxton Howard, "American Concentration Camps," *Crisis,* September 1942. Again, scholars such as Reginald Kearney depicted official Black responses to internment as too little and too weak. However, when viewed against a backdrop of virulent anti-Japanese sentiment and discrimination against minorities, these tentative gestures appear more significant. See Kearney, *African American Views of the Japanese,* 165–72.

18. Announcement of Conference on Interracial Cooperation, 10–11 January 1948, box 54, Charles Kikuchi Papers, collection 1259, Department of Special Collections, Charles E. Young Research Library, University of California, Los Angeles; Greenberg, "Black and Japanese Responses to Japanese Internment," 13–14; Edward Chew, "Election Fever Hot," *Chinese Press,* 3 November 1950.

19. Richard Moto, interview by Charles Kikuchi, 29 February 1944, Chicago Case Histories, box 47, Kikuchi Papers.

20. Robert Sakai, interview by Marsha Tagami, 24 September 1997, box 9, MIS; "Colorado Fair Play Committee," 1944, reel 83, JAERR; untitled article, *Crossroads: The Los Angeles Nisei Weekly,* 28 May 1948; Moto interview.

21. "Hold Japanese at S.F. Hotel" *Pacific Citizen,* 5 November 1942; Rose Kazuko interview by Harry Ando, 1943, reel 89, JAERR; *Of Civil Rights and Wrongs: The Fred Korematsu Story,* produced and directed by Eric Paul Fournier, National Asian American Telecommunications Association, 2000, videocassette; "First Case Filed in Supreme Court to Test Legality of Army Evacuation," *Pacific Citizen,* 12 February 1944.

22. Mary Oyama, "This Isn't Japan," *Common Ground* (Autumn 1942): 33; "Zoot Suit Gang Here," *Gila News-Courier,* 22 May 1943; Bill Katayama, interview by Charles Kikuchi, 1944, Kikuchi Papers; Tamie Ihara, interview by Charles Kikuchi, July 1943, reel 74, JAERR.

23. "Nisei: A Role in an American Minority," October 1944, JAERR; Tommy Yoneda to United China Relief, 1 May 1942, folder 2, box 8, Karl Yoneda Collection, collection 1592, Department of Special Collections, Charles E. Young Research Library.

24. Katayama interview; Chohei Sakamoto, interview, 10 September 1943, Kikuchi Papers.

25. Scholars have addressed the very different racial positions and understandings of Japanese Americans who settled in Chicago during the war as part of the government's relocation efforts. Charlotte Brooks and Jaclyn Harden both described how Nisei actively distinguished themselves from local African Americans, leaning more toward a White ethnic identity. See Charlotte Brooks, "In the Twilight Zone between Black and White: Japanese American Resettlement and Community in Chicago, 1942–1945," *Journal of American History* 86 (March

2000): 1655–87; Jaclyn Harden, *Double Cross: Japanese Americans in Black and White Chicago* (Minneapolis: University of Minnesota Press, 2003).

26. Kisako Yasuda, interview by Charles Kikuchi, 31 October 1944, reel 78, JAERR.

27. D. Michael Bottoms, "'Every Colored Man Is the Victim of Bitter Prejudice and Unjust Laws': Race and the Right to Be Heard in California's Courts, 1851–1873" (PhD diss., University of California, Los Angeles, 2004).

28. Jere Bishop Franco, *Crossing the Pond: The Native American War Effort in World War II* (Denton: University of North Texas Press, 1999), 106; Bernstein, *American Indians and World War II*, 83.

29. Bernstein, *American Indians and World War II*, 85. Roosevelt's remark was reported in the newspaper of Los Angeles City College: "Release of Japanese-American Internees Ends Argument Waged throughout U.S.," *Los Angeles Collegian*, 18 May 1943.

30. Agnes Savilla, interview by David Hacker, 8 April 1978, "Japanese American World War II Evacuation Oral History Project, Part V: Guards and Townspeople," ed. Art Hansen and Nora M. Jesch, California State University, Fullerton, 1993, 795; Simon Lewis and Iver Sunna, interviews by Scott Russell, 6 July 1993, in "Return to Butte Camp: A Japanese-American World War II Relocation Center," ed. Orit Tamir, Scott Russell, Karolyn Jackman Jensen, and Shereen Lerner, report prepared for the Bureau of Reclamation Arizona Project Office, 1993 (see appendix J for Sunna interview, appendix L for Lewis's).

31. *Gila News-Courier*, 1 April 1943, box 55, Kikuchi Papers.

32. Anonymous, interview by Orit Tamir, 14 June 1993, in Tamir, Russell, Jensen, and Lerner, "Return to Butte Camp," appendix J; "Indian Chiefs to Visit Here," 13 May 1943, "Indian Chiefs to Visit Camp," 22 May 1943, and "Indian Program to Be Presented," 22 May 1943, all in *Gila News-Courier*, box 55, Kikuchi Papers; *Kampus Krier*, 1943, Records of Colorado River Relocation, Huntington Library, San Marino, California.

33. Art Hansen, "Evacuation and Resettlement Study at the Gila River Relocation Center, 1942–1944," *Journal of the West* (April 1999): 45–46; Robert Spencer, "Gila Reports of Robert Spencer from Gila River Relocation Center," n.d., Kikuchi Papers. According to Hansen, Spencer led a small team of social scientists without government affiliation who hoped to learn about the enforced migration of the Japanese and design postwar solutions for the displaced people of Europe.

34. Kazue Tsuchiyama's "Indians of the Southwest" and the entirety of the Poston writings were republished in Vincent Tajiri, ed., *Through Innocent Eyes: Writings and Art from the Japanese American Internment by Poston I Schoolchildren* (Los Angeles: Keiro Services Press, 1990), 77.

35. Ishimi and Chiyoko Tagawa, interviews by Orit Tamar, 15 June 1993, in Tamir, Russell, Jensen, and Lerner, "Return to Butte Camp," 19.

36. Spencer, "Gila River Reports," Kikuchi Papers.

37. Savilla interview, 792, 805, 796.

38. Albert Cooley, interview, 1993, in Tamir, Russell, Jensen, and Lerner, "Return to Butte Camp," 100.

39. Ruth Cooley, interview, 1993, in Tamir, Russell, Jensen, and Lerner, "Return to Butte Camp," appendix K.

40. Bill Sorro's account of the silence his mother demanded as they walked past empty Japanese storefronts in the Fillmore District expressed the fearfulness so many non-Whites felt. This sense of peril pushed protest into less visible, more personal channels (Bill Sorro, interview by author, San Francisco, 3 August 2000; Bill Sorro, "A Pickle in the Sun," in Helen C. Toribio, ed., *Seven Card Stud with Seven Manangs Wild: Writings on Filipino Americans* (San Francisco: Eastbay Filipino American National Historical Society, 2002), 167–72.

41. Ruth Washington, "Black Leadership in Los Angeles," interview by Ranford Hopkins, July 5, 1984, Oral History Program, University of California, Los Angeles; Reginald Kearney, "Afro American Views of Japanese" (PhD diss., Kent State University, 1991), 185–87.

42. Charles Himes, *If He Hollers, Let Him Go* (1945; reprint, with a foreword by Hilton Als, New York: Thunder's Mouth Press, 2002), 3–4.

43. Peter Susuki, "Anthropologists in the Wartime Camps for Japanese Americans: A Documentary Study," *Dialectical Anthropology* 6 (1981): 29–30; Minutes of Joint Meeting of Japanese American Citizens League (JACL) Advisory and Executive Committees, 1942.

44. Patricia Justiniani McReynolds, *Almost Americans: A Quest for Dignity* (Santa Fe, NM: Red Crane Books, 1997), 200; Kim Fong Tom, interview by Beverly Chan, box 18, Southern California Chinese American Oral History Collection (hereafter SCCAOHP), collection 1688, Department of Special Collections, Charles E. Young Research Library; Vangie Buell, interview by author, Oakland, 24 May 2000.

45. Rose Kazuko Hayashi, interview by Harry Ando, 10 December 1943, Chicago Case Histories, box 47, Kikuchi Papers; Katayama interview; Charles Kikuchi, *The Kikuchi Diary: Chronicle from an American Concentration Camp: The Tanforan Journals of Charles Kikuchi*, ed. John Modell (Urbana: University of Illinois, 1973), 44.

46. Dionicio Morales, *Dionicio Morales: A Life in Two Cultures* (Houston: Pinata Books, 1997), 40, 113–14; Daniel Luevano, interview by Carlos Vasquez, 1988, Oral History Program, University of California, Los Angeles. In the introduction to his autobiography, Dionicio Morales described the story of his life as "not really much different from that of any other Mexican American who was young in the 20s and 30s."

47. Beatrice Griffith, *American Me* (Boston: Houghton Mifflin, 1948), 321.

48. The evidence does not allow more definite, quantified statements about Nisei opinions on the war. However, I believe the number and range of accounts I have collected permit reasonable generalizations.

49. Miné Okubo, *Citizen 13660* (New York: Columbia University Press, 1946), 79; Chiyeko Akahoshi to Mollie Murphy, 19 January 1945, Mollie Wilson Murphy Letters (hereafter MWML), Japanese American National Museum, Los Angeles; Sadie Saito to Murphy, 29 September 1942, MWML.

50. Violet Saito to Murphy, 3 January 1945; Akahoshi to Murphy, 25 December 1944; June Yoshigai to Murphy, 6 July 1944, all in MWML.

51. Kikuchi, *Kikuchi Diary*, 117; Rose Echeverria Mulligan, interview by Sherna Berger Gluck, 1983, "Rosie the Riveter Revisited: Women and the World

War II Experience," Oral History Resource Center, California State University, Long Beach; McReynolds, *Almost Americans,* 261.

52. "Commentary," *Rough Rider,* September 1939.

53. Ibid.; "The Colonel Speaks," *Rough Rider,* 19 March 1942.

54. *Los Angeles Collegian,* 10 April 1942.

55. "Minorities Play Important Part in Civilization," *Los Angeles Collegian,* 12 October 1942, and "Deltas Establish Role of Minority Groups in Establishing Post-War Reconstruction," *Los Angeles Collegian,* 18 June 1943.

56. "Resolutions," 1945, folder 18, box 1, Edwar Lee Papers (hereafter Lee Papers), ARC 2000/19, Asian American Archive, Ethnic Studies Library, University of California, Berkeley; Resolutions of 12th Annual Chinese Youth Conference, July 1944, ARC 2000/21, Lee Papers; Charter for Christian Youth, 2 July 1944, ARC 2000/16, Lee Papers; Charter of United Christian Youth Council, undated, ARC 2000/16, Lee Papers; "Newsclipping about Chinese Christian Youth Conference," 22–29 July 1945, ARC 2000/36, Lee Papers; Paul Louie, "Chinese Americans: What Course for the Future?" *Pacific Citizen,* 4 September 1943; Paul Louie, "A Challenge to Youth: Christian Ideals Must Be Based on a Solid Community Life of Mutual Achievement," *Chinese Press,* 20 August 1943; Moonbeam Tong Lee, *Growing Up in Chinatown: The Life and Work of Edwar Lee* (California, 1987), 56. In 1943, the youth movement added a New York branch of the conference to benefit East Coast youngsters. Although its members were primarily Chinese, the organization's charter invited all races to participate, and a 1945 resolution demanded more active recruitment of non-Chinese.

57. Daisuke Kitagawa, *Issei and Nisei: The Internment Years* (New York: Seabury, 1967), 60–61; "Statement of JACL," 15 September 1949, box 74, John Anson Ford Collection, Huntington Library; Helen Elizabeth Whitney, "Care of Homeless Children of Japanese Ancestry during Evacuation and Relocation" (master's thesis, University of California, Berkeley, 1948), 22.

58. Risa Hirao and a Professor Boskey, "Orphans of Manzanar: The Story of Children's Village," September 1998, Children's Village Project Materials, compiled by Art Hansen, Center for Oral and Public History, California State University, Fullerton. The quote appears in "Statement of JACL," 15 September 1949.

59. Whitney, "Care of Homeless Children of Japanese Ancestry," 26–33.

60. "Nisei Girl Postpones Wedding to Chinese until End of War," *Pacific Citizen,* 16 July 1942; Tetsuya G. Ishimaru to Ralph Merritt, 1 February 1943, and Paul Vernier to William Ball, memorandum, 5 June 1945, Children's Village Project Materials.

61. "WCLA Plays Cupid to Chinese-Japanese Pair," *Pacific Citizen,* 1942.

62. Jeanne Wakatsuki Houston and James D. Houston, *Farewell to Manzanar: A True Story of Japanese American Experience during and after the World War II Internment* (Boston: Houghton Mifflin, 1973), 35; Paul Spickard, "Injustice Compounded: Amerasians and Non-Japanese Americans in World War II Concentration Camps," *Journal of American Ethnic History* 5, no. 2 (Spring 1986): 16; Ellen Levine, *A Fence away from Freedom: Japanese Americans and World War II* (New York: G. P. Putnam's, 1995), 7, 65, 119.

63. Spickard, "Injustice Compounded," 6–22.

64. Statement to the Commission of Wartime Relocation and Internment of Civilians, n.d., box 3, Elaine Black Yoneda Papers, Labor Archives, San Francisco State University; Levine, *A Fence away from Freedom*, 219; Kim Fong Tom interview.

65. Vernier to Ball; "Nisei Girl, Wife of Filipino Held," *Pacific Citizen*, 9 July 1942; "Japanese Wife of Oakland Chinese Arrested as Alien," *Hawaii Chinese Journal*, 16 July 1942.

66. Oral Histories of Petaluma Jewish Community, 15 December 1977, folder 3, box 4, Elaine Black Yoneda Papers.

67. A sampling of such stories from the *Pacific Citizen:* "Nisei Girl, Wife of Filipino Held"; "WCLA Plays Cupid"; "Japanese Evacuee Supports Adopted Chinese Children," 24 December 1942; "Chinese American Gets into Difficulties over Nisei Experience," 4 March 1943; "Nisei Girl Arrested on Return to Evacuated Area," 4 August 1943; "Japanese American Woman, Wife of Chinese, Receives Permission to Return Home," 4 December 1943.

68. Arthur Caylor, "Behind the News with Arthur Caylor," *San Francisco News*, 18 April 1942.

69. Allen Mock, interview by Jean Wong, 13 December 1980, box 47, SC-CAOHP.

70. Beatrice Griffith, "In the Flow of Time," *Common Ground*, October 1948; Carey McWilliams, "Blood on the Pavement," in *Minorities in California History*, ed. George Frakes and Curtis Solberg (New York: Random House, 1971), 95; "Mexican Minority in Los Angeles," folder 10, box 4, Sleepy Lagoon Defense Committee Papers (hereafter Sleepy Lagoon Papers), collection 107, Department of Special Collections, Charles E. Young Research Library. For a more detailed discussion of the run-up to and aftermath of the Zoot Suit Riots, see Elizabeth Escobedo, "Mexican American Home Front: The Politics of Gender, Culture, and Community in World War II Los Angeles" (PhD diss., University of Washington, 2004), 198–220, and Eduardo Obregón Pagán, *Murder at the Sleepy Lagoon: Zoot Suits, Race, and Riot in Wartime L.A.* (Chapel Hill: University of North Carolina Press, 2003).

71. Edward Escobar, *Race, Police and the Making of a Political Identity: Mexican Americans and Los Angeles Police Department, 1900–1945* (Berkeley: University of California Press, 1999), 276; Ysmael "Smiles" Parra to Mrs. Cimring, 29 December 1945, folder 3, box 4, Sleepy Lagoon Papers; Kurashige, "Transforming Los Angeles," 384; "Race Unity Buttons May Be Had," *California Eagle*, 12 November 1942.

72. "Note to Disrupters: No Riot Here!" *California Eagle*, 3 June 1943, and Jeanette Cohen, "As I See It," *California Eagle*, 20 May 1943; undated report, folder 10, box 4, Sleepy Lagoon Papers.

73. "Mass Meet Charges Attempt to Goad Riot," *California Eagle*, 3 June 1943; advertisement for "People's Victory Market," *California Eagle*, 10 June 1943; Sides, *L.A. City Limits*, 49.

74. Parra to Alice Greenfield, 25 January 1944, folder 2, box 4, Sleepy Lagoon Papers; "Mexican Minority in Los Angeles"; undated press release from Sleepy Lagoon Defense Committee, Carey McWilliams Papers, collection 1319, Department of Special Collections, Charles E. Young Research Library.

75. Al Waxman's story in the *Eastside Journal* is quoted in Carey McWilliams, *North from Mexico: The Spanish-Speaking People of the United States* (New York: Greenwood, 1968), 249.

76. Alice McGrath, interview by Michael Balter for "The Education of Alice McGrath," 1987, Oral History Program, University of California, Los Angeles, 20, 43; "Mexican Minority in Los Angeles"; Kurashige, "Transforming Los Angeles," 380; David Leonard, "'No Jews and No Coloreds Are Welcome in this Town': Constructing Coalitions in Postwar Los Angeles" (PhD diss., University of California, Berkeley, 2002), 132.

77. "JACL Seeks Review of Indian Policy," *Pacific Citizen*, 7 January 1950.

78. Thomas Nakayama, ed., "Transforming Barbed Wire," booklet published by Arizona Humanities Council, Phoenix, 2003, 3.

79. Ibid.

80. Debate has long raged among home-front historians about the relative pace and degree of change brought by World War II. Some stress the gradualism of shifts, finding roots in the decades before the conflict. Others see quicker transitions beginning during the war itself. Marilyn Johnson aptly summarized these positions and urged a less polarized, more nuanced approach (Marilyn Johnson, "War as Watershed: The East Bay and World War II," *Pacific Historical Review* 64, no. 3 (1994): 315–31). Scholars should identify how and why different changes occurred and contributed to longer historical trajectories rather than adding up continuities and changes, she argued. The conversation about "war as watershed" started with these pioneering works: John Morton Blum, *V Was for Victory: Politics and American Culture during World War II* (New York: Harcourt, Brace, Jovanovich, 1976); Gerald D. Nash, *The Great Depression and World War II: Organizing America, 1933–45* (New York: St. Martin's, 1979); and Richard Polenberg, *War and Society: The United States, 1941–1945* (Philadelphia: Lippincott, 1972). More recent and specialized scholarship has considered war's effect on distinct social groups and regions. See Roger Lotchin, ed., *The Way We Really Were: The Golden State in the Second Great War* (Urbana: University of Illinois Press, 2000); Thomas A. Guglielmo, "Fighting for Caucasian Rights: Mexicans, Mexican Americans and the Transnational Struggle for Civil Rights in World War II Texas," *Journal of American History* 92, no. 4 (March 2006): 1212–37; Anthony Chen, "'The Hitlerian Rule of Quotas': Racial Conservatism and the Politics of Fair Employment Legislation in New York State, 1941–1945," *Journal of American History* 92, no. 4 (March 2006): 1238–64; Laura McEnaney, "Nightmares on Elm Street: Demobilizing in Chicago, 1945–1953," *Journal of American History* 92, no. 4 (March 2006): 1265–91; Gary Gerstle, "The Crucial Decade: The 1940s and Beyond," *Journal of American History* 92, no. 4 (March 2006): 1292–99.

5. MINORITY BROTHERS IN ARMS

1. Chester Himes, *If He Hollers, Let Him Go* (1945; reprint, with a foreword by Hilton Als, New York: Thunder's Mouth Press, 2002), 203.

2. In spotlighting the experiences of men, my intention is not to discount the value of women-centered approaches to military history. Brenda Moore's works on the lives of Japanese- and African-American women in the military are

particularly valuable. See Brenda Moore, *Serving Our Country: Japanese American Women in the Military during World War II* (New Brunswick: Rutgers University Press, 2003); *To Serve My Country, To Serve My Race: The Story of the Only African-American WACs Stationed Overseas during World War II* (New York: New York University Press, 1996).

3. Studies of military culture since World War II generally conclude that loyalty to one's fellow soldiers, cultivated by the routines and obligations of military service, more than ideology or patriotism, motivates fighting. See Stephen Ambrose and James Barber eds., *The Military and American Society: Essays and Readings* (New York: Free Press, 1972), 199; Don Snider, "An Uniformed Debate on Military Culture," *Orbis* (Winter 1999): 18–19.

4. Beth Bailey and David Farber, *The First Strange Place: The Alchemy of Race and Sex in World War II Hawaii* (New York: Free Press, 1992), 21, 167; Thelma Chang, *I Can Never Forget: Men of the 100th/442nd* (Honolulu: SIGI Productions, 1991), 116; Raul Morin, *Among the Valiant: Mexican Americans in WW II and Korea* (Los Angeles: Borden, 1966), 30.

5. Ben Kuroki, "Fighting Together," *Common Ground* (Summer 1944): 45; press release, unclear date, box 24, Carey McWilliams Papers, collection 1319, Department of Special Collections, Charles E. Young Research Library, University of California, Los Angeles.

6. Jacques E. Levy, *Cesar Chavez: Autobiography of La Causa* (New York: W. W. Norton, 1975), 84. A small sampling of general works on the history of minorities in military service includes Alex Fabros and Theo Gonzalves, " 'We Hold a Neatly Folded Hope': Filipino Veterans of World War II on Citizenship and Political Obligation," *Amerasia Journal* 21, no. 3 (Winter 1995–1996): 155–64; Stanley Falk and Warren Tsueneishi, eds., *American Patriots: MIS in the War against Japan* (Washington, DC: Japanese American Veterans Association, 1995); Albert Camarillo, "Research Note on Chicano Community Leaders: The GI Generation," *Aztlan* (Fall 1971): 145–50; K. Scott Wong, *Americans First: Chinese Americans and the Second World War* (Cambridge: Harvard University Press, 2005); Roger Lotchin, *The Bad City in the Good War: San Francisco, Los Angeles, Oakland, and San Diego* (Bloomington: Indiana University Press, 2003); Graham Smith, *When Jim Crow Met John Bull: Black American Soldiers in World War II* (London: Tauris, 1987).

7. Mario T. Garcia, *Memories of Chicano History: The Life and Narrative of Bert Corona* (Berkeley: University of California Press, 1994), 136; Jim Williams, interview by Maggi Morehouse, in her *Fighting in the Jim Crow Army: Black Men and Women Remember World War II* (Lanham, MD: Rowman and Littlefield, 2000), 123. Morehouse did not specify Williams's origins, but he was recruited in Virginia. I use his testimony here to represent racial sentiments and experiences likely shared by African-American Californians accustomed to diverse company.

8. Jim Williams interview, 123; Kiyoshi Kagawa, interview by Tom Sasaki, Daily Reports from Los Angeles, 21, 26 September 1946, RG 102, War Relocation Authority Records (hereafter WRAR), National Archives Building, Washington, DC. Most Filipinos who enlisted were organized into two all-Filipino regiments. See Luis Sanchez, interview by Ruben Buevara and Sojin Kim, 21 July 2002, Boyle Heights Oral History Project (hereafter BHOHP), Japanese American National

Museum, Los Angeles; Dawn Mabalon, "Life in Little Manila: Filipinas/os in Stockton California, 1917–1972" (PhD diss., Stanford, 2004).

9. Sanchez interview; Morin, *Among the Valiant*, 84.

10. Rudy Sanchez to Eduardo Quevedo, 16 June 1943, Eduardo Quevedo Papers, M0349, Special Collections, Stanford University Libraries; Morin, *Among the Valiant*, 56.

11. Garcia, *Memories of Chicano History*, 136; Levy, *Cesar Chavez*, 85.

12. David Colley, *Blood for Dignity: The Story of the First Integrated Combat Unit in the U.S. Army* (New York: St. Martin's, 2003), 27, 35; Atoy Rudolph Wilson, interview by Sojin Kim, 2000, BHOHP.

13. Al to "Sugar," 1 September 1943, "General Correspondence," Records of the Office of the Civilian Aide to the Secretary of War, Records of the Office of the Secretary of War, RG 107, National Archives, College Park, MD.

14. Arnett Hartsfield, interview by Morehouse, in *Fighting in the Jim Crow Army*, 41.

15. Alan Osur, *Blacks in the Army Air Forces during World War II: The Problem of Race Relations* (Washington, DC: Office of Air Force History, 1977), 97–98; Ulysses Lee, *The United States Army in World War II: The Employment of Negro Troops* (Washington, DC: Office of the Chief of Military History, US Army, 1966), 627. According to Beth Bailey and David Farber, the puzzled but warm reaction of Hawaiians to Black soldiers was a consequence of the island's uniquely multicultural composition, which tended to defuse racial tensions. See Bailey and Farber, *First Strange Place*, 133–66.

16. Adolph W. Newton, *Better Than Good: A Black Sailor's War, 1943–1945* (Annapolis: Naval Institute Press, 1999), 68; Walter Green, interview by Morehouse, in *Fighting in the Jim Crow Army*, 146; Newton, *Better Than Good*, 69. As in the case of Jim Williams, I use the firsthand account of Adolph Newton—a Baltimore native—because it speaks to the general experience of African Americans in the military, including Californians. Throughout this chapter I use representative experiences of various minorities, although not all were Californians.

17. Bill Downey, *Uncle Sam Must Be Losing the War* (San Francisco: Strawberry Hill Press, 1982), 170; Howard Hickerson, interview by Morehouse, in *Fighting in the Jim Crow Army*, 199.

18. Newton, *Better Than Good*, 77.

19. Nelson Peery, *Black Fire: The Making of an American Revolutionary* (reprint; New York: New Press, 1994). After World War II Peery became a prominent civil rights activist.

20. Peery, *Black Fire*, 277. For an engaging analysis of the social and political relations between Black soldiers and Filipinos during the Spanish-American War, see Scott Ngozi-Brown, "African American Soldiers and Filipinos: Racial Imperialism, Jim Crow and Social Relations," *Journal of Negro History*, 82, no. 1 (Winter 1997): 42–53; William Gatewood, *Black Americans and the White Man's Burden, 1898–1903* (Urbana: University of Illinois, 1975); Richard Welsch, *Response to Imperialism: The U.S. and Philippine-American War, 1899–1902* (Chapel Hill: University of North Carolina Press, 1979).

21. Geoffrey M. White and Lamont Lindstrom, *The Pacific Theater: Island Representations of World War II* (Honolulu: University of Hawaii Press, 1989),

29, 412; Geoffrey White, *Island Encounters: Black and White Memories of the Pacific War* (Washington, DC: Smithsonian Press, 1990), 29; Peter Schrijvers, *The GI War against Japan: American Soldiers in Asia and the Pacific during World War II* (New York: Palgrave, 2002).

22. Marc Gallicchio, *The African American Encounter with Japan and China: Black Internationalism in Asia, 1895–1945* (Chapel Hill: University of North Carolina Press, 2000); Annette Palmer, "The Politics of Race and War: Black American Soldiers in the Caribbean Theater during the Second World War," *Military Affairs* (April 1983): 59; Lee, *United States Army in World War II,* 429–30; 22 June 1948 excerpt from *Baltimore Afro-American,* Records of the Civilian Aide to the Secretary of War, Records of the Office of the Secretary of War, RG 107. Similar worries about how the deployment of Black troops in the Caribbean might unsettle islanders prompted the U.S. military to substitute Puerto Rican soldiers for African Americans.

23. George Lipsitz, "'Frantic to Join the Japanese Army': The Asia Pacific War in the Lives of African American Soldiers and Civilians," in *The Politics of Culture in the Shadow of Capital,* ed. Lisa Lowe and David Lloyd (Durham: Duke University Press, 1997), 338–39. Richard Welch is quoted in Ngozi-Brown, "African American Soldiers," 51.

24. Gallicchio, *African American Encounter,* 73.

25. Peery interview by Morehouse in *Fighting in the Jim Crow Army,* 142.

26. Gallicchio, *African American Encounter,* 26.

27. Newton, *Better Than Good,* 73; Felix Goodwin, interview by Maggi Morehouse, in *Fighting in the Jim Crow Army,* 105.

28. Sleepy Lagoon Defense Committee press release, n.d., McWilliams Papers; "As I See It," *California Eagle,* 20 May 1943; Bradley Biggs, *The Triple Nickles: America's First All-Black Paratroop Unit* (Hamden, CT: Archon Books, 1986).

29. *Hi-Times,* 28 February 1944, Records of the Colorado River Relocation Center, Huntington Library, San Marino, California; Christina M. Lim and Sheldon H. Lim, *In the Shadow of the Tiger: The 407th Air Service Squadron, Fourteenth Air Service Group, Fourteenth Air Force, World War II* (Brisbane: Fong Brothers, 1993), 35.

30. Peter Phan, "Familiar Strangers: The Fourteenth Air Service Group Case Study of Chinese American Identity during WWII," in *Chinese America: History and Perspectives* (Brisbane: Fong Brothers, 1993), 86.

31. Chang, *I Can Never Forget,* 125. Mike Masaoka, interview by E. Saul, 20 August 1982, 100th Infantry Battalion/442nd Regimental Combat Team, box 3, RCT Oral History Transcripts, National Japanese American Historical Society, San Francisco.

32. Masaoka interview; Takeo Kaneshiro, *Internees: War Relocation Center Memoirs and Diaries* (New York: Vantage, 1976), 9; *Los Angeles Tribune,* 23 January 1947.

33. Chang, *I Can Never Forget,* 124–26.

34. Raymond Nosaka, interview by E. Saul, November 1980, 100th Infantry Battalion/442nd Regimental Combat Team, box 3, RCT Oral History Transcripts, National Japanese American Historical Society (hereafter NJAHS), San Francisco; Harry Fukuhara, interview by Lonnie Ding, February

1986, box 5, Military Intelligence Service Oral History Project Transcripts (MIS), NJAHS.

35. "Some Aspects of Economic Losses Suffered by Japanese Evacuees," *Pacific Citizen*, 28 January 1943; "Filipinos Run Amok, Murder U.S. Japanese," *Rafu Shimpo*, 2 January 1942; "Gilroy Farmers Face Stiff Prison Sentence for Attack," *Pacific Citizen*, 2 July 1942; "Imperial Valley Merry-Go Round," *Philippines Mail*, 13 January 1942; miscellaneous newspaper clippings, December 1941, reel 17, Japanese American Evacuation and Resettlement Records (hereafter JAERR), Bancroft Library, University of California, Berkeley; Ben Ijima's diary, 25 August 1942, reel 17, JAERR.

36. Garding Liu, *Inside Los Angeles Chinatown* (Los Angeles: n.p., 1948), 114–15; *People v. Lim Dum Dong*, 26 Cal. App. 2d 135 (26 April 1938).

37. Sunao Ishio, interview by Stanley Falk and Warren Tsueneishi, *American Patriots*, 30.

38. Shigeya Kihara, interview, 21 January 1994, box 6, MIS. Jaclyn Harden discussed a similar case of ethnic misidentification in her work. Tom Watanabe, a native-born Californian who grew up in a farming community of Whites and Mexicans, was repeatedly called "John Chinaman" during his training in Texas by locals unsure what to make of the Counter Intelligence Corps member. See Jaclyn Harden, *Double Cross: Japanese Americans in Black and White Chicago* (Minneapolis: University of Minnesota Press, 2003), 106.

39. Stanley Mu, interview by author, Los Angeles, 23 October 2003.

40. Won-loy Chan, *Burma: The Untold Story* (Novato, CA: Presidio Press, 1986), 37.

41. Harvey Watanabe, interview by Ken Mochizuki and Pei Pei Sung, in *A Different Battle: Stories of Asian Pacific American Veterans,* ed. Carina A. Rosario (Seattle: Wing Luke Asian Museum, 1999); "Action Taken against Hostile Natives in Manila," *Yaban Gogai,* February 1946, file 64, RG 102, Records of the Civilian Aide to the Secretary of War, Records of the Office of the Secretary of War; Schrijvers, *GI War against Japan,* 142.

42. Jim Fung, interview by author, 7 May 2000; Committee on American Principles and Fair Play, "Fighting Men Speak Out," 22 May 1944, Charles Kikuchi Papers, collection 1259, Department of Special Collections, Charles E. Young Research Library; "Chinese American Backs Nisei in Letter to Soldier," *Pacific Citizen,* 23 December 1944.

43. Young Oak Kim, interview, 100th Infantry Battalion/442nd Regimental Combat Team, box 2, RCT Oral History Transcripts; Young Oak Kim, interview by Karen Ishizuka and Robert Nakamura, 28 August 1995, Veterans Oral History Project, Japanese American National Museum; untitled article in the *Korean Independence,* 12 July 1944.

44. Chan, *Burma,* 31, 39, 98–105.

45. Morin, *Among the Valiant,* 87; Karl Yoneda, interview by Yvonne Yoneda, 1982, collection 1992/055, box 3, folder 2, Elaine Black Yoneda Papers, Labor Archives, San Francisco State University.

46. Guy Gabaldon, interview by Ruchika Joshi, 25 July 2000, "U.S. Latinos and Latinas and World War II," *Narratives* 2 (Fall 2000), published by the Department of Journalism, University of Texas, Austin.

47. Among those works that trace postwar activism to wartime military service are Robert Williams, "Black Power and the Origins of the Black Freedom Struggle," *Journal of American History* (September 1998): 540–70; John Ditmer, *Local People: The Struggle for Civil Rights in Mississippi* (Urbana: University of Illinois Press, 1994); Camarillo, "Research Note on Chicano Community Leaders"; Carl Allsup, *The American GI Forum: Origins and Evolution* (Austin: University of Texas Press, 1982); Kevin Leonard, "Is That What We Fought For? Japanese Americans and Racism in California, the Impact of World War II," *Western Historical Quarterly* (November 1990): 463–82.

6. PANETHNIC POLITICS ARISING FROM THE EVERYDAY

1. Homer Jack, "Brotherhood Begins on Our Block," *Los Angeles Tribune*, 26 October 1946.

2. Daniel Crowe, *Prophets of Rage: The Black Freedom Struggle in San Francisco, 1945–1969* (New York: Garland, 2000), 55–57.

3. The survey is referenced in Thelma Gorham, "Negroes and Japanese Evacuees," *Crisis*, November 1945; "Divide and Conquer," *Pacific Citizen*, 1 February 1949; "The Moved-Outers," *Pacific Citizen*, 21 April 1945; untitled article, *Pacific Pathfinder*, June 1944.

4. Shizuko Kako, "Remembrances," in *Our Recollections*, ed. East Bay Japanese for Action (Tokyo: Tokyo Art Printing, 1986), 193; Art Takemoto, interview by Jim Gatewood, REgenerations Oral History Project (hereafter ROHP), Japanese American National Museum, Los Angeles; Larry Tajiri, "Nisei USA: Blueprint for Race Riot," *Pacific Citizen*, 6 January 1945; Katsuma Mukaeda, interview by Dave Biniasz, 28 November 1973, Japanese American Project, Center for Oral and Public History, California State University, Fullerton; Daily Reports from Los Angeles, September 1946, reel 108, Japanese American Evacuation and Resettlement Records (hereafter JAERR), BANC MSS 67/14c, Bancroft Library, University of California, Berkeley; Kariann Akemi Yokota, "From Little Tokyo to Bronzeville and Back: Ethnic Communities in Transition" (master's thesis, University of California, Los Angeles, 1996), 82–83.

5. Daily Reports from Los Angeles, September 1946, and Observations of Wholesale Market, Los Angeles, October 1946, both on reel 108, JAERR.

6. Yokota, "From Little Tokyo," 79; Tom Tiara, interview by Tom Sasaki, Daily Reports from Los Angeles, September 1946, JAERR; Sasaki, Daily Reports from Los Angeles, July 1946, JAERR.

7. "Japanese-Negro Relations Do Stink: Leaders Plan Action," *Los Angeles Tribune*, 8 March 1947; "The Mail box—Negro Japanese Relations," *Los Angeles Tribune*, 1 March 1947. Other sources that address the tensions precipitated by the reintegration of Japanese Americans are Togo Tanaka, "Price of Segregation," *Pacific Citizen*, 22 March 1947; Minnie Lomax, "Forum Says Few Japanese Live in Little Tokyo," *Los Angeles Tribune*, 19 April 1947.

8. Charles Kikuchi, Reception of the American Japanese in Southern California, January 1946, reel 74, JAERR.

9. "The Race War That Flopped," *Ebony*, July 1946; "Ebony Tells Us about 'the Race War That Flopped," *Pacific Citizen*, 13 July 1946; Elmer Smith, "Did

You Know?" *Pacific Citizen,* 23 December 1953. The Nisei sociologist is referenced in Tom Sasaki, Daily Reports from Los Angeles—First Impression of Little Tokyo, reel 107, JAERR.

10. Tom Sasaki, 20 August 1946, Daily Reports from Los Angeles, file series 64, box 1, RG 201, War Relocation Authority Records, National Archives Building, Washington, DC.

11. Ibid.

12. Interviews by Tom Sasaki, 17–18 September 1946, Daily Reports from Los Angeles, JAERR.

13. Samuel Ishikawa, *Common Ground,* 10 September 1945, box 74, John Anson Ford Collection (hereafter JAFC), Huntington Library, San Marino, California.

14. "DuBois Warns Minorities to Reason, Get Acquainted," *Los Angeles Tribune,* 22 March 1947; "Minority Unity," *Los Angeles Tribune,* 6 December 1947; Scott Harvey Tang, "Pushing at the Golden Gate: Race Relations and Racial Politics in San Francisco, 1940–1955" (PhD diss., University of California, Berkeley, 2002), 208–10. Although W. E. B. DuBois's ideas shifted over time, he consistently supported radical democratic movements in the United States and abroad. After World War II his attacks on corporate domination and imperialism earned him the tag "Communist" and triggered his departure from the NAACP in 1948. See Manning Marable, *W. E. B. DuBois: Black Radical Democrat* (Boston: Twayne, 1986), 159–63, 174–75.

15. *Providence Baptist Association v. Los Angeles Hompa Honowanji Buddhist Temple,* 79 Cal. App. 2d 734 (May 1947).

16. Remembered as a heterogeneous neighborhood of blacks, whites, Japanese, and Mexicans in the 1920s through the 1940s, Watts became steadily more Mexican and African American through the postwar period. Between 1920 and 1950 the black population grew from 14 percent to 71 percent of Watts's total. See James Allen and Eugene Turner, *The Ethnic Quilt: Population Diversity in Southern California* (Northridge: Center for Geographical Studies, California State University, 1997), 94.

17. Begun in 1937 in Mexico, the Sinarquista movement criticized the Mexican government for choosing collectivization and atheism over private ownership and Catholicism. In California Sinarquism won support among some Mexicans in the barrios with its antiracist message and promise to return the Southwest to Mexico if the Nazis triumphed. The U.S. Department of Justice, however, concluded that these supporters were few in number.

18. Quoted in 1945–1949 Watts Study: American Council on Race Relations, Los Angeles Neighborhood Study, box 8, Eshref Shevky Papers, collection 1279, Department of Special Collections, Charles E. Young Research Library, University of California, Los Angeles.

19. 1945–1949 Hollenbeck Study: American Council on Race Relations, Los Angeles Neighborhood Study, box 8, Shevky Papers; "Are the Police a Menace?" *Los Angeles Tribune,* 22 March 1947; "Second the Motion," *Los Angeles Tribune,* 11 May 1946. For a more thorough treatment of tensions between local law enforcement and African Americans, see Tang, "Pushing at the Golden Gate," 262–70, and Kristi Joy Woods, "Be Vigorous but Not Brutal: Race, Politics,

and Police in Los Angeles, 1937–1945" (PhD diss., University of Southern California, 1999).

20. 1945–1949 Watts Study.

21. 1945–1949 Hollenbeck Study.

22. Hollenbeck Study—General Description, box 8, Shevky Papers.

23. Ibid.

24. "Six Girls of Varying Racial, Religious Backgrounds Start U.S. Tour," *Los Angeles Tribune,* 1 February 1947; Esther Nishio, interview by Darcie Iki, 21 June 1999, ROHP.

25. "Church Youth Visit Areas of Racial Discrimination," *Los Angeles Tribune,* 27 April 1946; "Will Speak," *Penninsula Chimes,* 5 June 1947; "Third Annual Convention Los Angeles Youth Council," May 1948, box 60, JAFC; "Hollenbeck Youth Theatre in Intercultural Revue," *Los Angeles Sentinel,* 1 August 1946. The International Institute and public library system in Los Angeles also tried to bring about intercultural harmony. While the former offered programs that promoted "friendship between persons of different national origins," the latter sponsored displays of art and other exhibits that highlighted the cultural contributions of "the Negro, the Mexican, and the Oriental groups (International Institute Archives, YWCA of Lincoln Heights, Los Angeles; letter to Manuel Ruiz Jr., 24 January 1944, Manuel Ruiz Jr. Papers, Special Collections, Stanford University Libraries).

26. *Campus Crier,* April 1947, Oakland Technical High School.

27. *Girls High Journal,* June 1946, San Francisco History Center, San Francisco Public Library.

28. David Leonard, "'No Jews and No Coloreds Are Welcome in this Town': Constructing Coalitions in Postwar Los Angeles" (PhD diss., University of California, Berkeley, 2002), 145–55; Leo Frumkin, interview by Kenneth Burt and Sojin Kim, 19 December 2001, Boyle Heights Oral History Project, Japanese American National Museum; "79 Arrested in Uproar at Gerald Smith Meeting," *Los Angeles Times,* 4 November 1945.

29. Hisaye Yamamoto, "Small Talk," *Los Angeles Tribune,* 13 April 1946; Yokota, "From Little Tokyo," 70.

30. "Report of Director of Urban League Demonstration Project," January–March 1947, Community Welfare Council, California Federation of Civic Unity Records (hereafter CFCUR), C-A 274, Bancroft Library; Robert Gibson of Council of Civic Unity to Earl Warren, 17 April 1945, Administrative Files, Public Works—Race Relations, 1942–1943, Earl Warren Papers, California State Archives, Office of the Secretary of State, Sacramento. For more thorough treatments of how the politics of the developing Cold War shaped domestic struggles for civil rights, see Penny Von Eschen, *Race against Empire: Black Americans and Anticolonialism, 1937–1957* (Ithaca: Cornell University Press, 1997), 74–77; Mary Dudziak, *Cold War Civil Rights: Race and the Image of America* (Princeton: Princeton University Press, 2000), 9; Shana Beth Bernstein, *California Dreaming in a Divided World: Building Multiracial Bridges in World War II and Cold War Los Angeles,* forthcoming.

31. Press release by Richard Dettering, 1951, CFCUR; Harvard Sitkoff, "Racial Militancy and Interracial Violence in the Second World War" *Journal*

of American History 58 (1971): 661–81. First conceived in Chicago, the American Council on Race Relations had a well-established and active Pacific Coast chapter after the war. Noting the interdependence of racial, religious, and "nationality" groups, it offered technical and advisory services for existing indigenous community groups. The Council for Civic Unity, which described itself as a "public opinion forming agency," similarly played the role of coordinator and promoter of civil rights. The association had been started by the Hollywood Democratic Committee and drew members from varied community groups. In 1944 Los Angeles mayor Fletcher Bowron convened the Committee for Interracial Progress and Committee for Home Front Unity. Such committees sprung up in other American cities (Detroit, Chicago, New York) just after the war in the wake of interracial violence. Unfortunately, small budgets and conservative intentions—officials preferred superficial changes rather than significant socioeconomic reforms—limited their effect on interracial relations. Each boasted minority involvement and a commitment to better race relations (Human Relations Report Submitted for Human Relations Study Group, 11 January 1947, JAFC; Report on Interracial Committees in Los Angeles, 17 April 1944).

32. George Gelason to John Anson Ford, 18 January 1944; unsigned letter to Ford, 7 January 1944, all in box 72, JAFC; Minutes of Meetings, 1941–52, Scrapbooks of Human Relations Committee, Los Angeles Hall of Records.

33. "Civic Unity Council Extends Campaign," *Chinese Press,* 10 December 1948; "What the Federation Does," CFCUR.

34. Mark Wild, *Street Meeting: Multiethnic Neighborhoods in Early Twentieth-Century Los Angeles* (Berkeley: University of California Press, 2005), 176–77; 195–99; Bernstein, *California Dreaming in a Divided World;* Josh Sides, *L.A. City Limits: African American Los Angeles from the Great Depression to the Present* (Berkeley: University of California Press, 2003), 147; Larry Ceplair, *The Inquisition in Hollywood: Politics in the Film Community, 1930–1960* (Urbana: University of Illinois, 2003), 195, 197–98.

35. Fred Fertig, "Pilgrim's Progress: The Chronicle of a White Man in Search of God," *Los Angeles Tribune,* 4 January 1947; Hisaye Yamamoto, "Small Talk," *Los Angeles Tribune,* 4 January 1947. On the turn toward interracial civil rights activity in the postwar period, see Roger Lotchin, ed., *The Way We Really Were: The Golden State in the Second Great War* (Urbana: University of Illinois Press, 2000), 195; Kevin Leonard, "Years of Hope, Days of Fear: The Impact of World War II on Race Relations in Los Angeles" (PhD diss., University of California, Davis, 1992), 278–79, 281; "Civic Unity Council Extends Campaign."

36. Mark Brilliant, "Color Lines: Civil Rights Struggles on America's 'Racial Frontier,' 1945–1975" (PhD diss., Stanford University, 2002), 172; Human Relations Report.

37. Minutes of Meeting, 11 September 1944, and "Four Contributions to American Culture," Minutes of Meeting, 1947, Scrapbooks of Human Relations Committee, Los Angeles.

38. Chinese American Citizens' Alliance, Miscellaneous Organizational Materials, 1922–87, AAS ARC 2000/71, Asian American Studies Collection, Ethnic Studies Library, University of California, Berkeley.

39. Bill Hosokawa, *JACL: In Quest of Justice* (New York: William Morrow, 1982), 31.

40. Ibid.

41. Smith, "Did You Know?"; Minutes, National Board Meeting of JACL in Denver, 5 March 1946, JAERR.

42. Dorothy Fugita-Rony argued that Filipinos focused their civil rights energies on labor organization rather than legal challenges to discrimination in housing, immigration policy, marriage, or employment. See Dorothy Fugita-Rony, *American Workers, Colonial Power: Philippine Seattle and the Transpacific West, 1919–1941* (Berkeley: University of California Press, 2003). An important exception to this pattern, Dawn Mabalon noted, was the Committee for the Protection of Filipino Rights. Formed in 1930s Los Angeles by the prominent Filipinos Carlos Bulosan and Claro Candelario, the organization demanded naturalization rights for Filipino immigrants. See Dawn Mabalon, "Life in Little Manila: Filipinas/os in Stockton, California, 1917–1971" (PhD diss., Stanford University, 2004), 244.

43. Crowe, *Prophets of Rage,* 104–105; Bernstein, *California Dreaming in a Divided World,* 108, 207. The quote from Floyd Covington may be found in Carnegie-Myrdal Study, folder 6, box 2, Los Angeles Urban League, collection 2003, Charles E. Young Research Library.

44. Vern Partlow, "Much Good Results from United Effort," *Daily News,* 25 December 1950, folder 24, box 4, Fred Ross Papers, Special Collections, Stanford University Libraries; Mario Garcia, *Mexican Americans: Leadership, Ideology and Identity, 1930–1960* (New Haven: Yale University Press, 1989), 221–22.

45. Greg Ivers, *To Build a Wall: American Jews and the Separation of Church and State* (Charlottesville: University of Virginia Press, 1995), 37, 53; Marc Dollinger, *Quest for Inclusion: Jews and Liberalism in Modern America* (Princeton: Princeton University Press, 2000), 44–45; Svonkin, *Jews against Prejudice,* 18–22; Bernstein, *California Dreaming in a Divided World,* 155–57, 234; "Minority Groups Here Seek Unity," *California Eagle,* 25 December 1947.

46. Buell interview; Danny Kim, interview by author, San Francisco, 1 May 2000.

47. Fred Ross, "No More Bigotry for Bell Town," *Now: The War Worker,* August 1946; Tarea Hall Pittman, interview by C. L. Dellums, 1974, Earl Warren Oral History Project, Regional Oral History Office, BANC MSS 75/32, Bancroft Library.

48. Daniel Luevano, interview by Carlos Vasquez, 1988, Oral History Program, University of California, Los Angeles, 17.

49. Mario T. Garcia, *Memories of Chicano History: The Life and Narrative of Bert Corona* (Berkeley: University of California Press, 1994), 71, 132, 134.

50. Katherine Underwood, "Pioneering Minority Representation: Edward Roybal and the Los Angeles City Council, 1949–1962," *Pacific Historical Review* 66 (1997): 399–425.

51. Beatrice Griffith, "Viva Roybal-Viva America," *Common Ground* (Autumn 1949): 66. Joe Kovner is quoted in "Boyle Heights: California's Sociological Fishbowl," *Fortnight* 20–23 (20 October 1954): 23. Gus Hawkins, whose

district included Central Avenue, had himself won election because of multiethnic backing. Blacks, Mexicans, and some ethnic Whites voted him into office.

52. Tim Carpenter, "Nisei Progressives: A Link in the Chain of Social Democratic Movements in Twentieth-Century America" (master's thesis, California State University, Fullerton, 1998). Tats Kuchida, regional director of the JACL, also backed Roybal. See Tats Kuchida to John Anson Ford, 8 November 1950, box 74, JAFC.

53. "Councilman Discloses Housing Prejudice in Los Angeles," *Pacific Citizen,* 10 September 1949; "Demand for Negro Congressman Seen in Roybal Election Win," *California Eagle,* 2 June 1949. Richard Ibanez, a young Mexican-American lawyer running for a Superior Court judgeship, gained the support of the *Los Angeles Sentinel,* the all-Black Ministers Alliance, and the Nisei spokesman Arnold Nakajima. Frank Mankiewicz launched a campaign to become the assemblyman for Los Angeles's Sixteenth District with the help of important ethnic figures such as John Aiso, a Nisei judge, and Loren Miller, an NAACP attorney. Mankiewicz won the trust of the local Black community when he intervened on behalf of a Black postal worker who had been denied promotion after years of hard work (Chet Holifield, "Election of Roybal—Democracy at Work," *Congressional Record,* 81st Cong., Ernesto Galarza Papers, Collection M224, Special Collections, Stanford University Libraries; Luevano interview).

54. This section is not intended as an exhaustive discussion of the interethnic political coalitions attempted by minorities. It highlights those political efforts that most visibly bear the imprint of sociocultural connections. Discrimination in employment also mobilized minorities into multiethnic coalitions. The details of campaigns to create the Fair Employment Practices Committee have been so thoroughly documented by other historians, I chose not to reproduce the details in this chapter. I defer to other historical accounts for the full story of attempted but limited gains. See D. Leonard, "'No Jews, No Coloreds,'" 230–58; Tang, "Pushing at the Golden Gate," 234; Kevin Leonard, "Is That What We Fought For? Japanese Americans and Racism in California, the Impact of World War II," *Western Historical Quarterly* (November 1990): 462–83; Brilliant, "Color Lines," 190.

55. J. Chinn to Earl Warren, 26 April 1947, Warren Papers.

56. "California Supreme Court Refuses to Intervene in Restrictive Covenant Cases," *Pacific Citizen,* 9 August 1947; Grace Simons, "56th Street Whites Fight Chinese, Too," *Los Angeles Sentinel,* 30 May 1946. Minority veterans of World War II often became central figures in civil rights campaigns, both as organizers and as the victims of discrimination. In another case in point the NAACP defended the Mexican-American veteran Catarino Esparaza when he filed a breach-of-contract suit in 1949 against a housing developer who allegedly reneged on an agreement because of racial restrictions ("Mexican Veteran Sues Housing Developer for Contract Breach," *Los Angeles Sentinel,* 11 August 1949).

57. "Democracy Undoes Its Blunder," *Jewish Community Bulletin,* 20 December 1946; "California Supreme Court Refuses to Intervene"; Tang, "Pushing at the Golden Gate," 360. For more on the real estate practices that constrained the housing opportunities of minorities after the *Shelley* decision, see Deirdre Sullivan, "'Letting Down the Bars': Race, Space and Democracy in San Francisco, 1936–1964" (PhD diss., University of Pennsylvania, 2003), 127–30.

58. Carey McWilliams, *North from Mexico: The Spanish-Speaking People of the United States* (New York: Greenwood, 1948), 251–52.

59. Ross, "No More Bigotry in Bell Town."

60. Ibid. Mexican Americans and Blacks teamed up again in rural California. Represented by the NAACP and Alianza Hispano Americano, the parents of forty-four Mexican American and twenty Black children filed a class action suit against the school district of El Centro in 1951. See "NAACP Press Release," 7 February 1955, carton 1, CFCUR.

61. "*Méndez v. Westminster*" and "Transcripts," boxes 2 and 4, *Méndez v. Westminster,* Collection M938, Special Collections, Stanford University Libraries; Christopher Arriola "Knocking on the Schoolhouse Door: *Mendez v. Westminster,* Equal Protection, Public Education, and Mexican Americans in the 1940s," *La Raza Law Journal* 8 (1995): 166–207; *Gonzalo Méndez v. Westminster School District of Orange County,* 161 F.2d 774 (9th Cir. 1947).

62. Monthly Report of Legal Department, April 1947, carton 24, National Association for the Advancement of Colored Peoples, Region I, records, 1942–1986, BANC MSS 78/180c, Bancroft Library, University of California Berkeley; *Méndez v. Westminster,* amicus curiae briefs for the American Jewish Congress and JACL.

63. Cloyte Larsson, ed., *Marriage across the Color Line* (Chicago: Johnston, 1965), 62–65; "War Brides of Colored GI's Fare Very Well," *Los Angeles Sentinel,* 13 March 1948; "Intermarriage," *New World Sun,* 4 March 1936.

64. Larsson, *Marriage across the Color Line,* 62–65; George De Vos, "Personality Patterns and Problems of Adjustment in American-Japanese Intercultural Marriages" (master's thesis, University of California, Berkeley, 1959).

65. Larsson, *Marriage across the Color Line,* 63.

66. "War Brides of Colored GI's Fare Very Well"; "Negroes Come Back to Pro Football," *Ebony,* July 1946, 12–16.

67. Helen Elizabeth Whitney, "Care of Homeless Children of Japanese Ancestry during Evacuation and Relocation" (master's thesis, University of California, Berkeley, 1948), 66. Her conclusions were based upon interviews and reports of the War Relocation Authority.

68. "Japanese Evacuee Supports Adopted Chinese Children," *Pacific Citizen,* 24 December 1942.

69. "Seek Foster Homes for Nisei Children in Los Angeles Area," *Pacific Citizen,* 10 September 1949.

70. "Unwanted Children: A Chinese Tragedy," *Chinese Press,* 16 December 1949.

71. "Intermarriage," *New World Sun.*

72. Hisaye Yamamoto, "Wilshire Bus," in *Seventeen Syllables,* 34–38.

73. Marge Ong, interview, 11 December 1979, Southern California Chinese American Oral History Collection (hereafter SCCAOHP), collection 1688, Department of Special Collections, Charles E. Young Research Library; Mary Oyama, "A Nisei Report from Home," *Common Ground* (Winter 1946); Gloria Quan, interview by author, Orange County, California, 10 November 2003; Allen Mock, interview by Jean Wong, 13 December 1980, box 47, SCCAOHP. Another example of growing community comfort with inter-Asian matches was

that Vangie Buell's Filipino parents looked most favorably upon her Chinese dates, who seemed more culturally familiar than the Mexican and Black men who courted her (Vangie Buell, interview by author, Oakland, 24 May 2000).

74. *Perez v. Lippold,* 32 Cal. 2d 711 (1948). Among the legal precedents Dan Marshall cited during the case was *Shelley v. Kramer.* He compared the right to marry and procreate to another fundamental right recently upheld by the courts: equal access to housing. The California case triggered successful campaigns to repeal antimiscegenation statutes throughout the American West. See Dara Orenstein, "Void for Vagueness: Mexican Americans and the Collapse of the Anti-Miscegenation Law in California," *Pacific Historical Review* 74 (2005): 367–407.

75. Nellie Foster, "Legal Status of Filipino Intermarriages in California," *Sociology and Social Research* 16 (May–June 1942): 449.

76. "County Appeals Intermarriage Case to U.S. Supreme Court," *Los Angeles Sentinel,* 25 November 1948 (the U.S. Supreme Court affirmed the California decision); San Joaquin County Marriage Licenses and Certificates, 1943–46, available through the Los Angeles Regional Family History Center.

77. "County Acts on Racist Brief in Davis-Perez Case," *California Eagle,* 23 October 1947; "Catholics Start Attack on Statute," *Los Angeles Tribune,* 23 August 1947; "Suit Challenges California Mixed Nuptial Ban," *Los Angeles Sentinel,* 21 August 1947; Orenstein, "Void for Vagueness," 402–403.

78. "Mixed Couples in Three Big Cities Form Clubs to Fight against Social Bans," *Ebony,* January 1951.

79. Marc Gallicchio, *The African American Encounter with Japan and China: Black Internationalism in Asia, 1895–1945* (Chapel Hill: University of North Carolina Press, 2000), 175; "Chinese Exclusion Helps Minorities," *California Eagle,* 24 October 1943; "Exclusion Act Repeal Urged by Clare Luce," *California Eagle,* 8 July 1943; "Nisei Interested in Repeal of Chinese Ban," *Pacific Citizen,* 16 October 1943; Minutes of Meeting, 21 August 1941, Scrapbooks of Human Relations Committee, Los Angeles.

80. Bernstein, *California Dreaming in a Divided World,* 322–34. Japanese Americans also campaigned against alien land laws that prohibited new immigrants from owning property. The U.S. Supreme Court ruled in their favor in *Oyama v. State of California,* 332 U.S. 633 (1948). For a recent treatment of the legal battle and case see Brilliant, "Color Lines," 95–126.

81. Bernstein, *California Dreaming in a Divided World,* 295–334.

CONCLUSION

1. Marilyn Johnson, *The Second Gold Rush: Oakland and the East Bay in World War II* (Berkeley: University of California Press, 1993), 232; Eric Avila, *Popular Culture in an Age of White Flight* (Berkeley: University of California Press, 2004). George Lipsitz, George Sanchez, and Kenneth Jackson all note the discriminatory practices of the Federal Housing Administration, which effectively channeled loan money toward whites and away from those of color. The FHA consistently favored homogeneous subdivisions over older, industrial, more mixed neighborhoods. Federally funded highway projects, designed to get

suburbanites to and from their downtown neighborhoods, cut through non-White areas. See Kenneth Jackson, *Crabgrass Frontier: The Suburbanization of the United States* (New York: Oxford University Press, 1985), 206–15; George Lipsitz, "Possessive Investment in Whiteness: Racialized Social Democracy and the 'White Problem' in American Studies," *American Quarterly* 47 (September 1995): 369–88; George Sanchez, "Reading Reginald Denny: The Politics of Whiteness in the late Twentieth Century," *American Quarterly* 47 (September 1995): 388–95.

2. Deirdre Sullivan, "'Letting Down the Bars': Race, Space and Democracy in San Francisco, 1936–1964" (Ph.D. diss., University of Pennsylvania, 2003), 132–33.

3. Deborah Dash Moore, *To the Golden Cities: Pursuing the American Jewish Dream in Miami and Los Angeles* (New York: Free Press, 1994), 56–58; San Francisco City Planning Commission, *The Redevelopment of Blighted Areas— The Master Plan of San Francisco* (1945), 17–19; Sarah Deutsch, George Sanchez, and Gary Okihiro, "Contemporary Peoples/Contested Places," in *The Oxford History of the American West,* ed. Clyde Milner, Carol O'Connor, and Martin Sandweis (Oxford: Oxford University Press, 1994), 641.

4. James Allen and Eugene Turner, *The Ethnic Quilt: Population Diversity in Southern California* (Northridge: Center for Geographical Studies, California State University, 1997), 67, 120, 125–27; Moore, *To the Golden Cities,* 58; Lon Kurashige, "Made in Little Tokyo: Politics of Ethnic Identity and Festival in Southern California, 1934–1994" (Ph.D. diss., University of Wisconsin, Madison, 1994), 131; Scott Kurashige, "Transforming Los Angeles: Black and Japanese American Struggles for Racial Equality in the Twentieth Century" (Ph.D. diss., University of California, Los Angeles, 2000), 482.

5. Allen and Turner, *Ethnic Quilt,* 125–27; Jim Fung, interview by author, 7 May 2000; Davis McEntire, *Residence and Race: Final and Comprehensive Report to the Commission on Race and Housing* (Berkeley: University of California Press, 1960), 53, 63; Scott Harvey Tang, "Pushing at the Golden Gate: Race Relations and Racial politics in San Francisco, 1940–1955" (Ph.D. diss., University of California, Berkeley, 2002), 294.

6. Albert Camarillo, "Comparing Ethnic and Racial Borderlands in American Cities: Urbanization and Community Formation among African Americans, European Americans, and Mexican Americans between the World Wars," paper presented at the annual meeting of the Organization of American Historians, Washington, DC, April 1996; Dwight Waldo, *Minority Groups and Intergroup Relations in the San Francisco Bay Area* (Sacramento: Institute of Governmental Studies, 1963), 32–33; Kurashige, "Transforming Los Angeles," 493; McEntire, *Residence and Race,* 20; Phil Ethington, "Segregated Diversity: Race, Ethnicity, Space and Political Fragmentation in Los Angeles County, 1940–1994," Final Report to the John Randolph Haynes and Dora Haynes Foundation, 13 September 2000.

7. Shana Beth Bernstein, *California Dreaming in a Divided World: Building Multiracial Bridges in World War II and Cold War Los Angeles,* forthcoming; Mary Dudziak, *Cold War Civil Rights: Race and the Image of American Democracy* (Princeton: Princeton University Press, 2000); Thomas Borstelman, *The*

Cold War and the Color Line: American Race Relations in the Global Arena (Cambridge: Harvard University Press, 2001). Even in the face of intensified red-baiting during the 1950s, non-Whites maintained an activist and collaborative bent.

8. Doug Flamming, *Bound for Freedom: Black Los Angeles in Jim Crow America* (Berkeley: University of California Press, 2005); Tang, "Pushing at the Golden Gate"; Garin Burbank, "The Ambitions of Liberalism: Jesse Unruh and the Shape of Postwar Democratic Politics in California," *Southern California Quarterly* (1997): 487–502; Lawrence Crouchett, "Assemblymen Byron Rumford: Symbol for an Era," *California History* (1987): 12–23.

Bibliography

ARCHIVES AND COLLECTIONS

Asian American Oral History Composite. Bancroft Library, University of California, Berkeley.

Asian American Studies Collection. Asian American Archive, Ethnic Studies Library, University of California, Berkeley.

Children's Village Project Materials. Center for Oral and Public History, California State University, Fullerton.

Department of Social Welfare/War Services Bureau Records. California State Archives, Office of the Secretary of State, Sacramento.

Ford, John Anson. Collection. Huntington Library, San Marino, California.

International Institute Archives. YWCA of Lincoln Heights, Los Angeles.

Japanese American Evacuation and Resettlement Records. Bancroft Library, University of California, Berkeley.

Japanese American Research Project. Department of Special Collections, Charles E. Young Research Library, University of California, Los Angeles.

Kikuchi, Charles. Papers. Department of Special Collections, Charles E. Young Research Library, University of California, Los Angeles.

Lee, Edwar. Papers. Asian American Archive, Ethnic Studies Library, University of California, Berkeley.

McWilliams, Carey. Papers. Department of Special Collections, Charles E. Young Research Library, University of California, Los Angeles.

Méndez v. Westminster, Research Materials, 1879–1995. Special Collections, Stanford University Libraries.

Murphy, Molly Wilson. Letters. Japanese American National Museum, Los Angeles.

National Association of Colored Peoples, Region I, records, 1942–1986, BANC MSS 78/180c. Bancroft Library, University of California, Berkeley.

Quevedo, Eduardo. Papers. Special Collections, Stanford University Libraries.
Records of the Colorado River Relocation Center. Huntington Library, San Marino, California.
Records of the Office of the Secretary of War. National Archives at College Park, Maryland.
Ross, Fred. Papers. Special Collections, Stanford University Libraries.
Ruiz, Manuel Jr. Papers. Special Collections, Stanford University Libraries.
Scrapbooks of Human Relations Committee. Los Angeles Hall of Records.
Shevky, Eshref. Papers. Department of Special Collections, Charles Young Research Library, University of California, Los Angeles.
Sleepy Lagoon Defense Committee Papers. Department of Special Collections, Charles E. Young Research Library, University of California, Los Angeles.
Survey of Race Relations Records. Hoover Institution Archives, Stanford, California.
U.S. Latino and Latina World War II Oral History Project. Department of Journalism, University of Texas, Austin.
War Relocation Authority Records. National Archives Building, Washington, DC.
Warren, Earl. Papers. California State Archives, Office of the Secretary of State, Sacramento.
Yoneda, Elaine Black. Papers. Labor Archives, San Francisco State University.
Yoneda, Karl. Collection. Department of Special Collections, Charles E. Young Research Library, University of California, Los Angeles.

INTERVIEWS AND ORAL HISTORIES

Arlington, Dolores. Interview by author. 24 November 2004.
Buell, Vangie. Interview by author. 24 May 2000. Oakland.
Chin, Clara. Interview by author. 14 November 2003. Los Angeles.
De Santo, Sugar Pie. Interview by author. 16 February 2001. Oakland.
Erosa, Gloria, and Eddie Erosa. Interview by author. 6 December 2003. Gardena.
Escobar, Rose Mary. Interview by author. 8 March 2001. Oakland.
Fung, Jim. Interview by author. 7 May 2000.
Jamero, Peter. Interview by author. 10 August 2000. San Jose.
Japanese American National Museum, Los Angeles.
    Boyle Heights Oral History Project
    REgenerations Oral History Project
    Veterans Oral History Project
Japanese American Project. Center for Oral and Public History, California State University, Fullerton.
"Japanese American World War II Evacuation Oral History Project: Part V: Guards and Townspeople." Edited by Art Hansen and Nora M. Jesch. California State University, Fullerton, 1993.
Kaneshiro, Takeo. *Internees: War Relocation Center Memoirs and Diaries.* New York: Vantage, 1976.
Kim, Danny. Interview by author. 1 May 2000. San Francisco.
Kim, Jane. Interview by author. 6 December 2003. Los Angeles.

Latino Oral History Project, Oakland Museum of California.

Luevano, Daniel. Interview by Carlos Vasquez. 1988. Oral History Program, University of California, Los Angeles.

Marr, Frances. Interview by author. 11 November 2003.

Masumoto, David Mas. *Country Voices: The Oral History of a Japanese American Farm Community.* Del Rey, CA: Inaka Countryside Publications, 1987.

Mu, Stanley. Interview by author. 23 October 2003. Los Angeles.

Oral History Program, University of California, Los Angeles.

Oral History Project. National Japanese American Historical Society, San Francisco.

Paular, Jerry. Interview by author. 14 October 2003.

Paular, Paul. Interview by author. 21 October 2003. Gardena.

Quan, Gloria. Interview by author. 10 November 2003. Orange County, California.

Regional Oral History Project. Bancroft Library, University of California, Berkeley.

Repatriation Documents. National Archives, Laguna Niguel, California.

Rosario, Carina, ed. *A Different Battle: Stories of Asian Pacific American Veterans.* Seattle: Wing Luke Asian Musuem, 1999.

"Rosie the Riveter Revisited: Women and the World War II Experience." Oral History Resource Center, California State University, Long Beach.

Sorro, Bill. Interview by author. 3 August 2000. San Francisco.

Southern California Chinese American Oral History Collection. Department of Special Collections, Charles E. Young Research Library, University of California, Los Angeles.

Tateishi, John, ed. *And Justice for All: An Oral History of the Japanese American Detention Camps.* Seattle: University of Washington Press, 1984.

Wan, Cecil. Interview by author. 19 April 2000. San Francisco.

Watts '65 Project Collection. Southern California Library for Social Studies and Research, Los Angeles.

Westview Japanese Presbyterian Church Records. Special Collections, Stanford University Libraries.

Yung, Judy, ed. *Unbound Voices: A Documentary History of Chinese Women in San Francisco.* Berkeley: University of California Press, 1999.

PUBLIC DOCUMENTS

Los Angeles County Marriage Licenses and Certificates, Los Angeles Regional Family History Center.

Los Angeles Housing Authority. *Digest of Final Report: Housing Survey, City of Los Angeles.* 1940.

Louisiana Constitution, art. 220.

Oakland Housing Authority. *Annual Report.* 1945.

San Francisco Department of City Planning. *The Population of San Francisco: A Half Century of Change, 1900–1950.* San Francisco, 1954.

San Francisco. City Planning Commission. *The Redevelopment of Blighted Areas—The Master Plan of San Francisco.* 1945.

San Joaquin County Marriage Licenses and Certificates, Los Angeles Regional Family History Center.

U.S. Census Bureau. *Sixteenth Census of the United States: 1940, Population: Population Characteristics of the Non-White Population by Race.* Washington, DC: GPO, 1942.

——. *Sixteenth Census of the United States: 1940, Population and Housing: Statistics for Census Tracts, San Francisco—Oakland, California.* Washington, DC: GPO, 1942.

Young, Bryce. *Oakland's Changing Community Patterns.* Oakland City Planning Department, 1961.

NEWSPAPERS AND YEARBOOKS

California Eagle
Campanile
Campus Crier
Chinese Press
Common Ground
Crisis
Crossroads: The Los Angeles Nisei Weekly
Eastside Journal
Ebony
Gila News-Courier
Girls High Journal
Jewish Community Bulletin
Junior Campus
Korean Independence
Lincolnian
Los Angeles Collegian
Los Angeles Sentinel
Los Angeles Tribune
Mexican Voice
Negro Digest
New World Sun
Now: The War Worker
Olla Podria
Pacific Citizen
Philippines Mail
Railsplitter
Rough Rider

SELECTED SECONDARY SOURCES

Allen, James and Eugene Turner. *The Ethnic Quilt: Population Diversity in Southern California.* Northridge: Center for Geographic Studies, California State University, 1997.

Almaguer, Tomás. *Racial Fault Lines: The Historical Origins of White Supremacy in California*. Berkeley: University of California Press, 1991.

Asian American Women United of California, ed. *Making Waves: An Anthology by and about Asian American Women*. Boston: Beacon, 1989.

Austin, Joe and Michael Nevin Willard, eds. *Generations of Youth: Youth Cultures and History in Twentieth-Century America*. New York: New York University Press, 1998.

Avila, Eric. *Popular Culture in the Age of White Flight*. Berkeley: University of California Press, 2004.

Azuma, Eiichiro. "The Politics of Transnational History Making: Japanese Immigrants on the Western 'Frontier,' 1927–1941." *Journal of American History* 89, no. 4 (March 2003): 1401–30.

———. "Racial Struggle, Immigrant Nationalism, and Ethnic Identity: Japanese and Filipinos in the California Delta, 1930–1931." *Pacific Historical Review* 67 (1998): 163–200.

Bailey, Beth and David Farber. *The First Strange Place: The Alchemy of Race and Sex in World War II Hawaii*. New York: Free Press, 1992.

Bankston, Carl and Min Zhou. "The Social Adjustment of Vietnamese American Adolescents: Evidence for a Segmented Assimilation Approach." *Social Science Quarterly* 78 (June 1997): 509–15.

Basch, Linda, Nina Schiller, and Cristina Blanc, eds. *Nations Unbound: Transnational Projects, Postcolonial Predicaments, and Deterritorialized Nation-States*. Australia: Gordon and Breach, 1994.

Bernstein, Alison. *American Indians and World War II: Toward a New Era in Indian Affairs*. Norman: University of Oklahoma Press, 1979.

Bernstein, Shana Beth. *California Dreaming in a Divided World: Building Multiracial Bridges in World War II and Cold War Los Angeles*. Forthcoming.

Bogardus, Emory. "Gangs of Mexican-American Youth." *Sociology and Social Research* (September 1943): 55–66.

Brilliant, Mark. "Color Lines: Civil Rights Struggles on America's 'Racial Frontier,' 1945–1975." PhD diss., Stanford University, 2002; forthcoming from Oxford University Press.

Brodkin, Karen. *How the Jews Became White Folks*. New Brunswick: Rutgers University Press, 1998.

Brooks, Charlotte. "In the Twilight Zone between Black and White: Japanese American Resettlement and Community in Chicago, 1942–1945." *Journal of American History* 86 (March 2000): 1655–87.

Bryant, Clora, Buddy Collette, William Green, Steve Isoardi, Jack Kelson, Horace Tapscott, Gerald Wilson, and Marl Young, eds. *Central Avenue Sounds: Jazz in Los Angeles*. Berkeley: University of California Press, 1998.

Bulbulian, Berge. *The Fresno Armenians: History of a Diaspora Community*. Fresno: Press at California State University, 2000.

Burma, John. "Interethnic Marriage in Los Angeles, 1948–1959." *Social Forces* (December 1963): 156–65.

Camarillo, Al. *Chicanos in California: A History of Mexican Americans in California*. San Francisco: Boyd and Fraser, 1984.

———. "Comparing Ethnic and Racial Borderlands in American Cities: Urbanization and Community Formation among African Americans, European Americans, and Mexican Americans between the World Wars." Paper presented at the annual meeting of the Organization of American Historians, Washington, DC, April 1996.

Campbell, Malcolm. "Ireland's Furthest Shores: Irish Immigrant Settlement in Nineteenth-Century California and Eastern Australia." *Pacific Historical Review* 71 (2002): 59–90.

Catapusan, Benicio. "Filipino Intermarriage Problems in the United States." *Sociology and Social Research* (January–February 1938): 265–72.

———. "Social Adjustment of the Filipinos in the United States." Master's thesis, University of Southern California, 1940.

Chan, Sucheng. *Asian Americans: An Interpretive History*. Boston: Twayne, 1991.

Chang, Thelma. *I Can Never Forget: Men of the 100th/442nd*. Honolulu: SIGI Productions, 1991.

Chin, Soo-Young. *Doing What Had to Be Done: The Life Narrative of Dora Yum Kim*. Philadelphia: Temple University Press, 1999.

Cinel, Dino. *From Italy to San Francisco: The Immigrant Experience*. Stanford: Stanford University Press, 1982.

Cordova, Fred. *Filipinos, Forgotten Asian Americans: A Pictorial Essay, 1763–circa 1963*. Dubuque, IA: Kendall/Hunt, 1983.

Corona, Bert. "A Study of the Adjustment and Interpersonal Relations of Adolescents of Mexican Descent." Master's thesis, University of California, Los Angeles, 1955.

Corpus, Benicio Fermin. "An Analysis of the Racial Adjustment Activities and Problems of the Filipino-American Christian Fellowship in Los Angeles." Master's thesis, University of Southern California, 1938.

D'Emilio, John and Estelle Freedman. *Intimate Matters: A History of Sexuality in America*. New York: Harper and Row, 1988.

Dikotter, Frank, ed. *The Construction of Racial Identities in China and Japan*. London: Hurst, 1997.

———. *The Discourse of Race in Modern China*. London: Hurst, 1992.

Di Leonardo, Micaela. *The Varieties of Ethnic Experience: Kinship, Class, and Gender among California Italian-Americans*. Ithaca: Cornell University Press, 1984.

DuBois, Ellen and Vicki Ruiz, eds. *Unequal Sisters: A Multicultural Reader in U.S. Women's History*. New York: Routledge, 2000.

Dudziak, Mary. *Cold War Civil Rights: Race and the Image of American Democracy*. Princeton: Princeton University Press, 2000.

Escobar, Edward. *Race, Police and the Making of a Political Identity: Mexican Americans and the Los Angeles Police Department, 1900–1945*. Berkeley: University of California Press, 1999.

Escobedo, Elizabeth. "Mexican American Home Front: The Politics of Gender, Culture, and Community in World War II Los Angeles." PhD diss., University of Washington, 2004.

Espiritu, Yen and Wilbur Zelinsky. *The Enigma of Ethnicity: Another American Dilemma*. Iowa City: University of Iowa Press, 2002.

Espiritu, Yen Le. *Filipino American Lives*. Philadelphia: Temple University Press, 1995.

Ethington, Phil. "Segregated Diversity: Race Ethnicity, Space and Political Fragmentation in Los Angeles County, 1940–1994." Final Report to the John Randolph Haynes and Dora Haynes Foundation, 13 September 2000.

Flamm, Jerry. *Good Life in Hard Times: San Francisco's '20s and '30s*. San Francisco: Chronicle Books, 1977.

Foster, Nellie. "Legal Status of Filipino Intermarriages in California." *Sociology and Social Research* 16 (May–June 1942): 445–52.

Franco, Jere Bishop. *Crossing the Pond: The Native American War Effort in World War II*. Denton: University of North Texas Press, 1999.

Fugita-Rony, Dorothy. *American Workers, Colonial Power: Philippine Seattle and the Transpacific West, 1919–1941*. Berkeley: University of California Press, 2003.

Gabaccia, Donna. *We Are What We Eat: Ethnic Food and the Making of Americans*. Cambridge: Harvard Unversity Press, 1998.

Gabaccia, Donna and Fraser Ottanelli, eds. *Italian Workers of the World: Labor Migration and the Formation of Multiethnic States*. Urbana: University of Illinois Press, 2001.

Gallicchio, Marc. *The African American Encounter with Japan and China: Black Internationalism in Asia, 1895–1945*. Chapel Hill: University of North Carolina Press, 2000.

Garcia, Mario T. *Memories of Chicano History: The Life and Narrative of Bert Corona*. Berkeley: University of California Press, 1994.

Gordon, Linda. *The Great Arizona Orphan Abduction*. Cambridge: Harvard University Press, 1999.

Greenberg, Cheryl. "Black and Japanese Responses to Japanese Internment." *Journal of American Ethnic History* 14 (Winter 1995): 3–37.

Gregory, James. *American Exodus: The Dust Bowl Migration and Okie Culture in California*. New York: Oxford University Press, 1989.

Griffith, Beatrice. *American Me*. Boston: Houghton Mifflin, 1948.

Guglielmo, Thomas. *White on Arrival: Italians, Race, Color, and Power in Chicago, 1890–1945*. New York: Oxford University Press, 2003.

Gutiérrez David. *Between Two Worlds: Mexican Immigrants in the United States*. Wilmington, DE: Scholarly Press, 1996.

———. *Walls and Mirrors: Mexican Americans, Mexican Immigrants and the Politics of Ethnicity*. Berkeley: University of California Press, 1992.

Hansen, Art. "Evacuation and Resettlement Study at Gila River Relocation Center, 1942–1944." *Journal of the West* (April 1999): 45–55.

Hansen, Earl and Paul Beckett. *Los Angeles: Its Peoples and Its Homes*. Los Angeles: Haynes Foundation, 1944.

Harden, Jaclyn. *Double Cross: Japanese Americans in Black and White Chicago*. Minneapolis: University of Minnesota Press, 2003.

Hodes, Martha, ed. *Sex, Love, Race: Crossing Boundaries in North American History*. New York: New York University Press, 1999.

Hollinger, David. "Amalgamation and Hypodescent: The Question of Ethnoracial

Mixture in the History of the United States." *American Historical Review* 108, no. 5 (December 2003): 1363–90.

———. *Postethnic America: Beyond Multiculturalism*. New York: Basic Books, 1995.

Hosokawa, Bill. *JACL: In Quest of Justice*. New York: William Morrow, 1982.

Ichioka, Yuji. *The Issei: The World of the First Generation Japanese Immigrants, 1885–1924*. New York: Free Press, 1998.

Jacobson, Matthew Frye. *Whiteness of a Different Color: European Immigrants and the Alchemy of Race*. Cambridge: Harvard University Press, 1998.

Johnson, Marilyn. *The Second Gold Rush: Oakland and the East Bay in World War II*. Berkeley: University of California Press, 1993.

Kazal, Russell A. "Revisiting Assimilation: The Rise, Fall, and Reappearance of a Concept in American Ethnic History." *American Historical Review* 100 (April 1995): 438–71.

Kearney, Reginald. *African American Views of the Japanese: Solidarity or Sedition?* Albany: State University of New York Press, 1998.

Kenny, Kevin. "Diaspora and Comparison: The Global Irish as Case Study." *Journal of American History* (June 2003): 132–62.

Kolchin, Peter. "Whiteness Studies: The New History of Race in America." *Journal of American History* (June 2002): 154–73.

Kurashige, Lon. "Made in Little Tokyo: Politics of Ethnic Identity and Festival in Southern California, 1934–1994." PhD diss., University of Wisconsin, Madison, 1994.

Kurashige, Scott. "Transforming Los Angeles: Black and Japanese American Struggles for Racial Equality in the Twentieth Century." PhD diss., University of California, Los Angeles, 2000.

Larsson, Cloyte, ed. *Marriage across the Color Line*. Chicago: Johnston, 1965.

Lee, Erika. *At America's Gates: Chinese Immigration during the Exclusion Era, 1883–1943*. Chapel Hill: University of North Carolina, 2003.

———. "The Chinese Exclusion Example: Race, Immigration, and American Gatekeeping, 1882–1924." *Journal of American Ethnic History* 21, no. 3 (Spring 2002): 36–62.

Lee, Ulysses. *The United States Army in World War II: The Employment of Negro Troops*. Washington, DC: Office of the Chief of Military History, U.S. Army, 1966.

Leonard, David. " 'No Jews and No Coloreds Are Welcome in this Town': Constructing Coalitions in Postwar Los Angeles." PhD diss., University of California, Berkeley, 2002.

Leonard, Karen. *Making Ethnic Choices: California's Punjabi Mexican Americans*. Philadelphia: Temple University Press, 1992.

Leonard, Kevin. "Years of Hope, Days of Fear: The Impact of World War II on Race Relations in Los Angeles." PhD diss., University of California, Davis, 1992.

Levine, Ellen. *A Fence away from Freedom: Japanese Americans and World War II*. New York: G. P. Putnam's, 1995.

Lim, Christina M. and Sheldon H. Lim. *In the Shadows of the Tiger: The 407th*

Air Service Squadron, Fourteenth Air Squadron, Fourteenth Air Service Group, Fourteenth Air Force, World War II. Brisbane: Fong Brothers, 1993.

Lipsitz, George. "Possessive Investment in Whiteness: Racialized Social Democracy and the 'White Problem' in American Studies." *American Quarterly* 47 (September 1995): 369–87.

Liu, Garding. *Inside Los Angeles Chinatown*. Los Angeles: n.p., 1948.

Lotchin, Roger, ed. *The Way We Really Were: The Golden State in the Second World War*. Urbana: University of Illinois Press, 2000.

Lowe, Lisa and David Lloyd, eds. *The Politics of Culture in the Shadow of Capital*. Durham: Duke University Press, 1997.

Mabalon, Dawn. "Life in Little Manila: Filipinas/os in Stockton, California, 1917–1972." PhD diss., Stanford University, 2004.

Matsumoto, Valerie. *Farming the Home Place: A Japanese American Community in California, 1919–1982*. Ithaca: Cornell University Press, 1993.

McReynolds, Patricia Justiniani. *Almost Americans: A Quest for Dignity*. Santa Fe: Red Crane Books, 1997.

McWilliams, Carey. *North from Mexico: The Spanish-Speaking People of the United States*. New York: Greenwood, 1948.

Modell, John. *The Economics and Politics of Racial Accommodation: The Japanese of Los Angeles, 1900–1942*. Urbana: University of Illinois Press, 1977.

Moore, Deborah Dash. *To the Golden Cities: Pursuing the American Jewish Dream in Miami and Los Angeles*. New York: Free Press, 1994.

Moore, Shirley Ann. *To Place Our Deeds: The African American Community in Richmond, California, 1910–1963*. Berkeley: University of California Press, 2000.

Moorehouse, Maggi. *Fighting in the Jim Crow Army: Black Men and Women Remember World War II*. Landham, MD: Rowman and Littlefield, 2000.

Moran, Rachel. *Interracial Intimacy: The Regulation of Race and Romance*. Chicago: University of Chicago Press, 2001.

Morin, Raul. *Among the Valiant: Mexican Americans in WWII and Korea*. Los Angeles: Borden, 1966.

Nakayama, Thomas, ed. "Transforming Barbed Wire," booklet published by Arizona Humanities Council, Phoenix, 2003.

Nash, Gary. "The Hidden History of Mestizo America." *Journal of American History* 82 (December 1995): 941–64.

Nash, Gerald. *The American West Transformed: The Impact of the Second World War*. Bloomington: Indiana University Press, 1985.

Ngai, Mae. *Impossible Subjects: Illegal Aliens and the Making of Modern America*. Princeton: Princeton University Press, 2004.

Ngozi-Brown, Scott. "African American Soldiers and Filipinos: Racial Imperialism, Jim Crow and Social Relations." *Journal of Negro History* 82, no. 1 (Winter 1997): 42–53.

Nicolaides, Becky. *My Blue Heaven: Life and Politics in the Working-Class Suburbs of Los Angeles, 1920–1965*. Chicago: University of Chicago Press, 2002.

Nugent, Walter. *Into the West: The Story of Its People*. New York: Alfred A. Knopf, 1999.

Odem, Mary. *Delinquent Daughters: Protecting and Policing Adolescent Female Sexuality in the United States, 1885–1920.* Chapel Hill: University of North Carolina Press, 1995.

Omi, Michael and Howard Winant. *Racial Formation in the United States: From the 1960s to the 1990s.* New York: Routledge and Kegan Paul, 1994.

Orenstein, Dara. "Void for Vagueness: Mexican Americans and the Collapse of the Anti-Miscegenation Law in California." *Pacific Historical Review* 74 (2005): 367–407.

Pagán, Eduardo Obregón. *Murder at the Sleepy Lagoon: Zoot Suits, Race, and Riot in Wartime L.A.* Chapel Hill: University of North Carolina Press, 2003.

Palmer, Annette. "The Politics of Race and War: Black American Soldiers in the Caribbean Theater during the Second World War." *Military Affairs* (April 1983): 59–62.

Panunzio, Constantine. "Intermarriage in Los Angeles, 1924–1933." *American Journal of Sociology* 47(March 1942): 690–701.

Pascoe, Peggy. "Gender Systems in Conflict: The Marriages of Mission-Educated Chinese American Women, 1874–1939." *Journal of Social History* (1989): 631–53.

———. "Miscegenation Law, Court Cases, and Ideologies of 'Race' in Twentieth-Century America." *Journal of American History* 83 (1996): 44–70.

Pitti, Stephen. *The Devil in Silicon Valley: Northern California, Race, and Mexican Americans.* Princeton: Princeton University Press, 2003.

Portes, Alejandro and Min Zhou. "The New Second Generational: Segmented Assimilation and Its Variants." *Annals of the American Academy of Political and Social Science* 530 (November 1993): 74–96.

Roediger, David. *Wages of Whiteness: The Making of the American Working Class.* London: Verso, 1991.

Romano, Renee. *Race Mixing: Black-White Marriage in Postwar America.* Cambridge: Harvard University Press, 2003.

Root, Maria, ed. *Racially Mixed People in America.* Newbury Park, CA: Sage, 1992.

Sanchez, George. *Becoming Mexican American: Ethnicity, Culture, and Identity in Chicano Los Angeles, 1900–1945.* New York: Oxford University Press, 1993.

———. "Face the Nation: Race, Immigration and the Rise of Nativism in Late Twentieth-Century America." *International Migration Review* 31 (1997): 1009–30.

———. "Race, Nation, and Culture in Recent Immigration Studies." *Journal of American Ethnic History* 18 (Summer 1999): 66–84.

Saxton, Alexander. *The Indispensable Enemy: Labor and the Anti-Chinese Movement in California.* Berkeley: University of California Press, 1971.

Schrijvers, Peter. *The GI War against Japan: American Soldiers in Asia and the Pacific during World War II.* New York: Palgrave, 2002.

Shevky, Eshref and Marilyn Williams. *The Social Areas of Los Angeles: Analysis and Typology.* Berkeley: University of California Press, 1949.

Sides, Josh. *L.A. City Limits: African American Los Angeles from the Great Depression to the Present.* Berkeley: University of California Press, 2003.

Sitkoff, Harvard. "Racial Militancy and Interracial Violence in the Second World War." *Journal of American History* 58 (1971): 661–81.

Skenazy, Paul and Tera Martin., eds. *Conversations with Maxine Hong Kingston.* Jackson: University of Mississippi, 1998.

Spaulding, Charles. "Housing Problems of Minority Groups in Los Angeles." *Annals of the American Academy of Political and Social Science* (1946).

Spickard, Paul. "Injustice Compounded: Amerasians and Non-Japanese Americans in World War II Concentration Camps." *Journal of American Ethnic History* 5, no. 2 (Spring 1986): 5–22.

———. *Mixed Blood: Intermarriage and Ethnic Identity in Twentieth-Century America.* Madison: University of Wisconsin Press, 1989.

Sullivan, Deirdre. "'Letting Down the Bars': Race, Space and Democracy in San Francisco, 1936–1964." PhD diss., University of Pennsylvania, 2003.

Tajiri, Vincent, ed. *Through Innocent Eyes: Writings and Art from the Japanese American Internment by Poston I Schoolchildren.* Los Angeles: Keiro Services Press, 1990.

Tang, Scott Harvey. "Pushing at the Golden Gate: Race Relations and Racial Politics in San Francisco, 1940–1955." PhD diss., University of California, Berkeley, 2002.

Taylor, Quintard. *In Search of the Racial Frontier: African Americans in the American West, 1528–1990.* New York: W. W. Norton, 1998.

Thompson, Warren. *Growth and Changes in California's Population.* Los Angeles: Haynes Foundation, 1955.

Von Eschen, Penny. *Race against Empire: Black Americans and Anticolonialism, 1937–1957.* Ithaca: Cornell University Press, 1997.

Vorspan, Max and Lloyd Gartner. *History of Jews in Los Angeles.* Philadelphia: Jewish Publication Society of America, 1970.

White, Geoffrey. *Island Encounters: Black and White Memories of the Pacific War.* Washington, DC: Smithsonian Press, 1990.

Whitney, Helen Elizabeth. "Care of Homeless Children of Japanese Ancestry during Evacuation and Relocation." Master's thesis, University of California, Berkeley, 1948.

Wild, Mark. "'So Many Children at Once and So Many Kinds': Schools and Ethno-racial Boundaries in Early Twentieth-Century Los Angeles." *Western Historical Quarterly* 33, no. 4 (Winter 2002): 453–76.

———. *Street Meeting: Multiethnic Neighborhoods in Early Twentieth-Century Los Angeles.* Berkeley: University of California Press, 2005.

Wise, Harold. *Characteristics of the Low Rent Housing Market in Brawley, Holtville, Calexico, Imperial and Westwood, California.* Planning and Housing Research Associates, 1950.

Wollenberg, Charles. *All Deliberate Speed: Segregation and Exclusion in California Schools, 1855–1975.* Berkeley: University of California Press, 1976.

Wong, K. Scott. *Americans First: Chinese Americans and the Second World War.* Cambridge: Harvard University Press, 2005.

Wong, Scott and Sucheng Chan, eds. *Claiming America: Constructing Chinese American Identities during the Exclusion Era.* Philadelphia: Temple University Press, 1998.

Yakota, Kariann. "From Little Tokyo to Bronzeveille and Back: Ethnic Communities in Transition." Master's thesis, University of California, Los Angeles, 1996.

Yoo, David. *Growing Up Nisei: Race, Generation, and Culture among Japanese Americans of California, 1924–49.* Urbana: University of Illinois Press, 2000.

Yu, Henry. *Thinking Orientals: Migration, Contact and Exoticism in Modern America.* New York: Oxford University Press, 2000.

———. "Tiger Woods Is Not the End of History: Or Why Sex across the Color Line Won't Save Us All." *American Historical Review* 108, no. 5 (December 2003): 1406–14.

Yung, Judy. *Unbound Feet: A Social History of Chinese Women in San Francisco.* Berkeley: University of California Press, 1995.

MEMOIRS, AUTOBIOGRAPHIES, LITERATURE

Chan, Won-loy. *Burma: The Untold Story.* Novato, CA: Presidio Press, 1986.

Cheung, King-kok. *Seventeen Syllables and Other Stories.* New Brunswick: Rutgers University Press, 1998.

Chin, Duncan. *Growing Up on Grove Street, 1931–1946: Sketches and Memories of a Chinese American Boyhood.* Capitola, CA: Capitola Book, 1995.

Chin, Soo-Young. *Doing What Had to Be Done: The Life Narrative of Dora Yum Kim.* Philadelphia:Temple University Press, 1999.

Galarza, Ernesto. *Barrio Boy: The Story of a Boy's Acculturation.* Notre Dame: University of Notre Dame, 1971.

Himes, Chester. *Black on Black: Baby Sister and Selected Writings.* New York: Doubleday, 1973.

———. *If He Hollers, Let Him Go.* 1945; reprint, with a foreword by Hilton Als, New York: Thunder's Mouth Press, 2002.

Houston, Jeanne Wakatsuki and James D. Houston. *Farewell to Manzanar: A True Story of Japanese American Experience during and after the World War II Internment.* Boston: Houghton Mifflin, 1973.

Kikuchi, Charles. *The Kikuchi Diary: Chronicle from an American Concentration Camp: The Tanforan Journals of Charles Kikuchi.* Edited by John Modell. Urbana: University of Illinois Press, 1973.

Kingston, Maxine Hong. *The Woman Warrior: Memoirs of a Girlhood among Ghosts.* New York: Vintage, 1989.

Levy, Jacques. *Cesar Chavez: Autobiography of La Causa.* New York: W. W. Norton, 1975.

Morales, Dionicio. *Dionicio Morales: A Life in Two Cultures.* Houston: Pinata Books, 1997.

Newton, Adolph W. *Better Than Good: A Black Sailor's War, 1943–1945.* Annapolis: Naval Institute Press, 1999.

Peery, Nelson. *Black Fire: The Making of an American Revolutionary.* Reprint; New York: New Press, 1994.

Scharlin, Craig and Lilia V. Villanueva. *Philip Vera Cruz: A Personal history of Filipino Immigrants and the Farmworkers Movement.* Los Angeles: UCLA

Labor Center, Institution for Industrial Relations, and UCLA Asian American Studies Center, 1992.

Toribio, Helen C., ed. *Seven Card Stud with Seven Manangs Wild: Writings on Filipino Americans.* San Francisco: Eastbay Filipino American National Historical Society, 2002.

Yamamoto, Hisaye. *Seventeen Syllables and Other Stories.* Latham, NY: Kitchen Table—Women of Color Press, 1988.

COURT CASES

Bennett v. State Bar of California, 27 Cal. 2d 31 (1945).

Méndez v. Westminster School District of Orange County, 161 F.2d. 774 (9th Cir. 1947).

People v. Cabaltero, 31 Cal. App. 2d 52 (1939).

People v. Henderson, 4 Cal. 2d 188 (August 1935).

Perez v. Lippold, 32 Cal. 2d 711 (1948).

Providence Baptist Association v. Los Angeles Hompa Honowanji Temple, 79 Cal. App. 2d. 734 (1947).

Visco v. Los Angeles County State of California, No. 319408, Superior Court (1931).

Index

Text: 10/13 Sabon
Display: Sabon
Compositor: Binghamton Valley Composition, LLC
Cartographer: Bill Nelson
Indexer: Sharon Sweeney

CPSIA information can be obtained
at www.ICGtesting.com
Printed in the USA
BVHW032319280619
552258BV00001B/26/P